NOËL COWARD
ON (and in) THEATRE

NOËL COWARD
ON (and in) THEATRE

Edited and with commentary by

BARRY DAY

ALFRED A. KNOPF   New York
2021

THIS IS A BORZOI BOOK
PUBLISHED BY ALFRED A. KNOPF

Copyright © 2021 by Barry Day

All rights reserved. Published in the United States by Alfred A. Knopf,
a division of Penguin Random House LLC, New York, and distributed
in Canada by Penguin Random House Canada Limited, Toronto.

www.aaknopf.com

Knopf, Borzoi Books, and the colophon are
registered trademarks of Penguin Random House LLC.

Due to limitations of space, permissions to reprint previously
published material can be found following the index.

Library of Congress Cataloging-in-Publication Data
Names: Day, Barry, editor, writer of commentary.
Title: Noël Coward on (and in) theatre / edited
and with commentary by Barry Day.
Description: First edition. | New York : Alfred A. Knopf, 2021. |
Identifiers: LCCN 2020009461 (print) | LCCN 2020009462 (ebook) |
ISBN 9780525657958 (hardcover) | ISBN 9780525657965 (ebook)
Subjects: LCSH: Coward, Noël, 1899–1973—Criticism and interpretation. |
Coward, Noël, 1899–1973—Knowledge—Theater.
Classification: LCC PR6005.O85 (ebook) |
LCC PR6005.O85 Z78 2021 (print) | DDC 822/.912—dc23
LC record available at https://lccn.loc.gov/2020009461

Jacket photograph: Noël Coward, 1932, by Edward Steichen
© 2020 The Estate of Edward Steichen /
Artists Rights Society (ARS), New York.
Print: Courtesy Howard Greenberg Gallery, NYC

Jacket design by John Gall

Manufactured in the United States of America
First Edition

To the Master
(who else?)

Contents

List of Illustrations   *xi*

Prologue   *xiii*

INTRODUCTION   3

1. EARLY STAGES   5
    "But I Heard the Curtain Going Up"

    The Boy Actor · Prince Mussel in *The Goldfish* · Cannard the
    Page in *The Great Name* (Hawtrey) · *Where the Rainbow Ends* ·
    Mushroom in *An Autumn Idyll* · *A Little Fowl Play* · partnership
    with Esmé Wynne · meets Gertrude Lawrence when they both
    appear in *Hannele* · Slightly in *Peter Pan* · Charley in *Charley's
    Aunt* · *Hearts of the World* (film) · cabaret at Elysée Restaurant

2. ON WRITING A PLAY (1) FROM JUVENILIA TO *THE VORTEX*   33
    "Writing a Play Is Both a Craft and an Art"

    The Unattainable (1918) · *The Impossible Wife* (1918) ·
    The Rat Trap (1918) · *The Dope Cure* (1919) · *Humoresque* (1919) ·
    The Last Trick (1919) · *The Knight of the Burning Pestle* (1919) (actor) ·
    I'll Leave It to You (1920) · *The Young Idea* (1923) · *The Vortex* (1924)

3. ON MY FELLOW PLAYWRIGHTS   54
    "My Colleague Will" . . . and Others

    Shakespeare · George Bernard Shaw · Oscar Wilde ·
    Anton Chekhov · J. M. Barrie · Somerset Maugham ·
    T. S. Eliot · John Osborne · Arnold Wesker ·

Eugène Ionescu · Edward Albee · Samuel Beckett ·
Arthur Miller · Tennessee Williams · Eugene O'Neill ·
Terence Rattigan · Harold Pinter · Peter Shaffer

4. ON WRITING A PLAY (2) . . . TO WORLD WAR II   87

   "Success Took Me to Her Bosom Like a Maternal Boa Constrictor"

   The Rat Trap (1918) · *The Queen Was in the Parlour* (1922) ·
   Fallen Angels (1923) · *Hay Fever* (1924) · *Easy Virtue* (1924) ·
   This Was a Man (1926) · *Semi-Monde* (1926) · *Home Chat* (1927) ·
   The Marquise (1927) · *Sirocco* (1927) · *Private Lives* (1930) ·
   Post-Mortem (1930) · *Cavalcade* (1931) · *Design for Living* (1933) ·
   Point Valaine (1934) · *Tonight at 8:30* (1936)

5. ON ACTING . . .   135

   "Acting Is Acting—It's Giving the Impression of Feeling"

   THE ART OF ACTING   136

   Coward on · Auditions · Talent (or the Lack of It) ·
   Rehearsals · "Learning the Lines" · Clarity of Delivery ·
   Timing · "Control" · "Range" · "Stage Fright" ·
   Theatre Audiences · Fans · Vice and Squalor in the Theatre ·
   A Slice of Ham · Comedy · Overlapping Dialogue ·
   Style · Being "Noël Coward" · *Not* Being "Noël Coward" ·
   Revivals · Plays with a "Message" · Writing · Writing Fiction ·
   Writing Verse · Handwriting · Taste · Explicit Language ·
   Constructing a Play · Failure in the Theatre · Writing Plays vs.
   Writing Novels · Theatre vs. Cinema · Being Creative After Forty

6. . . . AND ACTORS   193

   "And One Man in His Time Plays Many Parts . . ."

   Consider the Public · "The Method" · John Gielgud ·
   Laurence Olivier · Gertrude Lawrence · THE LUNTS ·
   On Leading Ladies · Advice to Actors

   INTERMISSION: STAR QUALITY   231

   "I Don't Know What It Is—but I've Got It"

7. ON WRITING A PLAY (3) (1940–1960)   239

    "It Was the Best of Times, It Was the Worst of Times"

    Present Laughter (1939) · *This Happy Breed* (1939) · *Salute to the
    Brave* (1941) · *Blithe Spirit* (1941) · *Peace in Our Time* (1947) ·
    Island Fling (1949)/*South Sea Bubble* (1956) · *Relative Values*
    (1951) · *Quadrille* (1951/2) · *Nude with Violin* (1956) · *Look After
    Lulu* (1959) · *Waiting in the Wings* (1959/60)

8. THE CRITICS   271

    "O, You Chorus of Reviewers, / Irresponsible, Indolent Reviewers."

    James Agate · Alexander Woollcott · Graham Greene ·
    Kenneth Tynan · Consider the Public

9. PRODUCED BY . . . AND DIRECTED BY . . .   300

    PRODUCED BY . . .   300

    André Charlot · Charles B. Cochran · John C. (Jack) Wilson ·
    Hugh (Binkie) Beaumont

    . . . AND DIRECTED BY . . .   318

    Basil Dean

10. MUSICAL THEATRE, REVUE, AND CABARET   324

    ON TAKING LIGHT MUSIC SERIOUSLY   324

    MUSIC HALL   330

    REVUE   332

    London Calling! (1923) · *On With the Dance* (1925) · *This Year
    of Grace!* (1928) · *Words and Music* (1932) · *Set to Music* (1938) ·
    Sigh No More (1945)

    MUSICAL THEATRE   347

    Bitter Sweet (1929) · *Conversation Piece* (1934) · *Operette* (1938) ·
    Pacific 1860 (1946) · *Ace of Clubs* (1950) · *After the Ball* (1954) ·
    Sail Away (1961) · *The Girl Who Came to Supper* (1963) ·
    High Spirits (1964)

CABARET   394

Café de Paris, London (1951–1954) · Desert Inn, Las Vegas (1955)

TELEVISION   401

Together with Music (1955)

11. ON WRITING A PLAY (4) (1960–1970)   410

"Dad's Renaissance"

Volcano (1957) · *Suite in Three Keys (A Song at Twilight ·
Shadows of the Evening · Come into the Garden, Maud)* (1966)

12. CURTAIN CALLS   419

Envoi   424
Appendix "The Decline of the West End" (Coward)   429
Acknowledgments   435
Sources and Permissions   437
Index   439

Illustrations

xiv, 111, 121, 123, 125, 129, 133, 151, 156, 212, 343: Vandamm Studio © Billy Rose Theatre Division, The New York Public Library for the Performing Arts

xv: Guy Gravatt, courtesy of the Mander & Mitchenson Collection, University of Bristol

11, 20, 21, 31, 89, 160, 256, 285, 356: Courtesy of Noël Coward Collection, Special Collections, University of Birmingham

16, 91, 105, 246 (bottom): University of Bristol Theatre Collection

23, 91, 113, 214, 253, 358, 373 (bottom), 397: Courtesy of the Mary Evans Picture Library

24, 28, 57, 67, 104, 130, 202, 205, 211, 218, 221, 222, 243, 395, 402, 403 (top), 410: The Noël Coward Archive Trust

30: D. P. Cooper, courtesy of Noël Coward Collection, Special Collections, University of Birmingham

50: Sasha / Mander & Mitchenson Collection, University of Bristol / ArenaPAL

52, 109, 131, 134, 158, 359 (top left and right): Sasha, Hulton Archive, via Getty

59: Express Newspapers, Hulton Archive, via Getty

74, 416: L. Arnold Weissberger, Noël Coward Archive Trust

90, 313: Angus McBean, courtesy of Harvard University

92: Bill Hewison, courtesy of Noël Coward Collection, Special Collections, University of Birmingham

123: Vandamm Studio, Noël Coward Archive Trust

127: Peter Stackpole, The LIFE Theatre Collection, via Getty

132: Photograph by Leadlay-Dallison; Credit: Performing Arts Images / ArenaPAL

217: Courtesy of Ten Chimneys Foundation

242: Gordon Anthony, Moviepix, via Getty

244: CBS photo archive, CBS, via Getty

246 (top), 248, 250, 259: © Cecil Beaton Studio Archive

254: Mander & Mitchenson Collection, University of Bristol

256: Fred Fehl; Credit: Mander & Mitchenson / University of Bristol / ArenaPAL

262: Geoffrey Johnson Collection

293 (top): Courtesy of *The New Yorker*

303 (top left): Courtesy of the Max Beerbohm Estate

309: Photograph by Cannons of Hollywood (London), courtesy of the Mander & Mitchenson Collection, University of Bristol

334, 335: University of Bristol / ArenaPAL

338: William Rothenstein, courtesy of the Philip Mould Gallery

339 (top): Photograph by Lenare; credit: Mander & Mitchenson / University of Bristol / ArenaPAL

345 (right): Baron Studios, Geoffrey Johnson Collection, NCAT

351: Courtesy of the author

374: Kurt Hutton, Picture Post, via Getty

383: © Playbill

385, 386 : Photo by Friedman-Abeles © The New York Public Library of Performing Arts

400: Desert Sea News Bureau

403 (bottom): Courtesy of the William Claxton Estate

417: Composite by Angus McBean, Geoffrey Johnson Collection, Noël Coward Archive Trust

419: Courtesy of the Horst Tappe Foundation

420: ABC Photo Archives, Walt Disney Television via Getty

433: © William Hustler and Georgina Hustler / National Portrait Gallery, London

Image conversion on behalf of the Noël Coward Archive Trust by Nigel Hazle.

Prologue

"What's past is prologue..."
—SHAKESPEARE (*THE TEMPEST*)

"The Theatre still spells magic for many millions of people and that magic should be a source of deep pride to all those who are privileged to serve in it."

(1961)

.

"The theatre should be treated with respect. The theatre is a wonderful place, a house of strange enchantment, a temple of illusions."

.

"The primary purpose of the theatre is to amuse, not to reform, improve, or edify people."

.

"I write what I wish to write—later on the world can decide, if it wishes to. There will always be a few people, anyhow, in every generation who will find my work entertaining and true."

.

"Artistically it is very much better to make a suggestion rather than a statement."

.

HELEN: The great thing in this world is not to be obvious—over *anything*!
—*THE VORTEX* (1924)

.

"If you were to put me on a stage with Laurence Olivier, John Gielgud and Ralph Richardson, they would be acting me off the stage and out of the auditorium—but everyone in the audience would be looking at me."

"When I was one-and-twenty I was ambitious, cheerful and high-spirited. I had never heard of the death wish and I was blissfully unaware that I belonged to a dying civilisation. Today this dubious implication is pitched at me from all directions. Despair is the new religion, the new mode. It is in the books we read, in the music we hear, and far too often in the plays we see.

"Well, I am no longer one-and-twenty, I still have no preoccupation with the death wish. I am still ambitious, cheerful and I hope not offensively high-spirited and I am still unaware that I belong to a dying civilisation. If I do, there is really nothing to be done about it. So I am going to press on with my life as I like living it until I die of natural causes or an atom bomb blows me to smithereens."

"Writing and composing are the two most creative of my talents. I think that directing is very interesting and obviously fascinating, both theatrically and psychologically, but on the theatre side I really prefer acting."

At the piano in Goldenhurst. (Note the Grinling Gibbons wood carving that he took from home to home over the years.)

"So far as I am concerned, posterity isn't of any frightful significance. I think if it were, I'd become self-conscious and wouldn't be able to work at all. I could no more sit down and say—'Now I'll write an Immortal Drama' than I could fly, and anyway I don't want to. I have no great or beautiful thoughts."

(1931)

.

"First I was the *enfant terrible*. Then the Bright Young Thing. Now I'm a tradition."

.

"I have always prided myself on my capacity for being just one jump ahead of what everybody expects of me."

.

"With my usual watchful eye on posterity, I can only suggest to any wretched future biographer that he gets my daily engagement book and from that fills in anything he can find and good luck to him, poor bugger."

—*DIARY* (1969)

"How invaluable it would be...if just once, just for a brief spell, I could see myself clearly from the outside, as others saw me. How helpful it would be, moving so continually across the public vision, to know what that vision really observed, to note objectively what it was in my personality that moved some people to like and applaud me and aroused in others such irritation and resentment. How salutary it would be to watch the whole performance through from the front of the house, to see to what extent the mannerisms were effective and note when and where they should be cut down."

—*FUTURE INDEFINITE*

"Noël is the *enfant gâté* of the theatre. At his birth the two godmothers sat over his cradle. The benevolent one gave him one superb gift. The malevolent crone tossed in a handful of gifts almost as good and disappeared with a cackling laugh.

"He is aware of these gifts and feels that he must exploit them all—that is the trap she laid. This parable is just my Victorian way of saying that I don't think he will ever quite fulfil his great promise if he doesn't curb his versatility."

—DAME MARIE TEMPEST

NOËL COWARD
ON (and in) THEATRE

INTRODUCTION

The Theatre . . . a Temple of Illusions . . .

What it most emphatically is not and never will be is a scruffy, illiterate, fumed oak drill-hall serving as a temporary soap-box for political propaganda . . .

The primary function of the Theatre is to amuse, not to reform, improve or edify people . . . (I have a slight reforming urge, but I have rather cunningly kept it down.)

I will accept anything in the Theatre . . . provided it amuses or moves me. But if it does neither, I want to go home.

I believe the curtain should go up at eight o'clock and be down again two and a half hours later—or theareabouts . . .

If you're going to break the rules of your craft, you've got to learn them first.

There's room for everything in the Theatre. I think there's still room for a drama or a comedy or a play about kitchen sinks or tramps or whatever—that's fine, providing they're good enough. But there's still room for a charming upper middle-class family, who have hearts and limbs and feel and think, just the same as anybody else does. And even dukes and duchesses. There are still a few extant!

The Theatre still spells magic for many millions of people and that magic should be a source of deep pride to all those who are privileged to serve in it.

When I eventually write my book on the Theatre . . .

He often threatened to write his book on Theatre but never quite got around to it. Except . . . his opinions, as evidenced in his published writings, interviews, plays, stories, verse, lyrics, and other people's reminiscences over sixty years add up to a book. This one.

And I couldn't resist including some of his ironic asides. In addition to his many other talents, Noël was the Master of Sitdown Comedy.

His views on the medium were never formal and academic like those of, say, Stanislavski or Strasberg. Noël's—being both writer and performer—were more practical, pragmatic, and almost always delivered with an acceptable coating of wry wit.

It was a certain public self-deprecation, flavored with irony, that helped define him, endeared him to people, and made the medicine go down when what he had to say was critical.

Writer—Actor—often Director . . . Composer . . . Lyricist. Who has ever combined all those talents and continued to do so in various combinations for the best part of sixty years?

Shakespeare? If you insist but I don't remember seeing reviews of him in cabaret, exhibitions of his paintings, and we'll never know what he would have made of film and television. And was he the "celebrity" during his lifetime that Noël became in his?

He was a true Renaissance Man—who just happened to live in the twentieth century.

In *Noël Coward on (and in) Theatre* I have simply assembled, arranged, and put into context what he had to say on such subjects as the nature of theatre—what it should and shouldn't be—on the art of acting and actors, on plays and playwriting, and on the people he met on the stage and behind it.

And through it all I hope you will hear the voice of the man they rightly called—The Master.

It was a title that—being English—he couldn't publicly acknowledge, so he would turn it into a joke—"Oh, you know the old saying—'Jack of All trades—Master of None.'" In that at least he was wrong.

—BARRY DAY

1

EARLY STAGES

"But I Heard the Curtain Going Up"

As Slightly in *Peter Pan*, 1913.

The Boy Actor

I can remember, I can remember.
The months of November and December
    Were filled for me with peculiar joys
So different from those of other boys.
    For other boys would be counting the days
Until end of term and holiday times
    But I was acting in Christmas plays
While they were taken to pantomimes.
    I didn't envy their Eton suits,
Their children's dances and Christmas trees.
    My life had wonderful substitutes
For such conventional treats as these.
    I didn't envy their country larks,
Their organised games in panelled halls;
    While they made snow-men in stately parks
I was counting the curtain calls.
        I remember the auditions, the nerve-racking auditions:
        Darkened auditorium and empty, dusty stage,
        Little girls in ballet dresses practising "positions"
        Gentlemen with *pince-nez* asking you your age.
        Hopefulness and nervousness struggling within you,
        Dreading that familiar phrase, "Thank you, dear, no more."
        Straining every muscle, every tendon, every sinew
        To do your dance much better than you'd ever done before.
        Think of your performance. Never mind the others.
        Never mind the pianist, talent must prevail.
        Never mind the baleful eyes of other children's mothers
        Glaring from the corners and willing you to fail.
I can remember. I can remember.
The months of November and December
    Were more significant to me
Than other months could ever be
    For they were the months of high romance
When destiny waited on tip-toe,
    When every boy actor stood a chance
Of getting into a Christmas show,
    Not for me the dubious heaven

Of being some prefect's *protégé*!
    Not for me the Second Eleven.
For me, two performances a day.
        Ah, those first rehearsals! Only very few lines:
        Rushing home to mother, learning them by heart.
        "Enter Left through window"—Dots to mark the cue lines:
        "Exit with others"—Still, it *was* a part.
        Opening performance; legs a bit unsteady,
        Dedicated tension, shivers down my spine,
        Powder, grease and eye-black, sticks of make-up ready
        Leichner number three and number five and number nine.
        World of strange enchantment, magic for a small boy
        Dreaming of the future, reaching for the crown,
        Rigid in the dressing-room, listening for the call-boy
        "Overture Beginners—Everybody Down!"
I can remember. I can remember.
The months of November and December,
    Although climatically cold and damp,
Meant more to me than Aladdin's lamp.
I see myself, having got a job,
Walking on wings along the Strand,
Uncertain whether to laugh or sob
And clutching tightly my mother's hand,
    I never cared who scored the goal
Or which side won the silver cup,
    I never learned to bat or bowl
But I heard the curtain going up.

———

"I knew in my teens that the world was full of hatred, cruelty, vice, unrequited love, despair, destruction and murder. I also knew at the same time that it was filled with kindness, pleasure, joy, requited love, fun, excitement, generosity, laughter and friends. And through all my years I have never changed in my mind the balance of these absurd phenomena."

═══

Noël Coward was literally born to the sound of music.

At the turn of the century music in a domestic context meant the family gathered round the piano for a sing-song. Noël could sing those familiar songs and hymns word perfectly to the end of his life. But that early exposure certainly helped bring out the latent entertainer in him.

At the age of two he had to be forcibly removed from church for spontaneously dancing in the aisle to accompany the hymn being played. On another occasion he complained bitterly when his solo in the church choir earned no applause—merely the sight and sound of the congregation sinking creakily to its knees in prayer.

"I made my first public appearance at a prize-giving concert at the age of six. I was dressed in a white sailor suit and sang 'Coo' from *The Country Girl,* followed by a piping little song about the spring for which I accompanied myself on the piano. This feat brought down the house and I had to repeat it. I remember leaning over to Mother and Father in the front row and hissing exultantly—'I've got to sing again.' The evening ended in tears, however, because I was not given a prize. Mother tried vainly to explain to me that the prizes were for hard work during the term and not for vocal prowess, but I refused to be comforted, and was led away weeping."

But you can't keep a real "trouper" down and when the Cowards went to the seaside at Bognor for their traditional summer holiday, there was "Uncle George and His Merrie Men" concert party in their straw hats, colored blazers, and off-colored flannel trousers.

On the evening of the competition Noël donned his lucky sailor suit "and waited in a sort of pen with several aspirants," noting with satisfaction that "those who appeared before me were inept and clumsy. When my turn came I sang 'Come Along with Me to the Zoo, Dear' and 'Liza Ann' from *The Orchid.* I also danced violently. The applause was highly gratifying . . . At the end of the performance Uncle George made a speech and presented me with the first prize, a large box of chocolates, which, when opened in our lodgings, proved to be three parts shavings."

It was his first lesson that in the theatre the *appearance* of reality is all that matters.

"The reason I went on the stage was that I was set to go into the Chapel Royal choir, because I had a perfectly beautiful voice. I suppose the inherent acting in me headed its ugly rear, because I made Callas look like an amateur! And the poor organist fell back in horror. I gave it the expression. I did the whole crucifixion bit. And they turned me down because I was over-dramatic. And I was only nine and a half with an Eton collar going 'There was no other good enough to pay the price of sin.' I did the whole lot. So then Mother was very very cross and said the man was common and stupid anyway."

By now the urge to perform led him to begin writing his own material. A little later the Cowards were driven by an acute shortage of money to rent their London flat and live in the country for a while . . .

"Some little girls lived nearby and I forced them to act a tragedy that I had written, but they were very silly and during the performance forgot their lines and sniggered, so I hit the eldest one on the head with a wooden spade, the whole affair thus ending in tears and a furious quarrel between the mothers involved."

Nineteen nine now and he is concentrating on developing his singing voice . . .

"I occasionally sang anthems in churches but I hated doing this because the lack of applause depressed me."

There was the annual church garden party at Teddington with its apparently endless concerts run by his Aunt Myrrha—which provided a job for the boy . . .

"This was when I shone. I always sang a serious ballad to begin with, my principal successes being 'Through the Forest' and 'Cherry Blossom Time.' The latter was invariably a great favourite, possibly owing to the redundance of its 'Hey, Nonnys' and 'Ho, Nonnys' and its winsomely pastoral sentiments. After this, I returned, smiling to the applause, and rendered a light musical comedy number with dance. It must have been surprising and I should have thought, nauseating, to see a little boy of nine in a white sailor suit flitting about a small wooden stage, employing with instinctive accuracy, the gestures and tricks of a professional *soubrette,* but they seemed to love it and encored me vociferously."

For this he had his mother, Violet, to thank in large part, since she took him to the theatre (in the cheapest seats, naturally), where he could study the leading performers of the day and dutifully "borrow" elements of their routines. To the end of his life he continued to idolize the memory of stars like Lily Elsie in *The Merry Widow* and Gertie Millar in *The Quaker Girl.*

He was grateful to "those kindly old ladies in their garden party finery. After all . . . [he could confess when recalling this in the 1930s] . . . I act to them still at matinées and I have a sad suspicion that I don't give them half as much pleasure now as I did then."

He was also more realistic in retrospect about his youthful prowess . . .

"I am certain that, could my adult self have been present . . . he would have crept outside, at the first coy gurgle, and been mercifully sick outside . . . I was a brazen, odious little prodigy, over-pleased with myself and precocious to a degree . . . I was, I believe, one of the worst boy actors ever inflicted on the paying public."

═══

The breakthrough from amateur to professional came the following year, with an ad in the *Daily Mirror*.

Miss Lila Field was advertising for "a cast of wonder children" to appear in a play she had written called *The Goldfish* at London's Little Theatre.

This caught Violet's eye. "It stated that a talented boy of attractive appearance was required . . . This seemed to dispose of all argument. I was a talented boy, God knows, and when washed and smarmed down a bit, passably attractive. There seemed to be no practical reason why Miss Lila Field shouldn't jump at me and we both believed that she would be a fool indeed to miss such a magnificent opportunity."

So along they went to present Miss Field with her magnificent opportunity. "My heart sank when there was no piano . . . but I sang 'Liza Ann' and Mother la-la'd for the dance."

Miss Field was suitably impressed and said she would hire Noël for the part of Prince Mussel. The fee would be a guinea and a half a week. This caused Mrs. Coward great distress. She said she couldn't afford to pay that. Miss Field disabused her. The guinea and a half was what her little boy would RECEIVE! "Mother and I floated down the narrow staircase and into the street . . . I was now a professional actor."

As Prince Mussel, the court jester, "I had a good song in the last act . . . I sang it with tremendous passion, and at the end tore off a top B flat with a Pagliacci sob in it. I was invariably encored, sometimes twice."

He also received his first press review. The *Daily Mirror*—which had been complicit in the whole venture—declared that "Great success was scored by Master Noel Coward."

A fellow member of the cast was the young Micheál MacLiammóir on whom Noël made a clear impression . . .

ROYAL COURT THEATRE
SLOANE SQUARE.
Monday, April 17th, 1911, for Six Nights

Miss
LILA
FIELD'S
Company

"The
Goldfish"

SPECIAL MATINEES
Wednesday, Thursday and Saturday, April 19th, 20th and 22nd

"He was ten years old and already in manner and bearing a young man. The face, of course, was that of a child but the eyes were already amused and slightly incredulous, the voice was as crisply rubato then as it is today, and when he spoke after a few boyish grins, it was to ask me how much work I had done.

"'Work?,' I said aghast. 'Do you mean acting?'

"'But you've had your audition, haven't you?'

"'Oh, yes, I'm engaged.' And then—'What are you going to be when you grow up?'

"'An actor, of course. Why, what do you want to be?'"

Micky was not at all sure.

"'You'd better make up your mind, you know. People should always be quite clear what they want to be.'"

The Goldfish was to swim back into Noël's ken when he least expected it . . .

Thirty-seven years ago a children's play *The Goldfish* by Lila Field was produced at the Little Theatre, John Street, Adelphi. The months leading up to that moment had been fraught with tension and excitement. Rehearsals, sometimes sporadic, had taken place in basements, dance halls, even in the private homes of members of the cast, with the furniture pushed back and tea served afterwards, together with little cakes, drop scones and, on one occasion, watercress sandwiches.

During the weeks immediately before production, when there was no longer any doubt that the play really was going to open, the excitement rose to fever pitch.

Anxious mothers, clutching their offspring's shoes, shawl and "Dorothy" bags, lined the walls of rehearsal rooms, whispering sibilantly and now and then swaying slightly as the winds of rumour eddied round them.

"Miss Field said that Gladys's solo was to be cut." "Miss Field had said that Nora's bust was really too big and that she must come out of the ballet." "Miss Field said . . ." Everything, life and death and the stars in their courses depended upon what Miss Field said. Occasionally there was an outburst of hysteria—faces were slapped, tears were shed. Mothers bowed icily to each other and sat tight-lipped, staring with disdain at the cavortings of their rival's progeny who, serenely unaware of these primeval undertones, were enjoying themselves tip top.

Finally the great day dawned.

The curtain rose, I think at 2:00 pm but it may have been 2:30. However, it definitely did rise, disclosing a pretty garden scene, crowded with bright and eager children, all hell bent on a future, if not immediate stardom, and all under fourteen, with the exception of one, who shall be forever nameless—for we suspected then and I still suspect was nineteen if she was a day.

The opening chorus was led by a radiant fair little girl and a plumpish, very assured little boy in a white knickerbocker suit. The girl was described in the programme as "Little June Tripp" and the boy was "Master Noel Coward." They sang with extreme abandon "School, School, Goodbye to School."

Fifteen years later on that same stage "Master Noel Coward," now grown to man's estate, was playing with equal abandon a drug addict in his own play *The Vortex*. Twenty-two years later still with thinning hair but fortunately with most of his own teeth, he is playing at a different theatre a middle-aged, immoral, egomaniac with even more abandon [*Present Laughter*].

After a matinée of this rather shocking spectacle into Master Coward's orbit come Miss Lila Field, accompanied by her sister Bertha, and in a moment thirty-seven years drop away and the past and the present become as one. To begin with neither Lila nor Bertha have had the grace to change at all.

There is the same warm vitality, the same charming voices talking nineteen to the dozen, enthusiastically shouting each other down.

The Goldfish has been rewritten and is to be reissued in book form and possibly re-produced at Chichester. Would Master Noël Coward be a dear and write a foreword? Mr. Noël Coward, beguiled and charmed as ever and with much gratitude in his heart, says "Yes" immediately, for the very good reason that he would have been bitterly hurt if anyone else in the world had been asked to do so. This is the brief foreword . . .

The Goldfish is a play for children to be acted by children. It was written and has been rewritten by a lady forever young in heart. I have just finished reading this latest version of the play and for me to view it dispassionately is obviously out of the question. I cannot tell you if it is good, bad or indifferent, because every line of it is twined firmly round my Theatre roots.

Reading it again was an interesting personal experience. I discovered after reading the first line of a long speech I could close my eyes and say the whole speech through. The lyrics brought back to my ear the music, such pretty music it was—or was it? I don't know.

I remember so clearly, so very clearly, Master Alfred Willmore as King Goldfish singing "I lived within a bowl of glass. Heigho, a prince am I." Master Burford Hampden as the ruthless King Starfish "I am a really first class king/O'er the seas my praises ring." And, of course, my own song as Prince Mussel, the Court Jester—"Fairest Queen, you'll never guess/How I praise your loveliness/I've a heart that loves you so/ But alas, you must not know."

I remember hearing for the first time in my life an audience in a theatre laughing and applauding. I remember smelling for the first time the drying "size" on canvas, the pungency of the hot "gelatines" in the lime light and footlights, the unforgettable, indescribable dressing room smell—greasepaint, face powder, new clothes and cold cream. "I remember, I remember the house where I was born"—that actually I cannot remember at all but I certainly remember the theatre where I was born and the play in which I was born—and that play is *The Goldfish*.

Now perhaps a new generation of children will see it and act in it. I presume that it was with a weather eye on these chubby sophisticates that Lila has seen fit to interpolate some fairly up to date slang and other reminders that we are living in a changing world.

The Goldfish retains its magic and for one rapidly ageing little boy, a magic that will never die.

(June 1947)

The young Noël clearly caught somebody's eye, because by the time *The Goldfish* closed he'd been summoned to play a small role in the company run by Charles—later Sir Charles—Hawtrey at the Prince of Wales Theatre. Hawtrey was one of the leading actor-managers of the day and the play, due to open in three days, was a comedy called *The Great Name.*

Noël was to play a page boy in the last act, who addresses his one line to Hawtrey, who is supposedly playing the piano in the artist's room at Queen's Hall.

That one line was rehearsed by Noël and Violet with every possible inflection and several that were not. He was meant to enter and say— "Stop that noise at once, please. In there they're playing *The Meistersingers.* Making such a horrible noise. We're used to *good* music here."

That one line became a full production . . .

" 'STOP that noise at once, please' was to be said with tremendous force, with a barely perceptible note of awe creeping into the voice, 'in there (*big gesture to the left*) they're playing *The Meistersingers*' (*pause for effect*). Then, with biting contempt, 'Making such a horrible noise,' then (*swelling with pride*) 'we're used to *good* music here' (*rising inflection on the word 'good'*).

On the night . . . "I have seldom seen a human being so astounded. He swung round on the piano stool with a glaze of horror in his eyes. After I had made my dramatic exit there was a slight pause, and I heard Mr. Hawtrey say to the stage manager in a weary voice: 'Never let me see that boy again.' "

But he was to see "that boy" again many times and Noël was to say in years to come—"Hawtrey taught me everything I know. Every time now when I'm playing a comedy scene and I'm in trouble, and it's tricky to do, I think—'what would the Guvnor have done?' "

Hawtrey—having relented in the face of implacable ambition—took Noël aside . . .

" 'Listen, boy, I know you've been brought up as a little gentleman, but this is supposed to be a common little boy. Do you think you could speak Cockney?'

"So he said—'If you come on very quickly, say your line *very,* very quickly in Cockney, and go off, I'll give you an extra entrance. You can bring on a vase at the beginning of the scene and put it down. And walk off. *Quickly.*'

"So he bribed me with an extra entrance. A perfectly dear thing to do.

"I finished the brief run in what was almost certainly impenetrable Cockney."

"He was extremely kind to me as a little boy. I can't think why, I drove him mad. He used to say—'Keep away from me, boy,' I was always chattering at him. He signed an autograph book which I had, with sweet peas on the cover, seventeen times, then he gave up. And I was not allowed to stand in the wings, because I once made him miss an entrance by chattering to him.

"He was a perfectly brilliant comedian and one of the most sensitive directors . . . He used to watch me very carefully when I was rehearsing and he never bullied me. I was very precocious and I think quite a lot of other directors would have said 'Oh, shut up!' but I was eager to learn and he knew it. I used to stand at the side of the stage watching him, and he used to teach me—he taught me how to laugh. I remember him standing over me at rehearsal, in front of the whole company, and saying—'Now, boy, you've got to laugh. Now start with this. "Ho, ha, ha, ha, ha, ha, ha." But put your breath right.' And he stood over me till I did it. He said—'Now smile with it a bit,' and I'd go 'Ha, ha, ha.' And he said—'Now give way,' and I'd go 'Ha, ha, ha, ha.'

"That was entirely technical and, of course, it was an enormous help. He could laugh on the stage indefinitely. He taught me also to use my hands and my arms and swing them without looking as though I were acting at all. That was his great trick and it always used to infuriate me, even when I was quite young, because certain critics at the time, and certain members of the public, said—'Oh, Hawtrey's always exactly the same,' implying that he wasn't acting. But every time he went on to the stage, he raised his voice half a tone to pitch. He looked perfectly natural and relaxed, but he wasn't in the least natural and relaxed. One can never be natural and relaxed if one's a good comedian; there are too many things to think about."

"Hawtrey was the master of the naturalistic gesture.

"I honestly think that I've learnt practically everything I know about comedy playing from him, not only from what he actually taught me, but from his example."

Hawtrey had another production ready to go on. *Where the Rainbow Ends* had its initial production at the Savoy Theatre and was to become a classic children's Christmas play that came to rival *Peter Pan* for the next forty years.

Noël as Cannard the Page, with Sir Charles Hawtrey at the piano.

Noël was cast again as a page boy but in a much more important part.

Even more important as it turned out, was the fact that the leading lady was Miss Esmé Wynne, whom Noël described as "a podgy, brown-haired little girl with a bleating voice." Over the next few years she was to become Noël's closest friend and in many ways his Muse.

Ballet mistress was Miss Italia Conti. Miss Conti was responsible for casting any major production that required children. She and Noël did not get on, even though in later years she would claim credit for having discovered him.

Battle lines were effectively drawn the day she suggested to him that, as his part was only in the first act, he might like to appear as a hyena and a frog in the later scenes. Violet was firm on the point. His part, though small, placed him as one of the *principals*. He should not lower himself by crawling on all fours in a hot hyena suit!

Noël later enshrined Miss Conti in verse . . .

Ode to Italia Conti
Oh, Italia, with thy face so pale,
Why must thou float about the Stalls
Where Mr. Hawtrey sits?

Dost think that passing thus thou wilt prevail
Upon him to cut out the finest bits
Which we poor principals in our parts must speak?
We often hear the hapless tremble
When they're corrected by your raucous squeak.
To principals you like not you will serve
Out contracts in which cheek and guile are blended
And then you have the most appalling nerve
To say they must be yours till world is ended.
In vain you've tried to lure us to your classes—
We are not such unmitigated asses.

Ms. Conti had her own take on the young Noël.

"Little Noel was a shy, bashful child and used to sit on my knee in the lodgings and cry because he was so terribly homesick. Little Noel was a clever boy, but I never regarded him as normal, even in those days. He was very emotional, but full of brains."

In the same period he wrote a series of short verses he called "Concert Types." One of them he certainly knew something about. It was entitled . . .

The Child Prodigy
An infant prodigy of nine
Is shoved upon the stage in white.
She starts off in a dismal whine
About a Dark and Stormy Night,
A burglar whose heart is true,
Despite his wicked-looking face!
And what a little child can do
To save her Mama's jewel case!
This may bring tears to every eye.
It does not set my heart on fire.
I'd like to stand serenely by
And watch that Horrid Child expire!

Nineteen twelve saw him in a musical little piece ("Music by F. Chopin") called *An Autumn Idyll* starring a Miss Ruby Ginner. Miss Ginner herself appeared as an Autumn Leaf. "Rather too large to be blown about by the wind," as Noël noted.

"As a mushroom I provided a few of the more light-hearted moments. . . . I wore grey silk skin tights, a large grey silk hat like a gargantuan muffin and a diaphanous frill round my middle to conceal any unaesthetic protuberances. My entrance consisted of a series of abandoned high kicks, slightly higher with the right leg than with the left, typifying the carefree *joie de vivre* of the average mushroom."

The critic from *The Times* was suitably impressed.

"Miss Joan Carroll and Mr. Noel Coward as the Toadstool and the Mushroom headed delightfully a little troupe of various small and engaging fungi."

Then back to Hawtrey again for a sketch called *A Little Fowl Play* at the Coliseum. It was here that Noël's adolescent feelings about The Theatre started to come into focus . . .

With Joan Carroll in *An Autumn Idyll,* Savoy Theatre, 1912.

"In between the matinée and evening performances the Coliseum stage had an even greater allure for me; with only a few working lights left on here and there, it appeared vaster and more mysterious, like an empty echoing cathedral smelling faintly of dust. Sometimes the safety curtain was not lowered, and I used to stand down on the edge of the footlights singing shrilly into the shadowy auditorium. I also danced in the silence. Occasionally a cleaner appeared with a broom and pail, or a stage hand walked across the stage, but they never paid any attention to me. An empty theatre is romantic, every actor knows the feeling of it; complete silence emphasized rather than broken by the dim traffic noises outside, apparently hundreds of miles away; the muffled sound of a motor-horn and the thin reedy wail of a penny whistle being played to the gallery queue. As a rule there are a few exit lights left burning, casting blue shadows across the rows of empty seats. It seems incredible that within an hour or two this stillness will awake to garish red-and-gilt splendour, and be shattered by the sibilance of hundreds of voices, and the exciting discords and trills of the orchestra tuning up."

Another new and defining friendship began around this time.

Esmé Wynne—she of the bleating voice who had the starring role for those two productions of *Where the Rainbow Ends*—became an inseparable pal. "We alternated between childishness and strange maturity. The theatre had led us far in precocity and we discussed life and death and sex and religion with sublime sophistication.

"One of the most important aspects of this relationship was the fact that she was determined to be a writer, an ambition that filled me with competitive fervour. She wrote poems. Reams and reams of them, love songs, sonnets and villanelles; alive with elves, mermaids, leafy glades, and Pan (a good deal of Pan). Not to be outdone in artistic endeavour, I set many of the poems to music . . ."

On one occasion with disastrous effect. The poem was one of which Esmé was extremely proud. It ran . . .

Our little Love is dying,
On his head are lately crimson petals
Faded quite,
The breath of Passion withered them last night.

SAVOY THEATRE.

Licensed by the Lord Chamberlain to
Mr. G. A. Richardson (Secretary Savoy Theatre and Opera, Ltd.), Savoy Hotel, W.C.

ON THURSDAY EVENING, DECEMBER 21st, AT 8.

Mr. CHARLES HAWTREY'S PRODUCTION.

WHERE THE RAINBOW ENDS

By CLIFFORD MILLS and JOHN RAMSEY.
Music specially composed by Mr. ROGER QUILTER.

Characters
(in the order of their appearance)

Rosamund Carey	Miss ESMÉ WYNNE
Crispian Carey	Master PHILIP TONGE
William	Master NOEL COWARD
Cubs	Master GUIDO CHIARLETTI
Matilda Flint	Miss JEANNIE THOMAS
Joseph Flint	Mr. C. W. SOMERSET
Schlappe	Mr. HENRY MORRELL
The Genie of the Carpet	Mr. NORMAN MACOWAN
Jim Blunders	Master SIDNEY SHERWOOD
Betty Blunders	Miss DOT TEMPLE
St. George of England	Mr. REGINALD OWEN
The Dragon King	Mr. CLIFTON ALDERSON
Will o' the Wisp	Miss MAVIS YORKE
Danks	Mr. REGINALD P. LAMB
The Sea Witch	Miss HELEN VICARY
Captain Carey	Mr NORMAN MACOWAN
Mrs. Carey	Miss LYDIA BILBROOKE
The Slacker	Master HARRY DUFF
The Slitherslime	Mr. MAURICE TOSH
The Spirit of The Lake	Miss GRACE SEPPINGS
Dragon Sentry	Mr. J. K. EDRO
Hope	Miss ZOE GORDON
A Mother	Miss IVY WILLIAMS

Dragons, Hyenas, Elves, Flower Fairies, Dragon Flies, Rainbow Children, Spiders, Caterpillars, Toads, a Leopard, etc.

Flower Fairies:—Grace Sepping, Isla Raine, Rosie Block, Ruth Block.
Dragon Flies, Water Lillies, and Rainbow Children:—Ivy Bell, Edna Brown, Celia Block, Ella Jones, Eileen Grist, Rita Vivian, Irene Birch, Esmé Herzee, Ruby and Olga Warneford, Margaret Stuart, Dorothy Moody, Kathleen Jones, Marjorie Withey, etc.

Elves, Toads, Hyenas, etc.:—Leslie Ryecroft, Reginald Grasdorf, Philip Bates, Walter Woodgate, Norman Haddock, Jack Rea, John Renshaw, Robert Chapman, Maurice Hansard, Frank Bates, Jim Taylor, Sidney Spiro, Harry Withey, Ernest Wright, William Wodehouse, John Dixon, Arthur Brockner, etc.

Dragons:—Norman Wrighton, Arthur Grayson, Charles Gordon, Maurice Tosh, A. Charlwood, Stanley Ramsden, Leslie Rea.

Noël set them "to a merry lilt" . . .

Our little Love is dying on his head . . .

Ms. Wynne was not amused.

Noël began to write himself. "Short stories, beastly little whimsies, also about Pan, and Fauns and Cloven Hooves."

If anyone deserves the credit (or blame) for encouraging Noël to be a writer that person was undoubtedly Esmé Wynne.

In later years, when Noël was making his name, Esmé would send him her work for his professional critique. His notes to her offer some interesting sidelights on his own emerging theories of drama. In many ways they comprised a first draft for the book on the theatre he intended to write one day and never did.

You're at your old game—you *point* things too much. (Let the fact of there being a scarcity of men be apparent in their *attitude,* but don't mention it, because it's blatant!)

Your dinner scene is ridiculously short. You must give at least two pages to every course, if not more.

WHERE THE RAINBOW ENDS

in its twenty-first year

ITALIA CONTI

presents this Patriotic Fairy Play Featuring St. George

AT THE

HOLBORN EMPIRE

W.C.1.

SPECIAL MATINEE SEASON commencing
**Monday, December 21st, 1931, and Daily at 2.15,
till Saturday, January 23rd, 1932, inclusive**

All Star Cast and 50 of ITALIA CONTI'S Fairy
Sprites dancing to ROGER QUILTER'S Music

POPULAR PRICES AS USUAL

Special quotations to all members of The Boy Scouts and Girl
Guides, etc. and other associations.

F. H. CONTI (Manager for Italia Conti), Holborn Empire, W.C.1

PRICES (including tax): Orchestra Stalls, 7/6; Dress Circle,
7/6 and 5/9; Pit Stalls, 5/9 and 3/6.

In 1929 The Rt. Hon. The Lord Mayor of London said :—"Every boy and girl
in the British Empire should see this splendid Patriotic Play."

The Rt. Rev. Lord Bishop of London says :—I consider the Play is the most
beautiful Play in Christendom."

BOX OFFICE NOW OPEN

NOEL COWARD

WHEN A "CONTI" BOY (21 years ago)

HE APPEARED IN THE ORIGINAL
PRODUCTION OF

WHERE THE RAINBOW ENDS

You must not abbreviate words and use suburban slang such as "vamping," "coddling," etc., unless it's essential psychologically. (It's quite appalling and the obvious result of the people you're mixing with—you never used to do it.)

You have a serene and maddening disregard for superficial details which destroys atmosphere in exactly the places where you wish to use them to create it. (One bright moment that shattered my sensibilities is the thought that Peter's room in 1915–16 being filled with lusty photographs of Marie Tempest—then about 59—and Mrs. Patrick Campbell—then about 48.)

You've devoted your entire energy to the writing and haven't given a thought to *construction* or sense of the Theatre or Drama or climax—all of which are necessary in a good play.

You have a Prose mind not a dialogue mind. Novelists can't write plays and playwrights can't write novels—at least very *seldom*—Clemence Dane and Galsworthy.

(1915)

Fifty years later he would almost certainly have qualified some of his earlier commandments.

In early 1913 Italia Conti reenters the scene with an offer for Noël to join the cast of a play about to be produced at the Liverpool Repertory company. The play was *Hannele,* a translation from the German, and the director Basil Dean, who was to have a significant impact on Noël's career in the 1920s.

There were ten children on the train to Liverpool with Miss Conti but for Noël one of them stood out.

She was "a vivacious child with ringlets to whom I took an instant fancy. She wore a black satin coat and a black velvet military hat with a peak, her face was far from pretty, but tremendously alive. She was very *mondaine,* carried a handbag with a powder-puff and frequently dabbed her generously turned-up nose. She confided to me that her name was Gertrude Lawrence, but that I was to call her Gert because everybody else did, that she was fourteen. She then gave me an orange and told me a few mildly dirty stories, and I loved her from then onwards."

In her turn Gertie remembers Noël as "a thin, unusually shy boy with a slight lisp."

The Observer's verdict—"An excellent Slightly in Mr. Noël Coward"— would certainly have pleased him but hardly more than hearing a voice in the crowd at the Stage Door shout out—"Good old Slightly!"

As critic Kenneth Tynan concluded in later years—"In 1913 he was Slightly in *Peter Pan* and you might say that he has been *wholly* in *Peter Pan* ever since."

He was to play Slightly again the following year . . .

"I was immensely elated at the thought of actually appearing on the same stage with Madge Titheradge, who was playing Peter. . . . I had seen her in *Tiger Cub* at the Garrick and was deeply in love with her

"Poj" (Noël) and "Stoj" (Esmé).

"Isn't motor cycling glorious? I did it a lot on my cousin's cycle down in Cornwall. It certainly beats motoring for thrills! Good bye now, darling old Stodgekins, from your ever ever loving Pal to all eternity. PODGE. N.B. You got some Romantic in your last letter." A letter from "Podge" (Noël) to "Stoj" (Esmé). More often "Podge" would be spelled "Poj."

husky voice and swift, alert charm. That first matinée I was going down the stairs on to the stage for the underground scene when I met her face to face; she shook hands warmly with me and said: 'My name's Madge, what's yours?' A never-to-be-forgotten, most charming gesture."

Miss Titheradge was an actress of great power and in the scene where Tinker Bell will die unless the audience applauds loudly, she asked—"Do you believe in fairies?" so aggressively that small children burst into tears and clung to their parents instead of clapping their hands. She was not asked to play the part again.

———

Meanwhile Noël's literary creativity knew no bounds.

Apart from the "beastly little whimsies," there was the novel—*Cherry Pan* . . .

"*Cherry Pan,* I regret to tell you, was the daughter of the Great God Pan and was garrulous and tiresome to the point of nausea. Having materialized suddenly on a summer evening in Sussex, she proceeded with excruciating pagan archness to wreak havoc in a country parsonage before returning winsomely to her woodland glades and elfin grots. I

"In November I satisfied a long-cherished desire to be *in Peter Pan*, which was the Mecca of all child actors . . . I was engaged at four pounds a week to play 'Slightly' . . . It was all that I hoped it would be and more, and after the London run the entire company went on tour."

remember being bitterly offended by a friend who suggested that the title should be changed to *Bedpan*."

It took some thirty thousand words before *Cherry Pan* "finally petered out, owing to lack of enthusiasm on my part and lack of stamina on hers." She also persuaded her perpetrator to focus on writing plays.

Meanwhile, in the prose he did write—he would recall later—"I flung aside all bastard whimsies and concentrated on realism. No pert elf or faun dared even to peep round a tree at me. Pan and Pierrot retired disgruntled, into oblivion as far as I was concerned and, I am glad to say, have remained there. My mind, not unnaturally, jumped over-far in the opposite direction. I dealt, almost exclusively, with the most lurid types; tarts, pimps, sinister courtesans, and cynical adulterers whirled across my pages in great profusion. This phase finally passed owing to a withering lack of response from magazine editors, but it was all useful and I don't regret any of it."

——

And, indeed, these are the years when young talent is meant to make—and learn from—its mistakes.

As a young actor Noël was inclined to be overemphatic . . . to aspire to the highest note in a song . . . to exit with an unnecessarily high high kick.

At an audition "my bearing was a blend of assurance and professional vivacity; the fact that my bowels were as water I hope was not apparent to anybody. . . . My voice was small but my diction clear, assisted by a violent interplay of facial expressions. My rendition of a song in those days was a model of exhaustive technique. Sustained pauses, gay laughs, knowing looks."

In later years, when actors in his shows overstepped the mark, Noël wouldn't tolerate their excesses but he perfectly well understood them.

Nineteen sixteen saw him touring with Esmé in a revival of *Charley's Aunt*—for many years a surefire comedy. Noël played Charley.

He remembered that the producer (J. R. Crawford) directed rehearsals "with all the airy deftness of a rheumatic deacon producing *Macbeth* for a church social."

"We played at Glasgow, Edinburgh, Newcastle and Birmingham and all the suburban dates such as Wimbledon and Hammersmith and Kennington. When we were at Kennington Mother invited a lot of the company to tea between a matinée and evening performance and we were very excited when Pauline Chase consented to come. It's only a little way from Kennington Theatre to Clapham Common, most of us went by tram, but Pauline Chase and her friend Miss Berri (who played the Mermaid) drove to our house in a shining and smart yellow two-seater, which threw Miss Pitney, who was peering through the ground floor lace curtains, into transports of excitement. The tea was elaborate, the white Worcester cups (wedding present) were brought out and Mother insisted proudly that I should sing, which I did, to my own and everybody else's acute embarrassment.

"The tea party, however, on the whole was considered a great success and the remains of the home-made coffee sponge with walnuts and the Fuller's almond cake brightened our lives for the rest of the week."

For an actor in those days—and for many to come—touring the English provinces was a rite of passage. A little primitive radio but not even a rumor of television. And the internet? Something you caught fish in? Every town of even reasonable size had a theatre—sometimes two—and those theatres would be part of one "chain" or another. An actor in "variety" or music hall could and did make a living going round the "halls"— and never even needing to change their act.

For the ambitious—like the young Noël—the point of touring was to hope that some impresario would get to see your blazing talent and book you for the West End . . . so that you wouldn't *have* to tour the provinces and live in dubious "digs." Before you became a *tour de force*—you were forced to tour.

Meanwhile, you might as well make the best of your touring days. At least they provided him with the inspiration for a song—once they were safely behind him . . .

Touring Days

I've often wondered if it's possible to recapture
The magic of bygone days.
I feel that one couldn't quite resuscitate
All the rapture and joy of a youthful phase.
But still it's nice to remember
The things we used to do
When you were on tour with me, my dear
And I was on tour with you.

Touring days, touring days,
What ages it seems to be
Since the landlady at Norwich
Served a mouse up in the porridge
And a beetle in the morning tea.

Touring days, touring days,
Far back into the past we gaze.
The landlady was always drunk in Aberdeen,
She used to keep her money in the soup tureen.
One night you swallowed half a crown
And turned pea-green.
Those wonderful touring days.

We used to tip the dressers every Friday night
And pass it over lightly when they came in tight.
But somehow to us it seemed all right.
Those wonderful touring days.

By now Noël felt he was truly a part of what he liked to call "the mad, mad world of powder and paint"—a world in which every up seems to precede a down and both are a necessary part of the learning experience.

For example, later in 1916 he was cast in a play called *The Light Blues* by producer Robert Courtneidge, father of Cicely Courtneidge, who would go on to be a leading star of the London stage.

She remembered Noël as being "a thin, pale-faced youth who always seemed to know everything and infuriated me because he was always right."

Well, he wasn't always right as far as her father was concerned. Mr. Courtneidge considered Noël was taking far too much for granted for someone with limited experience. One day "he called me out before the entire company and mortified me to the dust. He informed me that I was not only a very young actor but a very bad actor, and that in addition to this I was practically a criminal for accepting a salary of four pounds a week when all I did to earn it was to fool about and giggle on the stage . . . I slunk away more bitterly humiliated than I had ever been in my life."

Cicely patted him on the back and said—"You mustn't mind Father."

"Currently resting," out of work, 1916.

But he did mind. The show ran for only two weeks and then he could take his humiliation elsewhere.

Up, down—and occasionally sideways—Noël persevered and continually extended his range of talents. Actor, singer, writer, composer . . .

"I appeared at crowded auditions wearing an immaculate suit and an air of amused condescension which deceived nobody and merely succeeded in irritating the other aspirants. I had written a number of light songs during the past years and I sang them repeatedly, accompanying myself on the piano.

"There was a bright 'point' number: 'Forbidden Fruit,' which I think is worthy of record, as it was the first complete lyric I ever wrote. The perceptive reader will, I am sure, detect, even in this very youthful effort, that unfortunate taint of worldly cynicism which I am so frequently told, degrades much of my later work."

Forbidden Fruit

Every Peach, out of reach, is attractive
'Cos it's just a little bit too high,
And you'll find that every man
Will try to pluck it if he can
As he passes by.

For the brute loves the fruit that's forbidden
And I'll bet you half a crown
He'll appreciate the flavour of it much, much more
If he has to climb a bit to shake it down.

In later years Noël professed himself less than satisfied with one phrase in his original lyric: "the suggested wager of half a crown rather lets down the tone. One cannot help feeling that a bet of fifty pounds, or at least a fiver, would be more in keeping with the general urbanity of the theme; for a brief moment the veneer is scratched and Boodle's, White's and Buck's are elbowed aside by the Clapham Tennis Club, but this perhaps is hypercriticism and it must be remembered that to the author half a crown in 1916 was the equivalent of five pounds in 1926. Also, it rhymes with 'down.'"

(It may have been his first complete lyric in 1916 but it didn't see the light of performance until 1924 and publication until 1953. Such being the vagaries of show business.)

"My actual achievements to date amounted to very little. I had written quite a lot, in spare moments, during the last few years: singly and in collaboration with Esmé, short stories, verses, and one meretricious full-length novel. I had also composed a good many songs and written lyrics . . ."

By no means all of their output ended up in the literary bottom drawer. A one-act play called *Ida Collaborates*—a joint effort by Noël and Esmé under the pseudonym "Esnomel"—was produced at the Theatre Royal, Aldershot, in August 1917 and had a subsequent short tour. Then, another one-act (*Woman and Whiskey*) appeared in January 1918 at the Wimbledon Theatre as a curtain-raiser to the evening's featured play.

━━

"Another brief engagement [in 1917] was as a 'super' in a D.W. Griffith film. I was paid, I think a pound a day, for which I wheeled a wheelbarrow up and down a village street in Worcestershire with Lillian Gish. The name of the film was *Hearts of the World* and it left little mark on me beyond a most unpleasant memory of getting up at five every morning and making my face bright yellow."

When he observed that in his key shot he would be pushing his wheelbarrow UP the hill—i.e., with his back to the camera—he suggested to Griffith that it might be more dramatic if he were to push it DOWN instead. Griffith couldn't have cared less. Down? Fine. And the cinemagoing public had their first glimpse of Noël Coward . . .

And Noël his first glimpse of Lillian Gish, who would be a lifelong friend.

Always ready to try his hand at some new form of artistic expression, on one occasion Noël decided to try his feet as a professional dancer . . .

"I became, briefly, a professional dancer. . . . I partnered a girl named Eileen Dennis, and we were engaged by the Elysée Restaurant [now the Café de Paris] to appear during dinner and supper. A slow waltz, a tango, and a rather untidy one-step, made up our programme. . . . We were neither of us ever invited to appear naked out of pies at private supper parties, in fact the whole engagement from the point of view of worldly experience was decidedly disappointing."

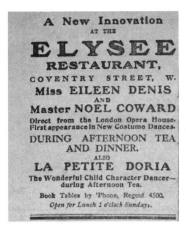

A New Innovation
AT THE

ELYSEE
RESTAURANT,
COVENTRY STREET, W.

Miss EILEEN DENIS
AND
Master NOEL COWARD

Direct from the London Opera House.
First appearance in New Costume Dances.

DURING AFTERNOON TEA
AND DINNER.
ALSO

LA PETITE DORIA
The Wonderful Child Character Dancer—
during Afternoon Tea.

Book Tables by 'Phone, Regent 4500.

Open for Lunch 1 o'clock Sundays.

Noël and Betty Chester,
Birmingham, 1919.

The low point was the evening when Noël decided to interpolate a song. Unfortunately, after one chorus he forgot the words. Murmuring a series of "la-la-las," he made an ignominious exit. A bewildered Colonel Blimp–type diner was heard to say—"What an *extraordinary* young man! Nothing but 'la-la-la.' I can't get over it."

Some years later when Noël appeared at the Café de Paris, he did rather better . . .

As the decade drifted to a close—having survived the first "war to end all wars"—Noël could honestly claim to have made some sort of mark. As a young actor, writer, singer, dancer (?), man-about-town. His options seemed virtually endless.

Oh, how fortunate I was to have been born poor. If Mother had been able to afford to send me to private school, Eton and Oxford or Cambridge, it would have probably set me back years. I have always distrusted too much education and intellectualism; it seems to me that they are always dead wrong about things that really matter, however right they may be in their literary and artistic assessments. There is something to me both arid and damp about dwelling too much among the literary shades of the past. My good fortune was to have a bright, acquisitive, but not, *not* an intellectual mind, and to have been impelled by circumstances to get out and earn my living and help with the instalments on the house. I believe that had my early formative years been passed in more assured circumstances I might quite easily have slipped into preciousness; as it was I merely had to slip *out* of precociousness and bring home the bacon. The world of the theatre is a strong forcing-house, and I believe I knew more about the basic facts of life by the age of fourteen than the more carefully untutored knew at twenty-five. In any event, my own peculiar circumstances suited me and on the whole the results haven't been too bad. After which encouraging self-slap on the back, I will bring this entry to a close.

All in all he felt that he had come to the end of "a somewhat elfin and whimsical phase."

And he'd just written this play that American producer Gilbert Miller had said he'd definitely—well probably/definitely—put on.

It was called *I'll Leave It to You . . .*

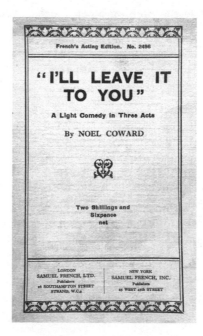

French's Acting Edition. No. 2496

"I'LL LEAVE IT
TO YOU"

A Light Comedy in Three Acts

By NOEL COWARD

Two Shillings and
Sixpence
net

LONDON
SAMUEL FRENCH, LTD.
Publishers
26 SOUTHAMPTON STREET
STRAND, W.C.2

NEW YORK
SAMUEL FRENCH, INC.
Publishers
25 WEST 45th STREET

2

ON WRITING A PLAY (1)

From Juvenilia to *The Vortex*

"Writing a Play Is Both a Craft and an Art"

"The most important ingredients of a play are life, death, food, sex and money—but not necessarily in that order."

———

The Unattainable (1918) · *The Impossible Wife* (1918) · *The Rat Trap* (1918) ·
The Dope Cure (1919) · *Humoresque* (1919) · *The Last Trick* (1919) ·
The Knight of the Burning Pestle (1919) (Actor) · *I'll Leave It to You* (1920) ·
The Young Idea (1923) · *The Vortex* (1924)

Being nothing if not a quick study, Noël soon felt he knew enough about writing plays.

He had already settled into his own style and was—as he was with most things he did—perfectly happy with it. In 1919 . . .

"I conceived a passably good plot for a play, and as, in those days, conception was only removed from achievement by the actual time required for putting the words on paper, it was completed within a week."

(Interestingly many of his biggest successes over the years—*Private Lives, Blithe Spirit,* for example—were written within a few days.)

"It was entitled *The Last Trick* and was a melodrama in four acts. The first and second acts were quite amusing, the third act good, and the last act weak and amateurish. The plot hinged on the 'revenge' motif and wasn't particularly original but the dialogue was effective, and showed a marked improvement on my other work. I took the play to Gilbert Miller [an American producer currently in London to whom Noël has been given an introduction] and he seemed to be impressed with it. He said he was leaving for New York . . . and would like to take it with him, and that he might possibly be able to arrange for it to be produced."

Miller, in fact, did eventually secure an option on it from producer Al Woods. Noël wrote to Violet: "Passing peacefully away." Woods offered $500 for one year, then increased it to $2,000 for outright purchase— a figure that was far beyond Noël's expectations. However, the play was never staged. Woods explained to Noël later that he had had the piece rewritten several times by different writers but had not been able to make it work. But in those far-off days $2,000 was reward enough for Noël.

The figure of $500 was to reappear two years later on that first visit to the U.S. *Metropolitan* magazine offered him that to adapt another of his plays, *I'll Leave It to You,* into a short story . . .

"I reflected gleefully that for $500 I would gladly consider turning *War and Peace* into a music-hall sketch."

———

"Buoyed up by Miller's encouragement, I wrote two bad plays—one of which was called *The Impossible Wife*—and one better one. The third, *The Rat Trap,* was my first really serious attempt at psychological conflict. Even in the light of later experience, I can still see in it two well-written scenes. As a whole, of course, it was immature, but it was much steadier than anything I had done hitherto. The last act, as usual, went to pieces, but when I had finished it, I felt for the first time with genuine conviction, that I could really write plays."

Incidentally, Noël was wrong when he said that he had written "bad plays that weren't worth considering."

They may have been juvenilia in terms of theatrical production but in them he's telling us a great deal about himself . . .

Coming, as he did, from a lower-middle-class/upper-working-class (and distinctly impoverished) background, he was aware of the rigid class boundaries in English society at that time and anxious to break through them personally.

It was a breakthrough when he got to meet Mrs. Astley-Cooper through a friend and was invited to stay for a weekend . . .

Rare photograph of Mrs. Astley-Cooper (center), with Noël (lower right) and house party at Hambleton Hall.

"It was a pleasant experience staying in a well-run country house. The trappings of life there were new to me; a fire in my bedroom every night, dinner clothes laid out neatly on the bed, brass cans of hot water and deep baths encased in shiny brown wood. People came over and lunched or dined occasionally. A flurry of wheels in the drive announced them and the murmur of different voices echoed up from the hall as I grandly descended the polished oak staircase, very careful not to slip in my new patent-leather shoes."

Mrs. Astley-Cooper was to prove something of a thread through these early years. Running into her in Italy a little later, he was to meet Gladys Calthrop, who was to become a designer for just about all of his theatrical work for many years and a friend for life. But from the outset Noël felt himself wary of judging her as a social equal . . .

"Her brain was alert, and her sense of humour keen, though somewhat impaired by a slight bias towards highbrow Bohemianism."

⸺

Those early plays provide fascinating glimpses of what was to come in his later work . . . and some of the stylistic excesses he would learn to correct.

For example . . .

The Unattainable (1918) is the dramatic equivalent of a series of piano exercises which feature characters and histrionic displays of sub-Wildean dialogue.

—Man always sighs after the unattainable.

—What about Woman?

—Oh, Woman never admits even to herself that anything IS unattainable.

The action is set in the Aston-Hoopers' Rutland home and features Mrs. Aston-Hooper (*née* Astley-Cooper), her married daughters—with whom she does not particularly get on—and various other young people who fall in love with each other, only to find that the object of their affection is otherwise attracted.

There is a great deal of talk about a forthcoming *soirée* at a neighbor's house and also an imminent garden party—although we never get to see either. There is also talk about taking drugs, which, not surprisingly, splits the characters by age groups in terms of their attitude towards it.

At one point one of the young men sits at the piano, while the others gather round, and sings "Forbidden Fruit." (This was Noël's first "complete" song for which he wrote words and music and, had the play ever been performed, this would have marked its introduction. As it was, it would not be heard in public until the biographical film on the life of Gertrude Lawrence, *Star!*, in 1968.)

Here's an example of early Coward . . .

The Unattainable (1918)

IRIS: Then you've been to China, Mr. Saville?

KATT: I've visited practically every interesting part of the world.

IRENE: Have you been to Paris?

KATT: Well yes, that is generally the first place to go.

IRENE: I've never gone farther than Ryde. But still that's something.

LADY
CARRINGTON: Undoubtedly.

IRIS: I like men who go about a bit and see life.

LADY C.: I suppose that is why so many women marry commercial travellers.

ALICE: But do go on telling us about the opium den, Mr. Saville. It's frightfully thrilling.

KATT: There's really nothing more to tell. The temporary satisfaction given by the drug doesn't last long, then one once more becomes normal and generally the victim of horrible depression.

ELVIRA: But really it's worth it. Think how glorious it must be to merge one's personality into a fantastic world of sensuous dreams.

LADY C.: Really, Miss Lestrange, some of your ideas verge on the indecent.

IRIS: I rather agree with Elvira. It must be a wonderful sensation.

MAJOR C.: Damned unhealthy form of amusement, I call it.

MRS. H-N.: One wouldn't expect a man like you to be in the least attracted to drug taking, dear Major. It appeals to the more degenerate natures.

NORMAN: I should love to try it.

LADY C.: My dear boy, your frantic efforts to be decadent are almost pathetic.

IRIS: I should love to smoke just one little pipe of opium, just to see what happened.

KATT: You'd probably be able to obtain the same result by crossing the Channel on a rough day.

IRENE: Oh, how disgusting! But I'm really a splendid sailor.

MRS. H-N.: But I thought you said you'd never been farther than Ryde.

IRENE: Those Solent boats rock dreadfully. Mother said it was splendid of me not to be ill.

LADY C.: If there's one topic of conversation I thoroughly dislike, it's *mal de mer.* Couldn't we talk of something else?

EDWARD: Democracy!

LADY C.: That's equally nauseous but less blatant.

IRIS: I'd prefer to continue our discussion of drugging.

KATT: Doping is the correct term.

ELVIRA: How *too* descriptive.

HILARY: Doping is quite a hobby among society women in Paris.

JIMMY POOL: By Jove, I'd like to see some of them at it!

IRIS: I knew a girl who used to drug a lot. Her descriptions of the sensation were most interesting.

KATT: What happened to her eventually?

IRIS: She went into a convent and now spends her time in penitence and prayer.

LADY C.: Praying only becomes really trying when one has linoleum in one's bedroom.

MRS. H-N.: Or furry rugs, they tickle one's knees.

MAJOR C.: So reminiscent of picture palaces. *(Laughs uproariously)*

LADY C.: Charlie, please remember that this is not the club.

MAJOR C.: Sorry, my dear.

MRS H-N.: Well, if a nunnery is the ultimate end of doping, I hope heaven will save me from it.

EDWARD: I hope heaven will save you from it anyhow, Mrs. Naigrill.

Not surprisingly—since Oscar Wilde had died only a few years earlier—he was a presence in Noël's literary life and remained an unwelcome guest for decades to come.

In a *Diary* entry as late as 1962 he shows his basic ambivalence . . .

"It is xtraordinary indeed that such a posing, artificial old queen should have written one of the greatest comedies of the English language [*The Importance of Being Earnest*]."

It was only a few years after he had adapted—with limited success—Wilde's *Lady Windermere's Fan* for the London stage as *After the Ball* (1954).

But to begin with, though, every other Coward line seemed to be a pseudo-aphorism. His characters always ran the risk of being struck by a flying epigram . . .

HE: *(having been told that a certain lady is an avid golfer)*
As Oscar Wilde might have said—golf is the massive in pursuit of the minute.

SHE: I don't see why you should imagine the poor man would ever say anything so unfunny.

·

NORMAN: To be artistic it is essential to be vicious.

ELVIRA: To be vicious it is preferable to be artistic.

—The Dope Cure (1919)

·

ELVIRA: I never altogether like her. She has no soul.

MRS. HOUGHTON-NAIGRILL: Women are not supposed to have souls, Elvira. It only makes things uncomfortable for their husbands.

—The Dope Cure

·

IRIS: It is very easy to abuse women.

KIT: Few husbands would agree with you.

—The Dope Cure

·

It's possible to begin to see some of what would become Noël's stamping grounds being marked out.

ANGELA (Lady Novelist): On most people Christian Science has the effect of a patent egg boiler.

PAULINE: You mean it makes them hard?

ANGELA: Exactly. Or so soft as to be almost unmanageable.

DENNIS: Is that in one of your novels?

ANGELA: No—but it's going to be.

—Humoresque (1919)

·

On Literary Ladies . . .

ALICE: Irene has always been a romantic little soul. She used to read Ella Wheeler Wilcox in a tree.

KIT: Is that the proper place in which to read Miss Wilcox?

—The Dope Cure

·

There was his early suspicion of classical music. ("There has never yet been composed a piece of classical music that was not too long"— *Diary*—1964) . . .

DENNIS: They've got a Swedish Quartette or something, I believe.

FELICITY: I do wish that Lady Battersby would realise that just because the instruments are large, the music isn't necessarily good.

MRS. ASTON-COOPER: She doesn't really mind what it is. She is perfectly happy as long as she can let her emeralds glitter to Chopin.

FELICITY: I've never heard Chopin there. They nearly always play Brahms with woeful faces and India-rubber collars.

—Humoresque

·

There was his fascination with the sound of place-names that led us remorselessly to "Very flat, Norfolk" . . .

IRENE: Why ever have we stayed so late? What will they say at Sydenham?

MRS. HOUGHTON-NAIGRILL: Whatever one does say at Sydenham under the circumstances, I suppose. There is very little variety in suburban conversation.

—The Dope Cure

·

EDWARD: Her mother is convinced that she's a wild woodland type.

MARGOT: St. John's Woodland.

—This Was a Man

·

MARGOT: You must *never* disapprove of things, Edward. It's so second rate.

—This Was a Man

·

ZOE: All your vitality seems to have been snuffed out by something. I expect it's success. That's always frightfully undermining.

—This Was a Man

·

ZOE: I must say I consider marriage an overrated amusement.

—This Was a Man

·

ZOE: There's no more glamour. Everything's indefinite and blurred except sex, so people are instinctively turning to that with a rather jaded vigour. It's pathetic when you begin to analyse it.

—This Was a Man

·

ZOE: I'm so old-fashioned—I like love stories without the slightest suggestion of sex.

EDWARD: You ought to be a critic.

—This Was a Man

·

NOTE: Noël never refers to them in his various writings—possibly because both plays were collaborations. *Humoresque* (1919) with Esmé Wynne and *The Dope Cure* (1919) with Aishie Pharall, an actress who appeared with them both in the 1916 tour of *Charley's Aunt.*

Interestingly, *The Unattainable*—one of the "bad" plays—contains elements and characters from the plots of both.

=====

Gilbert Miller was to be even more helpful but in quite a different way . . .

"He gave me some useful pieces of advice on the art of play-writing. He said, among other things, that although my dialogue was nearly always good, my construction was 'lousy.' He said that someone had told his father—Henry Miller, another powerful Broadway producer—who in turn had told him, that the construction of a play was as important as the foundations of a house, whereas dialogue, however good, could only, at best, be considered as interior decoration. This I recognized immediately as being authentic wisdom. He said, on parting, that he was quite convinced that before long I would write a first-rate play, and that when I did, he would be only too delighted to produce it."

Noël took Miller's words to heart . . .

"As long as I continue to write plays to be acted in theatres, I shall strain every fibre to see they are clear, well constructed and strong enough in content, either serious or funny, to keep an average paying audience from 8:30 until 11:15. Here endeth the first and last and, for me, only lesson."

=====

"Now that I considered myself definitely 'set' as a writer, the horror of being out of an engagement (as an actor) was less dreadful."

Noël may have considered himself "set" but London's theatre managers continued to feel that they could fill their houses without his help.

Luckily an "engagement" did materialize. In August 1919 he was cast as Ralph in a revival of the Elizabethan play *The Knight of the Burning Pestle,* to be directed by the eminent Nigel Playfair at the Birmingham Rep.

"I was not very good as Ralph, owing to a total lack of understanding of the play. It was my first and only experience of Elizabethan comedy and, being unable to detect any great humour in it, I played that poor apprentice with a stubborn Mayfair distinction which threw the whole thing out of key . . ."

Noël and Betty Chester in *The Knight of the Burning Pestle* (1919). "Betty played 'the Citizen's Wife' with youth, charm, and great vivacity, which, considering that she was supposed to be a bawdy matron of about fifty-five was hardly appropriate."

Shakespeare was someone Noël regarded with all due admiration. Several of his plays take their title from the Bard—*Blithe Spirit, This Happy Breed, Present Laughter*—but acting "my colleague Will" would remain quite another matter.

In an interview with the *Daily Mail* as late as 1969 . . .

"I was offered Hamlet five times . . . I just knew that the day I declaimed—'To be or not to be' in public, it would be the death of me."

Noël's review of his performance in *Pestle* was at variance with a review that claimed that "Ralph was delightfully handled by Mr. Noel Coward. There was no mistaking his vocation. He became the real fantastic knight of the flaming pestle and his knight errantries were carried out with a glorious flourish of voice and posture."

On balance one is inclined to accept Noël's own more modest verdict.

"I once played a performance of *The Knight of the Burning Pestle* with a temperature of 103 and gave sixteen members of the company mumps, thereby closing the play and throwing everybody out of work. There may be a moral lurking somewhere in this, but I cannot for the life of me discover what it is."

═══

Gilbert Miller returned to London and the lesson picked up where it had left off.

He deconstructed the plots of a number of plays and showed Noël the key elements of their construction. "He then went on to say that he himself had a good idea for a light comedy, but that he would like me to write it . . . and that if I did it well enough, he would produce it in London during the following spring.

"I was then, as I am now, extremely chary of the idea of writing anything based upon somebody else's idea, but I persevered, and within the next few weeks manufactured an amiable little play entitled (by Gilbert Miller) *I'll Leave It to You.*

"The dialogue, on the whole, was amusing, and unpretentious, and the construction was not bad, but it was too mild and unassuming to be able to awake any really resounding echoes in the hearts of the great public."

His own reservations were clearly shared by Miller, who was "not quite as enthusiastic as I had hoped he would be." He departed for America once again, having repeated his commitment to putting the play on as a tryout some months later at Manchester's Gaiety Theatre.

Although waiting patiently was never Noël's strong suit, he consoled himself with the thought that he had been careful to write in a good part for himself, "in which, I should undoubtedly, when the moment came, score an overwhelming personal triumph." He'd also written a part for Esmé.

═══

Miller had always envisioned the play as a vehicle for Hawtrey and towards the end of the first week in Manchester he sent his wife and Mrs. Hawtrey to see it.

To Noël's dismay they were not amused. Despite his disappointment he told them that "whether Gilbert Miller or Charles Hawtrey were interested, or whether they weren't, the play would definitely be produced in London within the next few months!"

Which, indeed, it was, opening at the New Theatre on July 21, 1920, under new management. (Ironically, the New Theatre—after going through various incarnations—ended up as the Noel Coward Theatre in 2006.)

The London critics quite liked *I'll Leave It to You*. "A Young Playwright of Great Promise" was the general tone of their reviews. Despite that, the paying public didn't take the piece to their hearts and after thirty-seven performances . . . they left it to him.

A definite disappointment but at least a start. A West End play with your name on it—at the age of twenty. And Heaven knows how many more gestating in your mind . . .

Meanwhile, back to the boards . . .

═══

In 1921 Noël decided that it was probably time he should see the New World—and the New World should see him. When the *Aquitania* docked in New York, it duly did.

During the months that followed he made friends of (among many others) Alfred Lunt and Lynn Fontanne (soon to be the Lunts), Edna Ferber, Fred and Adele Astaire, Dorothy Parker, Alexander Woollcott, George S. Kaufman (and the rest of the Algonquin Round Tablers), and on and on.

Ambitious plans were laid, many of which would come true in the years ahead. In terms of the theatre two became particularly significant . . .

He became the frequent house guest of the actress Laurette Taylor and her husband, Hartley Manners, in their West Side apartment, "an odd demi-Gothic edifice at 50 Riverside Drive."

Laurette was an imperious presence. "Her taste in dress was poor, and her loveliness triumphed over many inopportune bows and ostrich feathers, but her taste as an actress was unassailable."

The acting continued off-stage in the evening "parlour games" the family liked to play and insisted on their dinner guests playing too. Woe betide anyone "who turned out to be self-conscious, nervous, or unable to act an adverb or an historical personage with suitable abandon."

Inter-family arguments would break out with predictable regularity, often causing the hosts and their two children to storm out of the room. Later they would be discovered having a friendly cup of tea in the kitchen.

"It was inevitable that someone should eventually utilise portions of this eccentricity in a play, and I am only grateful to Fate that no guest of the Hartley Manners thought of writing *Hay Fever* before I did."

—————

Noël's other theatrical discovery on that first trip to New York was the way the actors spoke. Not that they spoke with American accents. What surprised him was the tempo, the timing . . .

"Bred in the tradition of gentle English comedy with its inevitable maids, butlers, flower vases and tea-tables, it took me a good ten minutes of the first act to understand what anyone was saying. They all seemed to be talking at once. Presently I began to disentangle the threads, and learnt my first lesson in American acting, which was the technique of realizing, first, which lines in the script are superfluous, and second, knowing when, and how, to throw them away."

In later years he would realize that it was the underpinning of the acting style adopted by his friends, Alfred and Lynn.

He couldn't wait to get back to put this technical revelation to the test in the West End.

As he sailed away from New York, "it seemed, in spite of its hardness and irritating, noisy efficiency, a great and exciting place" and one—he knew even then—would become his second home.

—————

Years later he would reflect on just how important that trip had proved to be . . .

I am in America's debt for many important moments in my life; for many close friends; much hospitality and kindness and, above all, a certain toughness of my fibres at a time of my life when I most needed it.

This was in 1921 when I first landed there with ten pounds and no return ticket. I spent six months in New York before I could earn enough money to go home. During some of this time I politely starved and this experience, which sounds more dramatic than it actually was, did me a power of good.

If I had been immediately successful there, I would have lost much that I value enormously. Apart from those black, scared moments of loneliness which are so depressingly good for the soul, I should have missed the initial contact with the ordinary people; the soda clerks; the cops; the struggling young theatre people living in digs up in the West Seventies. The people in the streets and cafeterias and subways and public parks. The real feeling of the city itself. Its utter callousness; its immensity, looking up at it from below, and its sudden sharp beauty.

All this I gratefully believe I have never quite lost. I know that New York is not representative of America, but for me it was a good enough beginning, a firm basis for what I have learned since. I remember, a few years later, when I acted there for the first time, I received on the opening night over fifty telegrams from complete strangers. Perhaps they were not strangers after all.

The American trip provided him with a valuable opportunity to stand back and take a reasonably objective view of what he was doing as a playwright and what he might do better. As the French say—*reculer pour mieux sauter.* And Noël was most definitely determined to *mieux sauter.*

He had been rushing things, trying to do everything as quickly as possible, easily and overly convinced that his way was the right way, despite the evidence that it frequently was not.

New York gave him professional perspective and was worth it for that alone. Exposure to another culture helped him to be more objective about aspects of himself.

It was obvious to him that his view of life was essentially ironic . . . wry-on-the-rocks. The *comédie humaine* was just that—a *comedy.* Not always a farce, by any means, but not a deep black tragedy either. He was not always able to strike the appropriate balance in years to come but he knew it was there somewhere.

Even though he would often not find the language to express his new insights until much later, it was now that they began to dawn on him and refused to go away.

For instance . . .

He was becoming well aware—and unduly proud of—the fact that he had the facility to write quickly. Later he would conclude and lecture others . . .

"I can see no particular virtue in writing quickly; on the contrary I am well aware that too great a facility is often dangerous and should be curbed when it shows signs of getting the bit too firmly between its teeth. No reputable writer should permit his talent to bolt with him." (Thank you, Gilbert Miller.)

Writing was not self-indulgence. It was work. "And the only way to enjoy life is to work. Work is much more fun than fun."

"Ideas do not come to you through wandering around in the woods, hoping for inspiration. It just isn't there. It's in your head."

"It seems to me that a professional writer should be animated by no other motive than the desire to write and, by doing so, to earn a living."

"Writing is more important than acting, for one very good reason: it lasts. Stage acting only lives in people's memories as long as they live. Writing is creative, acting is interpretive. Only occasionally does very good acting become creative."

"I consider myself a writer first and an actor second."

"It's no use to go and take courses in playwriting any more than it's much use taking courses in acting. Better play to a bad matinée . . . it will teach you much more than a year of careful instruction."

And in a late short story ("Bon Voyage") he would add . . .

"She felt suddenly cheerful, with that cheerfulness only writers know when they have successfully completed a morning's work."

Which is not to say that all of this came to Noël fully formed the moment he stepped on the ship taking him home. But the experience had certainly been transformative. Nothing would be taken for granted. The Boy Actor and Playwright was coming of age.

———

But first he had to deal with his pre–New York past, so to speak.

Before the trip he had finished another play—*The Young Idea*. Like much of his earlier unproduced work, it owed more than a little to playwrights who had preceded him.

This one—Noël knew all too well—owed just about *everything* to George Bernard Shaw's *You Never Can Tell*.

"Well, Shaw *could* tell when he was sent the script. He returned it carefully annotated with such remarks as 'No, you don't, young author!' and a note . . .

" 'I have no doubt you will succeed if you persevere and take care, above all, never to see or read my plays. Unless you can get clean away from me, you will begin as a back number, and be hopelessly out of it when you are forty.' "

Of course, Noël did evolve stylistically from Shaw—although the two would maintain occasional personal contact. He was forever grateful that Shaw had gone to so much trouble to set an arrogant neophyte straight.

In *The Young Idea,* 1923, with, from left to right: Kate Cutler, Herbert Marshall, and Ann Trevor.

The Young Idea was staged at the Savoy Theatre on February 1, 1923, and ran for sixty performances.

With his new self-awareness Noël (in the part of Sholto) could see that his own acting—although better than in *I'll Leave It to You*—was still not what Noël the Playwright was hoping for.

"I was still forcing points too much and giving knowing grimaces when delivering comedy lines. I had not learned then not to superimpose upon witty dialogue the top-heavy burden of personal mannerisms . . . I was both author and actor, and the former suffered considerably from the antics and over-emphasis of the latter."

On the positive side he was beginning to collect respectful reviews.

The less positive side he would summarize what he felt years later in retrospect . . .

"Wise beginners of playwrights will, of course, compare their press notices with their royalties and decide that they still have a great deal to learn."

The 1920s Noël knew a great deal about that even then. He might also have added on a more positive note . . .

"Work hard, do the best you can, don't ever lose faith in yourself, and take no notice of what other people say about you."

Easier said than done but he did take his own advice.

After his return from New York he wrote *The Queen Was in the Parlour* (1922), *Fallen Angels* and *The Vortex* (1923), *Easy Virtue* and *Hay Fever* (1924).

And there they sat until *The Vortex* opened the floodgates.

――――――

The Vortex cut through London theatrical convention with a scalpel.

Nicky Lancaster is a young drug addict—many people interpreted this as a thin disguise for homosexuality, which would be a crime in England for the next thirty years.

Nicky's mother, Florence, was taking a series of young lovers in a desperate and futile attempt to roll back the relentless years. In the third act of the play Nicky confronts his mother in her bedroom and berates her in a vain attempt to persuade her that both of them must give up the destructive courses their lives have taken.

Drama taken to melodrama. Never mind Shaw. Only borrow from the best—Shakespeare and the culminating scene between Hamlet and Getrude in *Hamlet.*

In those days every play script had to be licensed by the Lord Chamberlain's Office before production. Here was a clear case for rejection. Except . . .

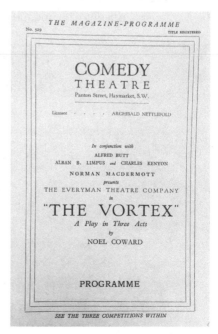

An inspector from the Office read the play and then reported to the Lord Chamberlain—"Milord, you do realise that if we ban this, we shall have to ban *Hamlet?*"

Noël himself went to see the Lord Chamberlain in person to plead his case. This was not a treatise about drug taking, he argued. This was a powerful tract AGAINST drug taking. Persuaded or not, grudgingly the Lord gave way and issued the license.

(Three years later, when the film version came to be made, producer Michael Balcon was not so fortunate. Film censorship was handled by a different branch of government. Balcon's emissary returned from his meeting—"Good news! The script's approved. Just a couple of small details. The son can't take drugs and the Mother can't have lovers." "Oh, great," said the about-to-be director, Adrian Brunel, "So now it's Mummy, if you'll give up tea dances, I'll give up cigarettes and aspirin!")

═══

As soon as the Everyman curtain came down on the evening of November 25, 1924, Noël knew . . .

"There it was, real and complete, my first big moment. . . . I recognized a solidity underlying all the excitement, this time I really had done it."

Lilian Braithwaite, his stage mother, asked wearily—"'Do you think we are all right?'" "And I knew, and she knew that I knew, that the question was merely rhetorical, a routine gesture of diffidence. We were all right. More than all right—we were a smash hit."

In an interview in the 1960s he was reminded of critic James Agate's review—"It was magnificently acted, particularly by Mr. Coward who lived every moment of it with his nerves and was so lifelike that one was in the same room with him."

Noël replied . . .

"Agate saw me give the opening performance when I did do a *tour de*

With Lilian Braithwaite, Mary Robson, Molly Kerr, Millie Sim, Bromley Davenport, Alan Hollis, Kinsey Peile, and Ivor Barnard in *The Vortex,* Everyman Theatre, 1924.

force of nervous acting. I got away with it. But from my point of view it was not a good performance. I'd had a lot of cast changes, darling Lilian Braithwaite had only rehearsed for a week, and I'd been so busy getting the play on, that I had not paid enough attention to my own performance. Fortunately, I think my talent saved me, and I did do it, I think, very well, otherwise I wouldn't have made the success I made. But about two weeks later I was playing it properly, when I could turn it on at will and not feel it.

"I've got a theory, which I've proved over and over again about emotional acting, as opposed to comedy. If you're playing a very strong scene, a moving scene, there is a moment at rehearsal when your words are clear, when you know it very well and it's beginning to flow, there is a moment when you really feel it. This is a very important moment. You cry, you overplay, but you have genuinely felt it. From then onwards until the opening night you have to begin to eliminate, because you cannot afford really to feel, when you're playing eight performances a week, and you're going to give the public their money's worth. Also it is not acting."

("Young Playwright of great Promise" . . . "an infant prodigy" . . . "an amazing youth with astonishing gifts") . . .

I relaxed, rather indiscriminately, into a welter of publicity. No Press interviewer, Photographer or gossip writer had to fight in order to see me. I was wide open to them all, smiling and burbling bright witticisms, giving my view on this and that, discussing such problems as whether or not the modern girl would make a good mother, or what would be my ideal in a wife . . . I made a few adequately witty jokes, which were immediately misquoted or twisted round the wrong way, thereby denuding them of any humour they might originally have had. I was photographed in every conceivable position.

I've never really minded publicity. In fact, sometimes I've been known to encourage it. But the thing about sitting up in bed with a cigarette holder was unfortunate, because I had Chinese pyjamas and a cigarette, and they insisted. They took it, and as the flash went my eyes shut, so the result was I looked like an advanced Chinese decadent in the last phases of dope.

That photograph was published all over the world.

I believe it did me a good deal of harm. People glancing at it concluded at once, and with a certain justification, that I was undoubtedly

"It doesn't matter about death, but it matters terribly about life."

a weedy sensualist in the last stages of physical and moral degenera-
tion, and that they had better hurry off to see me in my play before
my inevitable demise placed that faintly macabre pleasure beyond their
reach. This attitude, while temporarily very good for business, became
very irritating after a time and for many years I was seldom mentioned
in the Press without allusions to "cocktails," "post-war hysteria," and
"decadence."

My original motive was to write a good play with a whacking good
part in it for myself, and I am thankful to say, with a few modest reservations, that I succeeded. It is a good play, and although I am fully aware
that it could be a good deal better, I am quite reasonably satisfied with
it. At the time, I need hardly add, I considered it a masterpiece.

He was an early example of an emerging category—the *celebrity*. Someone well known for being famous and famous for being well known . . .

———

"The most difficult thing of all is to have a big hit very early in your
playwriting career. Suddenly you're the belle of the ball, and then they go
for you and, equally suddenly, chop-chop."

"Taken all in all the Twenties was a diverting and highly exciting decade in which to live and I wouldn't have missed it, not—as they say—for a King's Ransom."

"Between 1920 and 1930 I achieved a great deal of what I had set out to achieve and a great deal that I had not. I had not, for instance, envisaged in those early days of the Twenties that before the decade was over I would be laid low by a serious nervous breakdown, recover from it and return to London to be booed off the stage and spat at in the streets. Nor did I imagine, faced by this unmannerly disaster, that only a few months would ensue before I would be back again, steadier and a great deal more triumphant than before.

"The object of the enterprise for me then was to be a 'success,' a triumphant, inverted-comma'd, name-in-lights success and, lo and behold, after a few setbacks I achieved it. What is more—hold onto your hats, dear readers, and be prepared for a strange revelation—the Bitch Goddess was sweet to me when she came; she neither disillusioned me nor embittered me. She was warm and soothing and reassuring and I loved her as I love her now, for, odd as it may seem and in spite of journalistic rumors to the contrary, we still occasionally meet. If and when she chooses to leave me, I shall not repine nor shall I mourn her any more than I mourn other loved ones who have gone away. I do not approve of mourning, I only approve of remembering, and her I shall always remember gratefully and with pride."

3

ON MY FELLOW PLAYWRIGHTS

"My Colleague Will"...and Others

"That poor man. He's completely unspoiled by failure."
—NOËL ON A WELL-KNOWN BUT OVERRATED PLAYWRIGHT

———

Shakespeare · George Bernard Shaw · Oscar Wilde · Anton Chekhov ·
J. M. Barrie · Somerset Maugham · T. S. Eliot · John Osborne ·
Arnold Wesker · Eugène Ionesco · Edward Albee · Samuel Beckett ·
Arthur Miller · Tennessee Williams · Eugene O'Neill ·
Terence Rattigan · Harold Pinter · Peter Shaffer

"Poor Shakespeare"
Blow, blow, thou winter wind,
   Rough and rude like a goat's behind;
Helen of Troy and Lesbos fair,
   Catch a cloud in their matted hair
Eagerly seeking
   Raddled and reeking,
Speaking
       In
          Gasps
With tongues like Asps
   Fresh from the Convent of Sacré Coeur
And Queen Elizabeth's virginity.

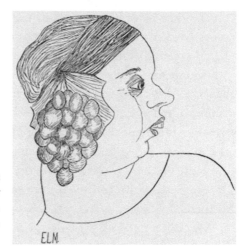

"Hernia Whittlebot," Noël's
fictional poetess, loosely
based on Edith Sitwell.
Drawing by Lorn Loraine.

ELM

Several of Noël's plays take their titles from Shakespeare quotations. *This Happy Breed* comes from *Richard II . . .*

> *This happy breed of men, this little world,*
> *This precious stone set in a silver sea.*

Present Laughter from *Twelfth Night . . .*

> *What is love? 'tis not hereafter,*
> *Present mirth hath present laughter.*

This Was a Man from *Julius Caesar . . .*

> *His life was gentle, and the elements*
> *So mix'd in him that Nature might stand up*
> *And say to all the world, "This was a man!"*

There was also an unfinished play, *A Summer's Cloud*, which drew on *Macbeth . . .*

> *Can such things be,*
> *And overcome us like a summer's cloud*
> *Without our special wonder?*

For other plays he would also use literary quotations. *Blithe Spirit* comes from Shelley's "To a Skylark," *On with the Dance* from Byron's "Childe Harold's Pilgrimage," and *Time Remembered* from Swinburne.

Shakespeare scholar Ivor Brown once wrote to Noël wryly noting that one "dry-as-dust academic" in criticising Brown's latest book had accused him of seeing Shakespeare "in the image of Noël Coward." Brown pointed out that he was merely seeing the Bard "in the image of all hard-working, gifted, stage-fascinated, audience-fascinating people of whom you are, most notably, one." Thus, Brown concluded, Mr. Dry-as-Dust, while trying to undermine, was actually underpinning his thesis.

"My colleague Will" was always somewhere near Noël's elbow. Not that he compared his achievements with Shakespeare's in terms of quality or potential immortality.

Facility of expression, perhaps. When he'd finished writing *Private Lives* in four days with an Eversharp pencil and a foolscap writing block—his constant companions in the 1920s and 1930s—he remarked rather smugly—"Shakespeare never wrote anything so quickly. Not even *Twelfth Night* or *Macbeth*." (Both of which are said to have taken ten days from writing to first performance.)

Noël's personal best was "good old *Hay Fever* . . . conceived and written in about three days in that little cottage in Dockenfield in 1924. What a profitable weekend that was."

Noël was approached several times to act in a Shakespeare production. His reaction? "I am probably the best comedian alive but the sort of acting I do wouldn't do at all at Stratford, though I'd probably have been quite good as Malvolio or Iago at one time." The Malvolio ambition—such as it was—died quite early. "I saw Larry [Olivier] and I stopped wanting to play it."

Would he contemplate some other role in the future?

"I think I've left it a bit late. I think I might play the Nurse in *Romeo and Juliet*."

Then as an afterthought—"I might be rather good as Madame Arcati."

George Bernard Shaw (1856–1950)

As we've seen, George Bernard Shaw was a key influence on Noël's early work—notably *The Young Idea.*

Shaw was to help him again as a middle-aged playwright—and the help had nothing to do with the theatre.

During the early part of World War II Noël was sent on various missions by the Ministry of Information . . . goodwill tours, fact-finding visits. The English press picked up on his absences and criticized him for leaving the country to avoid dangers like the Blitz. Noël was expressly prohibited from explaining the true situation.

He was sent to the U.S. on several occasions to assess the country's reactions to the war in Europe. At this point America was determinedly neutral, so, in effect, Noël was acting as a spy by projecting his views.

But then, in 1941 came another kind of bombshell. He was served with summonses for currency offenses. "I was told for the first time that on August 26, 1939 a law was passed decreeing that all English people with money in America must declare it and not spend it in any circumstances whatever. This was entirely news to me, and exceedingly unpleasant news, for it meant that by spending the money I had spent from my personal account in New York on work for my Government, I had been committing a criminal offence."

Since he was technically guilty, his lawyers recommended that he plead so. Then a surprising letter arrived . . .

4 Whitehall Court
London S.W.1
26/10/41

Dear Noël Coward,

The other day George Arliss [the actor], being in trouble about his American securities, pleaded Guilty under the impression that he was only admitting the facts and saving the Lord Mayor useless trouble. There was nothing for it then but to fine him £3,000.

He should have admitted the facts and pleaded Not Guilty, being as innocent as an unborn lamb. Of course the facts have to be established before that question arises; but when they are admitted or proved, they leave the question of innocence or guilt unsettled. There can be no guilt without intention. Arliss knew nothing about the Finance Clauses, and did not even know that he owned American securities. He was Not Guilty, and should have said so and thereby put his defence in order.

Therefore, let nothing induce you to plead Guilty. If your lawyers advise you to do so, tell them that I advise you not to. You may know all this as well as I do; but after the Arliss case I think it safer to warn you.

G.B.S.

Noël took Shaw's advice and got away with a relatively modest fine. From which he concluded that, while he knew he had enemies in high places, it seemed he had a friend or two as well.

⸺

He was able to repay Shaw in a sense.

Nineteen fifty-three was Coronation Year and everyone in the arts was anxious to make their contribution. Noël opted to play the part of King Magnus in a revival of Shaw's *The Apple Cart* (1929) opposite his old friend Margaret Leighton.

He had taken on one of the most demanding roles in contemporary theatre. The actor in him felt that the part needed some cutting, but the playwright in him said no . . .

"It's absolutely impossible to cut Shaw. It's so beautifully constructed that if you take out one line, you ruin the balance of the whole paragraph and the speech."

So he kept every word and told his director, Michael MacOwan . . .

"I will be word perfect. And there is no seagull in Jamaica that doesn't know that thirteen minute speech, because I did it hundreds of times. But I can't start to rehearse a play unless I know the words."

"It was very, very good for me, and I found it intolerably difficult at first. Playing Shaw is a completely different experience for an actor. In those long speeches I had to remember my scales, because you cannot do a long Shavian speech in a monotone. You must use your voice, without sounding theatrical, but it must hit this note, that note, that note, this note—you must go up and down without appearing to. But this is not done by just standing on the stage and doing it. When you're reading it and learning it, you've got to decide where you're going to take your voice up, where you're going to lower it, where you're going to do this; and the result has got to look as though you were doing it off the cuff."

He gave every credit to Michael MacOwan.

"I knew the words but I did not know how to play them quite accurately. It was you who gave me the clues. I could have played that part off my own bat very effectively, but without you, I couldn't have played it true. You told me the one thing that was important; you said—'Remember that this is basically a sad man'; and I don't believe that even Bernard Shaw was aware of that.

"I wish he'd seen it—[Shaw died in 1950]—I loved him so. I hope

1953, King Magnus, *The Apple Cart*.

he would have approved of me. But I wouldn't be certain, because we played that last act with sentiment and in the original production there was none."

Then he quickly added—"But it's a jolly good play!"

"I am not at all certain that in the future when I write a part I shall not write myself a king; it really is so satisfactory to have all the other characters standing up so often."

—*DIARIES* (1953)

Oscar Wilde (1854–1900)

"Am reading more of Oscar Wilde. What a tiresome, affected sod."

—*DIARIES* (1946)

Oscar Wilde became something of an obsession for Noël.

It may have started at the beginning of his career as a playwright, when his concept of wit was to give his characters sub-Wildean epigrams . . .

But as the years went by he began to see—with plays like *Hay Fever*—that the highly polished verbal jewels all too often turned out to be paste. Humor lay in juxtaposition and attitude rather than flashy wordplay.

Nineteen forty-nine finds him reading Wilde's *De Profundis* . . .

"Poor Oscar Wilde, what a silly, conceited, inadequate creature he was and what a dreadful self-deceiver. It is odd that such brilliant wit should be allied to no humour at all . . . The trouble with him was that he was a 'beauty-lover.' "

Some years later he read Wilde's letters and his feelings were confirmed.

"I have come to the conclusion that he was one of the silliest, most conceited and unattractive characters that ever existed. His love letters to Lord Alfred Douglas are humourless, affected and embarrassing, and his crawling letter from prison to the Home Secretary beneath contempt. *De Profundis* is one long wail of self-pity."

By this time he spoke from the hard-earned experience of hand-to-hand literary combat with the man. The process was competitive rather than complementary—and certainly not complimentary.

In 1953 Noël decided to turn Wilde's 1892 play *Lady Windermere's Fan* into a musical—and immediately ran into a problem.

The "book" for an operetta is traditionally a *soufflé*. Its main purpose is to get the audience painlessly from one musical number to the next. Noël was selling Wilde short when he only praised *The Importance*. *Lady Windermere's Fan* is also an extremely "well made play" and he had now given himself the uphill task of introducing his music into the fabric without tearing it.

There was also the question of style—or, rather, styles.

Because of his quick verbal wit, Noël was often compared to Wilde but comparable isn't the same as identical. There's an underlying affection in Noël's wit that's missing in the polished carapace of Wilde's. As a result he ended up competing instead of collaborating.

During the process of creation he confided to his *Diary* . . .

"I am forced to admit that the more Coward we can get into the script and the more Wilde we can eliminate, the happier we shall be."

Not everyone saw it that way. Robert Helpmann—who was the original director for the piece, which was now called *After the Ball*—took a more objective view . . .

"There was no way it would ever work. Everything that Noël sent up, Wilde was sentimental about, and everything Wilde sent up Noël was sentimental about. . . . It was like having two funny people at a dinner party."

If he was right, the critics didn't appreciate the combination. Despite one of Noël's most charming scores, *After the Ball* ran for a modest 188 performances.

"I have never felt obliged, like Oscar Wilde, to sit down at a dinner table and hold forth for a couple of hours. I'm not saying I couldn't— but oh! how boring for the poor guests. . . . All my life I've been accused of being like Wilde or Congreve, but the truth is—I'm not a bit like either!"

Anton Chekhov (1860–1904)

Although they rarely come up in his conversations, there is little doubt that Noël admired certain aspects of other classic playwrights.

One of them was Anton Chekhov.

·

ROLAND: Plots aren't important, it's ideas that matter. Look at Chekhov.

GARRY: In addition to ideas I think we might concede Chekhov a certain flimsy sense of psychology, don't you?

—*PRESENT LAUGHTER* (1939)

One could also trace a path between between Arkadina, the fading actress of *The Seagull,* and—say—Judith Bliss in *Hay Fever* and possibly even Florence Lancaster in *The Vortex.*

No, what seemed to irritate Noël were the obsequious, "intellectual" productions Chekhov seemed fated to receive on the London stage.

Of a particular production of *The Seagull* he said—"I hate plays that have a stuffed bird sitting on the bookcase screaming—'I'm the title! I'm the title!'"

And on another occasion, having sweated through a production of *The Cherry Orchard* set in the sweltering Deep South, he referred to it as "*A Month in the Wrong Country.*"

But when he came to stage *Waiting in the Wings* in 1961 he confided to his old friend Edna Ferber that he wanted to set it, "as Chekhov did his plays—without tricks and without the observance of trite usage."

And that—despite the predictable carping of the London critics—is what he succeeded in doing.

J. M. Barrie (1860–1937)

Noël always had a soft spot for James M. Barrie.

It was the ambition of every boy actor to be cast in Barrie's *Peter Pan* (1904) and he achieved that when he played Slightly, one of the Lost Boys, in 1913 and 1914 for £4 a week.

The play never left him . . .

> PERRY: I love *Peter Pan.*
> ZELDA: That's because you've got a mother-fixation.
>   All sensitive lads with mother-fixations love *Peter Pan.*
> *—WAITING IN THE WINGS*

There was an element in Barrie's writing that never failed to move him . . .

"I'm violently sentimental—I have to be led out of cinemas sobbing when a mother comes back to her son—or something ghastly . . . I cry like a baby. . . . A deliberately laid-on-with-a-trowel sweetness puts me into exactly the opposite mood. I become very sour.

"But, for instance, I cannot go to any play by James Barrie without crying before the curtain goes up. There are moments of Barrie's of such tremendous sentiment, like in *Dear Brutus* when the father realises that it has only been a dream. Barrie I love. I thought he was a marvelous playwright. Construction. His plays were made of steel. I played in *Peter Pan* for two years and there were moments that used to fix me. I used to cry. Not on the stage."

Noël got to know Barrie well enough for him to send one of his own plays to the playwright for comment.

After the runaway success of *The Vortex* there was a demand for anything else he may have written and from his proverbial "bottom drawer" he took *Sirocco,* a play he had written in 1921.

Barrie wrote back . . .

Dear Coward,

I have read *Sirocco* which you kindly sent me and in many ways I think it is a brilliant piece of work. In construction and the flow of it it is probably the best of your things, as far as I know them, but I don't think it really is worthwhile doing. There is nothing special of yourself in it—in structure or in thought—to give me at least the idea that I got from *The Vortex* that a real live new dramatist was appearing. (Of course it is live to the point of violence but that is not the kind of life I mean.) Change the scene to England (leaving out Sirocco, which has nothing to do with the play) . . . This may be all wrong—at any rate it is the view of one who has a warm belief in you.

Your sincerely,
J. M. Barrie

Don't think I am wanting you to "conceive" like your predecessors. No good in that. You belong to your time—they to theirs. Give us yourself or nothing, but your best self. (This is a little too solemn. Be gay also while you can.)

When *Sirocco* turned out to be the biggest flop of Noël's career, he would certainly have wryly remembered Barrie's advice.

Somerset Maugham (1874–1965)

An older playwright Noël felt close to—at least in the early days—was Somerset Maugham.

Before Noël's ascendancy in the 1930s England's preeminent playwright was undoubtedly Somerset Maugham. In 1930 in a preface to a collection of three of Noël's plays he publicly yielded the crown . . .

"For us English dramatists the young generation has assumed the brisk but determined form of Mr. Noel Coward. He knocked at the door with impatient knuckles, and then he rattled the handle, and then he burst in. After a moment's stupor the older playwrights welcomed him affably enough and retired with what dignity they could muster to the shelf, which with a sprightly gesture he indicated to them as their proper place . . . and since there is no one now writing who has more obviously a gift for the theatre than Mr. Noel Coward, nor more influence with young writers, it is probably his inclination and practice that will be responsible for the manner in which plays will be written during the next thirty years."

It could be argued that he missed his guess by only four years.

John Osborne's *Look Back in Anger* was produced in 1956.

For many years Noël regarded Maugham as something of a mentor.

He would follow the older man's rule of thumb, which was to write from seven o'clock to one—and then never go back in the afternoon, even if you're tempted.

He listened to Maugham's critique when he decided to add short-story writing to his armory. Of his 1939 story "Aunt Tittie" Maugham wrote— "You had material there for a great picaresque novel which probably no one but you could write and it is a shame to have squandered such a wealth of splendid stuff. Heaven knows I'm all for concision but there you had a subject that screamed to be treated on the grand scale."

―――

By the mid-1930s the balance between the two of them as playwrights was tilting steadily in Noël's direction and he felt able to critique Maugham's work. Writing to him about what would turn out to be the older man's last play, *Sheppey* (which he had not enjoyed) . . .

"Oh, Willie, Willie, how very naughty of you to write a play filled with subtle implications and exquisite satire and then cheerfully allow dull witted lunatics to cast it! I really wouldn't be so violent about it except that I really do mind."

Maugham replied . . .

Noel my pet,

I am sorry you were disappointed . . . I was a little, but I do not really care. I sat in my box at the first night feeling like a disembodied spirit. I have done with playwriting. I know now that I made a mistake in writing plays and then washing my hands of them . . . I cannot tell you how I loathe the theatre. It is all very well for you, you are author, actor and producer. What you give an audience is all your own; the rest of us have to content ourselves with at the best the approximation of what we see in the mind's eye. After one has got over the glamour of the stage and the excitement, I do not myself think the theatre has much to offer the writer compared with the other mediums in which he has complete independence and need consider no one.

Bless you, Willie

Maugham spent his many last years in his Villa Mauresque in Cap Ferrat and Noël was a frequent visitor. His *Diary* chronicles his feelings . . .

"Lunched with Willie, who is in fine form" . . . "Read Willie's *Writer's Notebook*. So clear and unpretentious and accurate" . . . "Lunched with Willie at the Dorchester. I only hope that when I am eighty I shall be as bright and charming" . . . "Willie I find enchanting when he embarks on literary criticism. . . . He is too sure an artist himself to lay down the law . . . he never overwrites. He has never, since his very early youth, become besotted with words, drunk on the *Oxford Dictionary*. . . . I am struck, all over again, with the lovely, lucid simplicity of his prose."

1957 . . . "Willie was really extraordinary. After all, he is eighty-three and should show some signs of wear and tear but he doesn't. He dived off the diving-board into the pool as usual and, as usual, the lunch was perfect. . . . We gossiped about everything under the sun and I drove home feeling happy and stimulated and deeply impressed by the charm of old age when it is allied to health and intelligence."

1962 . . . and the scales are beginning to fall from Noël's eyes . . .

"I've just re-read *Cakes and Ale*. A brilliant novel but, oh, how Willie's unfortunate character shines through it . . ."

(Noël had been particularly close to Syrie Maugham—Willie's former wife—whom Willie had continued to criticize mercilessly. He had
also tried to disinherit their daughter Liza in favor of his companion/gay
lover Alan Searle. All of which gave Noël cause to question his own feelings about the man he would later refer to as that "scaly old crocodile,"
"the Lizard of Oz.")

"I think this particular spiritual malaise, allied to certain annoying
literary mannerisms, may dim his posterity."

A few weeks later . . .

"William Somerset Maugham . . . [note the new formality] . . . had
adopted Alan Searle as his son and is suing Liza for, apparently, everything he has given her. It really is very silly indeed and he is making a
cracking fool of himself. The newspapers are sending him up sky-high,
of course. Perhaps it is not a good idea to live quite so long. . . . Disagreeable old sod!"

———

Noël stopped seeing Maugham but he hadn't quite finished with him . . .

In 1965 he felt that Time's wingèd chariot was beginning to goose him
too. Before he folded his "tattered wings" he felt the desire to act once
more on the London stage in a play of his own.

In March . . .

"Quite a good week I have written the first act of a new play called
A Song at Twilight. So far it is good, I know, and I've got the fireworks
still to come in the last act. The original idea has been in my mind for
some time. It was suggested by a scene in David Cecil's biography of
Max Beerbohm when Constance Collier, after years of non-contact, suddenly descends on him when he is an old man and flattens him with her
vitality. My play is more sinister and there is Maugham in it as well as
Max . . ."

The "fireworks" in the last act come when the Constance Collier character, who is in the process of writing her autobiography, which will feature her long-ago affair with the Max/Willie character, produces letters
detailing his homosexual love affair, which she intends to include in the
book, indelibly staining his "grand old man of letters" image.

Noël goes to see him not long before he dies . . .

"I'm glad I did because he was so wretchedly, pathetically grateful.
He was living out his last days in a desperate nightmare, poor beast. He

Noël, "Willie" Somerset Maugham, and Leonard Lyons at the Villa Mauresque.

barely made sense and, of course, he knew his mind had gone. Poor, miserable old man—not sadly missed, I fear."

"Maugham hated people more easily than he loved them. I love people more easily than I hate them. That is the difference between me and Somerset Maugham."

T. S. Eliot (1888–1965)

Then there was T. S. Eliot.

Eliot intrigued and irritated Noël in equal measure. "The pleasures of modern poetry—if there are any—elude me."

He enjoyed Eliot's *The Cocktail Party* (1949) but wondered why a writer who lacked the magic of the Elizabethan playwrights should go to the trouble of writing in pseudo-blank verse. An actor friend suggested that perhaps Eliot hadn't intended it to be blank verse—"Perhaps he has a narrow typewriter?"

With *The Confidential Clerk* (1953) . . . "It is not in verse although it is supposed to be, neither is it particularly 'significant,' which foxed the first night audience considerably. They were all coming to revere or deplore T. S. Eliot and all they got was a farcical idea which might have been conceived by Ben Travers in a *louche* moment, translated into over-literate English by Mr. Eliot."

At one point Eliot said that Noël hadn't spent one hour of his life in the study of ethics, to which Noël replied—"I do not think it would have helped me but I think it would have done Mr. Eliot a lot of good to spend some time in the theatre."

———

Dissolve to the 1950s . . . and the Angry Young Men . . .

Since the war a terrible pall of significance has fallen over plays. Lots of plays are about people who talk away for hours and still can't communicate with each other and become more and more wretched.

Nineteen fifty-six saw the arrival of the "new Noel Coward" . . . or did it?

John Osborne (1929–1994)

"I have just read *Look Back in Anger* and it is full of talent and fairly well constructed but I wish I knew why the hero is so dreadfully cross and what about? . . . I wonder how long this trend of dreariness for dreariness's sake will last. Apparently in the minds of the critics significance and importance can only be achieved by concentrating on unhappiness, psychopathic confusion and general dismay. No lightness is permissible."

A year later he saw the play . . .

"John Osborne's play was full of vitality and rich language. It irritated me at moments, as it did when I read it, but it was superbly acted and, on the whole, a rewarding evening in the theatre."

Two years later it was a different story . . .

He went to see Osborne's "musical"—*The World of Paul Slickey*—"and never in all my theatrical experience have I seen anything so appalling. Appalling from every point of view. Bad lyrics, dull music, idiotic, would-be-daring dialogue—interminable long-winded scenes about nothing, and above all the amateurishness and ineptitude, such bad taste that one wanted to hide one's head.

"I fear that Mr. John Osborne is not so talented as he has been made out to be. *Look Back in Anger* had vitality and too much invective. . . . *The Entertainer* was verbose, unreal and pretentious, and this is unspeakable.

"He is cashing in shamelessly on publicity, but this will soon die away and unless he reduces his head to normal size and gets down to genuine professional playwriting, he will die away too. . . . Destructive vituperation is too easy. I cannot believe that this writer, the first of the 'angry young men,' was ever angry at all. Dissatisfied, perhaps, and certainly envious and, to a degree, talented, but no more than that. No leader of thought and ideas, a conceited, calculating young man blowing a little trumpet."

And then a standoff—until Noël published his "Consider the Public" essays in *The Sunday Times* in 1961.

But there was to be a truce . . .

When *Suite in Three Keys* opened in 1966 Osborne wrote to Noël to congratulate him. And to add . . .

Now I would like to ask a favour of you. Could you, in future, stop assessing your fellow writers to newspaper reporters? Clearly it gives them pleasure but you scarcely need their approval. I have always had the profoundest respect for you, both for what you do, and as a unique and moving figure on our landscape. You are a genius. . . . But please say no more.

You may find it hard to believe, but there is more goodwill and kindliness here for you to draw on than you might expect to find . . .

Believe me, with respect and admiration always.

Yours sincerely,
JOHN OSBORNE

Noël replied by return post . . .

I really am very grateful for your letter. It gave me a sharp and much needed jolt. I absolutely agree that it is unnecessary and unkind to hand out my opinions of my colleagues to journalists. It is also pompous. . . . I regret very much that since we first met years ago we have known each other so little. This at least can be remedied. There is so much that I would like to talk to you about, even if our views on plays and playwrights may differ.

What you said in your letter about admiration and respect is entirely mutual.

NOËL

And so peace (of a kind) broke out.

Later Osborne would come up with the definitive comment on Noël . . .

"Mr. Coward is his own invention and contribution to this century. Anyone who cannot see that should keep well away from the theatre. To be your own enduring invention seems to me to be heroic and essential."

Noël's verdict on the two of them as playwrights?

"We both wrote about what we saw and didn't like. Mine was a more circumscribed dislike. Everything bothers him."

Noël felt a degree of sympathy for another of the "Angry Young Men" . . .

Arnold Wesker (1932–2016)

At least Wesker had some claim to be able to talk with some insight about Kitchen Sinks, coming, as he did, from a working-class background. Others—like Osborne—were middle-class intellectuals writing "down."

Wesker was certainly the genuine article and he took himself very seriously—as, indeed, so did the critics to begin with. Noël found it absurd to see him compared with Dickens and Tolstoy, "when he really happens to be an over-earnest little creature obsessed by the wicked capitalists and the wrongs of the world."

These sociological preoccupations—coupled with a poor sense of play construction—irritated him . . .

"What does he show? Lentils boiling in a pot while six men march up and down. He devotes far too much time to a perfectly sincere but slightly misguided sense of fighting for a cause. I think he has a rich and wonderful talent and he should write about PEOPLE, not about causes. Because for the causes he writes about, the battle has already been won."

Noël's articles in *The Sunday Times* drew Wesker's attention and, chancing his arm, he invited himself to visit Noël in Switzerland. Noël decided it might prove interesting to examine this "over-earnest little creature."

Wesker came with an agenda of sorts. He wanted Noël to help him raise funds for a venture to be called Centre 42, a project to bring culture to the masses.

Noël was predictably going to have nothing to do with that but the two of them talked amicably about the Theatre and life in general and

Wesker left him several of his plays to read. Noël duly wrote to him and, after critiquing the plays, went on to say . . .

I have got to talk to you more. . . . You have been victimized by these foolish men but your talent is too rich to be lastingly affected either by over-praise or over-blame. Please, dear Arnold, don't grumble so much in your heart over political and Governmental injustices and stupidities. You can't change human nature. All you can do with your gifts is observe and comment with compassion and humour AND as theatrically effectively as possible, so long as you continue to write plays. . .

And now you are going to waste an enormous amount of your energy and creative talent in coping with mediocre little bureaucrats and organizing a "Cultural Revolution"! Do me a favour! Leave those cheerful old girls to enjoy their Bingo. Let the great majority enjoy itself in its own way. Don't try to force them to stare at Henry Moore nudes with holes in their middles and sit on pre-fabricated mobile benches to see inevitably dodgy performances of plays in the Round. They won't go anyway. It will all turn out to be, as our mutual colleague Shakespeare said—"An expense of spirit in a waste of shame." Nor will it avail the world situation one iota for you and [fellow playwright] Robert Bolt to spend occasional weeks in the clink in protest against humanity's yearning for self-destruction.

To Hell with Centre 42! Those among the great masses who really want and need culture will manage to get it anyhow. Those who don't, won't. If this is cynicism, then I am a dyed-in-the-wool old Cynic, but it just may be common sense. One thing is clear to me, however, and that is that you are a strange, vulnerable and wonderfully gifted creature. Your first allegiance is not to Humanity or Political dogmas, or world reform, but to your talent which, incidentally, you are bloody lucky to have.

When you had left the house I had pangs of guilt for having been so unresponsive to your project, but they have since died away. I am unregenerate; still hopeful and eager to contribute to the world's entertainment and transient enjoyment, but ONLY AFTER I have contributed to my own integrity. I will enlarge on this jolly little theme when we meet again and I defy you to shout me down. In the meantime I wish you success and happiness in WHATEVER you do, even if it is only organizing Maypole dances in South Shields.

Wesker didn't give up so easily and there were further exchanges of letters and Noël's patience was increasingly tested . . .

I am perfectly prepared to admit that I may be dead wrong over all of this and, if the future proves me to be so, I shall be entirely delighted for your sake, because I am very fond of you and respect your sincerity. In the meantime be a dear and stop bullying me.

Yours with wicked, cynical love
NOËL

In June 1966 he was able to make amends—in a way—by spending "four hours at the Old Vic in wig, eyebrows and moustache, waiting to say my five lines in Wesker's *The Kitchen*—in a memorial performance for actor/director George Devine."

═══

On their first meeting . . .

"Arnold Wesker arrived looking grubby and peculiar in drab colours and his wife's sweater, which was definitely a mistake either for her or for him."

Eugène Ionescu (1909–1994)

Another "cult" playwright of the period was Eugène Ionescu, although Noël was inclined to let the intellectual parade pass him by.

He found *Rhinoceros* at the Royal Court "a tedious play, directed into the ground by Orson Welles. The beginning was brilliant . . . but then it began to drag, principally because after half way through the first act you know exactly what is going to happen and there is no more interest. I am sick of these amateur, pseudo-intellectual scribblings. Ionescu, in my opinion, is NOT a playwright and not a particularly original thinker. He merely tries to do, which is fatal."

═══

Then there were the more "experimental" playwrights . . .

Edward Albee (1926–2016)

There was Edward Albee . . . "very intelligent but badly tainted with *avant garde,* Beckett, etc."

In 1965 . . .

"We went to *Tiny Alice* and were as bewildered as everyone else including the cast. Edward Albee has a strong sense of theatre and he writes good parts. The first act was hopeful, after that a chaotic mess of sex and symbolism. . . . Altogether a maddening evening in the theatre, so nearly good and yet so bloody pretentious. I told Edward what I felt and he was very amiable about it."

Albee sent Noël a copy of the text, which led to Noël writing to him . . .

My dear Edward,

I have read *Tiny Alice* with the utmost concentration and considerable enjoyment. Your sense of Theatre is superb and your writing brilliant. You were right, I did get more of it from the printed page but not enough to clear up my confusion. I know now, or I think I know, what's happening but what I don't know is what YOU think is happening. . . . Perhaps my stubborn sanity clips my wings. Sex obsession and religious ecstasy, I agree, are on the same plane but it is not a plane on which I can move with much tolerance. I have enjoyed sex thoroughly, perhaps even excessively, all my life but it has never, except for brief wasteful moments, twisted my reason. I suspect that my sense of humour is as stubborn as my sanity, perhaps they're the same thing. Your seduction scene neither moved, shocked or appalled me, it made me want to laugh. You must forgive me for saying these things. I have a profound respect for your rich talent and a strong affection for you, although I only know you a little. Expert use of language is to me a permanent joy. You use it expertly all right but, I fear, too self-indulgently. Your duty to me as a playgoer and a reader is to explain whatever truths you are dealing with lucidly and accurately. I refuse to be fobbed off with a sort of metaphysical "What's My Line?"

Let me hear from you. Just an ordinary love letter will do.

NOËL

(At this time Albee and some colleagues were talking of doing a Coward Repertory Season on Broadway the following season but nothing came of it.)

"If Attila the Hun were alive today, he'd be a drama critic...

"It's not enough for a critic to tell his audience how well a play succeeds in its intention, he must also judge that intention by the absolute standards of the theatre as an art form."

—EDWARD ALBEE (1988)

Samuel Beckett (1906–1989)

Samuel Beckett was someone who was on a creative wavelength Noël could never connect with . . .

"I have been plodding through the works of Beckett etc., all filled with either pretentious symbolism or violent left-wing propaganda, and none with any real merit."

"I have just read, very carefully, *Waiting for Godot* and in my considered opinion it is pretentious gibberish, without any claim to importance whatsoever. I know that it has received great critical acclaim and I also know that it's silly to go on saying how stupid the critics are, but this really enrages me. It is nothing but phoney surrealism with occasional references to Christ and mankind. It has no form, no basic philosophy and absolutely no lucidity. It's too conscious to be written off as mad. It's just a waste of everybody's time and it made me ashamed to think that such balls could be taken seriously for a moment."

And later, seeing a photo of Beckett . . .

"He must have read too many of his own plays. It gets him down, I expect."

═══

Noël had less and less patience with the American playwrights. All too often he sensed theatrical pretension and self-indulgence.

Arthur Miller (1915–2005)

There was Arthur Miller.

It started harmlessly enough in 1949 when he saw the London production of *Death of a Salesman* and "had a long talk with the author, who was very nice." There was, perhaps, a warning note later when an over-enthusiastic playgoer told him that it was not a play but an "experience." Noël murmured that he rather wished it had been a play.

"I personally found it boring and embarrassing. . . . All that symbolic wandering about is considered to be an innovation. . . . The play is a glorification of mediocrity. The hero is a cracking bore and a liar and a fool and a failure, the sons are idiots. To me these ingredients do not add up to entertainment in the theatre. At odd moments the writing was literate and good and, when it was, it was out of key with the characters."

In 1962 he is chronicling the suicide of Marilyn Monroe, Miller's former wife.

"I am convinced that what brought her to that final foolish gesture was a steady diet of intellectual pretentiousness pumped into her over the years by Arthur Miller and 'The Method.' She was, to begin with, a fairly normal little sexpot with exploitable curves and a certain natural talent. I am sure that all the idiocies of her last few years, always being late on the set, etc., plus over-publicity and too many theoretical discussions about acting, were the result of all this constant analysis of every line in every part she had to play, and a desperate longing to be 'intellectual' without the brain to achieve it."

This may well have helped sour Noël's feeling about Miller—although there was not too much to sour. In 1964 he goes to a preview of Miller's *After the Fall*—a play which deals in part with the Miller-Monroe relationship . . .

"The play is a three-and-a-half hour wail about how cruel life has been to Arthur Miller. What it does NOT mention is that the cruelest blow life has dealt him is that he hasn't a grain of humour. He is capable of writing one or two fairly effective 'theatre' scenes. His philosophy is adolescent and sodden with self-pity. His taste is non-existent. The Marilyn Monroe part of the play is really vulgar beyond belief.

"Out of all this pretentious, turgid verbosity emerges the character of a silly, dull man with a mediocre mind. It has, needless to say, been hailed as a masterpiece and treated with the greatest possible reverence. There is more human truth in the first ten minutes of Neil Simon's *Barefoot in the Park* than in the whole three and a half hours of *After the Fall*."

Tennessee Williams (1911–1983)

With Tennessee Williams he detected humanity—albeit somewhat warped.

In 1948 he has dinner with Williams and Gore Vidal . . .

"Vidal intelligent and charming. Tennessee less charming but curious. They both gave out a sort of 'end of the world' feeling; they were good company but doomed. I felt sorry for them."

Four years later the "end of the world" almost came true when they met up in Rome . . .

"I dined with Tennessee, and we drove out along the Appian Way. And looked at all the ruins—lovely except for Tennessee's driving. I cannot imagine how he got a licence—he admits cheerfully that he cannot see with one eye and cannot drive at all. . . . On the way back we ran out of *essence,* but were able to coast to a petrol station. After this we got lost and drove about wildly in several different directions. It was all very light-hearted, although a trifle dangerous. . . . We missed a few trams and buses by inches and finally, at long last, I got to my bed."

In 1955 . . . "Went to Tennessee's new play *Cat on a Hot Tin Roof*—full of adolescent sex, dirty words and frustrations, but at moments very fine. It was beautifully played but over-directed by Elia Kazan."

He would find more of the same when it came to the 1959 *Sweet Bird of Youth* . . .

"Like all Tennessee's plays it has moments of brilliant writing but the play is not really good. None of the characters is really valid and the emphasis on squalor—drugs, syphilis, castration, sex, sex, sex—is too heavy and almost old-fashioned."

By now—in Noël's estimation—there was a predictable pattern in his work. In the film of *Suddenly, Last Summer* it was "poor Tennessee Williams at his worst. It was full of horrors, so many really that it was idiotic. Madness, brain operations, queerness, cannibalism and a few high-flown observations on life . . ."

Then came *Period of Adjustment* which he found "tasteless, dull and disgusting."

In 1967 Noël came full circle when he accepted the part of the Witch of Capri in *Boom*—the film version of Williams's play *The Milk Train Doesn't Stop Here Anymore.* The stars were his old friends Elizabeth Taylor and Richard Burton and the director Joseph Losey ("a dear man").

By this time Noël had given up stage acting and was playing character roles in other people's films for fun—and a great deal of money.

"I had a bit of trouble with Tennessee's curiously phrased dialogue, but apart from that everything was halcyon."

"Tennessee Williams has a strong streak of poetry, but I think he has run it into the ground, rather—what with all those neurotic mothers, castrations and things."

Eugene O'Neill (1888–1953)

"I've decided I'm not an O'Neill fan. . . . *The Iceman Cometh*—and I wenteth . . . *Long Day's Journey Into Night* turned into Day's short journey to the Exit at the first intermission."

Eugene O'Neill's marathon nine-act *Strange Interlude* (1928) tested his patience as well as his bladder. And with so many of those who came after he felt their attempt to be "significant" overshadowed their ability or, indeed, their inclination to entertain.

From the early days when he was given advice on constructing a play Noël became the messiah of the "well-made play" and his heroes—on a good day—playwrights like Pinero, Lonsdale, Shaw, and Maugham.

Terence Rattigan (1911–1977)

Of his own contemporaries he gave pride of place to Terence Rattigan.

Rattigan himself kept a watchful eye on Noël from very early on.

As an Oxford undergraduate Rattigan was asked to review *Cavalcade* for the undergraduate magazine, *Cherwell.* Since its more intellectual rival, *The Isis,* had already given the play a glowing review, the politics of university journalism forbade him from appearing a mere follower.

His review read . . .

"Coward has the happy knack of feeling strongly what other people are feeling at the same time. If he has this ability to transform this knack into money and success, we should not begrudge them to him. But such cannot be the qualities of genius."

Little did he know that in due time those very same qualities and qualification were to be applied to him.

In commercial context Rattigan's plays regularly outperformed most of Noël's at the box office . . . *The Winslow Boy* (1946), *The Browning Version* (1948), *The Deep Blue Sea* (1952), and *Ross* (1960).

Not surprisingly, the two became friends and Rattigan was happy to beat the drum for Noël, who was, he said, as a lyricist "the best of his kind since W. S. Gilbert" and went on to add . . . "he is simply a phenomenon, and one that is unlikely to occur ever again in theatre history. Let us at least be grateful that it is our own epoch that the phenomenon has so signally adorned."

(When Raymond Mander and Joe Mitchenson published their monumental *Theatrical Companion to Coward* in 1957 it was Rattigan who contributed the introductory essay—"An Appreciation of His Work in the Theatre.")

Came the mid-1950s and Rattigan shared with Noël the feeling of being edged into the wings by the Angry Young Men.

In 1960 Noël went to see *Ross*—Rattigan's play about Lawrence of Arabia—and said to his companion, "Wasn't it wonderful to see a play in which the hero was not a juvenile delinquent and the stage not cluttered up with dustbins?"

When Rattigan heard about it, he wrote to Noël . . .

"There is no judgment I would rather have about a play than yours (except perhaps the public's, which, I sincerely believe, you and I are the last 2 playwrights on earth to continue to respect) and a word of praise from you is worth a paean from the press."

And when Noël was to direct the revival of *Hay Fever* at the new National Theatre, he returned the compliment—"I hear you're going to be 'National Theatred.' . . . Any more such and I might get jealous. Enough is enough, please."

Their playwriting careers proceeded in parallel—sometimes collecting brickbats, sometimes bouquets. They both received knighthoods, Noël in 1970, Rattigan a year later. Rattigan wrote—"You know that you should have had yours forty years ago, at the time of *Cavalcade*."

There was always a slight sense that, friends though they were, Rattigan was envious of Noël's multiplicity of talents beyond simply writing plays.

After his *The Sleeping Prince* was tepidly received by the critics in 1953, Noël consoled him—"Don't worry, Terence. I not only fuck up some of my plays by writing them, but I frequently fuck them up by acting in them as well."

—————

In a turnaround that can only be called "theatrical" the contemporary playwright who came closest to Noël's ideal was not Osborne, Wesker, Beckett, or Bolt but . . .

Harold Pinter (1930–2008)

To begin with the outlook was decidedly unpromising . . .

March 1960 . . . "I went to see *The Dumb Waiter* and *The Room* at the Royal Court, two *soi-disant* plays by Mr. Harold Pinter. They were completely incomprehensible and insultingly boring, although fairly well acted. It is the surrealist school of non-playwriting. Apparently they received some fine notices. Nobody was there."

In that mood Noël tackled Pinter 2—*The Caretaker* . . .

"*The Caretaker* at the Arts, which I went to with fear and dread, was quite another cup of tea. I loathed *Dumb Waiter* and *The Room,* but after seeing this I'd like to see them again, because I think I'm on to Pinter's wavelength. He is at least a genuine original. I don't think he could write in any other way if he tried. *The Caretaker,* on the face of it, is everything I hate most in the theatre—squalor, repetition, lack of action, etc.—but somehow it seizes hold of you . . . NOTHING happens except that somehow it does. The writing is at moments brilliant and quite unlike anyone else's."

A little later, when it came to filming *The Caretaker,* Noël was one of the investors, thus putting his money where his mouth was.

He continued to follow Pinter's career and watched it develop. He was "immensely impressed" by *The Collection* (1961). "He is the only one of the *soi-disant avant garde* who has genuine originality."

He also found him to be "an absolutely meticulous director. Every pause is professionally timed and the net result is, I think, remarkable. I think he's not only a very extraordinary writer but also a remarkable theatre man."

Then *The Homecoming* (1964) . . . "an extraordinary play, fairly obscure, superbly done and utterly professional. . . . Pinter is a strange playwright. A sort of Cockney Ivy Compton-Burnett. The end of the play went off a bit, but I was never bored for an instant."

By this time Noël and Pinter were occasional correspondents and Pinter sent him a copy of the play text . . .

Dear Harold,

I have just read *The Homecoming* twice through. I had thought perhaps the impeccable acting and direction might have clouded my judgment of the play itself. But I was DEAD WRONG. It reads as well, if not better, than it plays. Your writing absolutely fascinates me. It is entirely unlike anyone else's. You cheerfully break every rule of the theatre that I was brought up to believe in, except the cardinal one of never boring for a split-second. I love your choice of words, your resolute refusal to EXPLAIN anything and the arrogant, but triumphant demands you make on the audience's imagination. I can well see why some clots hate it, but I belong to the opposite camp—if you will forgive the expression.

I have just written THREE new plays. One long and two short, so sucks to you! I am going to grace the London stage in all three of them next March!

———

With the perspective of time it's possible to see the pattern that linked Noël and Pinter.

In the 1936 *Shadow Play*—from the *Tonight at 8:30* sequence—Noël has the character Vicky say . . .

"Small talk—a lot of small talk with quite different thoughts going on behind it."

Years later in an interview Pinter described the revelation he'd experienced when he saw *Private Lives* for the first time and the Balcony Scene . . .

AMANDA: What have you been doing lately? During these last years?

ELYOT: Travelling about. I went round the world, you know, after—

AMANDA: Yes, yes, I know. How was it?

ELYOT: The world?

AMANDA: Yes.

ELYOT: Oh, highly enjoyable.

AMANDA: China must be very interesting.

ELYOT: Very big, China.

AMANDA: And Japan—

ELYOT: Very small.

AMANDA: And did you eat sharks' fins and take your shoes off, and use chopsticks and everything?

ELYOT: Practically everything.

AMANDA: And India, the burning Ghars, or Ghats, or whatever they are, and the Taj Mahal. How was the Taj Mahal?

ELYOT: Unbelievable, a sort of dream.

Pinter said it was the first time he realized that you could put a character on the stage and have him say one thing—and the audience KNEW he meant something entirely different.

It changed his whole approach to writing dialogue and influenced his whole approach to playwriting. So much so that people coming to Coward for the first time often comment that he is "Pinteresque."

Whereas the fact of the matter is that Pinter is "Cowardesque."

And he would have totally agreed with Noël's description of his own work . . . "Neither my lyrics nor my dialogue require decoration; all they do require are clarity, diction and intention and the minimum of gesture or business."

Peter Shaffer (1926–2016)

Of all the contemporary playwrights—Pinter excepted for the reasons given—Noël felt the greatest affinity for Peter Shaffer.

He particularly admired the 1964 *The Royal Hunt of the Sun* ("a beautifully written play"). "The difference between Peter Shaffer and all the Osbornes and Weskers is that he has no hatred in his heart and no partisan axe to grind. He writes compassionately about human beings. He also has more than a touch of poetry. I only wish he would write more."

Shaffer on Coward . . .

"Although people sometimes compare his plays with Oscar Wilde's, I don't think that's quite fair. Oscar was a very profound man, one of the truest voices of the 19th century. I don't think you can say Noel was one of the truest voices of the 20th century. But he belonged to that generation which felt it had a responsibility to engage an audience not just on the level of heart but also on the level of its pleasure in language and its pleasure in style."

———

CONSIDER THE PUBLIC
A Warning to Pioneers

In the last decade I have been a fairly detached spectator of what is described as "The New Movement in The Theatre," and I feel that now, after fifty years of activity in the profession as an actor, playwright and director, my age and experience entitle me to offer a little gentle advice to the young revolutionaries of today and also to those of our dramatic critics who have hailed their efforts with such hyperboles of praise.

My advice, in essence, is simple and can be stated in three words: Consider the Public. This I know may appear to be senile heresy to those who are diligently occupied in sweeping away, or attempting to sweep away, all the conventions and traditions which, with certain inevitable and gradual mutations, have kept the drama alive and kicking for several hundred years; but it would be unwise to dismiss it too contemptuously. If you intend to be a successful actor, playwright or director (and to embark on any of these three careers *without* intending to be successful would be plain silly), you must remember that it is the support of the public and only the support of the public that will earn you your living.

The Public! Exacting, careless, discerning, undiscriminating, capricious, loyal and unpredictable, is that goose that lays your golden eggs. To batter it with propaganda, bewilder it with political ideologies, bore it with class prejudice and, above all, irritate it with wilful technical inefficiency, is a policy that can only end in dismal frustration and certain failure.

Here I would like to quote my colleague Terence Rattigan, who writes in the preface to his second volume of plays: "A play can neither be great, nor a masterpiece, nor a work of genius, nor talented, nor untalented, nor indeed anything at all unless it has an audience to see it. For without an audience it simply does not exist. No audience means no performance and no performance means no play. This fact, sadly lamented though it may have been over the centuries by aspiring, talented but unperformed dramatists, is hard, I admit, but utterly inescapable . . . plays, though they may give incidental pleasure in the library are first intended for the stage. If they are not, they are not plays, but novels, poems or philosophies in dialogue form, and their author, writer of genius though he may well be, has no right to use the title of dramatist." Obviously I would not have quoted the above sensible statement if I were not entirely in agreement with it.

To my mind one of the principal faults of the "New Movement" writers is their supercilious attitude to the requirements of an average audience. Presumably this is accounted for by the fact that the majority of any average audience is usually composed of the despised "bourgeoisie." Another of their grave defects is what I will describe as "inverse snobbery." Their plays, to date, have dealt exclusively with the lower strata of society from which one concludes that, in their opinion, the people of these strata are the only people worth writing about. This is both didactic and inaccurate for it is absurd to imply that the problems, emotions, dramas and comedies of one class are intrinsically superior to those of another, particularly as the lower strata today represent merely a small minority of the population as a whole.

I am a staunch upholder of the theory that a beginner should first write about the class he knows best, but I also believe that, having done so, once or twice or even three times, his allegiance to his own creative talent should compel him to start learning about other classes as soon as he possibly can. It is as dull to write incessantly about tramps and prostitutes as it is to write incessantly about dukes and duchesses or even suburban maters and paters, and it is bigoted and stupid to believe that tramps and prostitutes and underprivileged housewives frying onions and using ironing boards are automatically the salt of the earth and that nobody else is worth bothering about. Equally bigoted is the assumption that reasonably educated people who behave with restraint in emotional crises are necessarily "clipped," "arid," "bloodless" and "unreal."

It is interesting to note that at the moment of writing there is only one "New Movement" straight play playing to good business in a London theatre—*The Caretaker* by Harold Pinter. This, to me, is in no way a strange phenomenon. Mr. Pinter is neither pretentious, pseudo-intellectual nor self-consciously propagandist. True, the play has no apparent plot, much of it is repetitive and obscure and it is certainly placed in the lowest possible social stratum but it is written with an original and unmistakable sense of theatre and is impeccably acted and directed. Above all, its basic premise is victory rather than defeat. I am surprised that the critics thought so well of it. Doubtless, they were misled by the comfortably familiar squalor of its locale and the fact that one of the principal characters is a tramp.

A few weeks ago Mr. Kenneth Tynan, that most articulate of *avant-garde* torchbearers, slithered gracefully backwards off the barricades and announced plaintively: "The present state of the English theatre is one of deadlock. Its audience is still predominantly conservative, wedded by age and habit to the old standards; its younger playwrights, meanwhile are predominantly anti-conservative, irretrievably divorced from the ideological status quo. Obviously they need a new audience; but in order to attract it they will have to define and dramatise the new values for which they severally stand. We know what they are *against*—the human consequences of class privilege, the profit motive, organized religion and so forth—but what are they *for?*"

In spite of Mr. Tynan's disillusional *cri de coeur* I cannot feel that this is really a very difficult question to answer. Having in the first place decided to become professional playwrights they must obviously be "for" the proven success of their plays. Not necessarily success in the *Chu Chin Chow / Mousetrap* sense, but at least success enough to relieve them of financial anxiety and bring them some of the material satisfactions that reward their, perhaps less earnest, but certainly more commercially popular, colleagues. I suspect, possibly unworthily, that their anti-class privilege, anti-profit theories might suffer a sea-change could they manage to achieve an eighteen months run in a largish West End theatre on a ten per cent of the gross contract.

It is well known that there are all sorts of audiences for all sorts of plays. The public that packs the theatre nightly for *Simple Spymen* or *Watch It, Sailor!* is entirely different from that which queues up for *Ross* or Shakespeare seasons at Stratford or the Old Vic. Somehow or other there always seem to be enough to go round. I disagree with Mr. Tynan when he says that the younger playwrights need a "new" audience. What they need is just an audience, new or old it doesn't matter which; and this, with one or two exceptions, they have so far been unable to get. They have received tumultuous acclaim from the critics (always a sinister omen). They have gained awards and won prizes and, in most cases, had their plays extremely well acted. But in spite of this and in spite of the fact that the plays themselves cost little in costume, decor and overhead expenses, they have failed to run. And their managements, who perhaps still retain a tiny interest in the "profit motive," have been forced to withdraw them.

Without wishing to be unkind, I must honestly admit, having read or seen most of the "New Movement" works under discussion, that I am not in the least surprised at the public's lack of response. In none of them to date, with a very few exceptions, have I observed any sign of genuine theatrical effectiveness. I have seen excellent acting, adroit direction and, once or twice, even good lighting, but nowhere among the torrents of words, propaganda, self-pity, vituperation, pretentiousness and self-conscious realism have I heard an original idea movingly expressed or a problem concisely stated.

I am aware that most of the young writers of today are obsessed by left-wing socialism and the grievances of the underprivileged, and that many of them, possibly owing to their own personal circumstances, are prejudiced against any form of what the Americans are pleased to call "Gracious Living." But the fact must be faced that a very large proportion of English people, even in our tax-ridden Welfare State, contrive to live, if not graciously, at least comfortably. The men manage to earn reasonable salaries in offices, banks, shops and factories; the women manage to run houses or flats, have children, bring them up and educate them and on the whole live fairly contented lives. For all the eager young talent of our day to be encouraged to dwell exclusively on the limited and monotonous problems of a fast diminishing proletariat seems to me to be not only foolish but very definitely old-fashioned.

In the early Twenties the *avant-garde* Piscator theatre in Berlin was presenting, to a bored and apathetic public, very similar plays to those which are being presented at the Royal Court Theatre today. There was the same "Down With The Rich—Up With The Poor" propaganda, there were the same sinks and dustbins and washtubs and onion frying; the same composite "imaginative" sets with different levels, and windows and doors opening onto nothing, and the same naïf conviction on the part of authors, actors and directors that they were pioneers sweeping away forever the moribund, fustian conventions and traditions of the commercial theatre.

To me these "new" values are as familiar as a maid and butler opening a first act with a brisk exposition of the characters about to appear. What neither the critics nor the contemporary pioneers take into consideration is that political or social propaganda in the theatre, as a general rule, is a cracking bore. In spite of much intellectual wishful thinking to the contrary, the theatre is now, always has been and, I devoutly hope, always will be primarily a place for entertainment.

If a young writer is burning with social injustice and quiveringly intolerant of "the ideological status quo," he would be well advised to choose some other medium in which to express his views. He can address crowds at Marble Arch, write pamphlets, novels or free verse, stand on soap boxes and incite factory workers and dock-hands to strike, or go into politics. He can even march up and down the main thoroughfares of London (protectively escorted by the long-suffering Metropolitan Police Force) waving banners and shouting at the top of his lungs that he is against this or that, or the other thing, but in fairness to himself and his future hopes, he had better keep away from the theatre; for theatre, after perhaps a brief start of surprise, will in a comparatively short space of time disown him, ignore him and ultimately forget him entirely.

The first allegiance of a young playwright should be, not to his political convictions, nor to his moral or social conscience, but to his talent. And what is more, over and above this initial talent, it is his duty as an artist to impose upon himself and his work, industry, lucidity, economy of phrase, self-criticism, taste, selectivity and enough technical ability to convey whatever he wishes to convey to a large audience. (I say "large" audience advisedly because it is palpably a waste of time to appeal merely to a minority of the already converted.) This cannot be achieved only by hatred of established conditions and the impulse to destroy. It can be achieved occasionally, however, by the forms of self-discipline I have outlined above, coupled with a certain humility, humour and an intelligent and respectful attitude to the public.

Consider the public. Treat it with tact and courtesy. It will accept much from you if you are clever enough to win it to your side. Never fear it nor despise it. Coax it, charm it, interest it, stimulate it, shock it now and then if you must, make it laugh, make it cry and make it think, but above all, dear pioneers, in spite of indiscriminate and largely ignorant critical acclaim, in spite of awards and prizes and other dubious accolades, never never never bore the living hell out of it.

(The first of three articles published in *The Sunday Times* in January 1961.)

4

ON WRITING A PLAY (2) . . . TO WORLD WAR II

"Success Took Me to Her Bosom Like a Maternal Boa Constrictor"

———

The Rat Trap (1918) · *The Queen Was in the Parlour* (1922) · *Fallen Angels* (1923) · *Hay Fever* (1924) · *Easy Virtue* (1924) · *This Was a Man* (1926) · *Semi-Monde* (1926) · *Home Chat* (1927) · *The Marquise* (1927) · *Sirocco* (1927) · *Private Lives* (1930) · *Post-Mortem* (1930) · *Cavalcade* (1931) · *Design for Living* (1933) · *Point Valaine* (1934) · *Tonight at 8:30* (1936)

Noël's advice to young would-be playwrights as expressed by actor Garry Essendine in *Present Laughter* . . .

GARRY: To begin with, your play is not a play at all. It's a meaningless jumble of adolescent, pseudo-intellectual poppycock. It bears no relation to the theatre or to life or to anything . . . If you wish to be a playwright, you just leave the theatre of tomorrow to take care of itself. Go and get yourself a job as a butler in a repertory company, if they'll have you. Learn from the ground up how plays are constructed and what is actable and what isn't. Then sit down and write at least twenty plays one after the other, and if you can manage to get the twenty-first producd for a Sunday night performance, you'll be damned lucky!

After *The Vortex* the floodgates opened in earnest.

What else had this brilliant young man done? Out from Noël's rather crowded bottom drawer came the other plays he'd written in which no one had been interested but now . . .

The Rat Trap (1918)

Noël never saw *The Rat Trap*. It was staged at the Everyman Theatre, Hampstead—scene of his breakthrough with *The Vortex* in 1924—while he was away in America in 1926 . . .

"It was written when I was eighteen, and was my first attempt at serious playwriting. As such it is not without merit. There is some excruciatingly sophisticated dialogue in the first act of which, at the time, I was inordinately proud. From the point of construction it is not very good except for the two principal quarrel scenes. The last act is an inconclusive shambles and is based on the sentimental and inaccurate assumption that the warring egos of the man and his wife will simmer down into domestic bliss, merely because the wife is about to have a dear little baby. I suppose that I was sincere about this at the time but I find it very hard to believe. I think it will be interesting as a play to ardent students of my work of which I hope there are several."

"It was produced while I was on the *Olympic* bound for New York, so I never saw it . . . in spite of the effulgence of the cast, the play fizzled out at the end of its regulation two weeks. I was not particularly depressed about this. *The Rat Trap* was a dead love."

In terms of his plays the rest of the 1920s might as well have been called the Post-*Vortex* Era . . .

Ironically the most decisive action was taken initially by New York producers. *Easy Virtue,* written in 1924, was modestly successful in a premiere production—*Hay Fever,* written in that same year, rather less so. Nonetheless, the name of Noël Coward was now established as a social and theatrical celebrity on both sides of the Atlantic.

Hay Fever (1924)

Typical of this overnight "canonization" was the example of *Hay Fever.* Prior to *The Vortex* Noël had shown it to Marie Tempest, arguably the leading *grande dame* of the West End. The lady was distinctly unim-

Noel Coward's " Clean " Play: " Hay Fever."

"*Hay Fever*, Mr. Noel Coward's play now running at the Ambassadors is the story of a 'Bohemian' household. The father is a romantic novelist, the mother an emotional ex-actress who loves scenes and likes flirting. The son and daughter are a pair of precocious, impudent children—a type pretty much in favor with both dramatists and novelists. The four of them, quite unknown to each other, invite guests to stay over the weekend. The latter are somewhat amazed at the household in which they find themselves, especially as Mrs. Bliss insists on everyone acting as though they were characters in a play. The children and husband know her little weakness but the visitors are completely bewildered and by Sunday morning find that they can bear it no longer and decide to go away before the Bliss family appear at breakfast. The family are busy quarrelling over the topography of Mr. Bliss's latest novel that they never notice their guests' departure. The play is not only very amusing but it gives Miss Marie Tempest a most admirable part. The husband is played by Mr. Graham Browne."

The flight from chaos in *Hay Fever* (1964 revival). A frequent
ending to a Coward comedy. (Think *Private Lives, Easy Virtue,*
and *Present Laughter.*)

pressed. She felt it was "too light and plotless and generally lacking in
action." Now—in the light of *The Vortex*—she could see its merits and
wanted to play it, which she duly did.

Looking back on it, Noël could see that it represented an evolution in
his approach to writing comedy. "I was passing through a transition; my
dialogue was becoming more natural and less elaborate and I was beginning to concentrate more on the comedy values of situation rather than
the comedy values of actual lines."

He needn't have worried. That initial production ran for 337
performances.

"*Hay Fever* is considered by many to be my best comedy. . . . At any rate it has certainly proved to be a great joy to amateurs, owing, I suppose, to the smallness of its cast and the fact that it has only one set, which must lead them, poor dears, to imagine that it is easy to act. This species of delusion being common to amateurs all over the world, no word of mine shall be spoken, no warning finger of experience raised, to discourage them, beyond the timorous suggestion that from the professional standpoint *Hay Fever* is far and away one of the most difficult plays to perform that I have ever encountered.

"To begin with, it has no plot at all, and remarkably little action. Its general effectiveness depends upon expert technique from each and every member of the cast. . . . I am very much attached to *Hay Fever*. I enjoyed writing it and producing it, and I have frequently enjoyed watching it."

Later Noël would reflect . . .

"Good old *Hay Fever* certainly has been a loyal friend.

"When I tapped out this little comedy on my typewriter in three days, I would indeed have been astonished if anyone had told me it was destined to emerge fresh and blooming forty years later.

"One of the reasons it was hailed so warmly by the critics was that there happened to be an ardent campaign being conducted against 'Sex' plays, and *Hay Fever*, as I remarked in my first-night speech, was clean as a whistle. True there has been no campaign against 'Sex' plays latterly. On the contrary rape, incontinence, perversion, sadism, psychopathology, flatulence, both verbal and physical, have for some time been sure bets in the race for critical acclaim. I was therefore agreeably surprised to wake up on the morning after the first night and read a number of adulatory and enthusiastic notices."

"Some of the Press naturally and inevitably described it as 'thin', 'tenuous,' and 'trivial,' because those are their stock phrases for anything later in date and lighter in texture than *The Way of the World*, and it ran, tenuously and triumphantly, for a year."

AMBASSADORS
THEATRE
West St. - Shaftesbury Avenue
W.C.2   *(Near Leicester Square Tube Station.)*
Proprietors . AMBASSADORS THEATRE LTD.   Licensee : HERBERT JAY
Sole Lessee . H. M. HARWOOD

ALBAN B. LIMPUS
presents

MARIE TEMPEST
in a New Comedy, entitled :

HAY FEVER
by
NOEL COWARD

PROGRAMME

In 1964 Laurence Olivier—first director of the newly formed National Theatre—invited Noël to direct a revival of *Hay Fever* in their temporary home, the Old Vic.

It would be the first revival of a play by a living writer.

Another pre–*The Vortex* play was *Fallen Angels.*

Fallen Angels (1923)

Written in 1923 but not produced until 1925, this could hardly be described as "clean as a whistle." Two youngish married women who had had affairs with the same French lover in their unmarried, if not exactly virginal, days hear that he is coming back to London and find their old feelings stirring. He arrives and we are left to speculate . . .

The two lustful ladies were to have been played originally by Gladys Cooper and Madge Titheradge but other commitments interfered with the pairing and the parts were finally filled by Tallulah Bankhead and Edna Best.

Noël recorded that the Press notices were "vituperative to the point of

Edith Evans and Maggie Smith in *Hay Fever* (1964).

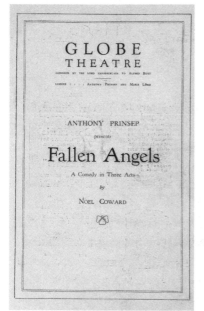

Julia Sherrol (Tallulah Bankhead) and Jane Banbury (Edna Best). "Mr. Coward," wrote *The Sunday Times* of *Fallen Angels*, "is a very young playwright of quite extraordinary gifts, who at the moment can no more be trusted with his talent than a schoolboy can be trusted who has stolen a piece of chalk and encountered a providentially blank wall" (1925).

incoherence. No epithet was spared. It was described as vulgar, disgusting, shocking, nauseating, vile, obscene, degenerate, etc., etc. The idea of two gently nurtured young women playing a drinking scene together was apparently too degrading a spectacle for even the most hardened and worldly critics. The *Daily Express* even went so far as to allude to these two wayward creatures as 'suburban sluts.' The whole thing was an insult to British womanhood. All this was capital for the box office." The play ran for 158 performances.

"At one performance a woman stood up in a box at the end of the second act and began to speak against the play but her words were drowned by the orchestra, which began to play 'I Want To Be Happy.'"

I certainly deny very firmly the imputation (made by several) that I wrote *Fallen Angels* in order to be "daring" and "shocking." Neither of these exceedingly second-rate ambitions has ever occurred to me.

It was, of course, none of these things. They might with truth have said that it was extremely slight and needed a stronger last act; they might, with equal truth and more kindness, have said that it had an amusing situation, some very funny lines, two excellent parts for two good actresses, and was vastly entertaining to the public.

I cannot honestly regard it as one of my best comedies but it is gay and light-hearted and British womanhood has been cheerfully insulted by it on various occasions. So has French womanhood, American womanhood, Italian womanhood, German womanhood, Spanish womanhood and, I believe, Scandinavian womanhood. Russian womanhood, up to date, has been spared, but I cannot help feeling, as the second act portrays two ladies of the *bourgeoisie* drinking too much champagne while waiting for their former lover, that it is likely to pop up in Moscow at any moment as a striking example of the decadence of Western democracy.

From the "Eighties" onwards until the outbreak of the 1914–1918 war the London theatre was enriched by a series of plays, which were described as "Drawing-room Dramas." All of them dealt with the psychological and social problems of the upper middle classes. The characters in them were, as a general rule, wealthy, well bred, articulate and motivated by the exigencies of the world to which they belonged. This world was snobbish, conventional, polite and limited by its own codes and rules of behaviour and it was the contravention of these codes and rules—to our eyes so foolish and old-fashioned—that supplied the dramatic content.

It is easy nowadays to laugh at these vanished moral attitudes but they were poignant enough in their time because they were true. Those high-toned drawing-room histrionics are over and done with. Women with pasts today receive far more enthusiastic social recognition than women without pasts. The narrow-mindedness, the moral righteousness and the over-rigid social codes have disappeared but with them has gone much that was graceful, well-behaved and endearing.

Easy Virtue (1924)

Easy Virtue was written immediately after *Hay Fever.*

The plot hinges on John Whittaker, who brings home his new wife to meet his very conventional extended family. The only problem is that Larita, the wife, has a somewhat questionable past and the family do their utmost to show their disapproval of the match. The situation continues to deteriorate until Larita—disillusioned with all of them, her husband included—makes a studied and theatrical exit from their lives.

This was the first of Noël's plays to have its premiere in America.

He writes of it . . .

"From the Eighties onwards until the outbreak of the 1914–18 war, the London theatre was enriched by a series of plays, notably by Somerset Maugham or Arthur Pinero, which were described as 'drawing-room dramas.' I suppose that the apotheosis of those was *The Second Mrs. Tanqueray.* . . . There were also the more specialized Oscar Wilde comedy-dramas.

"It was in a mood of nostalgic regret at the decline of such conventions that I wrote *Easy Virtue.* When it was produced several critics triumphantly pounced on the fact that the play was similar in form and tone and plot to the plays of Pinero. I myself was unimpressed by their perception, for the form and tone and plot of a Pinero play was exactly what I had tried to achieve."

The opening of the English production brought with it an element of off-stage farce . . .

The out-of-town tryout was in Manchester.

"The Manchester Watch Committee, for some strange reason known only to itself, refused to allow us to use the title *Easy Virtue,* and so it was announced merely as *A New Play in Three Acts.* (The Committee later claimed that, when they licensed it, they thought the title was *Easy Money.*) At the cinema next door to the theatre a film entitled *Flames of Passion* was complacently advertised for the whole week: the vigilance of the Watch Committee did not extend to mere celluloid."

On its arrival in the West End its original title was restored.

There was to be a small reprisal. When Noël came to write the script for the film *Brief Encounter* in 1945, there would be a scene where Celia Johnson and Trevor Howard leave a cinema, laughing at the film they have just been watching.

The cinema's neon sign blazes its title—*Flames of Passion!*

The New York production ran for 147 performances, the subsequent London one for 124 performances.

Nineteen twenty-six and 1927 saw no diminution in Noël's productivity—only in his ratio of success.

The Queen Was in the Parlour (1922)

There was *The Queen Was in the Parlour,* written in the spring of 1922 at St. Mary-in-the-Marsh, near Dymchurch in Kent, propped up against a family tombstone in the churchyard.

"Nothing could be further removed from that play than the surroundings in which I wrote it. Its passionate love scenes and Ruritanian splendours emerged from my mind to the gentle cawing of rooks and the bleating of new-born lambs.

"It was my one and only expedition into Ruritania and I enjoyed it very much. Ruritania is a dangerous country where romantic clichés lurk in every throne-room, but at that time I was young and eager and valiantly oblivious of them. Anthony Hope had blazed the trail and what was good enough for Anthony Hope was good enough for me.

"I thought, with an arrogant *naiveté* at which I can now smile tolerantly, that my brisk, modern mind could fill old bottles with heady new wine, that the dated glamour of Rassendylls and Flavias and crusty, lovable old generals could, by the application of some sophisticated 1920s spit and polish, be brought up to a nice shine. Here I was wrong. *The Queen Was in the Parlour* will be old-fashioned long before *The Prisoner of Zenda* and *Rupert of Hentzau.* However, on the whole, I didn't make a bad job of it."

The Queen reigned for 136 performances.

There were to be two film versions . . .

"The first was French and was played with excessive vivacity by Lili Damita. The second was made in Hollywood, and was called *One Wonderful Night* or *One Glorious Night* or *One Night of Something or Other.* I saw it once by accident in Washington and left the cinema exhausted from the strain of trying to disentangle my own dialogue from the matted mediocrity that the Paramount screen writers had added to it. It was performed doggedly by Claudette Colbert and Fredric March, who were so obviously bogged down by the script that I felt nothing but an embarrassed sympathy for them."

This Was a Man (1926)

After his successful run in *The Vortex* in New York Noël took a holiday in Palermo and to while away the time wrote *This Was a Man . . .*

"It was primarily satirical and on the whole rather dull; the bulk of its dullness being in the second act, which was an attenuated dialogue between two excessively irritating characters. The fact that the characters were intended to be irritating in no way mitigated the general boredom and this vital error in construction ultimately cost the play its life."

"The play failed in spite of some patches of expert acting and also, I hasten to add, some patches of expert writing, but these were not enough to relieve the general tedium. If it had been written with less meticulous veracity and more wit, it might have succeeded but even so, I doubt it. Bores on the stage, however ironically treated, inevitably bore the audience."

This Was a Man was produced in New York and ran for only thirty-one performances. It was never given a London production in Noël's lifetime.

During the American run and tour of *The Vortex* in 1926 "I had forced myself to write a play." He felt "it had been a tremendous strain and I felt that many months of creative impulse had been frustrated." (It was around this time that his aversion to long runs that limited his creative versatility began to harden.)

Semi-Monde (1926)

"The play I wrote was called *Semi-Monde* [originally *Ritz Bar*] and the whole action of it took place in the public rooms of the Ritz Hotel in Paris over a period of three years. It was well constructed and, on the whole, well written; its production in London or New York seemed unlikely, as some of the characters, owing to lightly suggested abnormalities, would certainly be deleted by the censor."

(Considering the difficulties Noël had experienced with the U.K. censor over *The Vortex,* it seems strange that he would embark on a venture that he admitted he knew would be doomed.)

"Max Reinhardt, however, was enthusiastic about it, and it was translated into German by Rudolph Kommer and taken in due course to Berlin, where for years it escaped production by a hair's breadth until eventually Vicky Baum wrote *Grand Hotel,* and *Semi-Monde,* being too closely similar in theme, faded gently into oblivion."

At the time, however, he clearly hoped that Reinhardt would go ahead, since "it would be one in the eye for everyone and place me on such an intellectual plane that I doubt I should ever come down!"

Semi-Monde had its long-delayed world premiere as written at the Citizens Theatre, Glasgow, in 1977 and was considered to be "probably the most accurate stage representation of the twenties *milieu* Coward inhabited that we have."

PREFACE TO *SEMI-MONDE*

I feel that a few words of explanation are necessary to exculpate *Semi-Monde* from the charges of "licentiousness," "decadence" and "sensationalism." Several times before with regard to my earlier plays these three qualities have been accredited to me in addition to several others equally vituperative. Therefore, in this case I wish to forestall the inevitable by laying at the disposal of whosoever cares to read it a brief outline of my real motives in writing of types and characters which, although constituting a comparatively small section of civilized society, are nevertheless just as valuable as factors in Human Drama as Gentlemen Burglars, Lancashire Homicides and Elizabethan Harlots.

At the time of writing this there is being waged in England a passionate campaign against what are described as "unpleasant" plays—that is, plays which utilize (perhaps a little more frankly than usual)—conflicting sex relationships for the furtherance of their dramatic values. There have been several hysterical demands—generally, it must be admitted, from elderly clergymen in Norfolk—that sex be abolished from the stage altogether. This suggestion, though too fatuous to be considered seriously, serves to illustrate the distressing trend of public opinion at a moment when the British Drama is tottering so visibly that artificial restoration has to be resorted to in the shape of imported American farces and musical comedies in increasing numbers.

The British nation since its deliverance from the horrors of war in 1918 appears in its attitude towards art to have become more and more lethargic—a comatose smugness seems to have swept over the land. In other countries tremendous efforts are being made in the progress of literature and drama. And for each forward step registered in America, Germany, France and Italy, England falls back two, completely undismayed in its serene and idiotic complacency. The younger writers are forced to compromise, because in most cases they are not in a position to fight and have a living to make. The slightest break away from tradition is greeted with fear and suspicion by the Church and State. Sincerely written plays by unknown young authors are turned down in feverish haste by the Lord Chamberlain, thereby being denied the judgment of the public, which is after all their right, solely because—in so many cases quite unwittingly— they present problems comic or tragic of the present day as contrasted with the standards of twenty-five years ago. These being unfortunately the only standard by which those in authority seem to be capable of judging.

During the years between 1914 and 1918 the general nerve tension was so great that with the sudden cessation of strain a complete psychological reaction was inevitable and it is in the midst of this reaction that we are living now. Moral values as they were have long since lost all significance. Ideals and ambitions as they were have changed likewise. This does not in any way mean abolishment, merely readjustment and it is this all important fact that the older generation seems incapable of grasping.

(1926)

Home Chat (1927)

Home Chat was written during the summer of 1927.

"It had some excellent lines and a reasonably funny situation, but I was not entirely pleased with it. However I read it to Madge Titheradge, for whom I had visualized the leading part, and she liked it . . . so we settled to do it in the early autumn.

"The opening performance was rendered agonizing by one of the more elderly actresses in the company forgetting her lines continually, with the result that the pauses she made while trying to remember them, coupled with the intentional pauses that director Basil Dean had carefully rehearsed, frequently brought the play to a standstill. There were boos at the end, and I bounded on to the stage with my usual misguided valour and had a brisk exchange of unpleasantries with the Gallery. However, no good came of any of it and the play closed after 38 performances. I do not think it would have lasted that long had it not been for the acting of Madge. When I wrote it, I naturally considered it good, so did she and everybody concerned, but we were wrong. It was a little better than bad, but not quite good enough, and that was that."

The Marquise (1927)

"It has long been a habit of wealthy American gentlemen to leave a standing order, with their measurements, with Savile Row tailors so that, at stated intervals, immaculately cut suits may cross the cold Atlantic and be stepped into without a button having to be altered.

"The writing of *The Marquise* was a reversal of the process. I left England in the autumn of 1926 with the line and measurements of Marie Tempest clearly in my mind."

At the time he was convalescing at the Greenbrier hotel in White Sulphur Springs . . .

I really should have rested completely but I had promised her that I would write a comedy for her and an idea had been kicking around inside me for some time. . . . She had played *Hay Fever* for over a year; her comedy technique was flawless and I knew from close and happy association with her the consummate grace with which she could handle a scene and the wit with which she could handle a line.

She, more than any other actress I have ever known—with the possible exception of Ina Claire—had brought to perfection the art of playing comedy with repressed laughter in her voice. I can still hear, over the years, that particular vocal trick of hers, that beguiling chuckle with which she could whisk a phrase, perhaps not in itself especially funny, into the realms of purest comedy.

I huffed and I puffed . . . with Marie Tempest speaking every line in my mind's ear . . . and finally completed a pleasant little eighteenth century joke called *The Marquise*. The last act was a bit weak but I thought on the whole it would make a good evening's entertainment.

I sent it to her. Some months later I arrived in England the day after she had opened in it.

I remember sitting in the stage box of the Criterion Theatre just before the rise of the curtain and wondering how much of the performance I was about to see would differ from the idealized, imagined performance. . . . It was a curious experience.

The curtain rose, the play started and presently in she walked through the French windows, accurate and complete. There was everything I had envisaged; the "tricorne" hat, the twinkle in the eye, the swift precision of movement. Every remembered intonation was there too, every sharply delivered line, every little gurgle. It was for me obviously an enchanting evening, and it has made me forever incapable of judging the play on its merits . . . I might perhaps see what a tenuous, frivolous little piece *The Marquise* is. . . . I might, bereft of her memory, read with disdain the whole play; sneer at its flippancy; laugh at its trivial love scenes and shudder at the impertinence of an author who, for no apparent reason, except perhaps that pictorially the period is attractive, elects to place a brittle modern comedy in an eighteenth century setting. But I am not and never shall be bereft of the memory of Marie Tempest and any reader who shares this privilege will, I am sure, agree that *The Marquise* is gay, brilliant, witty, charming and altogether delightful.

The Marquise remained "gay, brilliant, witty and charming" for 129 performances.

Sirocco (1927)

By 1927 Noël was suffering from post-*Vortex* reaction. The boy wonder had achieved some success in the three years since the tidal wave that show represented—but now the tide was turning, as it would turn again in the opposite direction with "Dad Renaissance" some thirty years later.

Part of the problem was his own facility and his own fault. A play would be written as soon as he'd thought of it and at this stage of his career he often lacked the critical faculty to assess it objectively.

A second problem was his inclination to dust off material written years earlier.

There was to be a full stop. It was called *Sirocco*. Written in 1921. Produced and reinterred in 1927.

In retrospect he had to wish it had stayed in the trunk. As he recalled the opening night. . . .

Probably nobody not connected with the theatre could appreciate fully the tension and strain of that dreadful evening. The first night of any play is uncomfortable for those who are intimately concerned with it. And in the case of *Sirocco* it was a losing battle from the word "Go." The first act was received dully. Ivor got a big reception from the Gallery when he came on. Apart from that there was nothing but oppressive stillness. The curtain fell to scattered applause.

The storm broke during Ivor's love scene with Bunny Doble.

Ivor was a difficult proposition. Although his looks were marvelous for the part and his name—owing to silent film successes—was a big draw, his acting experience in those days was negligible . . . Frances Doble was frankly terrified from beginning to end. She looked lovely, but, like Ivor, lacked technique.

The Gallery shrieked with mirth and made sucking sounds when he kissed her, and from then onwards proceeded to punctuate every line with catcalls and various other noises.

The last act was chaos from beginning to end . . . Ivor and Bunny and the rest of the cast struggled on doggedly, trying to shut their ears to the noise and get the torture done with as quickly as possible. The curtain finally fell amid a bedlam of sound.

Whether or not the demonstration was organized by personal enemies I neither knew or cared. I was conscious only of an overwhelming desire to come to grips in some way or other with the vulgar, ill-mannered rabble.

When I reached the side of the stage, Basil [the director] who had been quietly dining somewhere, was standing in the prompt corner, smiling and ringing the curtain up and down. From where he stood the tumult in the front of the house might conceivably be mistaken for cheering and he, having no idea of the horrors of the evening, was happily convinced that it was.

I quickly disillusioned him and walked on to the stage. Without once looking at the audience, I went along the frightened line of the company to the centre, shook hands with Ivor, kissed Bunny Doble's hand and walked off again.

This, as I expected, increased the booing tenthousandfold. I went on again and stood in the centre, a little in front of Bunny and Ivor, bowing and smiling my grateful thanks to the angriest audience I have ever heard in a theatre. They yelled abuse at me, booed, made what is known in theatrical terms as a "raspberry," hissed and shrieked . . . altogether the din was indescribable.

It was definitely one of the most interesting experiences of my life and, my anger and contempt having reduced me to a cold numbness, I was able almost to enjoy it.

I stood there actually for about seven minutes until their larynxes became raw and their breath failed and the row abated a little. Then somebody started yelling "Frances Doble." It was taken up and she stepped forward, the tears from her recent emotional scene still drying on her face and, in the sudden silence following what had been the first friendly applause throughout the whole evening, said in a voice tremulous with nerves—"Ladies and gentlemen, this is the happiest moment of my life."

I heard Ivor give a giggle behind me and I broke into laughter, which started a fresh outburst of booing and catcalls. Bunny stepped back, scarlet in the face, and I signaled to Basil to bring the curtain down.

(Noël and Ivor remained lifelong friends but somehow never worked together again, although Ivor did play Noël's part in the film version of *The Vortex*.)

The press reviews the following day were predictable.

"It seemed absurd to embark on another theatrical enterprise in London . . . An absence of a year or so would give the press and public time to forget and enable me to make a comeback with a more reasonable chance of success.

"Having decided upon this, we strapped on our armour, let down our visors, and went to the Ivy for lunch."

———

Music was to prove the answer—as it so often does.

Nineteen twenty-eight saw his successful revue *This Year of Grace!* open in London and then move to New York—this time with Noël in the cast opposite his old friend, Beatrice Lillie.

Then in 1929 came a major breakthrough, his first "book" musical—*Bitter Sweet*—his first operetta (or, as Noël insisted on calling the form—"operette").

It was as though the setback of *Sirocco* had reinvigorated him. No more looking back or disinterring youthful efforts. He would move on and the opening year of the 1930s would prove to be his *annus mirabilis* . . .

Private Lives (1930)

With *Bitter Sweet* more than safely launched on Broadway, Noël treated himself to an extended tour in the Far East with his frequent traveling partner, Jeffery Amherst. Arriving at the Imperial Hotel, Tokyo, where

"Gertie appeared in a white Molyneux dress on a terrace in the South of France and refused to go again until four a.m., by which time *Private Lives*, title and all, had constructed itself.

"For me the memory of her standing on that moonlit stage balcony in a dead white Molyneux dress will never fade. She was the epitome of grace and charm and glamour."

Jeffery was to join him, he was handed a cable advising him that Jeffery had missed a connection in Shanghai and wouldn't be with him until three days later.

"The night before he arrived I went to bed early . . . but the moment I switched out the lights Gertie [Lawrence] appeared in a white Molyneux dress on a terrace in the South of France and refused to go again until four a.m., by which time *Private Lives,* title and all, had constructed itself.

"In 1923 the play would have been written and typed within a few days of my thinking of it, but in 1929 I had learned the wisdom of not welcoming a new idea too ardently, so I forced it into the back of my mind, trusting to its own integrity to emerge again later on, when it had become sufficiently set and matured."

He then wrote to her . . .

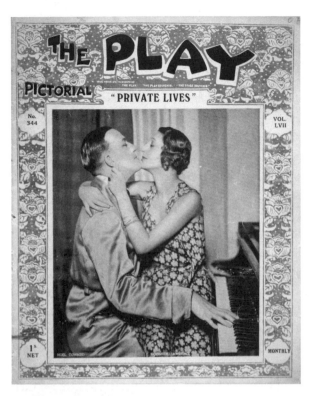

Hong Kong, January 7th 1930

Dearest Gertie,

Here is the play. I wish above all things I were there to read it to you, but I'm not, so you'll have to read it yourself, taking care to visualize my exquisite accents all the way through. Read it nice and slowly, darling, as though you were playing it, it will sound awfully scrappy read quickly, owing to the shortness of some of the sentences.

I've worked very hard on it, and I know it is good, but God knows it's going to be very tricky to play. The situation is obviously farcical, and our difficulty will be to keep it on a high comedy plane . . . The only place where we can really let go and enjoy ourselves will be the big quarrel scene at the end of the act. I do think that will be fun, though probably slightly painful. I'm all for being really abandoned in the love scenes, and doing a few things that will give the old ladies a treat at matinees. Copulation has been the basis of the dear old English drama for so long, we might just as well salute it. I shall write a sort of theme song, the one that brings us together in Act One, and for the rest, I think we might do any of the popular old songs that we feel like singing, changing lines every now and again when we get tired of them.

I am terribly anxious to keep the performance on such a level, that however lightly we may happen to be playing, we can always sw[i]itch to complete seriousness without too much of a jerk. But, of course, we can fix all that when we're working on it.

We can either do it ourselves and go halves or do it under Cochran's management and just own some of it, but discuss all that with Jack, there's really no hurry. I would like to open in London in September, play it there for three months, a month's holiday and come popping over to New York with it in January. (Please forgive business-like phraseology.)

I would like Edward (Molyneux) to make your clothes, you should get your shoes at Fortnums. You needn't worry about stockings, as my Aunt has some and, as far as dressing-room accommodation, I know you won't mind dressing under the stage, as I have a positive horror of stairs.

Years later Noël would admit that Elyot and Amanda were based on Lord and Lady Castlerosse, a prominent society couple. "Her wit, when she's in the mood, can be devastating but she doesn't give a tupenny damn about people's feelings—so watch it!"

"A bout of influenza laid me low in Shanghai, and I lay, sweating gloomily, in my bedroom at the Cathay Hotel for several days. The ensuing convalescence, however, was productive, for I utilized it by writing *Private Lives*. The idea now seemed ripe enough to have a shot at it, so I started it, propped up in bed with a writing block and an Eversharp pencil, and completed it, roughly, in four days. It came easily, and with the exception of a few of the usual 'blood and tears' moments, I enjoyed writing it. I thought it a shrewd and witty comedy, well constructed on the whole, but psychologically unstable; however, its entertainment value seemed obvious enough, and its acting opportunities for Gertie and me admirable, so I cabled her immediately in New York, telling her to keep herself free for the autumn and put the whole thing aside for a few weeks before typing and revising it."

One of the things he had to revise was the opening locale. Originally the terrace was in the South of France but when Elyot and Amanda decide to leave their new spouses and drive back to Paris overnight, Noël realized that the car ride would take too long—and moved the location to Deauville.

The plot itself was simple enough. Elyot and Amanda had been married to each other, then divorced. Each of them had now remarried and, by a convenient touch of theatrical fate, now found themselves on honeymoon in the same hotel in adjacent rooms with their adjacent balconies. When that same fate has them meet on those balconies, they realize that they still love each other. They run away to Paris and there it becomes clear that here are two people who are fated to be unable to live with or without one another. Their spouses (Victor and Sibyl) find them and begin to quarrel in much the same way. So much so that they fail to notice when Elyot and Amanda sneak away. And the wheel turns again . . .

The strategic departure of the principal characters was to become a convenient Coward ending.

Years later Noël reflected . . . "The thing about the play which went unobserved at the time is that it is the lightest of light comedies, based on a serious situation, which is two people who love each other too much. I wouldn't say it's a tragedy but there's a sadness below it."

And indeed, it can be argued that in recent years young directors, actors, and audiences from a totally different era have responded to what on the surface is a brittle story about superficial, selfish people because they detect that "sadness" beneath the wit. *Private Lives* is really about the difficulty and perhaps the impossibility of Love.

The Selwyn Theatre, New York, 1931.

The original London cast of *Private Lives*. Laurence Olivier (Victor), Adrianne Allen (Sibyl), Noël (Elyot), and Gertrude Lawrence (Amanda) (1930).

Adrianne Allen.

━━

Private Lives was presented as the opening production at the Phoenix Theatre, London, on September 24, 1930. (101 performances)

Noël records that "It was described in the papers variously as being 'tenuous,' 'thin,' 'brittle,' 'gossamer,' 'iridescent' and 'delightfully daring.' All of which connoted to the public mind 'cocktails,' 'evening dress,' 'repartee' and irreverent allusions to copulation, thereby causing a gratifying number of respectable people to queue up at the box office."

He himself didn't rate the play particularly highly . . .

It is a reasonably well-constructed duologue for two experienced performers with a couple of extra puppets thrown in to assist the plot and to provide contrast. There is a well-written love scene in Act I and a certain amount of sound sex psychology underlying the quarrel scenes in Act II.

As a complete play it leaves a lot to be desired, principally owing to my dastardly conscienceless behaviour towards Sibyl and Victor, the secondary characters [played by Laurence Olivier and Adrianne Allen]. These poor things are little better than ninepins, lightly wooden, and only there at all to be repeatedly knocked down and stood up again.

Apart from this, *Private Lives,* from the playwright's point of view, may or may not be considered interesting, but at any rate, from the point of view of technical acting, it is very interesting indeed.

To begin with, there is no further plot and no further action after Act I with the exception of the rough and tumble fight at the curtain of Act II. Before this there is exactly 40 minutes of dialogue between Elyot and Amanda, which naturally demands from them the maximum of resource and comedy experience, as every night, according to the degree of responsiveness from the audience, the attack and tempo of the performance must inevitably vary. This means a constant ear cocked in the direction of the stalls, listening for the first sinister cough of boredom, and, when it comes, a swiftly exchanged glance of warning and an immediate, and, it is to be hoped, imperceptible speeding up of the scene, until the next surefire laugh breaks and it is permissible to relax and breathe more easily for a moment.

This strenuous watchfulness is, of course, necessary in the playing of any high comedy scene, but as a general rule the considerate author provides life-lines for his actors in the shape of sharply-sketched cam-

eos for the subsidiary members of the cast, who can make bustling little entrances and exits in order to break the monotony. He may even, on occasion, provide a sustained plot for them to hang on to when all else fails.

By the second act of *Private Lives,* however, there was no help from the author over and above a few carefully placed laugh lines, and taken all in all, it was more tricky and full of pitfalls than anything I have ever attempted as an actor. But, fortunately for me, I had the inestimable advantage of playing it with Gertrude Lawrence, and so three-quarters of the battle was won before the curtain went up.

═══

The creating of *Private Lives* more than justified Noël's extended Asian trip, but, as he sat in his cabin on the P&O liner taking him home—the manuscript safely tucked away in his luggage—other thoughts took over.

He remembered his stay in Singapore, where he had run across The Quaints, a touring English repertory company. One of their offerings had been R. C. Sherriff's haunting war play, *Journey's End,* and Noël found himself agreeing to play the leading role of Stanhope for three performances.

A sell-out audience "politely watched me take a fine part in a fine play and throw it into the alley."

"I'd always longed to play Stanhope, because I thought it was a wonderful play. I had two days in which to learn it. I learned the words perfectly, and I came on and gave, I suppose, the worst performance I've ever given, because I'd not had the time to reach that point in rehearsal when the author's emotion got me. Instead of playing Stanhope as a tight-lipped, controlled military man, I played him as a sobbing neurotic. I cried steadily throughout the play and completely ruined it. The only thing that saved me was that, at the end of the play, when I was carrying Johnnie Mills (who was playing Raleigh), dying, and laid him tenderly on the cot, tears streaming down my face, my tin hat fell off and hit him in the stomach."

(Mills has a bawdier version of that incident. Earlier, he recalled, Noël had told him how pleased he was to be on the stage with him. "And I'm sure that unless I pull out all the stops at the right moment, I shall at the drop of a tin hat, be acted right off it.

("The first act went well. The second act really took off. Noël was giving a magnificent performance. He'd sparked off vibrations like a dynamo . . . My death scene finally arrived . . . I lay there on the bed in the dug-out . . . I sensed Stanhope rise to his feet, then heard him walk upstage; there was a pause, the rattle of machine guns, the footsteps returned, and I knew that, as rehearsed, he was standing at the bed giving Raleigh a last poignant look before his final exit. I was still holding my breath . . . when suddenly I let out a piercing scream, sat bolt upright and stared at the gallant captain, who was bare-headed—from quite a considerable height his tin hat had fallen on the most treasured and delicate part of my anatomy."

(In conversation he would add—"It fell on my cobblers—and I've never been the same since!")

———

Noël continued . . .

"By the third performance I began to be good. If I'd had three weeks' rehearsal and a week or so performing, I should have been very good as Stanhope, but I wasn't; because the emotion caught me unawares. I know this is dead against the modern trend, you have to be in the mood, and feel it. I think it's very good, sometimes, for actors to believe that, as long as they don't really do it.

"In the theatre the basis is always the author. If you're giving a true representation and the author is strong, it's up to you, as an actor, to adapt to the author."

Post-Mortem (1930)

War had long been a *bête noire* for him and now that he had time to contemplate . . .

"During that voyage I wrote an angry little vilification of war called *Post-Mortem.* My mind was strongly affected by *Journey's End* and I had read several current war novels one after the other. I wrote *Post-Mortem* with the utmost sincerity; this, I think, must be fairly obvious to anyone who reads it. In fact, I tore my emotions to shreds over it. The result was similar to my performance as 'Stanhope': confused, under-rehearsed and hysterical. Unlike my performance as 'Stanhope,' however, it had some very fine moments.

"I am exceedingly glad I made it, because, as a writer, it undoubtedly did me a power of good. It opened a lot of windows in my brain and allowed me to let off a great deal of steam which might have remained sizzling inside me and combusted later on, to the considerable detriment of *Cavalcade* and *Design for Living.*"

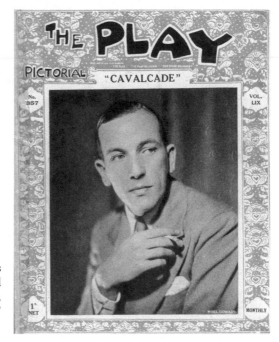

"Throughout the 1930s I was a highly publicized and irritatingly successful figure, much in demand."

During the run of *Private Lives* Noël began to discuss with C. B. Cochran the possibility of staging a big spectacular production.

"I toyed for a while with the thought of a French Revolution epic, a pageant of the Second Empire, and various other ideas which might give me enough scope for intimate characterisations against a background of crowd scenes.

"One day I happened to see in a back number of the *Illustrated London News* a photograph of a troopship leaving for the Boer War. Very soon after this the whole scheme of the play fell into my mind.

"I can't explain why it rang the bell so sharply, I only know that it did. The tunes came first, tunes belonging to my very earliest childhood— 'Dolly Gray,' 'Soldiers of the Queen' . . . I played them on the piano immediately."

Cavalcade (1931)

The emotional basis of *Cavalcade* was undoubtedly music.

The whole story was threaded on to a string of popular melodies. This ultimately was a big contributing factor to its success. "Popular tunes probe the memory more swiftly than anything else, and *Cavalcade,* whatever else it did, awakened many echoes."

He found people and events of the period cascading through his mind . . .

Mafeking Night . . . the Relief of Ladysmith . . . and newsboys— particularly newsboys, shrill Cockney voices shouting victories and defeats along London streets; cooks and housemaids running up foggy area steps to buy halfpenny newspapers; elderly gentlemen in evening capes stopping hansoms in order to read of "Bob's" latest exploits . . . Then the illness of the Queen—newsboys again—the Queen sinking— latest bulletin.

My original story was different from what finally emerged, but the shape was the same. New Year's Eve 1899 to New Year's Eve 1930. Events took precedence first in my mind and against them I moved a group of people—the bright young people of the nineties, the play was to finish with their children—the same eager emptiness, but a different jargon.

After a while I realised that the play should be bigger than that. I had flogged the bright young people, my vehemence against them had congealed, they were now no more than damp squibs, my Poor Little Rich Girls and Dance, Little Ladies. Thirty years of English life seen through their eyes would be uninspired, to say the least of it.

Presently my real characters appeared in two classes: "the Marryots," and "Ellen" and "Bridges."

In Noël's original version there were a number of other minor characters . . . "However, these fell away, still-born, into oblivion, discouraged by my firm determination to keep the whole thing as simple and uncomplicated as possible, and gradually the whole story completed itself in my mind."

Noël and Cochran had always had the London Coliseum in mind as their theatre of choice but, when it proved to be unavailable, they turned to Drury Lane. Yes, they could have it, provided they could guarantee

THE TOAST FROM *CAVALCADE* (1931)

JANE (*holding up her glass*): First of all, my dear, I drink to you. Loyal and loving always. (*She drinks.*) Now, then, let's couple the Future of England with the past of England. The glories and victories and triumphs that are over, and the sorrows that are over, too. Let's drink to our sons who made part of the pattern and to our hearts that died with them. Let's drink to the spirit of gallantry and courage that made a strange Heaven out of unbelievable Hell, and let's drink to the hope that one day this country of ours, which we love so much, will find dignity and greatness and peace again.

They both lift their glasses and drink as the lights fade.

a specific opening date. "I cabled back that the play would be ready for production by the end of September."

At this point Noël was in New York and playing in *Private Lives*. When he got back to London in May . . . "I carefully examined the facilities of the Drury Lane stage." Then, accompanied by Gladys Calthrop, his preferred designer of scenery and costumes, he settled down in his country home "after a series of conferences, to build the play according to blueprints, time-changes, electrical installations and hydraulic lifts. I had not one moment of patriotic fervour."

———

"The first night (October 13, 1931) will remain for ever in my memory as the most agonising three hours I have ever spent in a theatre."

The production was technically ambitious for its time. There were several lifts and their movement had to be synchronized. Side wings full of seated extras have to be rolled into place to meet them and complete a complex set. At the dress rehearsal everything clicked into place—but the machinery suffered from first night nerves and refused to budge.

Noël, seated in his box in full view of the audience, was told by the stage manager that it would take up to two hours to fix things. And then the gods of the theatre relented. The stuck became unstuck and the show continued.

From Noël's perspective the performance lost its edge but the audience didn't seem to share his doubts. At the curtain "the applause was tremendous . . . I appeared at the end against my will . . . It was one of the few occasions in my life that I have ever walked out on a stage not knowing what I was going to say. However, standing there, blinded by my own automatic lights, and nerve-stricken by the torment I had endured in course of the evening, I managed to make a rather incoherent little speech which finished with the phrase—'I hope that this play has made you feel that, in spite of the troublous times we are living in, it is still pretty exciting to be English.'

"This brought a violent outburst of cheering, and the orchestra, frantic with indecision as to whether to play my waltz or 'God save the King,' effected an unhappy compromise by playing them both at once. The curtain fell, missing my head by a fraction, and that was that."

The reaction of audiences and critics was overwhelmingly positive but Noël sensed a downside.

"Everybody seemed to be more concerned with *Cavalcade* as a patriotic appeal than as a play. This attitude I realised had been enhanced by my first night speech—'A pretty exciting thing to be English'—quite true, quite sincere; I felt it strongly, but I rather wished I hadn't said it, hadn't popped it on to the top of *Cavalcade* like a paper-cap. I hadn't written the play as a dashing patriotic appeal at all. There was certainly love of England in it, a certain natural pride in some of our very typical characteristics, but primarily it was the story of thirty years in the life of a family. I saw where my acute sense of the moment had very nearly cheapened it."

He needn't have been so concerned. In the context of time the heroine's "Toast to the Future"—"Let's drink to the hope that one day this country of ours, which we love so much, will find dignity and greatness and peace again"—has become what audiences want from the play.

Public reaction was immediate and enthusiastic . . .

A very gratifying Deluge. Letters of congratulation. Crowds in the streets. Superlatives in the Press. I was told, on all sides, that I had done "a big thing" and that a peerage was the least I could expect from a grateful monarch. I was also congratulated upon my uncanny shrewdness in slapping on a strong patriotic play two weeks before a general election, which was bound to result in a sweeping Conservative majority. (Here I must regretfully admit that during rehearsals I was so very much occupied in the theatre and, as usual, so bleakly uninterested in politics that I had not the remotest idea, until a few days before production, that there was going to be an election at all! However, there was, and its effect on the box office was considerable.)

The excitement continued for the two weeks that I remained in London after the play had opened, and I left for South America, flushed with heroism and extremely tired. I could relax on the boat and reflect that although it was undoubtedly very pleasant to read in the Press that my country was proud of me, I had escaped the grave danger of taking the idea seriously. True there had been a few uneasy highbrows who had deplored my fall from sophisticated wit into the bathos of jingoism, and had even gone so far as to suggest that the whole thing was a wily commercial trick, conceived, written, and produced in a spirit of cynical mockery, with my tongue fairly wedged in my cheek, but those shrill small voices were drowned out by the general trumpetings of praise.

Now that the whole thing is done . . . I can meditate blissfully upon the good fortune that prompted me to pick up just that particular number of the *Illustrated London News*, instead of one of a later date depicting the storming of the Winter Palace at St. Petersburg.

=====

Years later at a crowded cocktail party Noël, like the rest of the guests, was trying to balance his drink and a plate of canapés. Seeing his predicament, a waiter rushed up with a fork, causing a fellow guest to say— "How come YOU get a fork?" To which Noël calmly replied—"Well, I *did* write *Cavalcade*, you know."

NOTE: What Noël didn't realize was that he was inadvertently launching a saga. In the 1970s there was a series on British television called *Upstairs, Downstairs* that ran for several years and chonicled the doings of an aristocratic family (upstairs) and their servants (downstairs). Then in the 2010s came the phenomenon of *Downton Abbey*, proving that a good idea doesn't care who has it—or how often.

Design for Living (1933)

"I would like to explain here and now that to sit down and write an effective vehicle for one talented personality in the theatre is none too easy, to attempt to write one for three, particularly three of such equal status as Lynn, Alfred and me, seemed to me then, as indeed it seems to me now, an exceedingly tricky assignment. It was also, of course, one of the most stimulating challenges I have ever faced in my life."

This was Noël reacting to a cable he received while on a lengthy trip around South America. It was a terse message from the Lunts—"Darling, our contract with the Theatre Guild up in June, what about it?" Reminding him of the promise he had made on that first visit he'd made in New York back in 1921 to write a play for the three of them, once they had all reached star status.

At the time it had seemed "little more than a far-fetched and over-ambitious pipe-dream. But a lot can happen in eleven years and to Lynn, Alfred and me, a lot had . . . We were all three established stars in our own rights. The first move towards fulfilling the second part of the dream was now obviously over to me . . . I remember going to bed that night in a fairly pensive state of mind."

"We had met, discussed, argued, and parted again many times, knowing that it was something that we wanted to do very much indeed, and searching wildly through our minds for suitable characters. At one moment we were to be three foreigners. Lynn, Eurasian; Alfred, German; and I, Chinese. At another we were to be three acrobats, rapping out 'Allez Oops' and flipping handkerchieves at one another. A further plan was that the entire play should be played in a gigantic bed, dealing with life and love in the Schnitzler manner. This, however, was hilariously discarded, after Alfred had suggested a few stage directions which, if followed faithfully, would have landed all three of us in jail."

Once he'd absorbed the initial shock, "I knew from experience that, once I could snatch out of the air the right idea for a play, the actual writing of it would not take long. Once the basic theme of a play has been worked out in my mind, I have always written quickly.

"From that moment onwards my travelling lacked that sense of detachment which up to then had been its principal charm. Patagonia, Chile, Peru and Colombia presented themselves in turn, less as strange, thrilling countries brimming with historical interest than as painted theatrical backgrounds, against which three attractive, witty characters changed their minds and colours with the rapidity of chameleons, but failed, unlike chameleons, to achieve even the meagre satisfaction of being alive.

"The actual writing was done on a small Norwegian freight boat travelling from Panama to Los Angeles. The play suddenly emerged, and, with a superb disregard for the mountains and jungles and plains I had traversed in search of and, without even a salute to the flamboyant Mexican coastline on the starboard horizon, placed its own *mise-en-scène* firmly in Paris, London and New York.

"I had my typewriter on which, with no urgency, no consciousness of Time's wingèd chariot at my back, I began and completed *Design for Living*. The idea slipped into my mind, with neither prayer nor supplication, on the first evening out of Panama. I wrote it morning after morning almost effortlessly, with none of the routine moments of unbalanced exultance or black despair. It was a painless confinement and no instruments were required to ease the birth beyond an extra typewriter ribbon, which I happened to have with me. I finished it tidily two days before we were due to dock in Los Angeles and celebrated the occasion by having a royal piss-up with the crew."

On arriving in New York Noël read the script to Alfred and Lynn,

He would later describe to designer Gladys Calthrop a somewhat exaggerated view of audience reaction . . . "Capacity and standees at every performance and very common people, dear—not our class at all—given to spitting and coughing and belching during the quieter passages." (1933)

"who were even more enthusiastic than I had hoped they would be . . . Much as I dislike being read aloud to, I very much enjoy reading aloud, and the Lunts with loving indulgence resigned themselves to the inevitable. They sat like beautifully behaved mice, nobody sighed or yawned or coughed and Alfred mixed stimulating little drinks between acts. It was a very happy occasion. So often in our profession . . . dreams are dreamed which are never realised and hopeful plans made which ultimately come to dust. This was a long established dream for all three of us and that first reading was the moment when it actually came true. Fortunately later on it didn't let us down, the play was an enormous success and all was well, but that was the moment of magic."

"Gilda needs to have a touch of the gypsy. She needs to be a bit common." (1933)

DESIGN FOR LIVING

ALFRED LUNT, NOEL COWARD AND LYNN FONTANNE

ETHEL BARRYMORE
THEATRE

"*Design for Living* has been liked and disliked, and hated and admired, but never, I think, sufficiently loved by any but its three leading actors. This, perhaps, was only to be expected, as its central theme, from the point of view of the average, must appear to be definitely anti-social. People were certainly interested and entertained and occasionally even moved by it, but it seemed to many of them 'unpleasant.' This sense of 'unpleasantness' might have been mitigated for them a little if they had realised that the title was ironic rather than dogmatic. I never intended for a moment that the design for living suggested in the play should apply to anyone outside its three principal characters, Gilda, Otto and Leo. These glib, over-articulate, and amoral creatures force their lives into fantastic shapes and problems because they cannot help themselves. Impelled chiefly by the impact of their personalities each upon the other, they are like moths in a pool of light, unable to tolerate the lonely outer darkness, and equally unable to share the light without colliding constantly and bruising one another's wings.

"Different minds found different meanings in this laughter. Some considered it to be directed against Ernest, Gilda's husband, and the time-honoured friend of all three. If so, it was certainly cruel, and in the worst possible taste. I as author, however, prefer to think that Gilda and Otto and Leo were laughing at themselves."

After a short tour *Design for Living* opened at the Ethel Barrymore Theatre, New York, on January 24, 1933, and ran for 135 performances.

———

In 1935 critic Ivor Brown gave a halftime summary of *Design for Living* in *Theatre Arts Monthly* . . .

"It is Mr. Coward's peculiar genius to give theatrical value and the potentiality of wit to what appears in print to be next to nothing. Accordingly the comedy acting of our time has been specially developed to impose a personal glamour and to embroider with effects of humorous suggestion the stark bareness of the text.

"A player like Miss Gertrude Lawrence can, by her virtuosity, persuade us that Mr. Coward's text has brilliance of its own. What would an actress of her type do if, instead of imposing her own style (or bundle of tricks—if you prefer it so) on a negative surface, she had to subdue herself to the full, rich periods of Pinero, who wrote for players capable of rhetoric? In all probability she would flounder and drown, because realism has driven rhetoric as well as poetry out of the theatre.

"The ending is equivocal . . . the three of them are left together as the curtain falls, laughing . . . some saw it as a lascivious anticipation of a sort of triangular carnal frolic. Others . . . regarded it as a meaningless and slightly inept excuse to bring the curtain down." (1933)

"Our comedy is verbally limited to the hint or the flat assertion; if the water is to be aerated, the player must do it. That the players often can do it proves the resourcefulness of the human performer and the modern director. Just as French cooking has to be good because French meat is so tough, so English comedy has to be all the better acted because it is now so drably written. In the end style must show itself. But it is not style of composition. Mr. Coward, as author, kicks that downstairs as director and player he lets style of presentation slip in at the window."

Point Valaine (1934)

And then came a hiccup . . .

Point Valaine was certainly a departure for Noël. Set in a seedy hotel on an island in the Caribbean, the characters were a cross between sub–Somerset Maugham and early Tennessee Williams.

Lynn Fontanne plays Linda, the sleazy proprietess and Alfred is Stefan, her gruff Russian lover—characters far removed from those on which they had built their considerable reputations.

Considering the piece years later, Noël decided that "the fundamental weakness of the play was its basic theme. It was neither big enough for tragedy nor light enough for comedy; the characters were well drawn, but not one of them was either interesting or kind. . . . Somehow everything seemed to go wrong from the beginning. Alfred and Lynn and I were irritable with each other, which we had never been before and seldom have since . . . We all pressed on with 'old trouper' determination, but none of us was happy and none of us knew quite why until some time afterwards, and the revelation burst upon us that what was really wrong was the play."

Later . . .

"In fairness to myself, however, I must say that in conceiving and writing it I was honestly attempting to break, for me, new ground . . ."

(As Alfred would say when it was all over—with more than a touch of irony—"Well, Noely, you certainly succeeded there!")

"The heroine, or perhaps it would be better to describe her as the leading female character (Lynn), is curiously disagreeable and, what is worse, indefinite. The situation in which she finds herself should arouse, if not sympathy, at least compassion. But this it fails to do.

"'Stefan,' the sinister Russian waiter who is her secret lover (Alfred), should also particularly in the last act, strike a chord of pity, but he too fails, again, I think because of lack of definition . . ."

Audiences who had come to see the Lunts be the Lunts did not take kindly to what they saw. No matter what parts they were playing, the Lunts simply did not spit at one another!

Nor was the production helped on the technical side.

Symptomatic was the evening when Alfred was revealed standing on a high stage rock from which he was supposed to jump into the sea to be devoured by sharks. He would land on a mattress. An overly tidy stagehand had inadvertently removed the mattress. The curtain was hastily rung down and Alfred had to be helped down. For days afterward he insisted on bringing his own mattress to the theatre and placing it himself.

After fifty-five performances the play closed but the Lunts had long memories. They considered it to be their only flop and a decade later Alfred was heard to say . . . "All I can think and hope for is that that entire opening night audience was dead long ago."

Point Valaine (1934).

If you're Noël&Gertie, what do you do after *Private Lives*? That was the dilemma their success created.

Tonight at 8:30 (1936)

"In the year 1935, upheld by my stubborn faith in the 'star system,' I wrote the *Tonight at 8:30* plays as acting, singing and dancing vehicles for Gertrude Lawrence and myself. The success we had had with *Private Lives,* both in London and New York, encouraged me to believe that the public liked to see us playing together, and this belief, happily for us both and the managements concerned, turned out to be fully justified."

Noël determined that just another romantic comedy would simply invite comparisons and give the critics who had their "thin . . . brittle . . . gossamer" verdicts totally disproved a second chance to vent.

Then a lateral thought struck him, as he explained in the programme notes at London's Phoenix Theatre when the new show opened on January 9, 1936.

The idea of presenting three short plays in an evening instead of one long one is far from original. In fact, if one looks back over the years, one finds that the "triple bill" formula has been used, with varying degrees of success, since the earliest days of the theatre. Latterly, however—that is, during the last quarter of a century—it has fallen from favour. Occasionally still a curtain-raiser appears in the provinces, but wearing a sadly hang-dog expression, because it knows only too well, poor thing, that it would not be there at all were the main attraction of the evening long enough.

Its spirit is further humiliated by the fact that the leading actors treat it with the utmost disdain, seldom leaving their star dressing-rooms to glance at it. Therefore it has to get along as well as it can in the hands of small part actors and understudies who, although frequently far more talented and charming than their principals, have neither the name, authority nor experience to triumph over rustling programmes, banging seats and a general atmosphere of bored impatience.

A short play, having a great advantage over a long one, in that it can sustain a mood without creaking or overpadding, deserves a better fate, and if by careful writing, acting and producing I can do a little towards reinstating it in its rightful pride, I shall have achieved one of my more sentimental ambitions.

The press took note . . .

The outstanding event of the Autumn theatrical season is the renewed partnership of Gertrude Lawrence and Noel Coward in Mr. Coward's latest production, *To-Night At 7.30.*

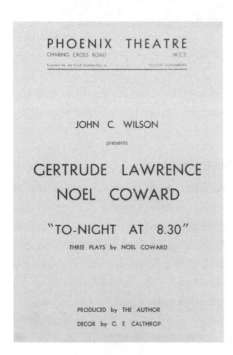

PHOENIX THEATRE
CHARING CROSS ROAD   W.C2
Licensed by the Lord Chamberlain to   VICTOR LUXEMBURG

JOHN C. WILSON

presents

GERTRUDE LAWRENCE
NOEL COWARD

"TO-NIGHT AT 8.30"

THREE PLAYS by NOEL COWARD

PRODUCED by THE AUTHOR
DECOR by G. E. CALTHROP

1936. Noël in his dressing room before the curtain goes up for *Tonight at 8:30.*

This will be their first appearance together since their sensational success in *Private Lives.*

Noel Coward can always be relied upon to provide something "different," and his latest venture will constitute an entirely new idea in the theatre. He has written six short plays and three of these will make up the programme of each performance—one comedy, one serious play and one play with music. . . .

In the musical shows Noel Coward and Gertrude Lawrence have several dances which have been specially arranged for them by Raph Reader, the young English dance producer, and they will also play the leading parts in all of the plays.

Noel Coward has for so long been the outstanding man of the English Theatre that a catalogue of his career would be tedious as well as futile. There is no aspect of the theatre of which he is not completely the master. Songs, sketches, operetta, revue comedy, farce, drama, flow readily from his pen. . . .

Think of all that is exclusive, witty, tasteful, smart and stylish—and you have Gertrude Lawrence. She has a greater flair for subtle comedy than any other actress on the English stage and has deservedly been the West End's leading star for some time.

John C. Wilson, Noel Coward, Alfred Lunt, and his wife, Miss Lynn Fontanne, form the company responsible for this production.

Messrs. Wilson and Coward are anxious to stress the fact that, although the plays will all be of short duration, they are not one act plays in the accepted sense. They will vary in length from 40 to 60 minutes each; in the number of scenes employed and in period. Each will be a complete little play.

At matinees the title will be changed from *To-Night at Seven-Thirty* to *To-Day at Two-Thirty*. A full orchestra will be travelled with the company.

———

"From our point of view behind the footlights, the experiment will obviously be interesting. The monotony of repetition will be reduced considerably, and it is to be hoped that the stimulus Miss Lawrence, the company and I will undoubtedly derive from playing several roles during a week instead of only one will communicate itself to the audience, therefore ensuring that a good time be had by all.

"All of the plays included in the programmes have been written specially. There has been no unworthy scuffling in cupboards and bureau drawers in search of forgotten manuscripts, and no hurried refurbishing of old, discarded ideas.

"The primary object of the scheme is to provide a full and varied evening's entertainment for theatre-goers who, we hope, will try their best to overcome any latent prejudice they may have against short plays and, at least, do us the honour of coming to judge for themselves."

He was not to be disappointed. The production in London and subsequently on Broadway were limited only by Noël's reluctance to be involved with long runs.

In the nine plays Noël and Gertie played a third-rate vaudeville couple, would-be suburban lovers, a psychiatrist and his mistress, a Victorian couple among others.

A tenth play—"Star Chamber," which only survived for one performance, dealt with a dysfunctional board meeting for a theatrical charity. It came just at the time that Noël was taking over a similar function from Sir Gerald du Maurier and the combination could have proved embarrassing.

Nonetheless, it was a pity that the world was prevented from seeing Noël as "Johnny Bolton"—a Max Miller–like low comedian.

Later Noël would write notes on the other nine . . .

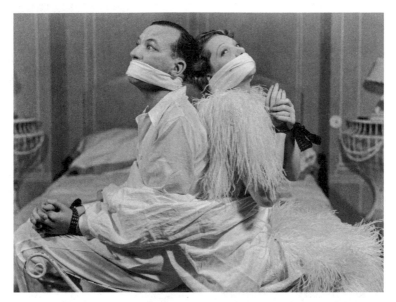

Ways and Means (1936).

"We Were Dancing" is a light episode, little more than a curtain-raiser. It was never intended to be anything more than this and, unlike its author, it fulfilled its promise admirably.

"The Astonished Heart" is more ambitious in intent than "We Were Dancing" but I thought then and still think that its theme, the decay of a psychiatrist's mind through a personal sexual obsession, was too esoteric to appeal to a large public. It gave us, however, good opportunities for dramatic acting and provided a strong contrast to "We Were Dancing," which preceded it and "Red Peppers," which followed it.

"Red Peppers" is a vaudeville sketch sandwiched in between two parodies of music-hall songs. We always enjoyed playing it and the public always enjoyed watching us play it, which, of course, was highly satisfactory.

"Red Peppers" gave him particular pleasure to write. During his own provincial "touring days" he had seen his share of incompetent variety acts drifting down the bill.

As he finished the plays in the sequence, he sent them in batches to Alfred and Lynn for comment. When she read this one Lynn wrote back . . .

"'Red Peppers' is very fine and very funny. Their utter third-rateness is so awfully pathetic. You know exactly why (aside from the pitiful business of their act) they have never been and never could be successful."

True in real life and yet . . . the affection with which Noël painted George and Lily Pepper and their way of life has brought them back for encore after encore over the last seventy years.

"Hands Across the Sea" is a satire on the confusions of a London society woman suddenly faced with the unexpected arrival of two colonials with whom she once stayed while travelling in the Far East. It is a gay, unpretentious little play, and it was acted by Gertie with incomparable brilliance. I cannot think of it without remembering the infinite variety of her inflexions, her absurd, scatter-brained conversations on the tele-

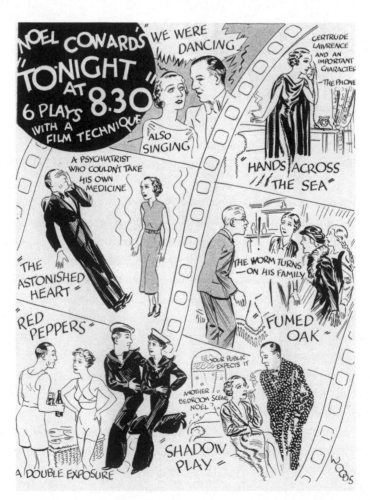

Victoria Gayforth (Gertrude Lawrence) and Simon Gayforth
(Noël) in "Shadow Play" from *Tonight at 8:30* (1936).

phone, her frantic desire to be hospitable and charming, and her expression of blank dismay when she suddenly realised that her visitors were not who she thought they were at all.

It was a superb performance in the finest traditions of high comedy, already now over and done with for ever, but, as far as I am concerned, never to be forgotten.

"Fumed Oak" is a comedy based on the good old "worm will turn" theme. I loved Henry Gow from the moment I started writing him, and I loved playing him more, I think, than anything else in the repertoire. A memorable performance was given in this by Moya Nugent as Elsie, the snivelling schoolgirl."

"Shadow Play," with which we finished the second bill, is a musical fantasy. It is a pleasant theatrical device which gave Gertie and me the chance to sing as romantically as we could, dance in the moonlight and, we hoped, convince the audience that we were very fascinating indeed. It always went extremely well, so I must presume that we succeeded.

"As we stroll down Picc-Piccadilly / In the bright morning air /
All the girls turn and stare . . ." Noël and Gertie Lawrence as
"The Red Peppers" in the song "Men About Town" (1936).

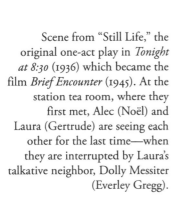

Scene from "Still Life," the original one-act play in *Tonight at 8:30* (1936) which became the film *Brief Encounter* (1945). At the station tea room, where they first met, Alec (Noël) and Laura (Gertrude) are seeing each other for the last time—when they are interrupted by Laura's talkative neighbor, Dolly Messiter (Everley Gregg).

The third bill started with "Ways and Means," a "twentyish" little farce set in the then fashionable South of France. I never cared for it much, but as an "opener" it served its purpose.

"Still Life" was the most mature play of the whole series (with the exception of "Hands Across the Sea," which was equally mature but in a different idiom). Later it was made into an excellent film and retitled *Brief Encounter*. I am proud of both the play and the film with, as usual, a slight bias in favour of the former. It is well written, economical and well constructed, the characters, I think, are true and I can say now, reading it with detachment after so many years, that I am proud to have written it.

"Family Album," the last of the series, is a sly satire on Victorian hypocrisy, adorned with an unobtrusive but agreeable musical score. It was stylised in both its décor and its performance, was a joy to produce and provided the whole talented company with good parts.

————

His next venture was to be the musical *Operette* followed by a revue for Broadway—*Set to Music*. Then back to being a playwright.

In 1939 he had two plays he intended to have produced . . .

"During April and May I stayed in my house in the country (Goldenhurst) and wrote two plays. *Present Laughter* and *This Happy Breed*. I planned to appear in both of these myself in the autumn, acting them on alternate nights with the same company. They both turned out well, in spite of the fact that while I was writing them I was aware that in all probability they would never be produced, at least not at the time I intended them to be. This dismal clairvoyance was ultimately justified."

On September 3 Prime Minister Neville Chamberlain declared war on Nazi Germany.

5

ON ACTING . . .

"Acting Is Acting—It's Giving the Impression of Feeling"

"I consider myself a writer first and an actor second."
—*PRESENT INDICATIVE* (1937)

·

"All acting worth the name is ham. We rehearse for weeks to hide it, but it's there all the time."
—NOËL TO MARIE TEMPEST (1934)

·

"Theatrical people are notoriously facile of emotion, and frequently victimised by their own foolish sentimentality."
—*PRESENT INDICATIVE* (1937)

·

"The purpose of playing . . . was and is to hold, as 'twere, the mirror up to nature . . ."
—HAMLET TO THE PLAYERS (ACT III, SCENE 2)

·

BRIAN (The Author)
Why can't people in the theatre behave like normal human beings?
TONY (Director's Assistant)
There wouldn't be a theatre if they did.
—*STAR QUALITY* (1967)

·

"You managed to play the first act of my little comedy tonight with all the Chinese flair and light-hearted brilliance of Lady Macbeth."
—NOËL COWARD

THE ART OF ACTING

You do not feel a comedy part to the extent that you feel a serious part. But, if you have an emotional scene to play, it is essential to feel it as early as possible in rehearsal and then set your feeling so that you can reproduce it without strain and in almost any adverse circumstances afterwards. I very much disapprove of the adage that you have to feel the performance completely every night on the stage. This is technically an impossibility, and really is the negation of the art of acting. The art of acting, after all, is not actual feeling but simulation of feeling, and it is impossible to feel a strong emotional part eight performances a week, including two matinées.

But if you are a good actor and an experienced actor, you can give the audience the semblance of the feeling you originally felt of the character and of the part, and this is to my mind what is great acting. I have seen many very, very great actors in my day, and I have never found one of them who comes off and says that they felt every minute of their performance that night. They know perfectly well I wouldn't believe them if they did. It is an impossibility. There is an old theatrical saying, "Lose yourself, lose your audience," and, even in an emotional part, you have to be aware with one part of your mind that the audience is there and that they are attentive; you have got, with a little extra sense, to listen for those coughs that might start, which may mean that you have either got to play more softly or hurry the scene a little bit or something; you have, in fact, to regulate your audience as well as be the character, as well as consider the other people on the stage with you. This is a very important aspect of acting: no really good acting is achieved without the complete co-operation of your fellow artists. You cannot play the scene by yourself unless you are alone on the stage. And if you are with somebody else on the stage you have to consider them and their reactions, help them to get their reactions, in return for which they will help you to get yours, and this is what makes fine acting.

This, of course, applies most particularly in comedy, when the getting of a laugh depends on a hairline of sensitivity and also must not always be considered the ultimate goal. It is not only getting laughs in comedy that is important; it is stopping them. There are certain laughs that have to be quelled in order to get a bigger one later. If you have a sentence, for instance, in which there is a titter in the first part of the sentence and probably a big laugh at the end of it, a technical comedian will see to it that he hurries the first part so that they hear it but have no time to laugh, so that he can get the full laugh at the end. Many inexperienced comedians will get the first laugh and lose the rest of the sentence in the laugh.

The whole of comedy depends on timing, and if you are really on your toes you play the audience and you control the laughter; you must never let the audience get out of hand—Rex Harrison today is a great exemplar of this exquisite timing—and this is achieved first of all, I suppose, by natural talent for comedy playing, but certainly by acquired technique. It is something that I am sad to see is not very prevalent in the theatre today, principally I think because there are not many comedies of wit and quick timing written.

This is all highly technical, but was drummed into my head as a small boy and as a young man by one of the greatest comedians of our stage, the late Charles Hawtrey. He taught me all I know about comedy acting, and I am grateful to him to this day. But then comedy is nearly always, in its time, treated as something trivial, whereas it is far and away the most complicated and the most difficult aspect of acting. Nearly all good comedians can play tragedy but very few tragedians can play comedy. Of course the great actors, such as Laurence Olivier, can play any part with the utmost ease. Larry, whose Macbeth at Stratford I think was one of the greatest performances I ever saw on the stage, also played Mr. Puff in *The Critic,* and it was one of the most brilliant, light, soufflé comedy performances that I have seen—incomparable technique. He can play anything. Edith Evans can play comedy as well as she can play tragedy. Nearly all the great ones can.

But I think that the nonsense that is talked today about the motivation of character and all these jargons that have developed is really a considerable waste of time. If a young actor comes up to me and I am directing a play, and says: "What is the motivation of this scene?"—well, there are one or two answers to that. One is: "Your salary cheque next Friday," and the other is: "If you haven't learned the motivation of the scene when you read the play, then you'd better not attempt to play it, because you must know that much by now." In fact a great deal of time is wasted in these dear, democratic days in the theatre with everybody giving their opinions. But it would be unwise for the captain of a ship when faced with a sudden storm to call all his crew together and ask their various opinions as to what to do about it, by which time I should think that the ship would have foundered. This, I feel, is rather the same for the director of a play. If he listens to all the actors giving their opinions about what they think their characteristics should be, the play is liable to founder. In fact, I have seen several submerge in the last few years for that very reason.

The last time I was directed by a director was when I did Bernard Shaw's *The Apple Cart,* and I was directed by Michael MacOwan. I explained to him that I always arranged to be word-perfect at the beginning of rehearsal, and when I was directing myself I always insisted that my actors should be word-perfect at the first rehearsal. This causes great rage and conflict among many actors, because they say that they like the part to grow with the movements they are given, and so on; and there might be cuts and they would have learnt a whole lot of stuff that was unnecessary. But actually it makes it much easier for an actor if only he has the sense to learn his part, not absolutely perfectly but well enough to be able to rehearse without a book, very early on; so many actors increase their own opening-night nervousness because they have not troubled to learn their parts accurately, and suddenly in the last week of rehearsal they realize this, and go home after a long day's rehearsal, which is very exhausting anyway, cut out all friends, all dinner parties, and everything, and try and cram the words into their tired brains. Whereas I always learn the part well in advance, so that at the end of a long day's rehearsal I go to another theatre or to a movie, or have a little quiet dinner or talk to my friends, and I wipe the play from my mind till the next morning rehearsal—because I know it, and this does eliminate the terrible fear of drying up on an opening night. You cannot, to my mind, rehearse too much.

It takes me a good three weeks' rehearsal, knowing the part, to give an adequate performance, and several weeks of performance with audiences to give a good performance, leaving aside a possible nervous *tour de force* on an opening night, when I might be very good indeed without quite knowing why. But with *The Apple Cart,* for instance, Michael MacOwan was courteous, wise, and sensible, and came up after each scene we had rehearsed with notes which we listened to, all of which were intelligent and sensible, and he did say one thing to me which completely made my conception of the part, and I am deeply grateful to him. He said: "I want you to understand that King Magnus is essentially a sad man." This, curiously enough, though I had studied the part, I had not thought of; it gave me the balance to play the part right, and I think I did play it right.

I don't think that a part possesses many actors outside the theatre, but there is a moment when you are playing an emotional part when the part gets hold of you. This occurs usually about the end of the first week of rehearsal.

This is what I would like to point out to many of the modern young actors who believe in the theory that you have to feel everything completely all the time. It is a mistake; it is not the art of acting, it is something entirely different, and the art of acting is really what they are trying to achieve.

Overacting is my pet loathing. There are several other things I hate about the theatre, but that, I think, is what I hate most. I don't entirely blame actors for this always; it depends on the circumstances. If an actor has been playing a part for months and months he is liable, even without knowing it, to come out and do much more than he was doing originally. I have often seen a subtle and beautiful performance on an opening night, and gone to see the play again a few months later and found that all the little nuances are over-emphasized. That is because when you play a play for a long run the quality—not the quantity but the quality—of the audience is liable to deteriorate; it is an actor's instinct to come out to the audience, and unless he is a very great actor indeed he often comes out too much without realizing it. The great ones seldom transgress in this way. Lynn Fontanne, for instance, will give as great a performance on the last night of a play as she did on the first, possibly a greater because she develops all the time.

From the actor's point of view, repertory is the answer to the long-run business; for to play three or four plays instead of one gives you a fresh edge on each one and does not allow monotony to creep in. I do not like long runs because my interests are so divided. I am a playwright and a composer, and when I am playing as an actor only it is a whole-time job. If I am playing eight performances a week of a star part, I can think of nothing else but that, and I have no time to write, to compose, or to do any of the other things I have to do. That is why, over so many years, I have limited my runs to three months, because to go on playing the same thing for a year, however successful it was, would turn out eventually to be a waste of time, because in the long run my writing is more important to me, much as I love acting.

Writing and composing are the two most creative of my talents. I think that directing is very interesting and obviously fascinating, both theatrically and psychologically, but on the theatre side I really prefer acting; I love performing, because I was, I suppose, brought up to it and I have been doing it since I was ten years old, on and off. But I do get slightly frustrated if I have to play for too long, for the reasons I've given. If I hadn't got the other talents to look after, I think I would be only too grateful to have a long run.

The prime purpose of the theatre is entertainment. I have always held that. Of course, I am far from infallible and I may be quite, quite wrong: the prime purpose of the theatre may be to show people how miserable life is, and how there is no hope for the human race. That may, indeed, be the prime purpose of the theatre, but I have never been brought up to view it that way. But at my age I can safely be called old-fashioned. I, personally, am still stage-struck after fifty-one years in the theatre, and it always gives me pleasure to go to a theatre and be entertained in it. It does not always give me pleasure to go to a theatre and be bored stiff in it, and therefore I hold grimly to my original training, which was that the theatre is primarily a place of entertainment.

If by any chance a playwright wishes to express a political opinion or a moral opinion or a philosophy, he must be a good enough craftsman to do it with so much spice of entertainment in it that the public get the message without being aware of it. The moment the public sniffs propaganda they stay away, and curiously enough, I am all in favour of the public coming to the theatre, paying for their seats at the box office, and enjoying themselves. If they enjoy themselves it means they come again, and if they come again it means so much more in the pockets of the playwright, the actors, and even the dear managements.

(Adapted from a radio interview "Talking of Theatre" [BBC Network Three] with Walter Harris and first published in the October 12, 1961, issue of *The Listener*)

Coward on Auditions

In his verse "The Boy Actor" . . .

> *"I remember the auditions, the nerve-racking auditions:*
> *Darkened auditorium and empty, dusty stage."*

To be an actor you need a stage.

And before you're allowed on a stage—there's the *audition*. A process which Noël could summon up with total recall—once he was safely on the other side of the footlights . . .

In all theatrical experience I know of nothing more dispiriting than an average audition; a bleak denuded stage only illuminated by one or two glaring working lights; a weary accompanist at a rickety upright piano; in the second or third row of the stalls, with the dim auditorium stretching behind them, sit a small group of people upon whom your livelihood depends, who mutter constantly to each other and whose faces, on the rare occasions that they are turned towards the stage, register such forbidding boredom that gay words stick in the gullet, and voice tones, so resonant and musical in the bathroom, issue forth in strangulated squeaks.

An additional horror is the awareness that the sides of the stage are packed with implacable ambition. Every watching eye is steely with determination, marking with satisfaction each nervous shudder and each false note. The inexperienced, of course, suffer the most. They usually embark upon some lengthy song or aria and are stricken into bewildered silence halfway through by a sharp "Thank you" from the stalls, and an abrupt cessation of all sound from the piano, after which, tremblingly, they give their names and addresses to the stage manager and go away, tortured by the knowledge that their top B flat, for which they had been conserving all their vocal energy, has not been heard at all. The wise ones sing only one refrain, sometimes only the last part of it, if it happens to be over-long.

Dancers have a very bad time as a rule, unless they bring their own accompanists, for in the hands of the lady provided by the management, their carefully rehearsed tempos change inexorably from fast to slow and slow to fast, heedless of their scurrying and gaspings and muttered supplications.

For most auditions ordinary day clothes are worn, embellished usually with borrowed finery. I believe that a white fox fur was actually identified in the course of one month on nineteen different people. There are always a few, however, who put on fancy costumes and make-up elaborately. Panniers, crinolines, insecure home-made bustles, and the inevitable pierrot suits with depressed tulle ruffles. Dancing girls used to wear imaginative "practice dress" but this in later years has gradually discarded its bows and frills and shrunk to nothing more or less than a plain one-piece swimming suit.

Noël then describes his own early approach to this chaotic process . . .

My own audition apparel was usually a navy blue suit with a colored shirt, tie, socks and handkerchief to match. I had not learned then that an exact duplication of colours ill becomes the well-dressed man.

My bearing was a blend of assurance and professional vivacity; the fact that my bowels were as water I hope was not apparent to anybody. I used to walk on to the stage, bow politely in the direction of the stalls and say "Good morning," sometimes, owing to nerves, a trifle more loudly than I had intended. Then, having banished the accompanist with a lordly gesture, I sat down at the piano on a stool that was invariably either too low or too high, and rattled off a few authoritative introductory chords, inwardly appalled by the tone and quality of the piano, but preserving an air of insouciance.

I then swiveled round sharply, announced my song and started it before anyone had time to stop me. My voice was small but my diction clear, assisted by a violent interplay of facial expressions. My rendition of a song in those days was a model of exhaustive technique. Sustained pauses, gay laughs, knowing looks. Frequently, if the dreaded "Thank you" came in the middle of a verse, I pretended not to hear it and continued with only a faint quickening of tempo until either a second and louder "Thank you" stopped me, or I was allowed to finish.

The experiences of aspiring youth never left the mature Noël but then neither did a lesson of later years when it was his turn to sit in the stalls and be on the receiving end of seemingly endless would-be versions of "Master Noël Coward" . . .

═══

"The nicest words I know in the theatre are—'That's all, sir,' which signifies the ending of a mass audition. It means we shan't hear 'Phil the Fluter's Ball' again that morning."

Coward on Talent (or the Lack of It)

Mrs. Worthington

Regarding yours, dear Mrs. Worthington,
Of Wednesday the 23rd,
Although your baby,
Maybe,
Keen on a stage career,
How can I make it clear,
That this is not a good idea.
For her to hope,
Dear Mrs. Worthington,
Is on the face of it absurd,
Her personality
Is not in reality
Inviting enough,
Exciting enough
For this particular sphere.

Don't put your daughter on the stage, Mrs. Worthington,
Don't put your daughter on the stage,
The profession is overcrowded
And the struggle's pretty tough
And admitting the fact
She's burning to act,
That isn't quite enough.
She has nice hands, to give the wretched girl her due,
But don't you think her bust is too
Developed for her age?
I repeat,
Mrs. Worthington,
Sweet
Mrs. Worthington,
Don't put your daughter on the stage.

Don't put your daughter on the stage, Mrs. Worthington,
Don't put your daughter on the stage,

She's a bit of an ugly duckling
You must honestly confess,
And the width of her seat
Would surely defeat
Her chances of success,
It's a loud voice, and though it's not exactly flat,
She'll need a little more than that
To earn a living wage.
On my knees,
Mrs. Worthington,
Please
Mrs. Worthington,
Don't put your daughter on the stage.

Don't put your daughter on the stage, Mrs. Worthington,
Don't put your daughter on the stage,
Though they said at the school of acting
She was lovely as Peer Gynt,
I'm afraid on the whole
An ingénue role

Would emphasize her squint,
She's a big girl, and though her teeth are fairly good
She's not the type I ever would
Be eager to engage,
No more buts,
Mrs. Worthington,
NUTS,
Mrs. Worthington,
Don't put your daughter on the stage.

Don't put your daughter on the stage, Mrs. Worthington,
Don't put your daughter on the stage,
One look at her bandy legs should prove
She hasn't got a chance,
In addition to which
The son of a bitch
Can neither sing nor dance,
She's a *vile* girl and uglier than mortal sin,
One look at her has put me in
A tearing bloody rage,
That sufficed,
Mrs. Worthington,
Christ!
Mrs. Worthington,
Don't put your daughter on the stage.

When he included the song in the 1953 *Noël Coward Song Book* Noël added an ironic tongue-in-cheek *apologia* . . .

"It is a genuine *cri de coeur* . . . Unhappily, its effectiveness, from the point of view of propaganda, has been negligible. I had hoped, by writing it, to discourage misguided maternal ambition, to deter those dreadful eager mothers from making beasts of themselves, boring the hell out of me and wasting their own and my time, but I have not succeeded . . . ninety-nine out of a hundred of the letters they write to me refer to it with roguish indulgence, obviously secure in the conviction that it could not in any circumstance apply to them. This is saddening, of course, but realising that the road of the social reformer is paved with disillusions, I have determined to rise above it."

His recollection of the song's genesis was that he was on a P&O liner sailing home from Singapore and found himself at the mercy of "the over-anxious mother who ultimately inspired the song."

An alternative account came from a young actress who recalled Noël visiting her producer father. The father tossed aside a letter he had been reading and, when asked what it was about the letter that had upset him, replied—"Oh, it's just a letter from some maddening woman called Mrs. Worthington asking me if I can put her daughter on the stage." Noël, the lady recalled, went straight upstairs and wrote . . .

History, of course, shows that Mrs. Worthington and her peers put many a daughter on the stage and that Noël played with more than a few of them with varying degrees of success and enjoyment.

Coward on Rehearsals

Then the *rehearsals* . . . and Noël had vivid memories of those . . .

For the benefit of the untheatrical public I would like to describe, briefly, the general horror of rehearsal rooms. There are several crops of them all over London, and they are a necessary evil, particularly in big musical productions. Stages are not always available, and even when they are it is usually only during the last week of rehearsals that they are occupied by the entire company. Until then a show is rehearsed in bits, dialogue scenes in one place, dance numbers in another and vocal numbers in another. This frequently necessitates members of a company scudding miserably from one side of the West End to the other. Touring companies are rehearsed almost exclusively in rehearsal rooms, seldom achieving the dignity of a stage at all until a hurried run through on the day of the opening night.

Each room in each place contains a tinny piano, too many chairs, a few mottled looking-glasses, sometimes a practice bar and always a pervasive smell of last week's cooking. Here rows of chorus girls in practice dress beat out laboriously the rhythms dictated by the dance producer. The chairs all round the room are festooned with hats, handbags, coats, sandwiches, apples, oranges, shoes, stockings and bits of fur. It is all very depressing, especially at night in the harsh glare of unshaded electric bulbs.

It is of little help at the first rehearsal to be able to translate Cicero.

There are two accounts that express the more common view of Noël's working methods. The first was written by a member of the cast of *Words and Music* and appeared in December 1932:

MR. COWARD REHEARSES

"I never lose my temper at rehearsals. But if I did, this would be my great moment." With these words Noël Coward annihilated eight trembling "Show Girls" who were rehearsing "Children of the Ritz," one of the hit numbers in his *Words and Music.* The words were delivered quite quietly, yet they had a quality behind them that froze the girlish giggles that had hitherto accompanied these beautiful young ladies' inability to cope with the task set them, which happened to be the movement of their heads in time with music.

Noël Coward is like that. He never loses his temper, and the only thing that makes him angry is slackness.

However, it is not so easy to slack with Mr. Coward. He is consumed with such a terrific smouldering activity that he automatically carries one along with him.

The sight of him rehearsing is awe-inspiring. He always rehearses with footlights as well as overhead lighting. When he stands on the front of the stage with these lights shining onto his working face, striking electric sparks from his already electric eyes, one is tempted to mistake him for some incarnate spirit.

All the critics in their reports of *Words and Music* seemed to have one thing in common—they all said that this show had a remarkable unity. This is not only due to the fact that Noël Coward wrote the "words" and the "music," but to the fact that in production he has made everybody do everything in his own way. Every important gesture, and most of the apparently negligible ones, were carefully thought out and demonstrated to the artiste by Noël Coward himself. He spent hours in getting the actors to play a scene exactly as he had shown them, with every gesture and every movement.

All the brilliantly timed movements of "Mad About the Boy," for instance, are the result of hours of intensive work on his part. The result is that the show has stylisation which is lacking in other shows, where actors are allowed to develop on what lines they please.

This stylisation may submerge the actors' personality a little, but without exception they are all giving better performances than they have ever given.

Noël Coward is the "be-all and end-all" of rehearsals. If he is unavoidably delayed and he is late for rehearsal (he is usually the first person there) the time is entirely wasted until he arrives. Various groups of actors may make a feeble effort to rehearse some scene or other, but the effort invariably peters out and riot reigns triumphant.

The moment he arrives on the scene, however, there is hush. The ear-splitting rhythm of the "dancing boys" practising stops, and "Mr. Cochran's young ladies" stop screaming at the top of their voices. It only needs, "Quiet, company, please!" from him, and the whole company settles down for a hard day's work.

And it certainly is a hard day's work. For Mr. Coward has taken his coat off and pulled down the "zip" fastener of his woollen sports shirt, and has announced that he will do a certain scene. The stage manager and his assistant rush on to the stage with chairs, which they place in position to represent scenery. The actors take a final glance at the parts they are supposed to have learnt and prepare to rehearse in real earnest. This goes on till midnight, with two short intervals for meals, and yet Noël Coward's eyes never stop blazing and his brain never flags from facilely directing his enormous company. Though it may be a hard day's work it is, however, a useful day's work, for Noël Coward never has to "scrap" a scene and start all over again. He knows exactly what he wants to do, and what effect he is going to get. No time is ever wasted.

This systematic way of working enables him to indulge a fad of his—that is not to rehearse over week-ends. Most companies when they start in to rehearse for the usual four weeks very rarely leave the theatre except to eat and sleep for the whole of that time. During the first week they may possibly get a night or two off, but they certainly rehearse every day, including Sundays. Noël Coward gives his company not only Sunday, but Saturday as well. An almost unheard of luxury. The result is that he and his company reassemble on Monday fresh and eager for a good week's work.

System is the keyword of his success as a producer. Even dress rehearsals—which are always a nightmare—are made almost bearable by the orderly way he conducts things. He generally has three or four dress rehearsals. At each one he concentrates on something different. The first one is generally an orchestral rehearsal. Noël Coward has an instinct for finding mistakes, and woe betide any musician who plays a wrong note! The second dress rehearsal is generally taken up with the question of scenery and the preliminary lighting. During the third he puts the final touches to the production, where all mistakes which are left over from the first two are rectified. He generally concludes with one complete "run-through" a few hours before the first night, after which he gives the company time to have a meal and rest before the show opens.

——

Norman Marshall, in his 1957 book, *The Producer and the Play*, renders this account of Noël at work:

Coward is today the only playwright of any note in the English theatre who still produces his own plays. He dictates every inflexion, demonstrates every bit of business in exact detail. He begins by reading the play to the company, portraying every part so vividly that some of the cast are apt to be reduced to a state of gloom because they doubt their ability to give a performance anything like as good as the author's own reading of their part. During rehearsals the actor never has that encouraging moment when he makes the rest of the cast laugh by neatly timing a line or a bit of business: Coward has got all the laughs in advance during that first reading. He insists on the cast reproducing exactly his own inflexions. Most actors and actresses willingly submit to this because they realise that Coward knows better than anyone else how to time his own laughs, how to point his own lines with absolute precision. His sense of audience is so unerring that he is quite confident that lines and bits of business which do not seem amusing during rehearsals will never the less get their laughs. He will say to an actor: "On the first night you will find your part is full of laughs where you didn't think there were any"—and the first night will prove Coward to have been right.

Coward's rehearsals are virtually a series of dictation lessons. In theory this should result in an atmosphere of dullness at a rehearsal because the actors feel they are being deprived of all initiative, but Coward is so electric a personality that he keeps his actors alert and eager. One of his cast told me that when Coward arrives for rehearsal in a chilly, dimly lit theatre on a dreary, wet morning, "you feel as if all the lights have suddenly been turned on and a glass of champagne put into your hand."

A peculiarity of Coward as a producer is that he insists on the cast knowing their lines at the first rehearsal. Engaging an actress for a part he will end the interview by handing her the script and saying: "Now, go home and learn your lines, duckie; that makes practising a pleasure"—advice that is usually followed up by a note from H. M. Tennent Ltd., politely intimating that "Mr. Coward would be very pleased if you would know your lines by the first rehearsal." Of course no actor can really be word-perfect until he has become accustomed to hearing the other actors and actresses speaking his cues, so for the first two or three days of Coward's rehearsals the cast are so busy trying to remember strings of words that they have no time for interpretation or characterisation. Presumably this is Coward's intention. All he requires from the actors is that they should present him with the skeletons of their parts to which he himself adds the flesh and blood.

=====

Over time, Noël the Director mellowed. When he directed the National Theatre's revival of *Hay Fever* in 1964, Lynn Redgrave recalls how he coaxed the performance from her and allowed her to improvise. Had she strayed too far, though, she would have found the path fairly narrow. Nonetheless, her experience was not commensurate with most recollections of Noël as director.

Big sister Vanessa fared less well. There was a period when she seemed to be in the news daily at some anti-Vietnam event or other. "She will keep on demonstrating," Noël remarked. "But then, she's a very tall girl and I suppose she's pleased to sit down."

Coward on "Learning the Lines"

A professional fetish of Noël's was *word perfection.* He believed actors should come to the first rehearsal knowing their lines. He did not always achieve that ambition . . .

> I believe in learning the part and each cue with a postcard over the page, which I do relentlessly, is the most horrible drudgery. And if I make one mistake on a page, I go right back to the beginning again, until I've not only learned it with this part of my mind, but with that part. I don't worry about whether I'm getting at the right meaning at this

point. When I get up on the stage the words give me the meaning; you can't know it better than the words. It's not only knowing it by heart; it's more than that. It's knowing it inside, getting to what the Lunts call the "silky stage."

There comes a moment half way through rehearsals when suddenly not only have you not got the book but—a certain feeling becomes injected. I cannot afford, and I am adamant about this, to take time off at rehearsals to learn words. I think those should be learned before you start.

I need three to four weeks rehearsal to decide how to play a part. I can't possibly decide that if I don't know my words . . . I always call for a reading a fortnight before we go into rehearsal, so that any wrong intonations can be corrected and marked. Then I send them away and say—"Now, learn it!" I can't rehearse people with books in their hands writing down things . . . You've got to be able to play it anywhere without depending on anything outward . . . When they have the words, I tell them—"Move where you feel. I'll tell you if you take a wrong turning."

I can't start to rehearse a play properly unless I know the words . . . How can you find out something about what you're going to do, if your mind is fluttering with anxiety about what you're going to *say* next?

If I have to go back and study after working hard all day and giving

Lynn Fontanne, Alfred Lunt, and Noël in *Design for Living* (1933).

out vitality rehearsing, it makes it terribly difficult. I can't understand actors who leave it to the last week of rehearsals and say—"Oh, I don't remember the last act. I must go home and study." This only results in panic.

Rules are one thing. Holding actors to them—particularly if they happen to be distinguished and often elderly actresses—was another.

Claudette Colbert and Gladys Cooper, for example, both insisted that they learned their lines as rehearsals went along.

Colbert he found "extremely tiresome" from the first when they acted together in the live TV version of *Blithe Spirit.* "She arrived at the first rehearsal not knowing the words, after I had particularly asked her to be word perfect, with the first act anyway. She explained that this was not her method and she *had* been a star for twenty-five years." Things did not go well from that point.

Sure enough she went on fluffing her lines and on one occasion smiled at him sweetly . . .

"Oh dear, and I knew them backwards last night."

"Yes, and that's just the way you're delivering them this morning, dear."

His verdict on the lady?

"I'd wring her neck—if I could find it."

═══

Gladys Cooper had cast herself in the same mold. She starred in his 1951 *Relative Values.* "Gladys obviously going to be wonderful, although slow at learning." Then "Disastrous rehearsal owing to Gladys knowing less and less. I am really getting worried. She faffs and stammers and we can never open as things are . . ."

Eventually he told her acidly—"I did not expect word perfection at the first rehearsal . . ."—he was learning to face the inevitable—"but I had rather hoped for it on the first *night.*"

It was not a subject to be trifled with when dealing with Noël.

He so annoyed Judy Campbell when they were touring the provinces during the war that she snapped—"Oh, I could just *throw* something at you!"

"Try starting with my lines."

But perhaps the encounter that Noël secretly relished, since, as usual, it gave him the last word—was with Edith Evans, when he was directing her in the historic 1964 revival of *Hay Fever* for the newly established National Theatre.

Edith as Judith Bliss has a line when she looks through the stage window and says—"On a *very* clear day you can see Marlow."

The "very" was superfluous to the line Noël had written. After several attempts to correct her, he finally said—"No, Edith dear, on a *clear* day you can see Marlow. On a *very* clear day you can see Marlows and Beaumont and Fletcher!"

After a later performance Noël noted that—

"[Edith] dried up and fluffed through all the performances, played slowly and down, and took her curtain calls as though she had just been un-nailed from the cross. . . . However, that is all part of the gay, mad world of powder and paint."

They never worked together again.

And then there was Beatrice Lillie.

Noël had worked with her several times since the 1920s and been frustrated by her apparent inability to learn words. He was careful to admit, though, that the business she created instead of the business she was *supposed* to create was invariably magical in its own right. She was the funniest woman he'd ever known.

He became philosophical about it . . .

"For an author, if he is wise and not too obsessed with the sanctity of his own words, will stay resigned in his seat and laugh. If not, he will fly out into the lobby and beat his head against the wall. In my own case, when faced with the erratic fantasies of Beatrice Lillie, I have found the former less agitating and more sensible."

Nonetheless, there are theatre lobby walls that bear the imprint of the Coward forehead.

Nineteen sixty-three brought *High Spirits*—the musical version of *Blithe Spirit* in which Bea played Madame Arcati.

With some trepidation . . . "I took Beattie to lunch. She looked wonderful and was very funny and sweet but also she couldn't even remember the beginnings of the sentences she'd started. And as she was NEVER good on words, this augurs ill for the future."

Their friendship barely survived the experience of the show.

It was only some years later that it became clear that what they were witnessing was the onset of Alzheimer's—the illness that ended her career.

———

There was to be an ironic aftermath a couple of years later.

Noël was playing his farewell roles on the London stage in his own *Suite in Three Keys*. To his chagrin he found himself having to be prompted by his leading ladies Lilli Palmer and Irene Worth. He was forgetting words he had written himself.

Coward on Clarity of Delivery

"Speak the speech, I pray you, as I pronounced it to you, trippingly on the tongue; but if you mouth it, as many of your players do, I had as lief the town-crier spoke my lines. Nor do not saw the air too much with your hand, thus; but use all gently."

—*HAMLET* (ACT III, SCENE 2)

.

He might say that word perfection was his highest priority but *clarity of delivery* wasn't far behind it.

The Scratch-and-Mumble of the Kitchen Sink era appalled him. "Realistic" it may or may not have been but in Noël's view it was just not what Theatre should be about . . .

"When young I remember having a downward-looking view from the Gallery of Tree and Hawtrey and I could hear every word. But now, swathed in stardom in the stalls, I find I don't hear as well as in the old days."

Coward on Timing

In Noël's opinion . . .

"Timing is 70 percent of acting." And timing in comedy is infinitely harder than in tragedy. Which is presumably why "Nearly all good comedians can play tragedy but very few tragedians can play comedy."

You can't do a play without an audience and in comedy the audience is effectively a character in the play and you've got to get them to realise that and play their part.

Sometimes they have to be goosed a bit. I nearly always play the first act of a comedy very quickly. I don't mean gabble; the difference between speed and pace. If you play quickly and articulately, it doesn't give them time, you throw away laughs; throw them away in the first act, pull them in in the last.

It's easy to get laughs and so difficult to control them. But that's the essence of comedy.

When you've got your audience where you want them, you can then afford to take some leisurely effects. But in the first act you've got to get their attention. If there are big laughs, stop them, except for the very big ones.

In all the plays I've been in—with Gertie and with Alfred and Lynn—we'd know whoever was on first, how a certain line went. If it got a laugh, we'd say—"Ha! We're home—nice, warm audience." If it got a titter, "Tricky." If it got silence—"Get to work, chaps!"

I used to give Gertie the wink, because I played the first scene in *Private Lives* with Adrianne Allen, and when I came off, Gertie was just going on with Larry, and I used to go "Quick"; and she'd know and be on it like a greyhound, and by the end of the first act we'd got them.

There are many tricks in the theatre that the comedian—not first-rate comedians, but quite excellent comedians use. They like upstaging, which is one of the most archaic forms of acting, and quite nonsense, and they do little tricks to spoil somebody else's lines, not realizing that by doing so they are destroying themselves and the play.

Now the Lunts do the exact opposite. They would spend minutes to enable me to get a laugh when I stubbed a cigarette out, and I would do the same for them. But, of course, we could experiment on stage after we'd played for a few weeks.

Suddenly Lynn would decide, maybe, to play by the fireplace instead of by the window, and I would be delighted, because it would give me a new approach. Then Alfred would come on and find us both in completely different places and it wouldn't faze him at all; we could play any way we liked.

Varying the performance is all very well when the actor is in control but there are times . . . and one of them occurred when Noël was playing with Alfred Lunt and Lynn Fontanne in *Design for Living* on Broadway in 1933.

The three of their characters are in a *ménage-à-trois*. Then Gilda (Lynn) leaves both of them and Otto (Alfred) and Leo (Noël) proceed to get drunk and feel sorry for themselves.

One evening . . .

"By accident, Alfred said one of my lines, and I gave him a quick look, and replied with his line, and with one glint he knew. It wasn't fooling on the stage, this was not jolly jokes. I wanted to do some of the bits of business he'd put in, because I admired them, and the same with him, he'd seen little bits that he fancied. We switched roles. It didn't matter psychologically because we were both drunk. So we played the whole scene reverse-wise, from different sides of the stage, playing each other's parts . . . Only at the very end of the scene there was a moment when I had to do a rather discreet little belch, because I knew Alfred couldn't belch. When we got to that moment—and I was thinking on all levels at once—I thought 'What am I to do?' So I answered his line and said mine quickly and got back, did my little belch, and the curtain came down. And people out in front who had seen the play before never noticed the difference."

One person who certainly did was Lynn.

Noël and Alfred found a frigid face waiting in the wings.

"Nothing either of you did out there was even remotely funny."

They were not inclined to try it again.

Coward on "Control"

"I believe that all acting is a question of *control*. The control of the actor of himself and, through himself, of the audience."

Even as experienced an actor as Laurence Olivier had Noël to thank for helping him master one specific aspect of control.

As a young actor in *Private Lives* he was given to "corpsing." The *Oxford English Dictionary* defines it as—"spoil a piece of acting by some blunder, as forgetting one's lines or laughing at an inappropriate moment."

Noël had had to conquer this himself . . .

"I very seldom giggle. I don't give it away. I used to be lectured by Hawtrey . . . I learned to be able to keep a straight face, which set me free to be able to upset everybody else. I nearly killed Larry's career when he was with me in *Private Lives* . . .

"He was playing this pompous prig and the only thing was, he was a terrible giggler and I had to stop him; it's all very fine to have a little actor's joke, but it's not very fair on the audience. If I did anything in the part that was at all impromptu and funny, I looked across the stage to see Larry in fits of laughter, when he was supposed to be very cross. So I said—'From now onwards, I'm going to try to make you laugh, and every time you do it, I'll kill you!' I'll throw in a line or piece of business when you least expect it."

Some of the diversions were surrealistic. Noël would pretend to detect a little piece of mouse-shit on the brioche Gertie had just handed him. Or he would address remarks to his nonexistent dog, Roger, and command him to bite Larry. Heaven only knows what the audience made of that night's performance.

On another evening, when Amanda was supposed to choke over something, Victor has to pat her on the back and on this occasion Larry was a little heavy-handed and Gertie, now really choking, couldn't get her words out. Finally she managed to croak—"You great clob!" Noël couldn't resist elaborating—"Clob?" Gertie, entering into the spirit of things—"Yes, *clob*!" "Ah," said Noël, now enlightened, "the man with the clob foot!"

Larry couldn't deliver his next line.

Nonetheless, he learned his lesson and was forever grateful that, at a key moment in his career, he had encountered a strict taskmaster in Noël, who had pulled him up and made him more self-critical, a charac-

Victor Prynne (Laurence Olivier) and Elyot Chase (Noël) clearly
have a difference of opinion in *Private Lives* (1930).

teristic that became very visible in the mature Larry. He was the first to
admit that it was Noël who made him use his "silly little brain."

Nonetheless, it was one of Olivier's boasts that he did once turn the
tables on Noël, which he regarded as one of his great triumphs in the
theatre . . .

Noël acknowledged that—"He completely broke me up. He was a
disgrace. He only did it once, though.

"I said to him—'Listen, if you do that again, I will have the curtain down and explain to the audience that you are not yet experienced
enough to play high comedy.'"

But their friendship did survive to play another day—though not on
the stage.

In Otto Preminger's 1965 film *Bunny Lake Is Missing* Olivier plays a
police inspector, while Noël is cast as the disreputable Horatio Wilson—

("an elderly drunk, queer masochist! Hurray! That's me all over, Mabel! Lovely lolly, too").

—————

Sometimes the actor and the play are an awkward fit—and the director doesn't help. Noël experienced that when he played Lewis Dodd in *The Constant Nymph* (1926) for director Basil Dean.

> Basil Dean was an excellent director and very meticulous. I was young and I'd had a lot of success, and he wanted, perfectly rightly, to rob me of Noel Coward mannerisms. I was not allowed to smoke a cigarette because I would smoke it like Noel Coward smoked it. He made me grow my hair very long and I never put any grease on it. Then he made me smoke a pipe, so that every time I lit it, I set fire to my hair and a lot of burning went on.
>
> Added to which it was an extremely difficult part. I had to express in the first few minutes of the play that I was a musical genius. I had some very charming music by Eugene Goossens to play on the piano, which was lovely, but it didn't absolutely establish me as Paderewski.
>
> In addition to the pipe, I wore purposely ill-fitting suits, and spectacles through which I peered short-sightedly ... I hated Lewis Dodd whole-heartedly from the first rehearsal onwards.
>
> Technically the play was constructed so that I had a series of ghastly thirty-second changes. I was in tails, in ordinary clothes, back to tails, so that when I wasn't actually on stage, which I was for most of the play, I was gasping away at the side, putting on my shoes or something.
>
> The only really emotional scene came at the end of the play, when Tessa, gloriously played by Edna Best, reached for the window and had a heart attack. I used to lift her on to the bed, gasping rather, she was quite heavy, and then the last line of the play was so touching. I used to fling up the window and say, "Tessa's got away; she's safe; she's dead." Tears, curtain. Unfortunately, on the third performance the window-cord broke and the window came down on to my hands, and so what I said was—"Tessa's got away; she's safe; she's—*ow!*" Whereupon the dead Tessa sat up and, of course, the curtain fell in roars of laughter.

He managed to arrange an "illness" to get him out of the show not long afterward. Once again the part went to his understudy—John Gielgud.

Noël as Lewis Dodd.

Noël's insistence on the importance of controlling an audience could easily be dated back to *The Vortex*.

After its groundbreaking reception in London, Noël and his leading lady, Lilian Braithwaite, took the production to Broadway with comparable success. Then it was decided to follow with a short tour.

All went well until they got to Chicago.

Chicago is not New York. Many miles and attitudes apart—as they found out the hard way. The company was all anticipation about the booking . . .

"Wait until we get to Chicago. There they'll really appreciate the play. There they'll eat it up!"

Successful as it had been, it must be admitted that *The Vortex* is an unbalanced play from a construction point of view. The opening acts are typical Coward social chat. The closing act high melodrama.

The Chicago audience was puzzled. Was this the play they'd heard so much about? Their reaction was subdued, to say the least. But by the second interval they'd got the point. This was a *comedy*.

Meanwhile, Noël and the cast were also trying to puzzle it out. At the end of the second act came the first big belly laugh . . .

"This struck me like a blow on the head. With every audience I had ever played it to, I had always been able to rely on complete absorption at the particular moment. It was really the most tragic scene of the play, when the son plays jazz more and more feverishly in order to drown the sight and sound of his mother abasing herself before her young lover.

"Chicago, however, saw it as only supremely comic and Lilian and I retired to our dressing rooms with prolonged laughter instead of prolonged cheers ringing in our ears. I was trembling with rage. I wanted to go out before the curtain and inform that gay holiday-spirited audience that this was the first and last time I would appear in their divine, breezy city and that to save themselves and me further trouble they could go back to their dance halls and speak-easies immediately as there was not

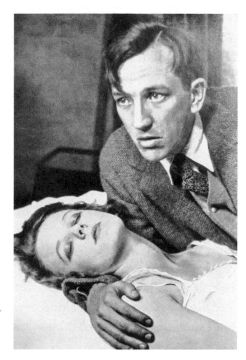

With Edna Best in *The Constant Nymph,* New Theatre, 1926.

going to be any last act at all. Lilian restrained me by gripping me by the shoulders and hissing in my face—'Remember you are *English*! Remember you are *English*!'

"The last act was worse than I could ever have imagined it to be. The sight of me in pyjamas and dressing-gown started them off happily, and from then onwards they laughed without ceasing. Never, since *Charley's Aunt* on a Saturday night in Blackpool, have I heard such uproarious mirth in a theatre. The curtain fell to considerable applause, and I even had to make a speech, which, remembering that I was English, was a model of graceful restraint."

Back in his dressing room Noël wrote on the wall in indelible pencil— "NOEL COWARD DIED HERE." His friend Clifton Webb, playing the same theatre years later, confirmed that the legend endured.

Coward on "Range"

"I wish I could only explain—it sounds almost pompous—but the decline of manners and the decline of elegance mean that it is much more difficult for young actors to achieve *range*.

"I remember when I was playing *Present Laughter* in the afternoon and *This Happy Breed* in the evening, it was with a sigh of relief that I got down to old shirt-sleeves and slouched on looking anyhow. It's so easy to play natural, when you can scratch yourself. Even then it's got to be well done; but it's so much easier than being slick, timing every line, being very sharp-looking; and I think that's what they're missing a bit. There are certain of them who could do it, given the plays.

"I think there's room for everything in the theatre, for a drama, or a comedy, or a play about kitchen sinks, or tramps, if necessary. That's fine, providing they are good enough.

"They are all human beings, so therefore to be a good actor you must constantly better yourself. If you come from humble beginnings you must then think—well, obviously I can play cockney, I can play north country; now I must learn how to play proper English, improve my voice, so that I've got range. Then I can play *Henry VIII* one night and *The Caretaker* the next. That kind of range is what actors should aim for, but I think that ambition has rather faded."

Coward on "Stage Fright"

Stage nerves.

Every actor has them at some point and for some it's a permanent condition. When he was casting *Sail Away* Noël had cause to reflect on the subject.

He was auditioning children for the six he needed in the show . . .

During the auditions they seemed not to have a nerve in their bodies. They just came on and belted it out. They're about seven years old. But you know, I remember when I was a little boy actor, I never had a nerve. It was only later, when I became more mature, that I began to be nervous.

The older you get, the more nervous you get. You know the hazards. But it also gets better as you get older, for over the years you've developed the experience—you know how to do it, which you didn't at first. In the beginning your talent dictated to you. Later you dictate to your talent.

Talent is the important thing. I've seen so many people who could sing, dance—very nice voices, move very charmingly, but they have no talent. Then you get someone who dances infinitely less well, and whose voice is lightweight, whose voice is infinitely less rich and resonant—but there's a talent for projection, which is a God-given gift. It's some way of communicating.

You go to the theatre, go to cabarets, and you see any number of adequate performers, but it's only very rarely that you see someone who knocks you for a loop.

But even they have nerves . . . they also know what it is to be up on that stage . . . and the words won't come at all?

Stage Fright—the specter that stands at the shoulder of every actor at times and behind some actors at all times.

Even someone as eminent as Laurence Olivier once admitted that he suffered from stage fright just before he made his first entrance.

Noël commented . . .

"It is only natural, I think, that established stars should become more and more prone to stage fright as the years stack up behind them . . . I have little patience, however, with those who indulge their nervousness to the extent of spoiling their performances . . . If an actor is undisciplined enough to allow his own self-consciousness to intervene between himself and his talent, he should leave the theatrical profession and devote himself to some less agitating profession."

He felt strongly enough to write a whole article on the subject . . .

STAGE FRIGHT

Stage fright is an occupational disease which attacks the middle-aged and elderly more than the young and grows with increasing malignancy over the years until it can become, in certain acute cases, a serious theatrical hazard. I have seen actors and actresses of established reputation, proven talent and technical brilliance acquired by decades of experience, sitting in their dressing-rooms on an opening night in a state of neurotic hysteria, staring at themselves in the mirror and quivering with fear to such an extent that they are almost incapable of coherent speech and frequently have to retire to the lavatory to be sick. To my mind such sensitivity to nervous tension is not only excessive but self-indulgent.

Nearly all actors who have achieved positions of responsibility suffer from first-night nerves to a certain degree. It is only natural that they should. To act in a play for the first time before an audience after weeks of rehearsing it without one is inevitably an ordeal, but it is an ordeal that one has been trained to endure, and any professional performer who permits herself to be so terrified of enduring it would be well advised to seek other employment.

One of the most irritating aspects of this particular malaise is that it is contagious and, to a large extent, self-induced. Not consciously, of course; no actress in her senses would consciously encourage herself to suffer the tortures of the damned before doing a job for which she is not only well equipped but extremely well paid. It is a subtle process which usually begins after a certain amount of success has been achieved. Before that, during the early struggles and ambitions, when the longing for personal recognition outweighs all other considerations, excesses of first night nerves are not so much in evidence; also small part actors are less burdened with responsibility and indeed less pampered than established stars.

Children, of course, have no nerves at all. When I was a child in the Theatre the idea of being scared on an opening night never occurred to me nor can I remember it affecting any of my pert and bouncing contemporaries. To us theatre children a first performance was an occasion of excitement and delight, a consummation devoutly to be wished, a red-letter day to which we had all been looking forward with the same degree of thrilled anticipation that civilian children look forward to birthdays and Christmases. Speaking for myself it was not until I had been a professional actor for ten years and had reached my twenty-first birthday that I began to view an imminent first night with less exuberance and more apprehension. Later still, at the hoary age of twenty-four, when I first experienced authentic stardom in *The Vortex,* the rot began to set in. Not to any alarming degree at first, but as the years went on and rehearsals and try-outs and opening nights followed each other in fairly rapid succession, I became more and more aware of my responsibilities to the public, the management and indeed to myself. I had sniffed much of the sweet smell of success and fear of this heady fragrance evaporating began to haunt me.

Happily for my ultimate sense of balance I didn't have to wait long for it to be blown away by a hurricane of critical and public abuse. I attained the curious distinction of being booed off the stage twice in the course of two months in 1927. Although this was as a playwright and not as an actor, it proved to me once and for all that disaster in the theatre, however unhappy and discouraging it may be at the time, is neither final nor irrevocable. It is indeed surprising how swiftly the pain passes and is forgotten, or if not quite forgotten, at least relegated to its proper perspective. At all events, I have never, since that singular experience, suffered more than the normal nervous reactions on opening nights. It must not be imagined that I recommend being shrieked at by a hostile audience as a specific cure for stage fright.

So far as I know, no specific cure has yet been discovered. Different actors have developed different methods of combatting it. Some of the more misguided ones find that a stiff drink before going onto the stage can allay the pangs. This, however, is dangerous because a stiff drink is liable not only to allay the pangs but to annihilate that extra sense of timing which is essential to all actors, especially comedians. Others, in later years, have taken to swallowing tranquillizing tablets with the object of inducing a state of euphoria in which they don't care if the play goes well or ill and whether or not they themselves are good, bad or indifferent. This course, quite obviously, has so many disadvantages that it would be a waste of time to enumerate them. Another method is the adoption of a "Christian Science-God-is-Love-there-is-no-pain" attitude. This, although comforting to the actress or actor who can believe in it, is apt to create a certain bland, arid serenity which is baffling to the other members of the cast and sometimes irritating to the audiences. It can also be carried too far.

Many years ago I remember a famous actress explaining to me with perfect seriousness that before making an entrance she always stood aside to allow God to go on first. I can also remember that on that particular occasion He gave a singularly uninspired performance.

There is one way, however, to mitigate first-night nerves if not entirely to banish them, and this is to see to it that you are absolutely sure of your lines, for the dread of drying up is for every actor the worst nightmare of all. Personally, I have always considered that the first essential in approaching a new part is to learn the words thoroughly and accurately before even beginning to rehearse. To me, the rehearsal period of a play is exacting, exciting and, above all, exhausting. At the end of a long day's rehearsal I am in no condition to go home and concentrate on cramming words into my brain for the simple reason that by that time my brain is too tired to register them. I much prefer to dine quietly with friends or go to a movie and not think of the play again until the next morning's rehearsal.

This theory of learning the words before rehearsal is viewed with disfavour by actors and actresses of my acquaintance. They argue hotly that the only way to create a vital and integrated performance is to allow the characterization to grow naturally during the rehearsal period; to co-ordinate the dialogue with the movements dictated by the director and to acquire, as they go along, a true understanding of the motivations and mood changes of the part until suddenly, just before the opening night or perhaps even *on* the opening night, the expected revelation occurs and the performance emerges shining and complete. This, on the surface, appears to be a perfectly valid method, if perhaps a little inconsiderate to the author, the director and the other members of the cast; and there is no denying that it has resulted in many fine and impressive performances. It can also result in a great waste of time, emotion and nervous energy. In fact on closer analysis it isn't nearly so valid as it looks. In the first place all star performers receive the script they have agreed to play a long while in advance so therefore they have ample time to discuss before-hand with the author and the director any psychological problems in the text that they find difficult to understand. To leave these vital discussions until rehearsals begin is, in my opinion, both arrogant and lazy.

The actor's first allegiance should be not to himself, but to the author and if, on his initial readings of the play, he considers it good enough to appear in, his first duty is to learn it accurately, to study it with a post-card over the cues for two or three hours a day, if necessary for weeks, so that he can utilise rehearsals as they should be utilised, to experiment with feeling, movement and implication, without embarrassing his colleagues and director by fluffing and insulting the author by paraphrasing.

I am aware that this regime that I have outlined is not easy. It is hard work, it is lonely, and for most of the time it is sheer drudgery, but it pays off in the end. I know that, within my limits, I am an accomplished actor. I also know that I am not so conceited as to imagine that I can build a good performance *and* learn the words in a brief four weeks. As a director I have for years resolutely refused to rehearse actors with books in their hands. I am willing to sit round a table with the cast and read the play through with them but the moment they get onto their feet they must know their words well enough to give me some idea of what they are going to do with them.

There are certain great stars with whom I have worked who fight me on this and, occasionally, *because* they are great stars I have allowed myself to be over-ruled, always with disastrous results. I have seen these great stars of glittering effulgence and with years of triumphant success behind them, stumbling through a final dress-rehearsal, fluffing their lines, muddling their effects, massacring my dialogue, casting agonized looks in the direction of the prompter and finally dissolving in panic-stricken tears in their dressing rooms afterwards. On the following night, after God knows what private hells they have gone through, I have seen these same talented, exasperating creatures sail onto the stage as though they hadn't a nerve in their bodies and play the whole play through with technical assurance and apparently a complete command of their dialogue (not always the author's) that is little short of miraculous. I have also on certain occasions seen them play the play straight down the drain. As a general rule however they manage to come through.

The audience, watching the play unfold for the first time, accepts this brilliant virtuosity with no surprise. They laugh and applaud and cheer, sublimely unaware of panic and strain and also happily ignorant that utter chaos is constantly being averted by a hair's breadth before their innocent eyes. To the author and director (in my case usually the dual capacity) sitting out in front, the whole evening is a nightmare. It is also a nightmare for the stage management and the supporting actors who, although they dutifully recognize the talent and reputation of their leading lady, know only too well that at any moment she may dry up dead, throw them inaccurate cues and very possibly cut several pages of plot. If the star in question happens to get away with this *tour de force,* she is acclaimed as usual, or even more than usual. One more histrionic victory is chalked up on her scroll of honour. The company crowd round her after the final curtain and overwhelm her with relieved congratulations; the author and director and management burst through the pass door and embrace her ardently, followed eagerly by hordes of enthusiastic first-nighters who belabour her with facile superlatives. She herself, benign and relaxed now that the ordeal is over, receives the plaudits with well trained graciousness, forgives, with weary magnanimity, the author and director and anyone else who has happened to irritate her during rehearsals and if she is a fool, which she usually is, accepts her very hazardous triumph as her natural due. It obviously does not occur to her that the frenzied nerve-strain she has undergone, the almost super-human effort of will and concentration she has forced herself to make and the frustrated anxiety she has inflicted on her fellow workers, were largely unnecessary. For if she had employed one quarter of that will power and concentration on doggedly learning the words by heart before rehearsals started, she could have stepped onto the stage for the first performance without her natural nervousness being exacerbated by the ghastly fear of drying up, ruining the play and making a cracking ass of herself.

To conclude: I have yet to discover a final and definitive cure for stage fright but the elimination of conceit and self-indulgence and a certain amount of disciplined homework and humility can help considerably to assuage the dreadful fears.

Coward on Theatre Audiences

"In England the public is more prone to think for itself. In America they have to be told what to enjoy and what to avoid, not only in the theatre but in every phase of life. They are told by television and radio what to eat, drink and smoke, what cars to buy and what laxatives and sanitary towels to use. They are told, in no uncertain terms, what movies to go to and what stars to admire. . . . The power of individual thought has been atrophied in them by the incessant onslaughts of commercialism."

"I am aware of a tremendous change in the quality of the New York audiences since I played here twenty-one years ago [this was written in 1957]. They used to be quick on comedy, quicker often than London audiences. Now, however, this quickness has gone. They are quite appreciative on the whole, but much dimmer. In fact they have lost the capacity for participation."

"Audience is like a great beast which the actor must tame into silence."
—THOMAS DEKKER

"All theatre is sharing . . . you share with the audience."
—MICHAEL HORDERN

"The public must not be underrated. They're not all that silly, and the reason so few go to the theatre now is that they're bored stiff by plays that are too long, and with the general atmosphere of 'down.' That is not what people go to the theatre for, unless it's done with genius—and it seldom is."

Coward on Fans

"Much as I adore my fans, they can be the second most irritating element of theatrical life . . ."

Social Grace

I expect you've heard this a million times before
But I absolutely adored your last play
I went four times—and now to think
That here I am actually talking to you!
It's thrilling! Honestly it is, I mean,
It's always thrilling isn't it to meet someone really celebrated?
I mean someone who really does things.
I expect all this is a terrible bore for you.
After all you go everywhere and know everybody.
It must be wonderful to go absolutely everywhere
And know absolutely everybody and—Oh dear—
Then to have to listen to someone like me,
I mean someone absolutely ordinary just one of your public.
No one will believe me when I tell them
That I have actually been talking to the great man himself.
It must be wonderful to be so frightfully brainy
And know all the things that you know
I'm not brainy a bit, neither is my husband,
Just plain humdrum, that's what we are.
But we do come up to town occasionally
And go to shows and things. Actually my husband
Is quite a critic, not professionally of course,
What I mean is that he isn't all that easily pleased.
He doesn't like everything. Oh no, not by any means.
He simply hated that thing at the Haymarket
Which everybody went on about. "Rubbish" he said,
Straight out like that, "Damned Rubbish!"
I nearly died because heaps of people were listening.
But that's quite typical of him. He just says what he thinks.
And he can't stand all this highbrow stuff—
Do you know what I mean?—All these plays about people being
    miserable

And never getting what they want and not even committing
    suicide
But just being absolutely wretched. He says he goes to the theatre
To have a good time. That's why he simply loves all your things,
I mean they relax him and he doesn't have to *think*.
And he certainly does love a good laugh.
You should have seen him the other night when we went to that
    film
With what's-her-name in it—I can't remember the title.
I thought he'd have a fit, honestly I did.
You must know the one I mean, the one about the man who
    comes home
And finds his wife has been carrying on with his best friend
And of course he's furious at first and then he decides to teach her
    a lesson.
You must have seen it. I wish I could remember the name
But that's absolutely typical of me, I've got a head like a sieve,
I keep on forgetting things and as for names—well!
I just cannot for the life of me remember them.
Faces yes, I never forget a face because I happen to be naturally
    observant
And always have been since I was a tiny kiddie
But names!—Oh dear! I'm quite hopeless.
I feel such a fool sometimes
I do, honestly.

And the *most* irritating?
"When that *doesn't* happen."

Coward on Vice and Squalor in the Theatre

There are still certain places in the Far East where the British inhabitants cherish the antiquated belief that life in the theatre is one prolonged orgy of vice and squalor. This, I must say, I found interesting, if a trifle annoying. It is always irritating to feel that one is being regarded with intense suspicion, especially when this suspicion emanates from that particularly unimaginative type of Colonial Englishman whose sense of humour begins and ends with a few old moth-eaten dirty stories, and whose only idea of a really successful evening is to sally forth *en masse* to some local brothel, where the sum total of pleasure achieved seldom exceeds a lot of noise and a few broken bottles.

One evening, at the end of an exceedingly long "stag" dinner party, during which I had answered, with as much evasive politeness as possible, a series of patronisingly lascivious questions about several of my best friends in the theatre. "Was Gladys Cooper hot stuff?" or "Was it true that Edna Best did such and such a thing?" etc., etc. I suddenly decided that it was high time somebody gave them a taste of the vicarious sensations for which they so obviously craved, so I started off with great solemnity, and discussed the moral degradation of theatrical life for at least an hour without stopping. I said I thought it was primarily the lime-light and make-up which caused the characters of our leading actors and actresses to disintegrate with such horrifying rapidity. I said I had known Gladys Cooper long before she ever went on the stage, when she was a simple parson's daughter in Warwickshire, when even the private behaviour of sheep was withheld from her, among all the other secrets of worldly life. Then came her disgrace and banishment from home—naturally "in trouble," and then finally as a last resource "The Stage," where after a few months painful struggling and deprivation, she fell into the clutches of Constance Collier, then at the height of her notoriety. I went on to describe her gradual degradation step by step, until now, although still the idol of an ignorant and misguided public, her private life was so thoroughly beastly that no one ever mentioned it, even in the Green Room Club.

I then told of my horrible experiences with Lilian Braithwaite when we played together in *The Vortex*. I had to admit in fairness to Lilian that it was the bad liquor in New York which was responsible for many of those unfortunate incidents, but even so, I said, it was a little humiliating to find my leading lady lying hiccoughing in the gutter outside the stage door five minutes before the curtain was due to rise on the first night. Of Sybil Thorndike, Madge Titheradge and Edith Evans I refused to speak at all, intimating subtly that there were some things that one didn't discuss even among men. But I did give a thrilling description of an average Sunday with the du Mauriers in Hampstead. I explained how Gerald always appeared at about twelve-thirty, unwashed and unshaven, and with a half-crazed, doped look in his eye, generally wearing rather torn pyjamas. I went on to describe the squalor of the lunch table with poor Lady du Maurier weeping at one end in a faded kimono, and

Edna Best, blind drunk, trying to prevent Herbert Marshall from hitting Viola Tree over the head with a beer bottle. I said that after lunch Gerald insisted on dragging us all upstairs to his bed-room in order to throw cream buns at a lot of naked negresses, which he always kept for the purpose. At this point I was almost defeated by somebody asking me about Tallulah Bankhead, but I had the presence of mind to remember that she came from Alabama, which accounted, I said, for her being so dull and straightlaced.

(? 1920s)

Coward on . . . a Slice of Ham

"In the world of the theatre there is an expression that is used a great deal; it is the word 'Ham.' It can be employed as an adjective or a noun or a verb or an adverb. To be Ham is a terrible sin in modern acting. It implies primarily a sort of 'cloak and sword' romanticism; artifice; falseness and modern acting resolutely disdains the full throated ringing tones of earlier days and goes in doggedly for realism. This, I think, is right although sometimes it is carried too far, often to such an extent that the actors, so haunted by the fear that they might be accused of ranting, frequently wind up by being completely inaudible, which to my mind is a worse sin yet. Hamming however is something we are all conscious of, all wary of. Actors who play a lot of Shakespeare or other plays in verse are those who have the toughest struggle, for it is virtually impossible to deliver long lyric speeches with the same degree of colloquialism as crisp, every-day modern dialogue. A few very fine actors who are accustomed to both modern and classic roles occasionally achieve a happy mean between the two extremes, but these are rare. A phrase can be ham; an idea can be ham."

Coward on Comedy

"Who can truly say there is more truth in tears than in laughter?"

═══

In any interview or sustained conversation about the theatre with Noël, the conversation would sooner or later come round to the creation and performance of *Comedy*.

In his early work that invariably took the form of pseudo-Wildean epigrams . . .

Later he would come to realize the error of those overly literary ways . . .

"To me the essence of good comedy writing is that perfectly ordinary phrases, phrases such as 'Just fancy!' should, by virtue of their context, achieve greater laughs than the most literate epigrams. Some of the biggest laughs in *Hay Fever* occur on such lines as 'Go on,' 'No, there isn't, is there?' and 'This haddock's disgusting.' There are many other glittering examples of my sophistication in the same vein."

"When they're laughing, an audience is less inclined to question the point being made."

In short—"Comedy is nearly always despised in its generation and honored more latterly—except by the public.

"It's treated, as something trivial, whereas it is far and away the most complicated and the most difficult aspect of acting."

In *Relative Values* he would have the butler Crestwell explain . . . "Comedies of manners swiftly become obsolete when there are no longer any manners."

Noël was also the first to point out that comedy is also essentially a team effort—the comedian, the audience, and the rest of the cast . . .

"You must always consider the other people on the stage with you. This is a really important aspect of acting; no really good acting is achieved without the complete co-operation of your fellow artists. You cannot play the scene by yourself unless you are alone on the stage. And if you are with somebody else on that stage, you have to consider them and their reactions, help them to get their reactions, in return for which they will help you to get yours, and this is what makes fine acting."

One can never be natural and relaxed if one's a good comedian; there are too many things to think about. You've got to have your mind working on several levels.

You've got first of all to remember the character you've learned and studied and know about. You've got to remember your voice pitch, which has got to reach the back of the gallery, without shouting. You've got to remember your other actors—vitally important to get their eye, speak to them, not to the audience, to them.

Then you've got to listen to the audience's reaction, because audiences vary at every performance. One night they're a lot of cods' heads, the next night they're marvellous; and you have to know how to handle them. If they're dull, then you've got to go a little quicker; if they're warm and responsive, you've got to watch yourself, otherwise they'll lead you astray and make you overplay. In fact, I believe that all acting is a question of control, the control of the actor of himself, and through himself of the audience . . .

The most dangerous thing . . . is when you're playing a high comedy part and you've got a wonderful audience, you begin to enjoy it a little bit too much. And the winks come and the face begins to react and you're having a ball; and it isn't till later that somebody tells you—and pray God that they do—that you were over playing.

"You, as a comedian, must enjoy what you're doing. I hate this new 'solemnity' in the theatre. If anybody says to me, 'She's a dedicated actress,' I'd like to strangle her. What's she 'dedicated' about? It sounds wretched. And this means all this gloomy searching for 'motives.' Acting must be a pleasure, even if you're playing something immensely tragic and dramatic—there's that sort of pleasure, too."

———

In the 1920s and 1930s, Noël made regular visits to New York to observe the speed and tempo of American comedy, which was much more sophisticated than the English equivalent. After the war, he found it much less so. English comedy, he felt, lost a great deal of its style because of a dearth of new light comedy playwrights. It was no longer fashionable to deal with the apparently trivial, although it became obvious with revivals that the "trivial" could deal with the fundamentals perfectly well.

Coward on Overlapping Dialogue

Noël's first experience of Broadway acting back in 1921 opened his eyes to a number of theatrical techniques. Perhaps the most illuminating was the way different characters' lines could overlap in such a way that the key part of a line would stand out.

It was a technique he would often experiment with himself . . .

"DROP IN FOR DRINKS" (SKETCH)

"You've done something to this room"

"Not much, really. I've just moved things about a bit"

"That Ming horse is new"

"Darling, the one thing a Ming horse *couldn't* be is new"

"*Touché*"

"Anyway it's Tang"

"Ming—Tang—Ping—Pong! What the hell!"

"You look wonderful. I suppose it's that mysterious professor in Switzerland"

"I've got 'Ewe' under my skin"

"That's marvellous. Bunny, did you hear what Maurice said?"

"What did he say?"

"I've got 'Ewe' under my skin"

"Cole Porter said it first"

"You've missed the whole point. This is 'Ewe' not 'You'"

"I'm worried about Caroline's hair"

"I expect she is too"

"I suppose that's either 'Ming' or 'Tang.' I can never tell the difference"

"I wonder why the Chinese were so crazy over horses"

"I don't know any Chinese except the man who does my feet. He lives in Onslow Gardens"

"But if I were shut up in a Capsule whizzing through outer space, I don't think I'd really *want* to!"

"Look out for those little biscuits with anchovies on them. They're hard as rocks"

"You'd never think that Maurice was in his sixties, would you"

"It's that man in Switzerland. He injects you with things"

"What sort of things?"

"I'm not quite sure. Something to do with goats, I believe"

"Bobbie's done something to this room"

"Not enough"

"I don't see how he can love Elizabeth Taylor *and* his wife at the same time"

"It's when you come back into the *earth's* orbit that's tricky, apparently"

"Sheila had a letter from Francis. She thinks that he *knows*"

"I'm not sure that I'd want to know, really. I'd much better (rather?) lie there and hope for the best"

"Poor Caroline. She looks madder than ever"
"It's her hair. All she needs is a red tunic and she could Troop the Colour"

In 1926 he used the device in *Semi-Monde* with a number of characters. His stage direction reads . . .

"The ensuing scene must be played simultaneously by everybody, the dialogue being immaterial but the general effect of noise essential."

OLD LADY I love anything a little *risqué.*

ALBERT Well, it's certainly that.

OLD LADY What?

ALBERT I say it's certainly that.

OLD LADY What a pity—she used to be so lovely.

SUZANNE I must say I see Marion's point.

GEORGE Who was the little fair girl who sang?

MARION I don't know—she made me feel uncomfortable.

SUZANNE Marie something or other—she used to be at the Casino de Paris.

GEORGE Damned attractive looking!

ALBERT Shall we go and have lunch now?

OLD LADY What?

ALBERT Lunch?

OLD LADY Oh yes—I'm dieting, you know—I shan't eat much.

ALBERT (*rising*) I'm not particularly hungry.

OLD LADY We might walk through to the restaurant.

ALBERT pilots her out.

SUZANNE Thanks for the cocktail, George—I wish you were eating with us.

GEORGE I shall wait ten minutes more.

MARION (*rising*) Come on, Suzanne.

SUZANNE Give us a call when you get back.

GEORGE We'll have a party.

MARION Lovely. Good-bye.

GEORGE I shall probably be at the Crillon—I'm sick of this place.

SUZANNE So am I—but it's a sort of habit one can't shake off.

Coward on Style

Noël firmly believed that a lot of younger actors had none of the sense of style that he and his contemporaries had.

In my early days in the theatre, in the actor-manager's time—which is certainly going back a bit—I would never go into a theatre belonging to Charles Hawtrey or Gerald du Maurier or Sir George Alexander or Sir Herbert Tree without being spick and span—whatever I was going to play. If I was going to play a dustman, I would have my suit pressed for rehearsals, out of respect for the theatre itself—the edifice, the building. You couldn't see a lot of people in denim and dirty old sweaters walking about the stage of the St. James's!

I don't know why I feel like this. I suppose it's old hat and senti-mental. It isn't, entirely. It's a question of discipline. I don't believe you can rehearse—easily—a highly articulate comedy, dressed in a slovenly manner. A young creature of twenty-one thinks it's perfectly all right to come slouching in without thinking of his poise, without thinking of his "line," his head, his stance. And now, when suddenly he's put into the clothes, he doesn't quite know how to wear them. I don't blame him. I blame the directors. I think a slovenly appearance indicates in some way a slovenly mind.

I wish I could only explain—and it sounds almost pompous—that with the decline of manners and of elegance, it's much more difficult for young actors to achieve "range" . . . It's so easy to play "natural" when you can scratch yourself—even then it's got to be well done—but it's much easier than being slick, timing every line and very sharp looking.

He returned to the subject frequently: "You must never appear in pub-lic looking less than your best. . . . God, how dismally bored I am with these people who slouch out of the stage door with handkerchiefs over their heads!"

Noël worried about the next generation of actors.

Talent wasn't the problem—but social conditioning wasn't helping . . .

"They've been caught by this awful solemnity bug . . . that the whole thing's so sacred. They fly like rabbits to the psychoanalyst's couch to have their own problems straightened out, but that's nothing to do with acting at all. . . . Too much emphasis is being placed on the lower orders of life, the young people have lost a certain style that we had in the old days."

Coward on Being "Noël Coward"

As he became more successful Noël found he'd created a personal problem—being Noël Coward . . .

"When I'd become a more experienced and a better actor, it was essential, with certain parts that I shouldn't be like me. I've been a personality actor all my life. I'd established, in my early years, the sophisticated urbane type, which is in tune with my own personality. But if, for instance, I play something that looks like me, but isn't like me at all, then I have to reconstruct in my mind, at rehearsals, my gestures so that I'm no longer like Noël Coward. But again you come up against this image you create of yourself in the public mind. When I was a little boy and a young man I always longed to be a big star and a great success. In those days I wouldn't have cared to put on too much nose paste and that sort of thing, because I was too occupied with somebody asking me for an autograph on a bus.

"I've become a more experienced and a better actor. And also, acting a character is far more interesting than anything else. To do my own sort of dialogue, flibberty-gibbet, witty, quick, and all that, is another sort of technique. I loved playing *Fumed Oak,* for instance, with that terrible moustache. I've loved the bits of character acting I've done in my life. I always forget, when I'm playing in my own plays, that I'm the author . . . I really prefer playing other people's plays to my own."

Coward on *Not* Being "Noël Coward"

His advice to actors playing the parts he had created was unequivocal: "Do not try and be me!" He was, as John Osborne said, "his own creation," and unfortunately, too many actors tried to re-create themselves in his image. Hugh Sinclair, Nigel Patrick, Donald Sinden, and countless others from West End revival to the humblest provincial repertory company tried to carbon-copy Coward. It only made one realize how original an "original" can be.

One actor who most certainly did not copy Noël was George C. Scott. In the 1982 Broadway revival of *Present Laughter,* he played Garry Essendine as a latter-day John Barrymore, complete with pouting profile and pseudo-Shakespearean rumble. Barrymore's narcissism was a relevant point of reference for a Broadway audience. It also saved George C. from having to attempt an English accent!

Noël the Actor. Robert Benchley once described "his scene-stealing stare" as "the look of a dead albatross."

Coward on Revivals

"Never boil your cabbage twice."

A memorable line but many of the items on Noël's theatrical menu were served to the public time and again. Nor did he seem to lose his appetite for them when they were cooked as well as the 1964 revival of *Hay Fever*.

Coward on Plays with a "Message"

"I remember Leonora Corbett once saying to me when I asked her out to the theatre in New York—'If it's a play with a message, I shan't dress.' I saw what she meant, because that was the great period of plays with messages. But most of my plays are absolutely crammed with messages, if you look carefully.

"*Cavalcade* that's home and dry. But there are some sharp messages in *Present Laughter* too. *Post-Mortem* was violently anti-war, and I wrote it too soon. I showed my hand too soon. It had some wonderful scenes in it. The cynic boy was very good, that long speech he had. But I wrote it too hot off the grid.

"Anyone with any sense is a pacifist, although 'pacifist' has such terrible connotations . . . all those terrible pale ladies at the Albert Hall making speeches."

"I am light-minded. I would inevitably write a comedy if—God help me!—I wanted to write a play with a message."

Coward on Writing

On Confidence
"When you're writing something, you know, at the time, that it is brilliant beyond belief. Otherwise you wouldn't go on with it. But then rehearsals

start and doubts begin to creep in and, even so, a success doesn't necessarily mean that it's all that good a play: It may mean that the leading
lady's got a wonderful part and is very good in it. It may mean a lot of
things. So may a real rousing failure. I've always done it the big way.
After the first night of *Sirocco,* they spat at me in the streets—literally
spat all over my tailcoat. And I thought: I must be a good playwright
because nobody's going to take all that trouble unless they feel badly disappointed. They needn't have made all that much fuss. It wasn't all that
terrible. In fact, there were many worse running triumphantly. But I'd set
a standard for myself. . . ."

═══

"Who is to say with any certainty which of an artist's works are his best?
Everyone knows that contemporary judgment is not to be relied upon
and in fact it is a fairly safe rule to take the opposite view to the current
one. Even Time will not tell, for an artist is sometimes remembered and
loved for his more popular works rather than his best."

(1939)

On Writing Fiction

"Being primarily a dramatist, short stories have been an absorbing
experiment in form, lying somewhere between a play and a novel. I
found them fascinating to write but far from easy. They demand perhaps a little less rigid self-discipline than a play, and a great deal more
than a novel. In a novel there is room for divergencies and irrelevancies.
In a play there is none; in a short story, just a little, but it must be strictly
rationed.

"I love writing fiction. It is hard going but it has the lovely satisfaction
about it that good, bad or indifferent, there it is and it has not got to be
translated through someone else's personality.

"My sense of words, a natural gift, is becoming more trained and
selective, and I suspect, when I next sit down to write a play, things may
happen that have never happened before."

(1949)

On Writing Verse

I can only assume that the compulsion to make rhymes was born in me.
It cannot have been hereditary, for neither my mother nor my father

nor any of my forebears on either side of the family displayed, as far as I know, the faintest aptitude for writing poetry or verse.

Throughout most of the years of my life, since approximately nineteen hundred and eight, I have derived a considerable amount of private pleasure from writing verse ... It is an inherent instinct in the English character.

I find it quite fascinating to write at random, sometimes in rhyme, sometimes not. I am trying to discipline myself away from too much discipline, by which I mean that my experience and training in lyric writing has made me inclined to stick too closely to a rigid form. It is strange that technical accuracy should occasionally banish magic, but it does. The carefully rhymed verses, which I find very difficult not to do, are, on the whole, less effective and certainly less moving than the free ones. This writing of free verse, which I am enjoying so very much, is wonderful exercise for my mind and for my vocabulary. Most of what I have already done I really feel is good and is opening up, for me, some new windows. My sense of words, a natural gift, is becoming more trained and selective ...

I have automatically enjoyed verse as a means of communication with my intimates ever since I can remember. Lorn Loraine, my beloved secretary and English representative for forty-six years, is an expert at squeezing the maximum of business information and personal news into rhymed cables and telegrams which, together with my own rhymed replies, has afforded us a lot of amusement.

Diaries (1956)

On Handwriting
"My handwriting looks as though Chinese ants have crawled all over the paper."

On Taste
"It can be vulgar, but it must never be embarrassing."

"There is to be a public lying-in-state for Gertie in which she will wear the pink dress in which she danced the polka in *The King And I.* Vulgarity can go no further."

(*Diary,* September 8, 1952)

On Explicit Language

"I'm not passionately interested in the moral aspect but artistically it is very much better to make a suggestion and not a statement. And I don't like a rash of four-letter words—for the simple reason that I use so many myself that I'm bored with them!"

Coward on Constructing a Play

"I wish they'd understand," he'd lament, "that writing a play is both a craft and an art." Whenever a "well-made" play, perfected by writers such as Shaw or Maugham, Lonsdale or Rattigan, was rejected in favor of inferior, poorly constructed work, he was genuinely appalled. Noël flirted unsuccessfully with more flexible forms, and he confided to his *Diaries* that, "I will never again embark on so much as a revue sketch that is not carefully and meticulously constructed beforehand." The discipline of structure gave him more, not less, freedom of verbal expression.

"I am also aware, though, from past experience, that when the right note is struck, and the structure of the play is carefully built in advance, it is both wise and profitable to start at the beginning and write through to the end in as short a time as possible . . . *Private Lives* lived in my mind several months before it emerged. *Present Laughter* had waited about, half formulated, for nearly three years before I finally wrote it . . . Before the first word of the first act is written the last act should be clearly in the author's mind, if not actually written out in the form of a synopsis. Dialogue, for those who have a talent for it, is easy; but construction, with or without talent, is difficult and is of paramount importance. I know this sounds like heresy in this era of highly-praised, half-formulated moods, but no mood, however exquisite, is likely to hold the attention of an audience for two hours and a half unless it is based on a solid structure."

(*Future Indefinite*, 1954)

Once construction was complete, the words became the paramount decoration, and few postwar playwrights ever matched Noël's exacting standards.

COWARD ON FAILURE IN THE THEATRE

When a play fails to please the general public it is, as a general rule, the fault of the author. This is a disconcerting, unpleasant little truism that many playwrights shrink from admitting and I do not blame them for their instinctive reluctance to shoulder the blame for, in the Theatre, there are so many wide margins for error. If a man sits down and writes a novel he knows, or should know, at the outset that nothing can go wrong with it except his own lack of talent. All he has to do, having written it, is to cut and polish where he considers it necessary, submit it to his publishers and later, if it is accepted, correct the proofs. No outside influences insinuate themselves between him and his opus. There it is, complete and whole as he wrote it, and if the reviewers and the public like it so much the better; if not, so much the worse. But whichever way the variable winds blow it is his own unaided and unencumbered work that either succeeds or fails.

For a playwright the process is infinitely more complicated. True, the writing of a play from the point of view of sheer manual labour is far less arduous and can be done in far less time than a novel, but to offset this there are desperate hazards with which the novelist need never be concerned. When a dramatist writes "Curtain" on the last page of his last act he experiences, like all creative artists, a feeling of immense relief. "At any rate," he says to himself, "good, bad or indifferent the thing is finished." Of course he doesn't really mean that his play could possibly be either bad or indifferent; he knows beyond a shadow of doubt that it is brilliant, provocative and startlingly original from the moment Eloise enters in Act One to her triumphant exit line at the end of Act Three, but what he does mean is, regardless of later disillusionments, that he has done his best and that the weeks or months of self-discipline and concentration are over and he can relax and perhaps take a little holiday. If he is an experienced playwright rather than a beginner, this sense of exaltation will last only a little while: memories of past productions will rise like phantoms to plague him. He will recall dreadful scenes between leading ladies and directors, interminable conferences in managerial offices and nightmare hours in provincial hotels when he has been forced by the director to sit up until dawn re-writing Scene One, Act Three and transposing a great deal of Act One into Act Two.

In my case some of these miseries are eliminated because I usually direct my own plays, but the same sort of crises have occurred and recurred monotonously with almost every production I have been associated with. Often, at a dress rehearsal in Manchester, I have stared gloomily at the stage and tried vainly to recapture that first fine careless rapture when I had just completed the play and loved it with all the uncritical tenderness of a doting mother. By now, sitting gloomily in an empty, darkened auditorium, abstractedly chewing a stale ham sandwich, I gaze without recognition at the characters I so cheerfully created. There is my heroine, whom I had envisaged tall, blonde and exquisitely witty, short, dark and walking through the part with nothing more than disagreeable professionalism because she had just had a flaming scene about her First Act dress and has, deaf to all entreaties, adamantly refused to wear a wig. There is my gay, insouciant hero, so very very unlike the star I had originally wished for and who unfortunately was unavailable.

There, overacting heavily, is the mildly eccentric dowager on whom I had lavished so much loving care, blissfully unaware that not only was she not my original choice for the part but the lowest on a fairly low list of "possibles." There is the play that I once loved, being obscured and distorted by the vanities of actors and their strutting egos. In general fairness it must be admitted that things are not always and inevitably as black as I have just painted them. Sometimes I have seen actors give wonderful performances of my plays, even at dress rehearsals in Manchester. Sometimes I have sat entranced, spellbound, hypnotised and ravished by the sorcery with which the leading lady endows my stilted heroine with new and vibrant life. These occasions are rare. However brilliant the leading actress or actor, however sensitively she or he plays the part you have written, there will always be something wrong, or if not exactly wrong, something different, from what you originally intended. Translations are seldom superior to the originals and only few of the greatest actors are more than translators of someone else's thoughts and words and mind. This is why the whole business of play production is so perplexing and tormenting for a dramatist who has never been an actor or a director himself. He has to sit quietly and watch his play prodded and poked into alien shapes; re-moulded, snipped and cut to fit individual artists whose personalities are frequently completely opposite to those he had first seen through his mind's eye. If he protests, he is taken out to lunch by the star and the director and bullied into submission. If he refuses to be bullied and to submit, he is taken out to lunch by the producing manager who coaxes and flatters him into a trance of weary acquiescence. If this gambit also fails, he is ruthlessly forbidden to enter the theatre until the opening night. If on the other hand he shows no sign of fight at all but merely an exuberant eagerness to co-operate in every possible way, he finds himself in even worse trouble. Before the first week of rehearsal is over he is taken out to lunch by the star who suggests that her two major scenes need lengthening, that the daughter's hysterical outburst in Act Two should be cut down to the bone because it holds up the action of the play and that the few oblique references to the heroine being middle-aged could quite easily be eliminated as they contribute nothing and will merely confuse the public. When the co-operative author has gladly agreed to all this, retired home, made the requested alterations and delivered them, he is immediately taken out to lunch by the director and told that the balance of the play has been completely upset, that the leading lady is a tiresome bitch, that her two major scenes were too long in the first place and must be cut relentlessly and that the daughter's hysterical outburst in Act Two should not only be strengthened but transposed to the end of the Act. The co-operative author is now in the soup, where he remains, struggling miserably, until the opening night when the play will either be a success, when he will be kissed by everyone, or a failure, when he will be cut by everyone with the exception of the character lady who has bored him stiff through-out rehearsals and invites him into her dressing-room to have some gin because she is sorry for him.

This, I admit, is a gloomy picture and strongly biased on the side of the author but then there are other points of view to be considered and in all justice, brushing aside the hoary old superstition that the author's work is sacrosanct, these points of view have considerable validity. Take that of the director for instance. If he is a good director he is probably an intelligent man who has studied the play carefully and knows a good deal more about the technical problems of stage production, the com-promises necessary and the elastic exigencies of casting, etc., than the author. He has taken on the job and is in a position of authority but however carefully he has studied the play it is unlikely that he knows absolutely what was in the author's mind. Nevertheless he proceeds to cast the characters to the best of his ability and to the best of the actors availability. The casting period of any play is always fraught with disap-pointment and frustration. The actor considered ideal for the part of "George" has just signed for an eight month's season at Stratford: the perfect "Rosemary" has retired to Thames Ditton with her new husband and is about to have a baby: the only actress with all the requirements for the part of "Mrs. Vereker" has a contract with Arthur Rank and is at the moment in the jungles of Borneo playing Gregory Peck's mother. The alternative to the original choice for "Rosemary" is available but well-known to be "difficult." When the author enquires what form her "difficultness" takes, looks are exchanged, lips are pursed and heads are shaken. It is admitted freely that she is a fine actress within her scope, a big draw in the right part and gave a really staggering performance of "Hedda Gabler" some years ago. It is admitted equally freely that she is actually a bit old for this particular part and that there *have* been rumours that she occasionally takes a nip. However, failing darling Gloria (the Thames Ditton one), there is no one else who so nearly fills the requirements, so a script had better be sent to her right away. While waiting for an answer from the difficult Miss X., the smaller parts are cast more or less satisfactorily, and suspense as to whether Miss X. will or will not accept the part steadily mounts until a high pressure of nervous anxiety is attained, not only in the minds of the author and the director but also in the sacred precincts of the Managerial Offices. As time goes on and the stately silence is maintained, an illusion takes root and grows out of all proportion. This illusion is that Miss X. is the only possible actress for the part and that if by any dreadful chance she should refuse it the whole project must be shelved and the play remain for ever unproduced.

Now we come to the point of view of Miss X. herself. Miss X. herself is perfectly aware that the domestic-minded Gloria has been offered the play first. She is also aware that with each day that passes the management will be growing more and more anxious to secure her services. Miss X. may be virtually illiterate, spoiled, conceited beyond belief and a monster of egocentricity, but she is no fool. She knows the part is good for her and that with a little re-writing here and there she can make a success of it. She also knows that to say Yes too soon would weaken her position and limit, to a certain degree, the contractual conditions she intends to impose, so she stays quietly in her overpoweringly rustic farm-house in Sussex, studies the script shrewdly from every angle and waits for the telephone to ring. When it does, her maid explains that she is unavailable, possibly out walking on the Downs and will Mr. Y. please call again at about six. When Mr. Y. does call again at six she is charming but evasive and says she cannot possibly commit herself until she has read two other scripts that are awaiting her immediate decision.

A week or so later she telephones the office and says she is coming up to Town for the day and would like to discuss the play, and if possible, meet the author.

If he is a young, eager beginner this first encounter with his star will be a complete rout. He will be charmed within an inch of his life and he will discover in this reputedly formidable lady a quality of simplicity that he had never suspected, a frank, disarming honesty and a warm, comforting friendliness. She may, before the lunch is over, ask him to call her by her Christian name, adding with a musical laugh that as she knows they are going to be friends they had better start as they mean to go on. He will find himself looking reproachfully at the manager or the director or whoever it is who is paying for the lunch, for so maligning this fascinating warm-hearted human being who is about to honour him by playing his play. How could anyone so gay and tolerant and amusing ever be tiresome in the theatre, ever complain about her dresses, ever in a thousand years be described as conceited or the least bit egocentric? He will finally leave the restaurant and walk home through the grey London streets, treading delicately like Agag for fear he might jolt himself out of his dreams.

A more experienced playwright will probably have known this particular star for years, brawled with her frequently and often longed to throttle her, in which case the inaugural lunch will be less charged with charm and be a good deal more business like. In either event the result will be the same. She will ultimately give exactly the performance she intends to give. She will undoubtedly end up with a completely new set of dresses for the London opening and if she is good in the part the critics will say how lucky the author is to have his mediocre work played with such brilliance, while if she is bad in the part they will say how grateful the author should be to have such a fine actress salvaging so unworthy a vehicle.

Personally I have been luckier than most in my dealings with my various leading ladies. I have only rarely been choked by the more obvious varieties of star-dust but on those few occasions the results were indescribably hideous and I still wake in the night sometimes, sweating and quivering with shameful memories of long past theatrical feuds. Nowadays, of course, there are fewer high-powered, one hundred per cent glamour actresses extant. The pattern has changed although the fundamental tiresomeness remains the same. To-day Theatrical Dragons are less obvious; they paw the ground and lash their scaly tails in a different way and the dangerous steam emitted from their flaming nostrils is a different sort of steam. There will still, always and for ever be "trouble about the dresses" but apart from this, old-fashioned shrieking temperament has been largely superseded by a disconcerting and most treacherous intellectualism. The new peril that faces the young dramatist of to-day is, if anything, harder to deal with than the old. Gone are the sables and minks and sudden unpredictable storms followed by the equally sudden and unpredictable blowing of kisses to everyone. Gone are the drumming heels, the flinging the shoes at the dresser, the monotonous and inevitable last minute refusals to appear. Gone also alas, with one notable exception, are the strong minded directors capable of saying firmly "Unless you are word perfect in your first act by to-morrow morning you will not play the part at all!"

Nowadays, at least in the higher strata of the Theatre, there is an entirely different approach. Technical efficiency, indeed many of the most useful "tricks of the trade" are banished into limbo, trodden out of sight. Nowadays no director will tell the leading lady how to play the part; on the contrary she will tell him how she is going to play the part. She will discuss it with him, if he will let her, until his head reels. She will discover, in the most innocent lines, Freudian significances which startle the author considerably. The actors too catch this sinister contagion and before you can say Stanislavski the rehearsal is brought to a standstill while the cast argue amongst themselves as to how the play should be played. This is not to say that many fine actors and actresses haven't emerged from highbrow acting groups, as indeed many of our greatest artists of a few decades ago began their careers in George Edwardes' Choruses. Genuine talent is the first and only prerequisite of good acting and as a general rule, talent wins through. The value of the acting schools is considerable. They teach young people to think about what they are doing and to approach their work from the inside rather than the outside. This is all very well when the young people thus trained have, in addition to talent, intelligence. But unfortunately there is no guarantee of this and if they are not intelligent enough and if their natural gift is limited in scope, they are liable to become not only pretentious but inaudible. I once saw a young, new-school intellectual actor playing a leading part in a successful play. His psychological approach to the character had obviously been meticulously thought out, his movements and gestures were accurate and he projected a sort of inner radiance which was fascinating to watch. Unhappily however, from my seat in the seventh row of the stalls, I was unable to catch more than half of what he said. Later, in his dressing-room, I suggested that he pitch his voice a tone higher and enunciate more distinctly, whereupon he looked at me with a withering smile and said he really couldn't think about such technicalities when he was right in the skin of a part and that if he did, he wouldn't be able to play it. Snubbed, but not defeated, I said that in that case the screen would be more suitable to his special talent than the theatre and withdrew in an atmosphere of glacial goodwill. I am proud to be able to record that he took my advice and is now a big movie star.

I am prepared to admit that one of my worst defects is intolerance of what I call pretentiousness in the Theatre. I am fully aware that I am not infallible and that what appears pretentious to me may not be so at all. But there it is; I approach the so-called highbrow, the artsy-craftsy and the intellectual do-gooders of my profession with deep-dyed prejudice. I know that this is a weakness and sometimes, to my surprise, I am proved wrong. I have seen some fine acting in some small, out of the way theatres, intelligent and imaginative productions and, every now and then, a good play. But this is very rare. Having worked in the theatre since I was a little boy of ten, which was all of a forty-seven years ago, I consider that I have earned the right to express at least one of my fuddy-duddy, old-fashioned convictions, and this is my unshakable belief that the Theatre is primarily intended for entertainment.

This I know runs directly counter to what is known as the "Modern Trend" but then in the course of forty-seven years I have seen a good many modern trends come and go, in fact I have been one of them myself except that I haven't gone yet. The present cult of depression, defeatism and long-winded metaphysical philosophy arouses no interest in me, theatrically speaking. I am aware that two major wars are apt to upset the world's equilibrium considerably but I still cannot quite blame the two wars for this dreadful cult of "Boredom" which seems to have the French, American and English Theatres so sternly in its grip.

When I was one and twenty I was ambitious, cheerful and high-spirited. I had never heard of the Death Wish and was briskly unaware that I belonged to a dying civilisation. To-day this dubious implication is pitched at me from all directions. Despair is the new religion, the new mode; it is in the books we read, the music we hear and, very much too often, in the plays we see. Well, I am no longer one and twenty but I still have no pre-occupation with the Death Wish. I am still ambitious and cheerful and not offensively high-spirited and still unaware that I belong to a dying civilisation. If I do, there really isn't anything I can do about it and so I shall just press on with my life as I like living it until I die of natural causes or an H-bomb blows me to smithereens. I knew, in my teens, that the world was full of hatred, envy, malice, cruelty, jealousy, unrequited love, murder, despair and destruction. I also knew, at the same time, that it was full of kindness, joy, pleasure, requited love, generosity, fun, excitement, laughter and friends. Nothing that has happened to me over the years has caused me to re-adjust in my mind the balance of these observed phenomena. I do become increasingly exasperated however when in my own beloved profession all that I was brought up and trained to believe is now decried. Nowadays a well constructed play is despised and a light comedy whose only purpose is to amuse is dismissed as "trivial" and "without significance." Since when has laughter been so insignificant? An actor-become-star who steps out and charms a large audience with his personality and talent is critically tolerated in a good-humoured way as though he were a performing bear. No merriment apparently must scratch the set, grim patina of these dire times. We must wait for death, or hurry it on, according to how we feel. To my mind, one of the most efficacious ways of hurrying it on is to sit in a theatre watching a verbose, humourless play acted with turgid intensity which has received rave notices and is closing on Saturday.

(The above was taken from Noël's introduction to *Play Parade* [1958]. He would use many of these observations in his last play *Star Quality* [1967], which was neither produced nor published in his lifetime.)

Coward on Writing Plays vs. Writing Novels

Reading the "exquisitely phrased verbosity" of Henry James caused Noël to reflect on the technical differences between the writing of a play and a novel:

"It is good for me technically because I am inclined to oversimplify my descriptive passages and reduce them to staccato interludes rather than letting them be part of the general structure. This is the natural result of years of dialogue writing. It is only when I have done a couple of pages of—to my mind—elaborate and drawn-out description that, on reading it over, I discover to my astonishment that it is neither elaborate nor drawn-out. On the contrary, it is usually on the skimpy side. This, I suppose, is the reason that so few playwrights write good novels and vice versa. Particularly vice versa. Most novelists overload their plays with masses of words. Personally, I am quite determined to be good at both!"

Coward on Theatre vs. Cinema

In his early years—which were also the early years of the cinema—Noël could be loftily dismissive.

He confided to *Picturegoer* magazine . . .

"You may take it that I am not interested in writing scenarios at all. I want to write words, not stage directions . . . As a dramatist, dialogue and its psychology are practically my whole career."

In later years he would moderate his views but . . .

"I'll always love the theatre a little better and I know why that is. It's the contact with an audience. I'd rather play a bad matinée in Hull . . . [what upset him in Hull we'll never know!] . . . than do a movie, even though I enjoy doing movies."

Admittedly he'd suffered the experience of seeing several of his early plays sacrificed to the silent cinema. A Coward play without the Coward dialogue was little more than a plot that any competent playwright could devise. Despite this Noël did write a "scenario" at that time. It was called *Concerto* and it was never made. He later used it as the basis for *Bitter Sweet*.

Later, of course, came *In Which We Serve* and all his creative reservations disappeared.

On Being Creative After Forty

When Noël turned forty on December 16, 1939, a magazine asked him if he would agree that a creative artist does his best work after the age of forty?

"Certainly. Look at Michelangelo, Leonardo da Vinci, Verdi, Bernard Shaw and me. Mind you, with regard to the last-named, opinion seems to vary as to whether it is my 'best' work, but I do not propose to let that worry me in the least. For who is to say with any certainty which of an artist's works are his best? Everyone knows that contemporary judgment is not to be relied upon and in fact it is a fairly safe rule to take the opposite view to the current one. Even Time will not tell, for an artist is sometimes remembered and loved for his more popular works rather than his best . . . You will notice that the artists I mentioned have one thing in common—certainly the only thing I have in common with them—*a large output*. They worked hard before they came to forty year, and then went on working hard for the rest of their productive lives. I do not see why a writer should lay down his pen on the stroke of forty any more than a mechanic his spanner or a surgeon his scalpel."

＝＝

So what does it all add up to . . . ?

"Wit and charm are not enough. The race is to the swift and you've got to work like mad in this world if you want to get anything and, above all, sustain anything."

(1947)

6

. . . AND ACTORS

"And One Man in His Time Plays Many Parts . . ."

—*AS YOU LIKE IT*

.

"If you were to put me on a stage with Laurence Olivier, John Gielgud, and Ralph Richardson, they would be acting me off the stage
and out of the auditorium—but everyone would be looking at me."

—NOËL COWARD

.

The actors are come hither, my lord.
The best actors in the world, either for tragedy,
comedy, history, pastoral, pastoral-comical,
historical-pastoral, tragical-historical,
tragical-comical-historical-pastoral, scene
individable, or poem unlimited . . . For the law
of wit and the liberty, these are the only men.

—POLONIUS IN *HAMLET*

.

JOANNA: I expect it's because you're an actor, they're always a bit
papier-mâché.
GARRY: Just puppets, Joanna dear, creatures of tinsel and sawdust,
how clever of you to have noticed it.

—*PRESENT LAUGHTER* (1939)

.

"Actors are incredibly silly and leading ladies idiotic."

—NOËL COWARD

"The players . . . are the abstracts and brief chronicles of the time."
—*HAMLET*

CONSIDER THE PUBLIC
A Warning to Actors

Having, in a previous article, delivered a measure of warning and advice to our pioneer playwrights, I should like, in this essay, to give a few pointers to our young actors and actresses. Before I begin laying about me, however, I must say in all fairness that the standard of acting among the youth of our New Movement in the theatre is, within its limits, remarkably high. Nevertheless, "within its limits" is the operative phrase, for these limits, imposed principally by left-wing socialism, are dangerously narrow.

To perform small grey plays in small grey theatres with the maximum of realism and the minimum of make-up is a great deal easier than to play classic drama or modern comedy with enough style and technical assurance to convince an audience of fifteen hundred to two thousand people.

This is largely the fault of contemporary playwrights and directors but not entirely. It is also the fault of the actors themselves for they should realise that *one* approach to the mastery of their medium, however intelligent that approach may be, is not enough. The duty of every young actor, regardless of what political beliefs he may hold, or what particular class he comes from, is to widen his views and his scope as much as possible.

Many of our greatest and most distinguished actors and actresses have come from humble beginnings and one of the principal contributory causes of their later greatness and distinction was the fact that they were not content to stay as they were. With determination, hard work and concentration they strove during their early years to improve themselves. They studied dancing, fencing and elocution; they banished from their speech, both on the stage and off it, the tell-tale accents of their early environments; they trained their ears and their tongues to master alien dialects, and to many of them the most alien of these was the speech of the educated. In fact they rigorously disciplined themselves to a point where they could play Kings and Queens, north country farmers, foreign diplomats, Cockney cab drivers, Irish colleens, Welsh miners and average middle-class business men, without strain and with equal authenticity. I have noticed few signs of this deliberately and painstakingly acquired versatility to-day.

Theatrically, one of the more depressing aspects of the present transition phase through which the civilized world is passing, is the monotonous emphasis on the lot of the Common Man; for the Common Man, unless written and portrayed with genius, is not dramatically nearly so interesting as he is claimed to be. A glance at the list of currently successful plays in London will show that the public, on the whole, prefer to see extraordinary people on the stage rather than ordinary ones; fantastic situations rather than familiar, commonplace ones, and actors of outsize personality and talent rather than accurately competent mediocrities.

I am quite prepared to admit that during my fifty odd years of theatre going, I have on many occasions been profoundly moved by plays about the Common Man, as in my fifty odd years of restaurant going I have frequently enjoyed tripe and onions, but I am not prepared to admit that an exclusive diet of either would be entirely satisfying. In this I am fully convinced that the general public is in complete agreement with me.

From the acting point of view, of course, the Common Man is the easiest and most immediately rewarding assignment in the theatre, particularly in straight, down-to-earth plays where no comedy values are involved. For any experienced actor who has mastered the poetic nuances of Shakespearean verse and the intricate subtleties of modern high comedy, "Dear Old Dad" in a kitchen sink drama is the equivalent of a couple of aspirin and a nice lie-down. Some years ago when I was giving alternate performances of *Present Laughter* and *This Happy Breed* at the Haymarket Theatre I can remember to this day the relief I used to feel when, after a matinée of the former with its tension and tempo and concentrated timing, I returned in the evening to play Frank Gibbons in *This Happy Breed.* To wander about in shirt-sleeves, take off my boots, pick my nose and drink cups of tea was so infinitely less demanding than dashing about at high speed in coloured dressing gowns and delivering comedy lines accurately enough to reach the back of the gallery.

This brings me, with a slight yawn, to what is colloquially known as The Method.

A number of years ago Vladimir Ilitch Lenin was conveyed, in a sealed compartment, across Europe to Russia. This furtive adventure resulted in a great deal of trouble for a great many people. A few years later, whether in a sealed compartment or not I have no idea, a book by Constantine Stanislavski found its way to America where it, in its turn, caused a great deal of trouble to a great many actors, actresses, directors and, ultimately, to the unfortunate public. The only ones who benefited from it being a few performers who, having proved themselves dismally inadequate on the stage, decided to set themselves up as teachers.

Actually there were two books, *My Life in Art* and *An Actor Prepares*, in both of which Mr. Stanislavski states his views on the art of acting. In the former, which is autobiographical, he explains without humour but in merciless detail, his psychological, spiritual and technical approach to every part he played in the course of his distinguished career. These esoteric soul-searchings are accompanied by a series of photographs which prove at least that he was a great one for the nose paste and crepe hair and not above a comical posture or two when the role demanded it.

In *An Actor Prepares* he is more objective and, under the thin disguise of a director called Tortsov, he sets out to explain his theories to a group of embarrassingly earnest young drama students. That this book should become a sort of theatrical bible in Russia is quite understandable. It is written by a Russian for Russians with, naturally enough, a proper appreciation of the Russian temperament, but that it should be regarded as holy writ to the theatrical youth of the Western world is less understandable and to my mind excessively tiresome.

It would be foolish to deny that among Mr. Stanislavski's analyses of acting there are not a few simple and basic truths concealed beneath his laboured and tortuous verbiage, but these truths are so simple and so basic that I doubt if they would have called forth more than a casual grunt of agreement from the late Sarah Siddons.

There is quite a lot to be said in favour of certain aspects of The Method. It stresses a few essential "musts" such as the necessity of finding the correct psychological values of the part to be played and concentrating first on the interior truth of a character before attempting the exterior projection of it.

In my opinion The Method places too much emphasis on actual realism and too little on simulated realism. To Be, up to a point, and Not To Be, over and above that point, is the whole art and craft of acting. Every intelligent actor realises the impossibility of *genuinely* feeling the emotions necessary to his part for eight performances a week over a period of months or even years. His art lies in his ability to recreate nightly an accurate simulation of the emotions he originally felt when he was first studying and rehearsing it. If acting were actually a state of "Being," anybody playing a heavy dramatic role in a smash success would be in a mental home after a few weeks. In any event, emotion on the stage without the technique to project it and the ability to control it merely results in mistiming and untidiness and has nothing whatsoever to do with acting.

Technique, although a much despised word nowadays, is, beyond a shadow of doubt, indispensable. It is impossible to give a consistent and continued performance without it. However progressive and revolutionary a young actor's theories may be and however many rules, conventions and traditions he may hold in contempt as being "ham" and old fashioned, he would be well advised to learn these rules, conventions and traditions before attempting to break them. It is as palpably foolish for an actor to try to play a major role, or even a minor one for that matter, without first learning to move about the stage and speak audibly, as it would be for a budding pianist or violinist to embark on a concerto without first having mastered his scales. And it is here that I feel that The Method, as a method, breaks down. I myself have heard a famous Method teacher in New York inform a student that audibility was unimportant compared with "the moment of truth!" This lofty statement of course evaporates immediately when even cursorily examined, for how can *fifty* moments of truth be of the faintest significance on the stage if no one in the auditorium can hear what the actors are talking about?

In addition to a large number of grimy, introspective, megalomaniacs, The Method has undoubtedly produced a small number of brilliant actors. But then so has the Royal Academy of Dramatic Art, The Old Vic Drama School and every other sort of acting school down to "Miss Weatherby's Shakespeare in Twelve Easy Lessons, 36, Station Approach, Sidcup."

Genuine talent can profit from or survive any given system of instruction, although unquestionably the best training of all is acting to paying audiences either in touring companies or repertory companies. Audience reaction is of paramount importance to learning the job, for without it, the acting, however brilliant, has no point. To perform to a handful of fellow students and relatives in a small fit-up studio theatre is a waste of time and not even good practice; in fact it is very often bad practice because the reaction, both from teachers and prejudiced spectators, can be misleading. The aim of every budding actor should be to get himself in front of a paying audience, no matter where, as soon as he possibly can.

This salutary experience might conceivably rub off a little of the solemn, dedicated gloom that Mr. Stanislavski and his disciples have imposed on our hitherto cheerful and fairly ramshackle profession. The Theatre may be regarded as an Art with a capital letter, a craft, a means of earning a living or even a showcase for personal exhibitionism, but it is not and should not be a religion. I am all in favour of actors taking their work seriously, in fact on many occasions I have been accused of being a martinet in this respect. But I am definitely not in favour of every member of the company embarking on endless, ego-feeding, quasi-theological discussions of the possible reactions and motivations of the parts they have to play. If they have studied the play intelligently and learnt the words they should *know* the necessary reactions and motivations already and not waste my time and their own in gabbing about them. All this tedious argument, recapitulation and verbose questing after "Truth," apart from giving the individual actor an overblown opinion of his own intellectual prowess, is pretentious nonsense and not to be tolerated for a moment by a director of integrity. The director of a play is analogous to the Captain of a ship, and few ships' Captains in moment of crisis lend a benign and tolerant ear to the suggestions of every minor member of the crew.

Another, to my mind, dangerous assumption on the part of the Method teachers is that actors are cerebral and can be relied upon to approach the playing of a part intellectually. In my experience, the really fine actors whom I have known and admired and often worked with have been, in varying degrees, intelligent, shrewd, egotistical, temperamental, emotional and, above all, intuitive, but never either logical or intellectual. Their approach to their work, according to their respective characters and techniques, is guided almost mystically by their talent.

It is this that has propelled them up from the ranks of small part players into the position of loved and envied stardom. It is this, combined with every trick and technical device they have acquired on the way, which enables them on a nerve-strained, agonized opening night to rise supremely to the challenge and sweep the play into success. And it is this, curiously enough, in which most of them have the least confidence and for which they require the most reassurance. However much self-confidence they may appear to have, this basic uncertainty is their most valuable and endearing asset. It is also the hallmark of the genuine article. I have encountered few fine actors and few real stars in the true meaning of the word who, beneath God knows how much egotism, temperament and outward flamboyance do not possess a fundamental humility.

Alas and alack, I have encountered quite a number of our young actors and actresses of to-day who, sodden with pretentious theories and trained to concentrate solely on their own reactions and motivations to the exclusion of their fellow actors and the audience, have not even a bowing acquaintance with humility. They apparently despise the far past as thoroughly as they despise the immediate past. They arrogantly condemn the "commercial" theatre, which in essence means the public that they must hope ultimately to please, thereby, it seems to me, spitting in the eye of the golden goose before it has even met the gander.

It is this innate contempt for the values of other days which accounts, I presume, for their physical slovenliness on the stage. I have watched, with Edwardian dismay, these talented young creatures arriving at a rehearsal. The boys, unshaven, wearing grubby open-necked sweaters and stained leather coats, and with dark finger nails. The girls, in strained jeans, equally grubby sweaters, with their hair unwashed and unbrushed or twisted into unalluring pony-tails. Admittedly this very young sartorial defiance is perfectly consistent with most of the parts they are called upon to play, but my point is that if they are really to succeed over the years they will be called upon to play all sorts and kinds of parts and that all this initial grubbiness will suddenly turn out to be a severe handicap. There is, after all, no theatrical law decreeing that an actor should identify himself off stage with whatever he is going to play on stage. In point of fact it is a dangerous and confusing premise. Slovenliness of appearance all too often indicates slovenliness of mind and no actor can afford to have that.

I do not wish to imply by the above that I am so advanced in my dotage as to be entirely out of sympathy with the facile defiance of the young. I was young myself once; defiant, pushing and self-confident— outwardly at least—and, like most intelligent, ambitious youngsters, I imagined I knew a great deal more than I actually did. But never, in all my youthful arrogance, was I idiotic enough to allow myself to be influenced by any current political creed, nor conceited enough to curl my lip contemptuously at the "great" of the theatre because they happened to be commercially successful.

On the contrary, I was deeply in awe of them and blushed with pride whenever one of them deigned to speak to me. I had only two presentable suits, but these were daily pressed within an inch of their lives. I would never have dreamed of attending even an understudy rehearsal, and in those days I attended many, without going to immense pains to look my very best.

The theatre should be treated with respect. The theatre is a wonderful place, a house of strange enchantment, a temple of illusion. What it most emphatically is not and never will be is a scruffy, ill-lit, fumed-oak drill-hall serving as a temporary soap-box for political propaganda.

The theatre still spells magic for many millions of people and that magic should be a source of deep pride to all those who are privileged to serve in it.

(Originally published under the title "The Scratch-and-Mumble School" in *The Sunday Times* on January 22, 1961.)

Coward on "The Method"

He would have more to say on the subject . . .

"What is my motivation here?" an actor would start to ask. "Why do I put the drink down here—and not there? Would my character even have a drink at all?"

Noël had no patience with it. "Every star I've ever known has had a method. But there can be no one Method." His concern was that an actor's excessive search for "motivation" encouraged too much introspection and too often broke up the rhythm of rehearsal.

"The influence of psycho-analysis on acting is a great bore. Whether the actor is right with himself is not in the least important. It's being right with the part that matters . . . When you've learned the words, analyse the part. Find out what it's about.

"When he goes out on that stage, an actor should forget himself and remember the part . . . remember the other actors who are sharing the stage with you. Look at them. Not at their foreheads. Not at their ears. But at their eyes. Then learn to laugh and cry—without feeling happy or sad."

He parted company with Method actors who felt they should inhabit and "live" their parts . . .

"You cannot 'be' on stage. You can only create the *illusion* of being . . . You must create a replica that can be delivered to every audience."

Only when the intellectual approach to the role had been settled did the technical aspects of the performance come into play . . .

"Take care to project, pushing the words forward in the mouth. The good actor projects without shouting. He must appear intimate and at ease—but every individual word must be heard.

"Do justice to the playwright first and only then to yourself as an actor.

"Oh, and it's still a good idea not to bump into the furniture—or your fellow actors."

———

To describe all the actors who came hither in Noël's life would take an encyclopedia. But key elements of his personal and professional life can be seen by examining his relationship to . . .

His key competitors—John Gielgud and Laurence Olivier.

Sir John Gielgud (1904–2000)

Late in life Noël would record . . . "I'm proud to say that in an earlier stage of my career Johnny was my understudy . . . To work with he was absolutely extraordinary. A most generous, genuinely modest big actor. There's nothing fake about him, he is absolutely true . . . I've always loved working with Johnny . . . I think he's wonderful."

Their working relationship began with *The Vortex* in 1924 and Noël recalled—"I had arranged to stay off for the Monday and Tuesday performances and allow my understudy to play for me. I would never behave so casually to the public nowadays, but then I was new to stardom and unencumbered by any particular sense of responsibility. Incidentally, my understudy happened to be a keen young actor called John Gielgud, so in the light of later events, the public were not really being cheated at all."

Noël might not have been so laudatory had he known what Gielgud wrote in his first night programme . . .

After admitting that it was a "very brilliant play, with a fine third act" and that Lilian Braithwaite "in a magnificent part, has never done anything better," he decided that "Coward himself lacked charm and personality and played the piano too loudly, though he acted sincerely

John Gielgud (June 1939).

and forcefully as far as he could. The play is certainly an amazing achieve-ment for him, and the end of the 2nd act and all the third are really fine."

However a second visit persuaded him that Noël's performance at the end of the second act convinced him—

"In the tiny auditorium the atmosphere was extraordinarily tense, and the curtain of the second act, with Noël sitting in profile to the audience, his white face lifted, chin jutting forward, head thrown back, playing that infuriating little tune over and over, louder and louder, until the curtain fell, was one of the most effective things I had ever seen in the theatre."

He could also admit that when he played Nicky himself—"It seemed to me that the only way to say the lines was to imitate as nearly as pos-sible the way he had said them, and this kind of mimicry led me into some rather mannered habits. Coward's style of speech and manner is not quite the same as mine, although my clipped vowels and rather stacccato manner are not altogether unlike his. Perhaps in the twenties we all talked a bit like that . . . a brittle, crackling staccato . . . Coward, after all, was the angry young man of the day, and we all thought it smart to copy him."

And years later he would write to Noël that "In a way I have always thought that my success in the theatre only began after *The Vortex* time."

The "keen young actor" was to step in again when Noël was appearing in *The Constant Nymph* a year or two later. The role of Lewis Dodd was not a comfortable fit and it wasn't long before Noël contrived an "illness" that forced him to leave his passive pipe-smoking character. His guilty conscience was somewhat put to rest when "John Gielgud took over my part—pipe and all—and played it beautifully, and the play continued for a considerable time after I left."

Gielgud's own recollection—"Noël realized he must try to supress his characteristic mannerism of clipped speech for the first time. With the help of director Basil Dean he succeeded in giving a character performance of greater variety and depth than he had attempted since *The Vortex*."

———

Much as he admired John over the years, there were certain philosophical differences.

In his acting style Noël often found him "a little false in his performance . . . but very effective." He would also worry about what mounted to an obsession with John about possessing the "Terry voice," inherited from his family and in describing him as being "verbally beautiful," which was qualified praise.

Gielgud also questioned Noël's insistence on an actor arriving at first rehearsal word perfect . . .

"In my view, it is much easier to learn the words when you have the movements and the business. It is important to know how the other actor is going to speak his lines, so that both of you can react properly. If you start absolutely word-perfect, like a parrot, I think it makes everything flat and dull."

Despite that, Noël said frequently that he admired Gielgud because "he has never been afraid to fail. As a result, he has the greatest range of all of them."

———

In the world of Theatre Gielgud achieved a second eminence—as a dropper of verbal bricks. He himself admitted that he had dropped enough "to build a new Wall of China." They came to be known as "Gielgoodies."

Example. At lunch in the Ivy a man passes their table. "Thank God he didn't stop," says Gielgud, "he's a bigger bore than Eddie Knoblock." His host was Eddie Knoblock.

Two West End theatres were back-to-back. Gielgud was going in one stage door when he saw an actor he knew going into the one next door. Gielgud greeted him cheerfully. "Your show not going too well, I hear." Then lightning struck. "Oh, my God, I directed it, didn't I?"

As the years went by their personal friendship deepened and Noël found "Johnny G." to be a highly entertaining houseguest, the words tumbling out of his mouth, frequently having to stop and wipe away his own tears of laughter at the funniness of the disasters he recounted, disasters always against himself.

═══

Noël and Johnny G. were not to work together again for another thirty years.

Noël was approached to play a scene in producer Mike Todd's film of *Around the World in 80 Days*. He was meant to be cast with Laurence Olivier but Larry predictably dithered and finally said no. Gielgud was signed instead . . .

"On Tuesday I got up at crack of dawn and went to Elstree. It was a very successful day and Johnny and I managed to do the whole scene. Johnny was charming to work with. He was, as usual, a little false in his performance but very effective. If Larry had played it in a dreadful, refined Cockney accent it would have been hilarious; as it was, it was perfectly all right. All the people at the studio were extremely nice and I thoroughly enjoyed the day."

═══

In 1956 Noël wrote a play that been loitering at the back of his mind for ages. The subject was modern art and he was motivated by a book he was reading . . .

The result was *Nude with Violin*. Gielgud was signed to play the lead, Sebastien, and also direct.

It was to be their final collaboration but their personal friendship would only end when Noël made his final Exit.

Laurence Olivier (1907–1989)

There are few who would deny that Laurence Olivier was the greatest actor of his generation.

His professional path first crossed Noël's with the 1930 *Private Lives*. He was cast as Victor, current husband of Amanda opposite Sybil (Adrianne Allen), current wife of Elyot. Even though Noël had written the parts as little more than foils for the two leads—Gertie and himself—he realized that the other two characters had to come across as credible replacement partners. The parts must be strongly played if the balance was to be credible.

By the time Noël cast him, "Larry Boy" was beginning to make a name for himself as a romantic lead and was perhaps a little too full of himself. Before Noël disciplined him ruthlessly for "corpsing" (see the chapter on "Acting") he had acquired something of a reputation for behaving inappropriately on stage.

As a young actor with the Lena Ashwell Players he was playing the small part of Flavius in *Julius Caesar*. At one point he was required to tear down a couple of tatty-looking wreaths. In doing so, he found that by a twist of the wrist he could take with them the black velvet backing.

On the SS *Normandie* (1937).

Fellow cast members were treated to a tantalizing glimpse of the bare bottoms of several ladies who were changing costumes behind it. Miss Ashwell saw to it that he was soon looking for a new job.

Noël saw to it that he dropped the habit.

He was also among the first to spot Larry's obsession with changing his physical appearance onstage . . . "I cannot think of any living actor who has used such quantities of spirit-gum with such gleeful abandon. I believe that this rather excessive determination to be old before his time is the result of an integral shyness in his character. He has never had the smallest inclination to look or be himself on the stage."

They were never to appear together onstage again but their friendship remained close, surviving troubling episodes such as Larry's tortured marriage to and divorce from Vivien Leigh . . . and Larry's strong disapproval of Noël's decision to leave England and become a tax exile in the mid-1950s.

Even so they both made sure during this thirty-year professional hiatus to see any stage or film production the other appeared in and convey their professional opinion.

Then in 1964 came a reunion.

The long-planned National Theatre was finally a reality and its first Director General was—Sir Laurence Olivier.

Since the actual building was yet to be completed, the production would be housed at the Old Vic and Olivier wanted the opening season to include *Hay Fever*. He also wanted Noël to direct it.

Much as he wanted to, Noël felt he shouldn't undertake what was bound to be a challenging task. His health had been deteriorating for some time. He wrote to Larry . . .

I've learned a pretty severe lesson and have accordingly promised myself (and the doctor) not to engage in any directorial activities whatsoever for at least a year. I may write fourteen plays, seven novels and appear in a series of ravishing movie cameos but I would rather undertake to play *Peer Gynt on Ice* than show one actor, however talented, how to walk across the stage. (Incidentally, I find that very few actors nowadays know how to achieve this minor miracle.)

I know that you, of all people, will understand this very well.

I hate letting you down like this and please believe that I wouldn't, unless it were absolutely unavoidable.

It is being slowly and painfully beaten into my skull that I am no longer a precocious boy of nineteen, although when I look into the mirror at this lovely little heart-shaped face with all those pretty little jowls hanging from it, I find it hard to believe.

Please cable or write to me when you get this letter saying that you understand and forgive your loving old Noëlie.

A little later either his health improved dramatically or the lure of *Hay Fever* proved too much . . .

There were to be two footnotes.

The following year Noël played one of his "ravishing movie cameos" in Otto Preminger's *Bunny Lake Is Missing* as a rather effete landlord. Playing a stolid police inspector was—Larry.

The circle was completed at a celebration of Noël's seventieth birthday at Claridge's. When Noël finally made his way to the piano, it was Larry who was on hand to push the chair beneath him. If he hadn't, Noël would have found himself sitting on thin air!

After all his other achievements in forty years Larry had learned to be the ideal supporting player.

Gertrude Lawrence (1898–1952)

"Gertie lived her entire life in an imaginary screening room, forever watching her own rushes."

"Gertie was always acting out some role. Most actresses when they write a book about their youth recall the crunch of carriage-wheels in the drive. Gertie recalled eating kippers in the gutter, which, of course, was completely untrue."

In the obituary for the London *Times* he wrote—"No one I have ever known, however gifted or however brilliant, has contributed quite what she has contributed to my work."

When Noël Peirce Coward (thirteen) and Gertrude Alexandra Dagmar Lawrence-Klausen (fourteen), both child actors, met on a train in 1913, it was the beginning of a unique theatrical partnership—'Noël & Gertie."

They were both cast as angels in a rather dreary play which they accidentally enlivened with a piece of business that was definitely not in the script. They had overindulged in peppermint creams and the curtain rose to reveal two little cherubs being comprehensively sick over the scenery.

Their first professional collaboration as adults would be in the 1923 revue *London Calling!* for producer André Charlot—to which Noël contributed significantly.

That was interrupted by Charlot's decision to take a show to Broadway which would be a composite of several of his previous revues. It would star Jack Buchanan, Beatrice Lillie, and Gertie—but not Noël.

Their reunion would have to wait another seven years and a degree of happenstance.

On a 1929 trip to the Far East Noël wrote *Private Lives.*

That was the easy part. Pinning down Ms. Lawrence was not.

He cabled her . . .

HAVE WRITTEN DELIGHTFUL NEW COMEDY STOP GOOD PART FOR YOU STOP WONDERFUL ONE FOR ME STOP KEEP YOURSELF FREE FOR AUTUMN PRODUCTION

The lady replied . . .

HAVE READ NEW PLAY STOP NOTHING WRONG THAT CAN'T BE FIXED STOP GERTIE

Then . . .

THE ONLY THING THAT WILL NEED TO BE FIXED IS YOUR PERFORMANCE STOP NOËL

Private Lives opened London's new Phoenix Theatre, and "Noël&Gertie" became established in the public mind as a single entity.

Many people came to believe that—like the Lunts in the U.S.—they acted exclusively together but that was not to be the case. Six years later they would costar again in Noël's *Tonight at 8:30*. Later there were several projects but none came to fruition. Nor did they need to. A legend was already born that lives on.

Around that time Noël tried to pin down what he felt about his "other half" . . .

She has an astounding sense of the complex reality of the moment, and her moments, dictated by the extreme variability of her moods, change so swiftly that it is frequently difficult to discover what, apart from eating, sleeping and acting, is true of her at all. I know her well, better, I believe, than most people. The early years of our friendship set her strongly in my mind. I knew her then to have quick humour, insane generosity and a loving heart, and those things seldom change. I see her now, ages away from her ringlets and black velvet military cap, sometimes a simple, wide-eyed child, sometimes a glamorous *femme du monde,* at some moments a rather boisterous "good sort," at others a weary, disillusioned woman battered by life but gallant to the last. There are many other grades also between these two extremes. She appropriated beauty to herself quite early, along with all the tricks and mannerisms that go with it. In adolescence she was barely pretty. Now, without apparent effort, she gives the impression of sheer loveliness. Her grace in movement is exquisite, and her voice charming. To disentangle Gertie herself from this mutability is baffling, rather like delving for your grandmother's gold locket at the bottom of an overflowing jewel-case.

Her talent is equally kaleidoscopic. On the stage she is potentially capable of anything and everything. She can be gay, sad, witty, tragic, funny and touching. She can play a scene one night with perfect subtlety and restraint, and the next with such obviousness and over-emphasis that your senses reel. She has, in abundance, every theatrical essential but one: critical faculty. She can watch a great actor and be stirred to the depths, her emotional response is immediate and genuine. She can watch a bad actor and be stirred to the depths, the response is equally immediate and equally genuine. But for this tantalizing lack of discrimination she could, I believe, be the greatest actress alive in the theatre today.

Her greatest fault is to embroider her performance after a few weeks with improvisations and funny business, which sometimes spoils the clean line of her otherwise brilliant readings.

It may amuse her but it drives me mad.

On October 13, 1931, Noël's pageant/play *Cavalcade* opened at the Theatre Royal, Drury Lane, and Gertie was in the first night audience. She wrote to him . . .

Noel, my darling,

Here I am down on my knees to you in humble admiration and complete adoration.

I didn't wire you last night because I felt too NEAR you to mix my stupid pence worth of good wishes with those many who couldn't have been feeling as deeply as I was; but please believe me when I tell you that I spent the whole evening from eight 'til eleven with my hand tightly clasped in yours—ANYTHING just to feel that I might perhaps be of some some subconscious support to you. As you say, it's "pretty exciting to be English." But also it's pretty exciting to love you as I do!

This, you may be surprised to see is from
"Ole Gert"

In 1940 Gertie married Richard Aldrich, the son of a well-connected "society" family and the owner of the Cape Playhouse in Massachusetts.

Noël could not resist a teasing cable to mark the event . . .

DEAR MRS. A HOORAY HOORAY AT LAST YOU ARE DEFLOWERED STOP ON THIS AS EVERY OTHER DAY I LOVE YOU STOP NOEL COWARD

A little poetic license here, as Gertie would have been the last to claim to be an innocent modest maiden.

She would devote much of her time to the Playhouse in the years ahead and during the war years—like Noël—she would travel a great deal entertaining the armed forces. She also found time to star on Broadway in the Kurt Weill–Ira Gershwin musical *Lady in the Dark*.

Again, it was Noël who made up her dithering mind for her. And on opening night another Coward cable . . .

HOPE YOU GET A WARM HAND ON YOUR OPENING

As the war ended she was still being offered plays but none of them appealed. Like Noël, she was in the theatrical doldrums and their personal past was still all too present.

In 1947 she suggested to him that they might revive *Tonight at 8:30* because "It stands to reason that SOMEONE will get the bright idea and we shall only have ourselves to blame." Noël was not at all keen to repeat himself but, when he realized that Gertie was having money troubles— not for the first time—he reluctantly agreed to a short U.S. tour but with Graham Payn playing his own original parts.

The tour was modestly successful—with one particular highlight.

In San Francisco . . .

"Went down to see Graham (before the show). He felt weak and so we decided that he had better lay off the matinée and only play tonight. Suddenly decided to play the matinée myself. 'Shadow Play' and 'Hands Across the Sea.' I flew down to the theatre and started rehearsing at 1:20 and was on at 2:30. I was proud of the fact that I didn't dry up once. The performance was not bad. The company and audience were thrilled but it was all rather exhausting."

It was also the last time he would play opposite Gertie. It brought back so many memories. For her part—"I would so much like us to be back once more hand in hand at curtain calls."

But they were so much two sides of the same coin that there would inevitably be a professional encore . . . another musical, another play.

Golden days at Goldenhurst. Left to right: Bea Lillie, Bobbie Andrews, Gertie, and Noël.

Private Lives (1930).

But there wasn't. Several possibilities, several near misses.

Then Gertie starred on Broadway in *The King and I.* She'd bought the rights to *Anna and the King of Siam,* so that she could play Anna Leonowens, the Victorian lady who goes to work in the Court of the King. She persuaded Rodgers and Hammerstein to turn it into a musical for her and wanted Noël to play the King opposite her.

Noël could see perfectly well that the show was likely to be a big hit and involve the kind of long run that was anathema to him. He refused and recommended a young cabaret performer he'd seen in a Greenwich Village nightclub. His name was Yul Brynner.

He was correct in his prediction of the show's success. But a problem appeared quite early on. It was to do with Gertie's voice. Never strong, it was finding it increasingly difficult to cope, even though Rodgers had written the score specifically to fit her limited vocal range.

There came a point when both Rodgers and Hammerstein came to Noël for help. Could he help devise a plan to lure Gertie to leave the show? Write a new vehicle for the two of them, perhaps? Noël understood the situation all too well and tried his best to persuade her . . .

April 29, 1952

Lunched with Gertie, who was at her best. Advised her to leave *The King and I* for good. I did not say they were anxious to get rid of her because of her singing, but I think I convinced her that she ought to do a straight play. I also said I would be prepared to rewrite *Island Fling* for her. I am sure that, with some reconstruction, it would be a success with her playing it.

He was overconfident. Gertie was determined to take *The King and I* to London the following year, which would be Coronation Year. She soldiered on.

Then . . .

November 6

A day that started gaily ended in misery. The happy part was going to the Folkestone races with Coley [his assistant Cole Lesley] and Gladys. I backed several winners and it was great fun. Just as I was leaving Coley told me it was in the Stop Press that Gertie Lawrence was dead. I drove home to Goldenhurst feeling dreadful. The telephone never stopped ringing. The Press all agog.

I dined with Gladys and then came home and wrote an obituary for *The Times*. This was agony and I broke down several times, but pressed on and finished it . . . Poor, darling old Gertie—a lifelong friend. With all her overacting and silliness, I have never known her do a mean or an unkind thing. I am terribly, terribly unhappy to think that I shall never see her again.

Not for a moment had he—or, indeed, anyone else close to her—realized how ill she was. She'd written to him not long before . . .

Well, whadderyerno??

After that short siege of vocal doldrums my voice suddenly returned, my spirits rose, and my hackles fairly bristled with vitality . . . So it seems there is not too much to worry about—I just struck a bad patch and you came and sat in it!!

Oh, dear—and it's always you I want to please above ANYONE.

The definitive portrait of Gertie and Noël that had pride of place on his piano at Chalet Coward.

But it wasn't just a "bad patch." The only one with a premonition was her friend and sometime lover, Daphne du Maurier, who later wrote to Noël . . .

I was pretty sure something was wrong and had been for some time. That real exhaustion to do anything every Sunday but just lie on the *chaise longue,* turban on her head, Nivea skin oil on her face, plaid rug over the knees, steam heat on at full blast, enough to kill anyone. Angus the Scottie lying panting at her feet.

Why, oh why should someone with the mind of somebody of ten— with whom one really had no thought in common, no topic of real conversation, no sort of outlook resembling one's own at all, who frequently lied, who never stopped doing the most infuriating things—have the power to so completely wrap herself around the heart that, because of her, one became bitched, buggered and bewildered?

The night before I left—and it will be my last memory of her—she had the eternal radio switched on, it went on through the night, and suddenly your *Bitter Sweet* song came over, the "I'll See You Again" song, and she began to sing it from her pillow, in that lilting sexless, choirboy voice that was her true voice, very softly, and I told her that was what I meant, to sing always like that, but she said I was being sentimental, and rushed off to some new teacher who was to make her sing like Patti, Melba, Fladstadt, the works.

I'll see you again
Whenever Spring breaks through again.
Time may lie heavy between,
But what has been
Is past forgetting.
Your sweet memory
Across the years will come to me.
Though my world may go awry,
In my heart will ever lie
Just the echo of a sigh,
Goodbye.

Though my world
Has gone awry
And I never said Goodbye,
I shall love you till I die—
Goodbye.

——

"Sometimes I would look across the stage at her—and she would take my breath away."

——

A decade later in *The Girl Who Came to Supper* he wrote a song which echoed his feelings for her . . .

I'll Remember Her
I'll remember her,
How incredibly naive she was,
I couldn't quite believe she was
Sincere
So alert
So impertinent
And yet so sweet.
My defeat was clear.
I'll remember her,
Her absurd exaggerating
And her utterly deflating

Repartee
And the only thing that worries me at all
Is whether she'll remember me.

I'll remember her
In the evenings when I'm lonely
And imagining if only
She were there.
I'll relive,
Oh, so vividly,
Our sad and sweet,
Incomplete
Affair.

I'll remember her
Heavy-hearted when we parted.
With her eyes so full of tears she couldn't see
And I'll feel inside a foolish sort of pride
To think that she remembers me.

THE LUNTS

ALFRED LUNT (1892–1977)
LYNN FONTANNE (1887–1983)

On his first trip to New York in 1921 Noël met a number of people who would become friends for life.

One of them was Lynn Fontanne, a young English actress who had moved to America. When he wrote to his mother . . .

"Do you remember Lynn Fontanne? She played some small parts in London, was 'adopted' by Laurette Taylor—now there's a character— and came to New York. Well, she's had a huge success in a play called *Dulcy* (she's Dulcy). I went to see her opening night with her fiancé, an actor called Alfred Lunt and, my dear, a star was born. Well, two stars, actually, as Alfred is also making a name for himself in these parts.

"They're quite wonderful and couldn't have been kinder to me. They haven't any money either—though they soon will have, I'm sure—and they helped keep me body and soul together by sharing their last crust

At Ten Chimneys, Genesse Depot, c. 1930.

(not quite that really!). They're going to be huge stars and, since we all know that yours truly is going to be one, too, we've decided that, when that great day arrives, we shall act together in a play I shall write for us and the cosmos will have a new galaxy."

In *Present Indicative* he elaborated . . .

"She and Alfred were, to put it mildly, 'courting' at the moment, and lived in a theatrical lodging-house somewhere in the West Seventies . . . The food was good, and the house comfortably untidy . . . From these shabby, congenial rooms, we projected ourselves into future eminence. We discussed, the three of us, over delicatessen potato salad and dill pickles, our most secret dreams of success. Lynn and Alfred were to be married. That was the first plan. Then they were to become definitely idols of the public. That was the second plan. Then, all this being successfully accomplished, they were to act exclusively together. This was the third plan. It remained for me to supply the fourth, which was that when all three of us had become stars of sufficient magnitude to be able to count on an individual following of each other, then, poised serenely upon that enviable plane of achievement, we would meet and act triumphantly together.

Laurette Taylor (1884–1946).
The inspiration for Judith Bliss in
Hay Fever. After she saw the play,
Taylor didn't speak to Noël for
several years.

"After these prophetic orgies, we ofen found it necessary to bring ourselves down to earth by taking brisk walks to the corner of the street and
back, or going to the pictures. Once Lynn and I even sank so low as to
make a charabanc trip to Chinatown."

Twelve years later in 1933 Plan 4 duly came to pass.

The three of them acted in Noël's *Design for Living* and, as he would
recall—"All three of us gave the worst performances of our careers every
night for months—and managed to be very good indeed!"

———

In later years he would say that it was his favorite play.

World War II caused an Intermission but the friendship continued
to flourish. Lynn was busily keeping the home fires burning, even at a
distance . . .

January 8, 1940

Darling, darling,

We received your lovely letter intact, uncensored, it was wonderful.
It made us laugh an awful lot, such a good letter and we were so glad
to get it, the first since that dark cloud closed down on us . . .

We had a party on the train in the club car, quite unexpected like. It was the day of the British victory over the *Graf Spee*. It began with Frank Compton, who was a little, not very tight, suddenly beginning to sing in a very pleasing voice, "Rule Britannia," at which everyone joined in hysterically. We went from there to all the old war songs—"Tipperary," "Pack Up Your Troubles," "Keep the Home Fires Burning," "Long, Long Trail," "Mademoiselle from Armentiers"; it was lovely.

The party ended with the only German in the company (whom we strongly suspect of having pro-Nazi sympathies) standing up with Frank Compton and me, the only English, and singing with tears rolling down his cheeks, "God Save the King."

Alfred and Lynn fretted increasingly that they would never be able to face their English friends unless they came to England while the war was going on—which they eventually did.

Absence gave Noël the opportunity to assess his friends more or less objectively . . .

"They are strange and wonderful personalities—very difficult to understand until you realise that they are not two but one personality. Each is the other's complement. Together they are marvelous, their artistry amazing. Apart, they are oddly ineffectual.

"Alfred, a vaguely wandering soul who looks at you like a lost dog who is afraid of being washed. Lynn, splendidly null, a sort of highly intellectual ice maiden. Alfred's genius illuminates Lynn. Lynn's strong brain and well-balanced judgement keeps Alfred within bounds and brings him back to earth when he soars skywards. I love them both but the Alfred-Lynn combination is the real person, not the component parts."

He recalled his own experience sharing the stage with them . . .

"To play with those two is quite, quite unlike playing with anybody else; quite, quite different. Lynn, of the two, has a slightly slower-moving technique, but can play it more swiftly and more mercurially than anybody I've ever seen, once she gets it. She takes a little longer to learn it. Alfred, on the other hand, is tremendously quick. But the mixture of the three of us—the whole of America was waiting for us to have dreadful rows. Well, we had one row, at rehearsal, which lasted for two days. Exactly the opposite from what you'd think, because in the theatre, where

we were going to play, there was underground—below the stage floor—
a big star dressing room and a little one immediately opposite. Obvious,
I thought for the Lunts. So I said, 'I'll dress upstairs.' 'No,' they said, 'you
are the author, you have both the dressing rooms downstairs, and we . . .'
I said, 'I'm not going to have people coming round and seeing . . .' and
this became very tough. Finally, I had to go to Macy's and buy a whole
lot of drapes, chaise-longue, and telephone, and make the chorus room
upstairs look so glamorous that they gave in."

"Lynn Fontanne, for instance, will give as great a performance on the
last night of a play as she did on the first, possibly a greater, because she
develops all the time."

He recalled that when they were playing *Design for Living* Lynn came
up to him and said—" 'Noëlie, darling, I've just realized how to make
that trick with my handbag work in the second act.' 'I'm afraid you're a
little late, my darling. We're closing the show tonight.' But she did get to
do it once and got the laugh she'd been missing for months."

=====

They were to work together on only one other occasion.

Design for Living had been a hit. *Point Valaine* a flop. Noël felt he had
something to prove to his old friends and—just as important—to his
postwar English critics (of whom there were many).

In early 1952 he cabled the Lunts . . .

QUADRILLE IS FINISHED I LOVE IT VERY MUCH AND ONLY HOPE
THAT YOU WILL

What he didn't realize—having not worked with them for the best
part of twenty years—was that they had crafted their joint professional
persona in the interim and now had the influence to adapt their material
to fit. As *they* saw fit.

Cecil Beaton, whom Noël had selected to design the sets and costumes, felt the project would be "all a great lark—long may it remain so!"

Lynn saw things quite differently and said so—"It will be a lot of hard
work, anxiety, worry. We will very likely fight to the death, we will hope
to win through to success, but it won't be fun."

Nor was it. The play would open in London after a provincial tour.
The tour seemed to go well but the London critics were in no mood to
like anything Noël put out there.

In addition he found himself on the receiving end of what other playwrights had been experiencing with the Lunts at this stage of their joint

career. They would insist on rewrites as they went along for what they claimed performance had revealed as "soft spots" in the play.

———

During the next decade Noël and Alfred and Lynn met from time to time in various parts of the world but it seems to have taken time for the old closeness to return. Correspondence from that period is sparse.

Then in 1961 Noël came to New York with his musical *Sail Away* and in November he dined with the Lunts . . .

"Just the three of us. We started at a quarter to eight and finished at a quarter past one, during which time we never drew breath. We wandered back and forth happily over the forty-one years we have known and loved one another and it was altogether enchanting and, above all, comforting. Lynn looks marvelous and Alfred much better than he has for years. They are a fabulous couple."

In February 1965 they visited him in Jamaica ("gay and well and as dear as ever") to be present when the Queen Mother came for lunch to Firefly.

In the New Year's Honours List for 1970 came the long-deferred knighthood for Noël and later in the same year a special Tony award for "lifetime achievement."

At a celebratory dinner the seating plan was preordained forty-nine years earlier . . .

"The Day the Queen Mum dropped in" Noël with Lynn Fontanne, the Queen Mother, Alfred Lunt, and Blanche Blackwell (Firefly, Jamaica, February 28, 1965).

Noël&Alfred&Lynn.

Then there was another time Alfred and Lynn visited Noël in Jamaica. It was meant to be a break from the theatrical grind—a time to relax and enjoy Nature. Noël took Lynn to the top of a local mountain and proudly showed her the view . . . the terraces, the jungle in the valley below, the sandy beaches and the sparkling blue Caribbean beyond, "There," he said, "what do you think?"

The lady replied—"It looks like rows and rows of empty theatre seats."

——

This was by no means Noël's only social encounter with the Queen Mother.

After the visit he received a thank-you letter, recalling:

Many delightful memories of that heavenly luncheon party. . . . It was the nicest bit of my visit to Jamaica and I can quite see what a wonderful and inspiring place it must be to work in.

I hope so much to see you when you come to England . . . Could you not come down to Sandringham for the night of Tuesday July 20th? . . . It would be such fun to see you, and show you dear Edwardian Sandringham.

I am, Yours very sincerely
Elizabth R.

Noël duly accepted the invitation—but even Royalty can't command the English weather.

Noël's Review of *Stagestruck* (1965)

Mr. Maurice Zolotow was faced with a difficult task when he sat down to write a dual biography of Lynn Fontanne and Alfred Lunt. I am now faced with a less arduous but also difficult task, which is to write my opinion of it. The hazard confronting Maurice Zolotow was, that with the best will in the world, he did not and could not have known the Lunts well enough. My almost insurmountable hurdle in writing a comment on the book is that I know them far too well.

In the first place let me say that *Stagestruck* is lucid, affectionate without being over-eulogistic, most readable and fairly accurate. I say "fairly" accurate advisedly, because some of the anecdotes, of which to my mind there are rather too many, have been twisted out of shape and occasionally misdated. This is only a minute personal criticism based on my own elephantine memory and does little damage to the book as a whole.

The author, a thoroughly professional writer, has assembled a mountain of facts about their respective childhoods, their early struggles, their hobbies, their way of living and their relatives and friends. He has quoted widely from me, from the late Alexander Woollcott and various other of their more articulate adorers. He has also quoted extracts from some of Lynn's private letters, which are quite enchanting and most vividly indicative of her character. There are few, if any, quotations from Alfred's letters which is a pity, because they also are enchanting, if perhaps a trifle less elegant in tone.

What is wrong with the book in my opinion, and it must never be forgotten that mine in this case is an extremely personal opinion, is that the Lunts themselves have been too much involved with it. It is quite apparent that there have been detailed conversations between them and the author at Genesee Depot and elsewhere where he has encouraged them both to talk expansively. I am not implying that anything either of them told him was remotely dishonest or untrue, although some of it may have been the teeniest bit exaggerated, but, knowing them as I do, I think it would have been wiser now and again if he had made notes of what they didn't say rather than what they did. The result of this collaboration has robbed the book of true objectivity and without true objectivity a biography, however entertaining, loses quality.

It has been suggested many times over the years that I myself should write their strange, loving story, and on each occasion the subject came up my heart sank like a stone and I burst out into a sort of spiritual sweat. Not that anything I would say about them could ever be in the slightest way deprecating or unkind, I love them dearly and for ever and they know it, but it must be remembered that they are magic creatures and magic creatures are touchy and vulnerable in different ways from ordinary mortals. In the long wonderful years of our friendship I have frequently insulted them roundly, chided them and laughed at them, on which occasions they have usually insulted and chided me back and laughed themselves. True and intelligent criticism, however devastating, they will accept like lambs, but there is a world of difference between spoken criticism and written criticism. The written word is irrevocable. There is nothing on earth that I couldn't say to Lynn or Alfred face to face, but if I criticised quite mildly any aspect of their character or behaviour in print they would, I know, be deeply hurt. There they would lie, the teasing, wicked words, leering up at them from the printed page and this they would find hard to forgive. As I would cheerfully plunge into a vat of boiling oil rather than hurt a hair of their heads, my pen will remain firmly sheathed.

Fortunately in Maurice Zolotow's book there is little that I could see that might upset them although here I may be talking out of turn, because I havn't yet discussed it with them. This will be a voluble and dubious treat in store for they are coming to me in Jamaica in February. *Stagestruck,* as I said before, is eminently readable and I am certain that hundreds of thousands of people to whom they have given so much of themselves in course of their fabulous careers will read it with immense pleasure. As one of the many nuns in *Sound of Music* remarked, a trifle effusively I thought, of Miss Mary Martin. "How can you catch a moonbeam in your hand?" I can only conclude by saying that catching a moonbeam in your hand would be falling off a log compared with catching and holding the truth about the Lunts between the covers of a book. Neither Mr. Zolotow nor I nor anyone in this world could do it entirely successfully. Perhaps in some future existence Henry James, Anton Chekhov and Sir James Barrie might have a bash at it, but I don't envy them the assignment.

On Leading Ladies

There were many more "asides" . . .

The *Theatrical Dame* (or Would Be Dame)
"Great big glamorous stars can be very tiresome."
—*DIARIES* (1956)

"It is sad to think how many of our glamorous leading ladies are round the bend."
—*DIARIES* (1958)

"She stopped the show—but then the show wasn't really traveling very fast."

He once attended a session of the Actors Studio and heard Lee Strasberg recall Eleanora Duse . . .

"He explained that when she smiled, she didn't merely smile with her mouth, but with every part of her body! Which comes under the heading of the neatest trick of the week."
—*DIARIES* (1965)

"I remember once saying—'God preserve me in future from female stars.' I don't suppose He will."

And, indeed, He didn't . . .

Epitaph for an Elderly Actress
She got in a rage
About age
And retired, in a huff, from the stage.
Which, taken all round, was a pity
Because she was still fairly pretty
But she got in a rage
About age.

She burst into tears
It appears
When the rude, inconsiderate years
Undermined her once flawless complexion
And whenever she saw her reflection
In a mirror, she burst into tears
It appears.

She got in a state
About weight
And resented each morsel she ate.
Her colon she constantly sluiced
And reduced and reduced and reduced
And, at quite an incredible rate
Put on weight.

She got in a rage
About age
But she still could have played Mistress Page
And she certainly could have done worse
Than *Hay Fever* or Juliet's Nurse
But she got in a terrible rage
About age.

And she moaned and she wept and she wailed
And she roared and she ranted and railed
And retired, very heavily veiled,
From the stage.

———

Dame Laura, Dame Rosie, and Dame Margaret could look back without anger. But then—they were Noël's own invention (with just a vestige of certain real Dames) . . .

Edith Evans and Sybil Thorndike, contemporary critics surmised.

Three Theatrical Dames

DAME LAURA

Verse 1 I started from scratch
In a house with a thatch
With two very unpleasant old ladies.
My parents were dead
So I finally fled
And appeared in a tent
Outside Burton-on-Trent
In a very small part in *Quo Vadis*.
I toured in *East Lynne*
And *The Wages of Sin*
Till I couldn't tell one from the other,
Then a rich friend
And achieved the West End
In a farce called *She Did It for Mother*.

ALL

Refrain 1 Three theatrical Dames,
Eminent and respectable,
Our accents are undetectable
And though we've achieved our aims
If they knew what we'd done
In Eighteen Ninety-One
They certainly wouldn't have made us Dames.

DAME ROSIE

Verse 2 My very first step
Was Shakespearian "rep"
Where an awful old "Ham" used to train us.
I'd nothing to do
In *The Dream* and *The Shrew*
But I carried a spear
In *King John* and *King Lear*
And a hatchet in *Coriolanus*.
I ranted for years
In pavilions on piers
Till my spirits were really at zero,

Then I got a small role
Of a Tart with a soul
In a play by Sir Arthur Pinero.

ALL

Refrain 2 Three Theatrical Dames,
Models of prim propriety,
Accepted by High Society
Because of our famous names,
If they'd asked us to tea
In Eighteen Ninety-Three
They certainly wouldn't have made us Dames.

DAME MARGARET

Verse 3 I made my début
In a canvas canoe
In a horrid American drama.
It wasn't a hit
So I left the "Legit"!
And I got myself backed
In a musical act
Called "A Night in the Garden of Karma."
An agent called Klein
Said, "I'm willing to sign
Whoever that girl who unveils is"
So I got my first chance
With a Biblical dance
In a flop at the Old Prince of Wales's.

ALL

Refrain 3 Three theatrical Dames,
Each of our houses we adorn
With photographs of the highly-born
In elegant silver frames.
If they'd caught us in Crewe
In Eighteen Ninety-Two
They certainly wouldn't have made us Dames.

Refrain 4   Three theatrical Dames,
              Prominent high and mighty girls,
              The fact that we once were flighty girls
              Our manner today disclaims,
              If they'd seen our high kicks
              In Eighteen Ninety-Six
              They certainly wouldn't have made us Dames.
                    —"Three Theatrical Dames" from *Hoi Polloi* (1949)

His Advice to Actors . . .

"My dear, always make sure your eyebrows are properly lit. You can't play comedy without eyebrows."

—NOËL TO ACTRESS PATIENCE COLLIER

.

"You know you've arrived in the profession when you don't have to read *The Stage* every week."

.

"Acting is an instinct. A gift that is often given to people who are very silly as people. But as they come on the stage, up goes the temperature."

.

"I would like to prove that talent and material count for more than sequins and tits."

—*DIARIES* (1950)

.

"An actor is a recollection with a lot of gold dust on it."

.

GARRY: You must admit that my opinion, based on a lifelong experience of the theatre might be the right one.
ROLAND (*contemptuously*): The *commercial* theatre.
GARRY: Oh dear. Oh dear. Oh dear!
ROLAND: I suppose you'll say that Shakespeare wrote for the commercial theatre and that the only point of doing anything with the drama at all is to make money! All those old arguments. What you don't realise is that the theatre of the future is the theatre of ideas.

GARRY: That may be but at the moment I am occupied with the
theatre of the present.

—PRESENT LAUGHTER (1939)

.

"Always take your disappointments bravely. No tears, no fuss, no rows
or sulks or bitterness. Take it cheerfully. Always be cheerful. That is
true professionalism. Nothing kills a career more speedily than bitterness and self-pity. Better to be a bad actor than like that."

(1947)

.

"It's so easy to play Americans. All you have to do is to say—'Hi, folks'
very loudly—and then do the rest in English."

.

"There is too much busy-ness on the stage. Ruth Draper is enthralling,
but she never went leaping all over the stage."

.

"I don't care for the present trends either in literature or the theatre.
Pornography bores me. Squalor disgusts me. Garishness, vulgarity
and commonness of mind offend me, and problems of social significance on the stage, unless superbly well presented, to me are
the negation of entertainment. Subtlety, discretion, restraint, finesse,
charm, intelligence and good manners, talent and glamour still
enchant me. Is it because I am so much older that I am unable to
distinguish these qualities in the majority of present day books I read
or shows I see?"

(1961)

.

"As an actor your mind must work on several different layers at once.
You must think of many things simultaneously. It's like reflexes in driving a car. It becomes so automatic that it isn't even conscious thought."

Intermission

STAR QUALITY

"I Don't Know What It Is—But I've Got It"

"If you're a star, you should behave like one.
I always have."

E ven though he claimed not to know what the phrase "star quality" meant, Noël never stopped trying to define it and in 1967, in his last completed play—of that name and unproduced in his lifetime—he handed the task to the director . . .

Director

I leave to the last the question of talent. That's the pay-off, the definitive answer to all the silly riddles. That's their basic power, their natural gift for acting. I don't suppose a star has ever acted really badly in her life. I don't believe she could if she tried. That is her one reality, the foundation upon which the whole structure of her charm and personality rests, and, believe you me, it's rock solid. But that Star Quality is what transcends everything else. It's beyond definition and beyond praise. Whether they're born with it or how and where they managed to acquire it, I neither know nor care, but it's there all right. It's there as strongly in comedy as it is in tragedy.

You can be at a matinée in Manchester—or even in Hull. The play is lousy, the fortnight's notice is up on the board and the audience is so dull, you think half of them must be dead. That was the first act.

By the last they're sitting on the edge of their seats and at the final curtain they scream the place down. The hair rises on your scalp, the tears are cascading down your face and you solemnly bless the day that you were born.

And that, my friends, is Star Quality.

Among his papers there is an essay on the subject—undated but clearly somewhat earlier than the play.

The play manuscript also contains a handwritten annotation . . .

"Come to think of it, I don't remember ever playing a good matinée in Hull!"

"how i wonder what you are"

Throughout all the years that the living theatre has existed the "Star System" has been decried and abused by devotees of the drama who are dedicated to the idealistic theory that "The play's the thing" and should rank first in importance in any theatrical enterprise. This theory is entirely admirable and, if only it were as realistic as it is admirable, the "Gay mad world of powder and paint" would be a great deal more comfortable than it is.

Every now and then a gleam of hope is discernible on the Utopian horizon. Somebody puts on a play with a cast of virtually unknown actors and is a "smash." A repertory company appears from some alien land devoid of any outstanding personalities and is crowned with laurels, but also, these shining auguries, unlike Mr. Christopher Fry's Phoenix, are *not* too frequent. The "Star System"—like some brash, bejewelled courtesan, remains triumphantly in power, smiling contemptuously at all abortive efforts to dislodge her.

The grim fact must be faced: that the majority of the theatre-going public would rather pay their money to see an extraordinary creature than an ordinary one. An extraordinary actress playing a relatively ordinary part may indeed lay waste the author's original intentions, but she will bring to that part a certain quality, a composite of her own personal magnetism, her reputation and her acquired technique which will hypnotize the audience into loving her. An ordinary, possibly better actress, playing the same part honestly and with loyal adherence to the author's text, will usually succeed in being little more than accurate. She will, of course, be effusively thanked by the author, director and the management and, if she happens to be an understudy, cheered to the echo by the gallery, but the business will drop steadily until the star returns to the cast. From the point of view of the dedicated drama enthusiasts this is indeed a desperate injustice, but then the theatre world is as packed with desperate injustice as is the world outside it.

Now we come to the burning question. "What is it that stars have that others haven't?" Is it an earthy quality or a spiritual quality? Is it concrete, abstract, animal, vegetable or mineral? There will obviously never be a satisfactory answer. A young girl decides to go on the stage. She is strikingly beautiful and by no means untalented. She is adequately taught at an acting school or by the better method of playing small parts in a repertory company. After a year or so she procures a job in London for which she receives honourable mention in *The Sunday Times* and an "Among others" in *The Daily Telegraph*. She at once acquires an agent, or has one thrust upon her, and her future is shining with promise. Twenty years later, having played two leading parts, one on tour and one in the West End in a play that ran only a fortnight, bits in movies, snippets on the radio and an endless succession of heroine's friends, she one day looks at herself in the mirror, and, if she is wise, notes that she is not quite so strikingly beautiful as she was, marries a well disposed dentist in

Kettering and is heard of no more. If she is not wise she sticks doggedly to the Theatre and finally has to be assisted to the grave by the Actors' Benevolent Fund.

This, I admit, is a gloomy picture but it is not an unusual one. It is astonishing how often it has been proved in the Theatre that good looks, even when bolstered with talent, are not enough. Something extra is required and what that extra something is has never been satisfactorily explained. Of course, there are thousands and thousands of actors and actresses in the theatre who earn reasonable salaries and manage to live useful and happy lives. In fact, without these the Theatre would cease to exist. But surely at the very beginning of all their careers "To be a great star" must have been the ultimate goal? And surely, somewhere along the line there must have been a dismal moment when they realise that they hadn't made it and were never likely to?

Then, on the other side of the coin you take another young girl who decides that she wants to be an actress. She may not be outstandingly pretty and her talent may be negligible but these defects are mercifully veiled from her by the possession of a strong ego and a plentiful supply of ruthless determination. She will endure, possibly only briefly, the routine early struggles. Somebody will spot her either in a leading role in a repertory company or in a small part in a London production. It may not be because she is particularly gifted that they spot her, it is because she possesses an extra "something" that demands attention.

This extra "something" is an amalgam of various elements: vitality, sex-appeal, an intriguing voice (nearly all big stars have distinctive voices), an individual style of movement and some sort of chemical emanation, of which she may or may not be conscious, which places her on a different plane from her possibly more talented colleagues. The balanced mixture of all these ingredients is recognized as "personality" or, in other words, "Star Quality." Very very occasionally this "Star Quality" may be acquired by years of experience, determination and the assurance of polished technique, but as a general rule it is something that people either have or have not and when they have, it is unmistakable.

In any event this fortunately endowed creature, whoever she may be, is hailed, within a relatively short space of time, as a Star, and it is in this glorious moment that the rot usually starts to set in. Her hitherto unblemished character begins, subtly at first, to suffer that "sea change— into something rich and strange." The name in lights, tumultuous applause, hosts of admirers, acres of first-night flowers and extravagant publicity all contribute their insidious magic until, a few years later, we see, bowing graciously to us on an opening night, a triumphant, assured, fascinating, adored, rip-snorting megalomaniac. During the few weeks immediately preceding that glamorous moment, Heaven alone knows what hair-raising scenes and dramas have taken place.

At least, it isn't Heaven alone that knows, everybody backstage from the director to the assistant stage manager knows only too well. From the first reading of the play until about the end of the second week of rehearsal all goes smoothly. The star behaves like an angel—who, oh who, invented those unjust rumours about her being "difficult" in the theatre? She is modest, unassuming, almost over-considerate to the minor members of the cast. She lunches daily with the director and returns radiant to be both comradely and coquettish with the leading man. She is easily adored by everyone but the stage manager who has worked with her before and is inclined to be cynical. She is sometimes late for the morning rehearsal but so enchantingly apologetic that she is immediately forgiven. She is not quite happy about the second act scene with Hubert, because she has to sit still for such a long time without doing anything so she cajoles the besotted author to write in a few extra lines. This upsets the balance of the scene and also the leading man who has to be comforted. This tiny warning of the shape of things to come however is swiftly glossed over and rehearsals proceed, perhaps without quite the enthusiasm with which they started, but smoothly enough.

Then suddenly, like a thunderbolt falling from a cloudless sky, the first major row occurs. Any number of trivial reasons may spark this off; a bit of direction of which she doesn't approve, a headache from having been up too late the night before, an onset of panic, because she isn't sure enough of her lines or an inadvertent prompt from the assistant stage manager when she is experimenting with a pregnant pause. Anyhow, the battle is joined and the angel is transformed into a fiend. The company is stunned, the director enraged and the author in despair. The fiend, after getting a great deal more off her chest than should ever have been on it, either stamps out of the theatre vowing never to return, or bursts into floods of tears and has to be led to a dressing-room and cosseted. In either event the day's rehearsal is ruined and the One-big-happy-family atmosphere completely disrupted.

From then on the climate changes, the barometer plummets down and grey clouds gather. A week or so later the real trouble starts with the first dress-rehearsal. Everything is in the wrong place, the colour of the set is entirely different from the one she passed in the original sketch. The scene designer takes exception to her favourite dress and the director suggests, with quivering tact, that she must either wear a wig or do her hair differently. After a series of blistering exchanges her agent is sent for and all hell breaks loose, while the company wander about looking mournful and munching thick sandwiches.

The opening performance of the try-out is sheer misery. The fiend-angel has refused to rehearse on the Sunday evening, because she has lost her voice. On the opening night she finds it, but loses a lot of laughs, the blame for which she places squarely on the shoulders of the author, the director and her fellow actors. She is, of course, rapturously received by the audience, but this in no way mollifies her. By this time the director and she are not on speaking terms and the author is locked in a hotel room cutting his favourite lines and rewriting his favourite scenes. There are dreadful conferences after each night's performance in the managerial suite at which everyone talks a great deal, nothing much is achieved and wild suggestions are put forward of other actresses for the part who may or may not be available. These suggestions are patiently dismissed by the producing manager who is aware that, good, bad or indifferent, the fiend-angel is a big box-office draw and has a run-of-the-play contract.

At long last, after several weeks of arduous re-rehearsing, foot stampings, incessant scenes and oceans of tears, the long dreaded moment arrives when the star steps onto the stage on the opening night in a West End theatre. The atmosphere backstage is crackling with tension, nerves are lacerated and everyone is exhausted. She, the angel-fiend, receives an ovation on her first entrance from which moment on she plays the part as she has never played it before. Her timing is flawless, her charm devastating and in the new dresses, which have cost the management fourteen hundred pounds, she looks utterly ravishing. At the supper party after the performance she publicly kisses the leading man, the author and the director, while her dresser is left to engage two taxis to take her floral tributes back to her flat. The next morning she reads five ecstatic notices about herself and one not so good, upon which she bursts into tears and telephones her agent immediately to start legal proceedings. The play may be a success or a failure but, whichever way it goes, she is all right and she knows it, but what she doesn't know, what she never for an instant realises is that, without the author's lines, the director's skill, the talented support of her fellow players and, above all the indefinable gift of personality bestowed on her by benevolent destiny, she might be playing a muted revival of *The Last of Mrs. Cheyney* in Norwich.

It is obviously unnecessary to state that the rather florid example of megalomania I have described does not apply to *all* star actresses. There are many who are intelligent enough to employ their precious, indefinable quality with grace and humility, but these, regrettably, are far far rarer than they should be. Megalomania in the theatre is an insidious disease and there are, like Mr. Heinz's pickles, at least fifty-seven varieties. It is liable to attack females more than males as a general rule, possibly because it is in the nature of things for women to attract more of the outward attentions and trappings of success than men, although I must admit to having encountered a few male stars who were not entirely displeased with themselves. The original cause of infection is a combination of adulatory press notices, over-flattery and the heady sound of personal applause. Certain egos expand under these stimuli with lightning rapidity; others, more controlled, accept them calmly and concentrate on more lasting values. The angel-fiend type I have just sketched so affectionately swiftly grows to accept the praise and the cheering as her natural right and, if she is fortunate or unfortunate enough to go on receiving it night after night for a number of years, her megalomania becomes chronic and she is as near barmy as makes no matter. Her exigence increases with every play she plays, her demands for various privileges outstrip all sanity and yet—and yet—without her the Theatre would lose much of its fascination.

In most adventurous vocations there are unexpected hazards to be dealt with and vanquished. The captain of a ship scans the heavens for evil portents; the air pilot braces himself to combat fog, sudden electric storms and any form of what is comprehensively described as "engine trouble." The Big Game hunter dreads the stampeding elephant and the sly, irrelevant cobra, and I can only conclude by saying that in all my long years of directing straight plays and musicals, I would rather face any of the above-mentioned perils than be forced to cope with a glamorous female star on the rampage about her dresses or her hair.

"When I eventually write my book on the theatre there will be a whole chapter devoted to leading ladies' dresses and hair. They are invariably the main stumbling-blocks. Leading ladies' husbands may also come in for some acrid comment."

—*DIARIES* (1961)

7

ON WRITING A PLAY (3)
(1940–1960)

"It Was the Best of Times, It Was the Worst of Times"
—DICKENS, *A TALES OF TWO CITIES*

———

Present Laughter (1939) · *This Happy Breed* (1939) · *Salute to the Brave* (1941) · *Blithe Spirit* (1941) · *Peace in Our Time* (1947) · *Island Fling* (1949)/*South Sea Bubble* (1956) · *Relative Values* (1951) · *Quadrille* (1951/2) · *Nude with Violin* (1956) · *Look After Lulu* (1959) · *Waiting in the Wings* (1959/60)

September 3, 1939, changed things for everyone.

Noël had two plays in rehearsal—*Present Laughter* and *This Happy Breed*. Both were put on hold for the unpredictable duration, since London theatres were temporarily shut down. They eventually had their premiere on a provincial tour in 1942, when they were joined by a third play—*Blithe Spirit.*

When war was declared Noël was sent to Paris to open a propaganda bureau—a venture that turned out to be a good deal less significant than he'd been led to believe. The following year his lords and masters detected "a frenzied beating of wings" and sent him to the USA on a fact-finding mission to gain a perspective on American opinion.

Since the country was neutral, Noël was technically a spy as he went around projecting the Allied point of view. What he detected was the presence of a significant pro-Nazi faction in high places. He decided to encapsulate his case in the way he knew best. He would write a play.

The result was *Salute to the Brave.* It told of an upper-class English-woman who decides to bring her two young sons away from the London bombing to the safety of her American friends. To her dismay she finds that to many of them the war is an irrelevant disruption in their social lives—but not their business. They don't want to hear the horror stories she has to relate. Disillusioned, she decides to return home and do what she can to help.

Realizing in his first draft that he had perhaps depicted the horrors too graphically, Noël toned them down in his second draft, which he called *Time Remembered.* As it was, neither version was to see a stage. Pearl Harbor saw to that. America was now committed. The Yanks would be coming again after all.

======

Perhaps the most predictive lines in the play . . .

"This war's making most people feel bloody in one way or another—apart from the actual immediate horror of it, it's planting a fine crop of neuroses in all of us. God knows what we shall be like when it's over."

======

May 1941 found him back in England after his American assignment, followed by a goodwill trip to the Antipodes. His overlords at the Ministry of Information suggested he take a break . . .

"On Friday May 2, Joyce Carey and I caught a morning train from Paddington bound for Port Meirion in North Wales. For some time past an idea for a light comedy had been rattling at the door of my mind, and I thought the time had come for me to let it in and show it a little courtesy. Joyce was engaged in writing a play about Keats, so here we were. 'Hurrah for the holidays,' without buckets and spades, but with typewriters, paper, carbons, bathing suits, suntan oil and *bézique* cards.

"We arrived on a golden evening, sighed with pleasure at the mountains and the sea in the late sunlight and settled ourselves into a pink guest-house. The next morning we sat on the beach with our backs against the sea-wall and discussed my idea exclusively for several hours. Keats, I regret to say, was not referred to. By lunchtime the title had emerged, together with the names of the characters, and a rough—very rough—outline of the plot.

"At 7:30 the next morning I sat, with the usual nervous palpitations, at my typewriter. Joyce was upstairs in her room wrestling with Fanny Brawne. There was a pile of virgin paper on my left and a box of carbons on my right. The table wobbled and I had to put a wedge under one of its legs. I smoked several cigarettes in rapid succession, staring gloomily out of the window at the tide running out. I fixed the paper into the machine and started: *Blithe Spirit. A Light Comedy in Three Acts.*"

The only thing to change was the subtitle. It now read—"An Improbable Farce in Three Acts." Harold Pinter was to disagree. When he directed a revival at the National some years later, he warned his cast that he considered it neither "improbable" nor a "farce."

Noël continued . . .

"For six days I worked from eight to one each morning and from two to seven each afternoon. On Friday evening, May 9, the play was finished and, disdaining archness and false modesty, I will admit that I knew it was witty, I knew it was well constructed, and I also knew that it would be a success. My gift for comedy dialogue, which I feared may have atrophied from disuse, had obviously profited from its period of inactivity. Beyond a few typographical errors, I made no corrections, and only two lines of the original script were ultimately cut. I take pride in these assertions, but it is a detached pride, natural enough in the circumstances and not to be confused with boastfulness. I was not attempting to break any records, to prove how quickly I could write and how clever I was. I was fully prepared to revise and rewrite the whole play had I thought it necessary, but I did not think it necessary. I knew from the first morning's work that I was on the right track and that it would be difficult, with that situation and those characters, to go far wrong. I am also aware though, from past experience, that when the right note is struck and the structure of a play is carefully built in advance, it is both wise and profitable to start at the beginning and write through to the end in as short a time as possible."

Margaret Rutherford, the original Madame Arcati.

Programme cover for the U.S. production of *Blithe Spirit* at the Morosco Theatre, 1941.

Noël, Lauren Bacall, Mildred Natwick, and Claudette Colbert in the CBS-TV version (1956).

Years later he would reflect . . .

"Perfection in art is, like anything else, a question of degree. All creative artists strive to achieve it within the limits of the form they have chosen. I must admit, with what must seem to be a refreshing gust of modesty, that I have never yet achieved the great play that I have always longed and will always long to write. But I am forever grateful to the almost psychic gift that enabled me to write *Blithe Spirit* in five days during one of the darkest years of the war.

"It was not meticulously constructed in advance. In fact, only one day lapsed between its original conception and the moment when I sat down to write it. It fell into my mind and on to the manuscript. Six weeks later it was produced and ran in London for four and a half years and I am still wondering whether or not it was important. Only time will tell."

Which, of course, it has. *Blithe Spirit* is revived more than any of his other plays.

Blithe Spirit was put into rehearsal in record time and proceeded to run for 1,997 performances—a record for a straight play on the London stage until it was surpassed by Agatha Christie's *The Mousetrap*. It was

In 1956 Noël starred in a live
TV production for CBS.

then included with a touring company in a sequence called *Play Parade*
that also featured *Present Laughter* and *This Happy Breed* making their
delayed debuts.

———

Graham Greene in his review called it "a weary exhibition of bad taste."
He was later to retract that opinion.

———

When Noël was asked if he'd ever had any ambition to play Shakespeare,
he would turn the question aside with a quip. But on one occasion at
least he added that he'd often thought that he'd like to play Madame
Arcati. . . . "I think I'd have been rather good!"

He wasn't joking, and he probably would have. As it is, we'll all live
with our indelible memory of Margaret Rutherford. It's hard to believe,
but she originally turned the part down. Margaret respected spiritual-
ism and felt the play was an attack on it. It took producer Binkie Beaumont's most lavish lunch and silken manner to talk her into it. It was,
he claimed, an *attack* on fraudulent mediums. In that case, the lady per-
sisted, how can Madame Arcati raise two ghosts? "Ah," replied Binkie,

"that was a stroke of luck that can happen to even fraudulent mediums!" There was a pause before Miss Rutherford nodded her several chins in agreement. "Very well, but I must warn you that I regard this as a very serious play, almost a tragedy. I don't see it as a comedy at all." Which is precisely the way she played it, and why it was so funny.

Present Laughter (1939)

"*Present Laughter* is a very light comedy and was written with the sensible object of providing me with a bravura part. It was an enormous success. I received excellent notices and, to my bewilderment and considerable dismay, the play also was reasonably acclaimed. This so unnerved me that I can say no more."

But there is a little more to be said. The hero, Garry Essendine, is a matinee idol beginning to feel a little concern about the fragility of fame. The line between "being" and the illusion of being (otherwise known as "acting") is not always clear.

As Garry says—"I'm always acting—watching myself go by—that's what's so horrible—I see myself all the time eating, drinking, loving, suffering . . . my life is not my own . . . I belong to the public and to my work."

Garry is clearly Cowardesque but it was not until much later that—after the umpteenth question on the subject—he finally admitted. "Of *course* Garry is me!"

The sadness is that he never committed his own performance to film. There was talk of it and it was one of the two plays he had intended to be performed live as part of his three-part contract with CBS in 1955.

Front Office, however, stepped in: Bill Paley, head of CBS. Noël recalled in his *Diary*—"Bill Paley is frightened of the sex angle and

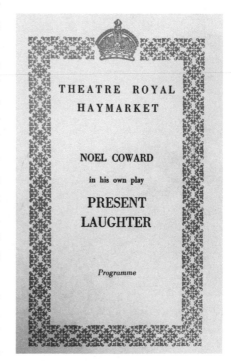

THEATRE ROYAL
HAYMARKET

NOEL COWARD

in his own play

PRESENT
LAUGHTER

Programme

With Judy Campbell in *Present Laughter*, 1942.

The set from the 1947 revival of *Present Laughter* at the Haymarket Theatre, London. Once again Noël starred as Garry Essendine.

fears angry letters rattling in the mail-box, written by outraged Method-ists in Omaha complaining about illicit love being brought into their very houses by me and my sponsors."

So *Present Laughter* was replaced by *Blithe Spirit.*

=====

The only black spot for *Present Laughter* was in 1948 when a translated version by André Roussin called *Joyeux Chagrins* was presented at the Théâtre Edouard VII in Paris with Noël playing Garry (now called Max Aramont).

Noël recorded . . . "The play is a flop and it is no use pretending for one instant that it is not. Personally I want to close as soon as possible and call it a day. Roussin tells me that the day I was taken ill and couldn't be photographed the Press took against me. Personally I am convinced that, although the Press have been cruel, the truth is that the French people didn't care for the play. It is, of course, bitterly disappointing. I suppose this succession of failures is good for my soul but I rather doubt it. I feel rather depressed tonight. I know it will pass and fade into its right perspective but the disappointment of having worked so hard, hav-ing had the bad luck to be ill and then having a flop is a little heavy on the heart."

This Happy Breed (1939)

This Happy Breed is a suburban middle-class family comedy covering the period between the Armistice in 1918 to the humiliating year of 1938, when the late Neville Chamberlain spent so much time in the air.

Many of the critics detected in this play an attitude on my part of amused patronage and condescension towards the habits and manners of suburban London. They implied that in setting the play in a milieu so far removed from the cocktail and caviare stratum where I so obvi-ously belonged, I was over-reaching myself and writing about people far removed from my superficial comprehension.

In this, as usual, they were quite wrong. Having been born in Ted-dington and having lived respectively at Sutton, Battersea Park and Clapham Common during all my formative years, I can confidently assert that I know a great deal more about the hearts and minds of ordi-nary south Londoners than they give me credit for. My metamorphosis into a "Mayfair playboy" many years later was entirely a journalistic con-

As Frank Gibbons in *This Happy Breed*.

ception. Since I achieved my first real theatrical success with *The Vortex* in 1924, I have moved observantly and eagerly through many different cliques and classes of society.

Being a natural writer with a constant eye on human behavior, I have also moved without undue imaginative strain, through Regency and Victorian society as well. I have also a sound working knowledge of the navy, the army and the air force. To ascribe preconceived social limitations to a creative writer is a common error of the critical mind; it is also a critical revelation of the common mind.

I wrote *This Happy Breed* in the spring of 1939. My personal criticism of it as a play is that the character of Frank Gibbons is a fraction more than life-size. His views are too clearly expressed to be quite true to life. I have no doubt whatever that he would hold such views, but to my mind, his articulateness throughout the play concedes too much to theatrical effectiveness. Had he been a character in a novel, this error could have been eliminated; the author could have explained his feelings and reactions without imposing upon him the burden of speaking them aloud. However, *This Happy Breed* was a play written for the theatre and must stand or fall within the theatre's necessary limitations.

The other characters are well drawn . . . They were none of them written with the faintest patronage or condescension but with sincerity, affection and the inherent understanding that is the result of personal experience.

Peace in Our Time (1947)

Nineteen forty-five and World War II was finally over. The curtain rose on what was, hopefully, a brave—if impoverished—new world. But for Noël things began to go worse.

His war had been a personal triumph . . . Apart from his undercover work for the Government, there were three successful plays . . . *In Which We Serve* . . . a recommendation for a knighthood from King George himself (which Churchill put a personal stop to) . . . and *Brief Encounter*.

Opinions vary as to what went wrong. Was it the postwar mood determining that things were going to change and there should be no going back to the prewar world of privilege in Labour Britain? Did a country that could turn its back on Churchill, the man who had done more than anyone to see it through, need a playwright like Noël Coward, who only wrote about people who seemed to do nothing for a living?

Whatever the reason, that was what happened. Noël pretended the prevailing mood had no effect on him but the evidence tells a different story. The critics carped at anything he put before them and producers, who had been taking anything he offered them, began to question and demand changes. It disrupted Noël's longtime *modus operandi* and affected the quality of the work he produced.

He began by repeating an earlier misjudgment.

He had expressed his emotional reaction to the First World War in *Post-Mortem* and—as he admitted "tore my emotions to shreds over it." But at least he got it out of his emotional system.

His reaction to the second war to end all wars was more considered but no less emotional and personal.

He wrote *Peace in Our Time*—mimicking Neville Chamberlain's fatuous claim just before that war was declared. It opened in the West End in 1947.

The play is set in a typical London pub. It is only when the news comes through on the radio that we realize that the authorities referred to are German. Britain has lost the war!

Needless to say by the end of the play we are reassured that an underground Resistance movement is at work and presumably all will eventually be well. "Britons never, never, never shall be slaves."

The idea was not exactly original. In 1913 "Saki" (H. H. Munro), one of Noël's favorite writers, had published a novel, *When William Came,* in which "William" (Kaiser Wilhelm II) and his fellow Germans had conquered Britain. Ironically, Saki was killed in that conflict.

Noël wrote . . .

The idea was conceived in Paris shortly after the Liberation . . . I spent the first eight months of the war there, in course of which I came into contact with more varieties of French people than I ever had before. I also grew to understand them and appreciate them more than I ever had before. The Fall of France, therefore, had more personal implications for me than it had for many others. I had countless friends to wonder about and worry about and my imagination was plagued with visions of Nazis swaggering along under the arcades of the Rue de Rivoli and Gestapo officials letting themselves in and out of my flat in the Place Vendôme (which incidentally they occupied for the duration).

When I returned soon after the Germans had been driven away, the city itself seemed to be unchanged, physically at least untouched by the horror of enemy occupation. It didn't take me long, however, to realise that behind the facade a great deal had changed, the sense of immediate relief and exaltation had faded and there was an atmosphere of subtle disintegration, lassitude and, above all, suspicion.

The pervasive atmosphere of suspicion, malice and unease was horribly depressing and I began to suspect that the physical effect of four years of intermittent bombing is far less damaging to the intrinsic character of a nation than the spiritual effect of four years of enemy occupation. This in time led me to wonder what might have happened to London and England if, in 1940 the Germans had successfully invaded and occupied us, which they so very nearly did.

I began to make mental lists of those of my friends and acquaintances who would be one hundred per cent loyal and get shot, those who would manage a compromise without actually letting down the side and those who would collaborate whole-heartedly in order to save their own skins . . . Nevertheless, it is a sobering thought to imagine for a little what so easily might have been. Four years is a long time and anti-climax is a lethal enemy of heroics. Life, of a sort, would have to go on . . . People would have to continue to make and sell things. Singers would have to sing, dancers would have to dance and actors would have to act. Would they be considered contemptible if they performed before the German invaders? Would a leading lady be branded as a collaborator if an eminent German general called on her in her dressing-room after her performance and handed her a bunch of flowers. Should she refuse to receive him? Throw the flowers in his face? What should she do? She would have to go on acting in order to live.

This, of course, would be only one of a million dilemmas that English civilians would find themselves faced with. How soon, I wondered, would it be before an underground resistance movement got under way and who in the end would liberate us? . . . But how would they set about it and from where? How and when would that most poignant D-Day be launched?

It wasn't long after these reflections that the play began to take form in my mind. I decided to place the entire action in the bar-parlour of a London pub, that being the most easily manageable setting for various types of Londoners . . . Personally I thought it an exciting play and a stimulating evening in the theatre, but then I am devoured by

Original production of
Peace in Our Time (1947).

stubborn prejudice about my work. I just cannot get it out of my head that it is good.

Peace in Our Time ran for a modest 167 performances but that was not attributable to the quality of the cast, which was made up of such established and emerging actors as Bernard Lee, Elspeth March, Kenneth More, Ralph Michael, Dora Bryan, Dandy Nichols, and Alan Badel.

In retrospect Noël had to admit that what undermined its chance of commercial success was one simple fact. After five harrowing years of war, British theatregoers were in no mood to relive those years—especially what it would have been like had we lost.

.

"I know nothing so dreary as the feeling that you can't make the sounds
or write the words that your whole creative being is yearning for."
—*DIARIES* (1945)

.

A look at the Coward canon indicates one indisputable fact. His most successful plays emerged fully formed and were committed to paper within days. *Hay Fever, Private Lives, Blithe Spirit, Design for Living.*

Many of the others—particularly during his "wilderness years"— suffered to one degree or another from revision.

Pensively into the fifties in his New York East River apartment, formerly the home of Alexander Woollcott.

That was certainly true of the one that ended up, reasonably success-fully, as *South Sea Bubble*.

Diary, *April 2, 1949*
"Had a long think about what I want to do. A play for Gertie, or for me, or for both . . ."

April 6
"Suddenly an idea for a comedy for Gertie fell into my mind. It rang a loud bell, so I constructed it then and there and everything seemed to fall into place. The title is *Home and Colonial,* theme—Lady 'Sandra' Magnus (a combination of Diana Cooper and Edwina Mountbatten), Government House, Samolo, scandal with local politician [Jamaican prime minister at the time]. There is more to it than that, but it's a heaven-sent opportunity to get in a lot of Jamaican stuff. Felt really happy."

Then the first warning signs . . .

May 3
"Finished the play at five o'clock. It is very funny, I think, but it has been extraordinarily hard work. Whenever Gertie (Sandra) was on it floated easily but the rest has been tricky. Sandra is a glorious part. My only deep fear is that Gertie may overplay it."

He needn't have worried. Having initially been excited by it, Gertie turned against it. Which caused Noël to tell her husband, Richard Aldrich, that his wife "should mind her manners and if she wants another play from me, she can fish for it." At the same time Kay Hammond and her husband, John Clements, whom Noël had also wanted for the play, turned it down too.

Disappointment followed disappointment. What about Vivien Leigh for Sandra?

"Binkie phoned to say that Vivien and Larry violently disliked poor old *Home and Colonial* and flew at him for encouraging me. They said they loved me far too much to lie to me and that I was not to do the play, as it was old-fashioned Noel Coward and would do me great harm. This is a surprising and salutary jolt, and I have a strange feeling that they are right. At all events, I love them for their honesty and moral courage. They may be wrong, but I must admit that the play didn't come easily in the first place and I don't think my heart has ever been deeply in it. I

Act 1. The Hon. Maud Witterby (Edith Meiser), Lady Alexandra Shotter (Claudette Colbert), and the Earl of Sharpenhoe (Chester Stratton) (1951).

shall think carefully and probably shelve it for at least a year. It is all very peculiar but I feel a sense of relief."

A year later he has significantly rewritten it as *Island Fling* and it is being produced at the Westport Country Playhouse in summer stock. The Playhouse in Connecticut at this point was being run by Jack Wilson, Noël's former lover and business manager. By this time the personal relationship is long since over and the business one noticeably shaky.

Nonetheless Jack feels he has pulled off a coup by signing Claudette Colbert to play Sandra.

July 25, 1951
"Cable from Jack—my play is apparently a success and Claudette is wonderful in it. After a talk with Binkie have decided to fly to America and see it before it closes. I must know whether it is good or not and what Jack has done with it."

From there things began to unravel . . .

July 29
"Another long cable from Jack literally beseeching me not to come to America. He has obviously bitched the play by bad direction and doesn't want me to see for myself. He is behaving like an abject fool."

August 26

"Wrote a long letter to Jack accepting his suggestion that we finish our theatrical association. This is a relief as I think very little of him as a theatre man."

Meanwhile, back to the Smith-Corona . . . and four years later . . .

March 10, 1955

"I have been pressing on with *Home and Colonial* and have rewritten the whole play except for the hut scene and a few good bits here and there. It has been a salutary experience. It really wasn't good enough and was curiously overwritten. I seem, in later years, to have lost my gift for economy. This has been, and in the future must continue to be, remedied. It is now very good, I think, light and undated. I have reverted to one of the other original titles, *South Sea Bubble.* I am reading it to Claudette tomorrow. I think she will probably play it. This has all been hard work but worthwhile and I feel relieved to have salvaged a play which was really too intrinsically good to be allowed to moulder away."

Claudette had been too badly scarred by the Westport experience to wish to risk repeating it—whatever the title.

Even then he couldn't leave it alone . . .

April 10

"I've finally finished . . . written in a new scene and made the whole of act one much stronger. It now has a shape and a plot, which it didn't have before."

By September—ironically—he has Vivien Leigh, obviously forgetting her earlier reservations, "madly enthusiastic" about the revised play.

South Sea Bubble ran for 276 performances and would certainly have run longer, if Vivien hadn't become pregnant and left the cast rather precipitately.

"I think from Vivien's point of view that it is a highly perilous enterprise. If anything goes wrong, it will very possibly send her round the bend again; she is over forty, very, very small and none too well balanced mentally."

Noël's instinct didn't let him down. Vivien had a miscarriage almost straightaway.

Reflecting on the play later. . . . "I am quite prepared to admit that *South Sea Bubble* does not rank among my best comedies . . . but it has, to my prejudiced eye, a good deal to recommend it. I find Sandra a gay

With Ian Hunter in *South Sea Bubble* (1956).

and enchanting character, so much so that I have reintroduced her in my recent novel, *Pomp and Circumstance.*

"To be honest, I consider the first act to be rather verbose and lacking in action, but from then on the play gathers momentum and I have found it highly entertaining both to write and read. The fact that my inner vision of it has never been distracted by seeing it performed may have a lot to do with my pleasure in it."

At this point (1956) Noël was a U.K. tax exile and only permitted a limited number of days' residence.

He then ends up where he would have wished to come in . . .

"I still envisage it being played by Gertrude Lawrence and, with all loving respect to Vivien and courteous bows to Claudette Colbert and whoever else decides to have a bash at Sandra, I still know that no one in the world, however gifted and charming, could endow her with the unique quality that was Gertie's own special enchantment."

Nineteen fifty-one also showed the critical tide beginning to turn for Noël . . .

March 23

"Good Friday. Very good Friday, really. Suddenly evolved a comedy called *Moxie*. It feels the sort of play I want to write."

A few days later . . .

"Eight pages done of *Moxie* and rather good. The flow is beginning, and oh, the bliss of writing dialogue."

Moxie is the personal maid and confidante of the widowed Countess of Marshwood. The Countess is waiting for the arrival of her son and his fiancée, a budding film starlet, when she is shocked by Moxie handing in her notice. Pressed to say why she wants to leave after all these years, she finally admits it's because the starlet, Miranda Frayle, is her younger sister from whom she is estranged. She cannot bear to be seen as a lowly domestic, even though her sister is originally Freda Birch and they are both daughters of a Brixton greengrocer.

On the surface the play could easily be dubbed "old-fashioned Coward" with its class-conscious theme. The fact that it transcended the

The young Gladys. His nickname for her would be "Darling Hag."

obvious pitfalls and ran for 477 performances at the Savoy Theatre was attributable, in Noël's view, to the fact that it "was beautifully played by an excellent cast . . . Gladys Cooper (Felicity Marshwood) gave one of the most incisive, witty and altogether enchanting comedy performances that it has even been my pleasure to see. But then Gladys Cooper learned her job in her young days from four of the most brilliant actor-manager-directors who ever graced our theatre—Seymour Hicks, Charles Hawtrey, Dennis Eadie and Gerald du Maurier.

"To watch the precision with which she timed her lines (not, I hasten to add, until she had learned them, which took quite a while) was to me an exquisite pleasure. She also continued, obviously because she made no effort to do so, to look as lovely as she has ever looked, even in the old days when her picture postcards could be bought by the bushel, two-pence *glacé* and coloured but never penny plain. From the above eulogy the perceptive reader may gather that I am very fond of Gladys Cooper."

Moxie did not survive as a title and the play became *Relative Values*.

━━━

Re-enter the Lunts . . .

May 18, 1951

"I want to do a Victorian comedy for Alfred and Lynn, if only I can get a good enough idea."

The idea didn't take too long to arrive and, although he was heavily involved with *Relative Values* and several other projects, he managed to commit it to paper by year end. He met with the Lunts in New York and Noël read them the first draft of what was now *Quadrille*.

"They are absolutely ecstatic about it," he wrote in his *Diary*, "and really could not have been more grateful and sweet."

But they were no longer the Lunts he had worked with two decades ago. Having acted exclusively together ever since, they had perfected their own *modus vivendi*, which included modifying a playwright's work to achieve what they considered would be best for them. The professional chemistry had changed—even when it came to working with Noelie.

Noelie found the new experience unnerving—and told them so . . .

The play is yours to do as you like with. I wrote it for you and there it is. I will not rewrite or alter one more line. You can cut it to bits, play it backwards, engage Shirley Temple to play Octavia. I shall not be pleased but I shan't mind all that much because, unless it is played as I wrote it, I shall never come and see it.

I expect this letter will make you hopping mad but that can't be helped either. I am, as you may have gathered, hopping mad myself.

I feel terribly sad about all this. The principal cause of my sadness is that you have apparently so little faith in the play I wrote for you.

Some poor tortured playwright should have written this letter to you years ago.

Love, love, love as always and for ever (although at the moment vitiated by desperation!!!)

NOELIE

Quadrille opened at New York's Coronet Theatre on November 3, 1954, and ran for 150 performances. (It had run for 329 at London's Phoenix Theatre.) The U.S. run could have been longer but the Lunts decided

Alfred and Lynn in *Quadrille*—Phoenix Theatre, London (1952).

to end it and canceled the national tour that could have put the production into profit.

Noël wrote in his *Diary*—"This is a sad blow and a very nasty little surprise . . . Whether this is because they are old or cross or tired or just stubborn, I don't know, probably all four. I don't know what is really going on in their minds . . . I have said nothing one way or the other."

Nude with Violin (1956)

Back in October 1950 Noël was "suddenly struck with a really wonderful idea for a light comedy . . . It fell into place easily, which is always a good sign . . ."

Over the next few days "The idea matured and grew. No title yet but it really could be a wonderful satire on the dear old art lovers. It will have to be kept at a high artificial pitch throughout."

"Suddenly thought of a title, *Nude with Violin,* which is really right for the play."

Noël was himself a painter in what he called the "Touch-and-Gauguin Style" of Primitive art. He had little time for art critics and after reading Wilenski's *Lives of the Impressionists* he confided to his *Diary* in 1954 . . .

"Really no burlesque, however extravagant, could equal the phrases he uses to describe the 'Abstract' boys. Quite a lot of it is completely unintelligible. He talks a great deal of 'emotive force' and 'lyrical colour' and 'constant functional forms,' etc., and after he has described a picture in approximately these terms you turn to a coloured plate and look at a square lady with three breasts and a guitar up her crotch. At any rate I am grateful to him for giving me a lot of hilarious material."

From there a short step to *Nude with Violin* . . .

The plot is a typical farce. The famous, if eccentric, painter Paul Sorodin has died. His manservant and confidant, Sebastien, is waiting in the apartment for the estranged family to return from the funeral. They arrive with Jacob Friedland, the art dealer who handled Sorodin's pictures. He explains that the work falls into four distinct periods—the Farouche (1927 to the early 1930s), the Circular (1933–1939), the postwar "Jamaican," and, finally, the Neo-Infantilism, which lasted until his death.

Then everything begins to unravel as it is revealed that Sorodin never painted a picture in his life and the four individuals who actually did the work arrive one by one to claim what they see as their inheritance.

Nineteen fifty-six now and the play is out of town—a long way out of town. In Dublin, to be precise.

Noël's recent decision to become a tax exile meant that at this point he could not visit the U.K. So he went to Ireland to see what John Gielgud—who was directing as well as starring—had done to the play . . .

September 27

Well, I now know the worst and the best and the in-between about *Nude with Violin* and can act accordingly. Actually I have been the centre of such a carry-on during the last few days that I can hardly see straight, but I can at least see straight enough to realise that the play needs stringent cutting, a bit of rewriting, and a hundred per cent redirecting.

John, to my infinite relief, is so very much better than I thought he would be that my real apprehensions are gone. He looks fine and, although not yet comedically sure, is neither embarrassing nor mannered, both of which I dreaded he would be. There are a few "Terry" ringing tones in his voice but these can be eliminated. David Horne is hopelessly miscast and moos and bellows like a mad water-buffalo, thereby completely upsetting the balance of the play. The set is very good but the lighting far, far too dim.

John has directed the play with loving care and reverence and given everyone so much fussy business to do that most of the comedy lines are lost. They get up, sit down, carry trays in and out, change places and move around so incessantly that I nearly went out of my mind.

However, all this can and will be rectified. The play, I think, is genuinely funny and should be successful, but this I cannot be sure of until I cut away all the fussy inessentials and see it clear. It is extraordinary that a fine director like Johnny, who can do *The Cherry Orchard* and *A Day by the Sea* so superbly, should have gone so very far wrong. I can only conclude that it was over-anxiety.

Noël really should not have been surprised. Much of Gielgud's early career had been spent as Noël's understudy and he had somehow cast himself in The Master's shadow.

Noël continues . . .

"I am certainly glad now that I did not see *South Sea Bubble,* for had I done so there would have been no time to get it right. I wonder why it is that my plays are such traps for directors, as indeed my lyrics are for singers. Nobody seems capable of leaving well enough alone and allowing the words to take care of themselves. Neither my lyrics nor my dialogue require decoration, all they do require are clarity, diction and intention and a minimum of gesture and business."

The play—with Noël still *in absentio*—opened at the Globe Theatre on November 7 of that year. As he recorded, "It received almost unanimous abuse from the critics and ran to capacity for 18 months . . . After playing it for nine months John Gielgud left the cast and was replaced by Michael Wilding, who brought to it even larger audiences, immense personal charm and startling inaudibility. After six months he in turn was replaced by Robert Helpmann who, from all accounts was extremely funny and enjoyed it almost as much as the audience."

In May . . .

"The time has come for me to stir my stumps . . . and being temperamentally restless, I am now sniffing the sawdust again . . . I think seriously of playing *Nude* myself for a limited season on Broadway. With me in it it would be practically surefire and also make an attractive television and movie proposition."

In November he admits that he miscalculated . . .

"I always serve myself the best!" says NOËL COWARD

It's beer as beer should be   **Rheingold** EXTRA DRY *Lager Beer*   Always refreshing – never filling

"Both Brooks Atkinson [*New York Times*] and Walter Kerr [*New York Herald Tribune*] were contemptuous of the play, although they praise me as a comedian . . . There is obviously a quality in *Nude* which irritates the critical mind. Perhaps because the whole play is a blistering satire on the critical mind? At all events, in London it didn't receive one even civil notice and has played to capacity for over a year . . . I fear, even with me in it, that it will not do that here. In England the audience can identify with the family and its dilemmas. Here there is no line of identification with what, to us, is the ordinary well-behaved middle class. Such a class really doesn't exist in America."

That observation sent him off on a comparative sociological riff . . .

"Also, in England the public is more prone to think for itself. In America they have to be told what to enjoy and what to avoid, not only in the theatre but in every phase of life. They are told by television and radio what to eat, drink and smoke, what cars to buy and what laxatives and sanitary towels to use. They are told, in no uncertain terms, what movies to go to and what stars to admire. They are allowed to choose, admittedly from not too glamorous a selection, what gods to worship. The power of individual thought has been atrophied in them by the incessant onslaught of commercialism. Their reading matter, for the large majority, consists of columnists' gossip, headlines and magazines. Among the so-called intelligentsia there is only one trend at the moment, a sort of defeated psychopathic despair."

Having got that off his chest, he was still left with the dilemma of a faltering Broadway run . . .

"I am aware of a tremendous change in the quality of the New York audiences since I played here twenty-one years ago. They used to be quick on comedy, quicker than London audiences. Now, however, this quickness has gone. They are quite appreciative on the whole, but much dimmer. In fact they have lost the capacity for participation.

"Possibly this change has been caused by the 'theatre party' habit, which to my mind is a dangerous and intolerable racket. Charity organisers buy out the theatre at the box office prices. They then proceed to sell the tickets at exorbitant prices to the supporters of some given charities. Thus, most of the members of the audience, particularly the men, arrive at the theatre either consciously or subconsciously aware that they have paid too highly for their seats and that whatever show they see has got to be super-good to justify their expenditure. These 'theatre party' audiences are hell to play to.

"The managements, unwisely I think in the long view, encourage this racket. For them it is, of course, a form of insurance. If they have sold the house out for five or six performances a week for two or three months before the play has even opened, they can at least have a chance, in the face of bad notices, of getting some money back . . . It is another ghastly example of the all-pervasive commercialism . . ."

As the year ended . . .

"A beastly week. All the dreary Christmas fuss and half-empty houses."

Noël then made a New Year's resolution. No way was he going to limp out of America, tail between legs. When they moved on to San Francisco . . . "I have decided to play *Present Laughter* alternately with *Nude* and use the same set with a few slight alterations."

Which in due course is what he did, having tried it out in New York, where he did *not*—repeat *not*—invite the critics!

Although he was not to know it, it was his farewell to Broadway as an actor. The next time he appeared onstage there it would be to receive a Tony "for lifetime achievement" in 1970.

Look After Lulu (1959)

Look After Lulu (1959) was another in what was becoming a long line of Coward comedies that found favor with nobody—but the public.

The play was a translation/adaptation of *Occupe-toi d'Amélie,* a farce by the French writer Georges Feydeau (1862–1921). It was an unlikely choice of subject for Noël, who found the work of adaptation unrewarding . . .

"The trouble is that none of it, apart from visual action, is very funny." He considered Feydeau to be "a very untidy playwright. He leaves characters around all over the place and disposes of them without explanation."

However, he completed work on it by the end of 1958 and productions were planned for both Broadway and the West End.

For Broadway he had hoped for Shirley MacLaine but her film commitments ruled that out. Carol Channing? She didn't want to play a prostitute.

Having seen her in cabaret, Noël discovered the young Tammy Grimes and cast her in the part. Vivien Leigh—forgiven after *South Sea Bubble*—would star in the London production.

The U.S. run turned out to be more of a stagger for only thirty-nine performances. In summing it up . . . "The general consensus of opinion is that Cyril Ritchard over-directed it, that Tammy didn't quite come up to expectations . . . All of this, I think, is quite true, but it doesn't really explain the failure. The reasons for that are deeper. The Broadway theatre for some years has been in the doldrums, owing to . . . the sheep-like attitude of the public to the two leading critics, Brooks Atkinson and Walter Kerr . . . Also the American public is not attuned to stylised farce, neither are the American actors. Personally, I have few regrets. I saw the play rapturously received in New Haven by audiences who had not been told much about it one way or the other. I found it, in spite of the above-mentioned defects, very enjoyable. It was a bit common and lacked coherent style."

On to London . . .

Here the theatrical drama lay not so much in the play as in the fact that it was being staged at the Royal Court Theatre, the crucible of the Angry Young playwrights like John Osborne. The Royal Court was meant to conquer the West End—yet it seemed that the reverse was happening. Blood pressure returned to normal when *Lulu* was transferred to the New Theatre for a modest run of 110 performances.

Waiting in the Wings (1960)

April 13, 1958
"I have some ideas beginning to burgeon. One is a play called *The Wings* about a home for retired actresses. I really do think that this has great possibilities."

In an introduction to the published text Noël puts the play in context . . .

"The Wings is a small charity home for retired actresses. It differs from other organisations of its kind in that it provides only for those who have been stars or leading ladies and who, through age, lack of providence, misfortune, etc., have been reduced to poverty.

"No actress under the age of 60 is eligible for admittance to the home."

The subject matter had a personal resonance for Noël. He had taken over the running of the Actors' Orphanage from Sir Gerald du Maurier in 1934 and only gave up that particular role when he left England as a tax exile in 1956. In addition he was known to make personal cash "gifts" to supporting actors who had worked with him over the years and who now found themselves in difficult circumstances. *Waiting in the Wings* offered employment to a number of them.

May 1
"In a wild resurgence of energy I rushed at *Waiting in the Wings* and wrote away like mad, getting up at 6:30 every morning and fairly flogging myself. Alas, two days ago, when I had nearly finished the second act, I realised with dismay that although the characters are good and the dialogue, of course, excellent, there is no play. I had started too soon and

too quickly, without taking enough care to construct properly. I was horribly discouraged by this and felt wretched.

"I love the idea and it should and must be carried out really well. I am no longer twenty-eight but fifty-eight and my processes are inevitably a little slower and my critical standards are higher. I find I can no longer dash off things with quite the insouciance I used to have . . . Since I made the decision to abandon the play for the time being, I have felt much better. Also ideas about how it should be done are beginning to flow unbidden into my mind."

April 5, 1959

"I read through what I had written last year. I found it much better than I had thought it was and so I set to work and finished it. I think I have done a good job and that it is a moving and valid play . . . my hopes are high and I certainly do know that one or two of the scenes in it are among the best I have written."

Waiting in the Wings opened at the Duke of York's Theatre on September 7, 1960 . . . ("It's a real 'theatery' theatre and dead right for it.")

U.S. production (1999).

"From the moment the curtain rose on the opening performance I knew instinctively that that particular audience was warm, well-disposed and eager to find the play good. Actually it was one of the most moving first nights I have ever attended. The audience reaction was marvellous, swift in all the laughs and quiet as mice when required. At the end there was a really tremendous ovation and when I finally emerged from the theatre an hour later there were cheering crowds on both sides of St. Martin's Lane.

"The next morning the notices!

"I was accused of tastelessness, vulgarity, sentimentality, etc. To read them was like being repeatedly slashed in the face. I don't remember such concentrated venom for many a long day . . . In this play Sybil [Thorndike's] great performance, to say nothing of Marie [Lohr's] and the others, was barely mentioned . . .

"Meanwhile the business looks healthy and the advance is good, but this blast of spleen has, of course, altered the atmosphere. We are not a 'smash' hit, which we should be judging by the audience reaction, and, I fear, we may have to fight a bit to survive. I am terribly sad for the company's sake. This ghastly cold douche after that heart-warming triumph cannot but have laid them low inside. I know it made me frankly miserable. To be the target of so much virulence is painful, however much one pretends it doesn't matter. It breeds hatred in the heart and that is unedifying and uncomfortable. I suppose it is foolish to wonder why they hate me so. I have been too successful too long."

Later he was fortunately able to record that *Wings* was able to play to capacity for three months (188 performances) and to add in the published version—"I recommend this play, more than any I have written for many years, to the reader's most earnest attention."

But it would be many more years before he wrote another.

Even though he felt disinclined to write another play for the theatre, he was prompted to write *about* the theatre.

October 9

"I have written a 2,500-word article on 'The New Movement in the Theatre' which really is rather good, I think. When I've done one or two more I shall send them to the *Sunday Times* and later use them as the nucleus of a book on theatre. I think, by now, my age and experience entitle me to write one."

(In the end he wrote five articles, which are reproduced in the relevant places in this book.)

======

"The American theatre, with the exception of a very few exceptional hits, seems to be falling off considerably. I think that this is inevitable, because what with the Unions and Equity and one thing and another and everybody's salaries being far too high, it is impossible to have a moderate success. I always suspected that the Unions and Equity would kill the living theatre far more effectively than the talkies or television could ever do, and it looks to me as if this is coming to pass. I think the only thing to do, when eventually I appear again on Broadway, is an eight-week season with one set and a small cast, but we shall see."

(1950)

"Oh how nice it would be, just for today and tomorrow, to be a little boy of five instead of an aging playwright of fifty-five and look forward to all the high jinks with passionate excitement and be given a clockwork train with a full set of rails and a tunnel. However, it is no use repining. As things are, drink will take the place of parlour games and we shall all pull crackers and probably enjoy ourselves enough to warrant at least some of the god-damned fuss." (*Diary*, December 24, 1954)

Noël entered the sixties—his own and the century's—questioningly.

Time's wingèd chariot, he felt, was beginning to goose him.

In *Waiting in the Wings* he has Maudie say . . .

"Who was it who said there was something beautiful about growing old?"

To which Bonita replies . . .

"Whoever it was, I have news for him."

And as Noël himself remarked—"It is said that old age has its compensations. I wonder what they are?"

One of them was the revival of *Private Lives* at the tiny Hampstead Theatre on April 24, 1963. The production was well reviewed and transferred to the West End. It seemed to renew interest in his earlier work and is now generally considered to mark the beginning of what came to be called "Dad's Renaissance."

In a musical he was contemplating there was a serendipitous song . . .

Later than Spring
Have no fears for future years
For sweet compensation you may find,
Make your bow
To the moment that is now
And always bear in mind:

Refrain 1

Later than Spring
The warmth of Summer comes,
The charm of Autumn comes,
The leaves are gold,
Poets say
That the blossoms of May
Fade away
And die.
Yet, don't forget
That we met
When the sun was high.
Later than Spring
Words that were said before,
Tears that were shed before
Can be consoled.
Realize that it's wise to remember
Though Time is on the wing,
Song birds still sing
Later than Spring.

Refrain 2

Later than Spring
Though careless rapture's past
No need to gaze aghast
At days gone by,
You can still if you will
Feel the thrill
Of a new desire,
Still
Feel that glow
When you know
That your world's on fire.
Later than Spring
Remembered April showers
May bring our present hours
A clearer sky.
We pretend and pretend it's the end

But the pendulum must swing,
Nightingales sing
Later than Spring.

Reprise
Later than Spring
Much disillusion comes,
Sometimes confusion comes,
You lose your way.
Need it be such unbearable sadness
To face the truth?
Love, with its passionate madness
Belongs to youth.
Later than Spring
Our values change, my dear,
It would be strange, my dear,
If they should stay.
Waste no tears
On the hurrying years,
For whatever they may bring
Song birds still sing
Later than Spring.

8

THE CRITICS

"O, You Chorus of Reviewers,
Irresponsible, Indolent Reviewers."
—TENNYSON (AFTER CATULLUS)

———

James Agate · Alexander Woollcott · Graham Greene · Kenneth Tynan

"I can take any amount of criticism, so long as it is unqualified praise."

·

"I have always been fond of them...I think it is so frightfully clever of them to go night after night to the theatre and know so little about it."

·

"If I had really cared about the critics, I would have shot myself in the Twenties."
—PLAY PARADE 4 (1954)

·

"Criticism and Bolshevism have one thing in common. They both seek to pull down that which they could never build."
(1925)

·

"They—the Critics—search busily behind the simplest of my phrases, like old ladies peering under the bed for burglars, and are not content until they have unearthed some definite, and usually quite inaccurate, reason for my saying this or that. This strange mania I can only suppose is the distinctive feature of a critical mind as opposed to a creative one."

·

"A young playwright who believes that it is possible to achieve critical acclaim AND a successful career is doomed to disillusionment. He may have one or the other, but he cannot have both, at least not for very long."

·

"I could learn from Gielgud, from Olivier, from Somerset Maugham, from the public. Never from the critics."

·

"Oh, Lordy, Lordy, there is quite an accumulation of bitterness in my heart for those mean, ungenerous, envious, ignorant little critics."

—JANUARY 1961

·

ZOE:

I'm so old-fashioned—I like love stories without the slightest suggestion of sex.

EDWARD:

You ought to be a critic

—THIS WAS A MAN (1926)

·

Routine for a Critic (Dirge)
Night after night my weary body slumps
Into my usual complimentary seat,
Hedged in by those I envy and detest,
The rich, the "chic," the fashionably dressed,
The over-publicised, effete, elite,
Shrill-voiced young introverts,
Authors and actors reeking with success,
Earning ten times my income more or less
And stumbling, as they pass, across my feet.

Night after night when I have judged the play
And sent "collect" a cable to New York on it,
Stated my opinion, burnt my boats,
Typed out my notice from my programme notes

And maybe written out a broadcast talk on it,
I then go home to my suburban wife,
Still querulous, still having "change of life."
Still in the pink kimono with a stork on it.

Night after night I go to sleep and dream
My latest play has been a huge success,
I see myself, a flower in my lapel,
Returning to my luxury hotel,
Wearing, as usual, my faultless evening dress.
The lift boys bow to me, the waiters beam,
They know and I know that soon I'll be knighted.
Also they're all aware I've been invited
To champagne supper with a Duchess.

.

"I don't know what makes them so vitriolic; I suppose it's my continued success and something about my personality that infuriates them, in which case I fear they will have to get on with it."

On Good Reviews

"Such allusions are immensely agreeable. Unimportant, perhaps, in their essence, but in their implication very important indeed. Just as millions of little coral animals in so many years construct a barrier reef against the sea, so can these small accolades, over a period of time, build, if not quite a barrier reef, at least a fortification against the waves of oblivion."
—EVAN LORRIMER IN "WHAT MAD PURSUIT?"

.

"Shaw's plays are the price we pay for Shaw's prefaces."
—JAMES AGATE

.

For most of his career Noël was critical of critics.

In the main he had a point. Many of them for much of the time seemed to be somewhat jealously condemning the theatrical phenomenon he rapidly became and remained in the U.K.—even during the Siberia of the late 1940s and 1950s. If you disapprove of the man, how can you possibly see merit in what the man writes?

Noël's relationship with some of them was a piece of theatre in and of itself.

And yet . . . there was perception in what some of them wrote—particularly in the early years before judgment became clouded by personal chemistry.

James Agate (1877–1947)

In the 1920s, for example, London's leading critic was undoubtedly James Agate. The fact that he entitled his nine-volume diary/autobiography *Ego* gives some indication of what he felt his words were worth.

Before they fell out on a personal basis, Agate offered the young Noël—who had just written and played in *The Young Idea* (1923)—some worthwhile advice in his review . . .

"One remembers Mr. Noël Coward's first play [*I'll Leave It to You*] as a very light and entirely admirable comedy. His second, *The Young Idea,* if you examine it closely, reaches after more than it can grasp—a good fault in a young writer. Superficially it is exhilarating and great fun. The two plays together suggest original talent, a feeling for the theatre, and a quite extraordinary belief in the existence of an audience capable of intellectual delight. It is unusual to find an actor sufficiently interested in plays to undertake the writing of them, and perhaps I may suggest that Mr. Coward is not, primarily, a player. He always seems to me to stand beside his impersonations, to turn them inside out for curious inspection, to quiz them. Whatever character he essays at once becomes unoriginal, and the original fellow is always the actor's own self. . . .

"Mr. Coward has spun this play out of his own wit and entrails but hardly out of human nature. If he will only be content to observe a little more, and give observation back in his own way, he bids fair to become . . . etc."

"As Sholto Mr. Coward gives an admirable performance of—Mr. Coward."

Agate neatly echoed Noël's own interior feelings about the piece—which he could easily accept because it had, after all, been conceived and written before his American Epiphany.

In many ways the most valued souvenir of the production was "a letter of the most generous praise from Mr. Charles Blake Cochran"—one of the most important producers of the day.

═══

Agate continued his encouragement with *The Vortex*.

"There is the imprint of truth upon this play. These creatures are nauseating as *animalculae* in a pond, but they interest. The craftsmanship is beyond reproach, and the dialogue is taut and spare and of an admirable *vraisemblance*. The piece was magnificently acted."

═══

While their mutual admiration was still in full flower Noël was asked by Agate to write the introduction to one of many volumes of *Contemporary Theatre* . . .

I was very appreciative of the honour Mr. James Agate has done me to ask me to write an introduction to this volume. I believe he is one of the few critics in England who make a genuine effort to be constructive.

The mental equipment of the average critic consists of an enthusiastic knowledge of Fleet Street and a faint contempt for the commercial theatre (fostered doubtless by the mildly bitter realisation that plays though easily written are not so easily accepted) and a partiality for presenting whatever opinions they may have in uninspired but adequate journalese.

Mr. Agate—by means of his nimble mind and a definite love of the stage rises up like a Triton among these minnows. Though even he couldn't be absolved of certain prejudices. The greatest of which is his unbridled passion for dead dramatists and deader plays!

Maugham, Shaw, Galsworthy, Barrie and all contemporary writers shrink into insignificance before the ardent flame of devotion to the Restoration Playwrights.

He rushes into the Lyric Theatre, Hammersmith with all the force of his dynamic intelligence concentrated on enjoying himself and finally emerges proudly flushed and inebriated with the pirouettings and gambollings of his pet Restoration lambs.

His enthusiasm even carries him so far as to say in his criticism of *The Way of the World* that "Wit of Millimant's order is imperishable for the simple reason that her creator gave her a mind" and there are more Millimants around town today than there are Hedda Gablers. But later on in another outburst of exuberant enjoyment of *The Country Wife* he has apparently already sacrificed his passion for Millimant on the altar of his adoration for Wycherley's Mrs. Pinchwife.

Surely the dust of ages cannot for Mr. Agate have so enshrouded them in glamour that he fails to observe the infinite superiority of Mr. Somerset Maugham's polished finesse. I have a sneaky suspicion that had the Duchess and Pearl Grayston been christened respectively "Lady Lovesick" and "Mistress Faithless" he would have appreciated them more.

In spite of the fact that he occasionally drags the Restoration herring across the path of unbiased criticism, the truth reward that his selective mind and an extraordinary sublety of perception are of unmeasurable service to the English Theatre. There are practically no other critics of the present day who successfully eliminate the personal element in their tirades against the wretched Actor, Author and Producers but Agate possesses the full courage of his convictions and doesn't wait to see which way the wind is blowing before voicing them. Nor does he assume that Patronising Air of Condescension and Patronage which sits so heavily upon his younger associates. It is also a great comfort when reading his current notices in *The Sunday Times* to stumble across such shy-making phrases as—"Methinks there will be no grounds for this right merrie little comedy to be removed from the London stage for many a long day."

Unfortunately even Mr. Agate falls for the prevailing mania for comparisons. He seems unable to write a notice of one Author without mentioning at least sixty-five others in various stages of mental or physical decomposition. It is a little disheartening for an Ambitious Author waiting anxiously for either praise or blame to be greeted with the following sort of notice . . .

ROLLING STONES
by Petra Luck Minaver

Miss Minaver's play has one great thing in its favour—it presents its problem honestly. What matters is that the selfsame problem had been handled by Stephen Bloodworthy in *Fate Enchained*. Who can forget that memorable scene when Tessie, soaked in absinthe, rounds on her embittered Auntie Jessie crying—"Don't touch me, don't touch me! It is your upbringing that has brought me down!" Or yet again that scene of exquisite pathos in De Vriaac's *La Vache Espagnol* when Juanita returned from the bull fight to find her lover, crazed with wine, tearing up all the photographs of her mother's wedding group. She goes up to him tenderly— *"Pourquoi est ce que tu fais ça dans la cuisine, mon cher?"*

Then the almost stark realism of the reply—*"Parcequ'il fait moins chaud ici qu'a la salle a manger!"* There is always a certain defiance in De Vriacc's work coupled with a quality of sex psychology unequalled in the English Theatre since Edgar Shepmeadow's *Girls Will Be Girls* and Norman Chudd's miracle play in seventeen scenes. Miss Minaver's second act reminds one of Barrel's *Strange Experience of Miss Barnet,* except that in this case Osric is in the Guards and Violet is a society girl rather than an inn keeper's daughter.

Nevertheless, the play has many good points and was competently handled by Sir Gerald du Maurier (in extremely baggy trousers) and Mr. Ivor Novello (in a long red beard). The heroine was in the capable hands of Miss Gladys Cooper (who should get out of that tiresome habit of smoking backwards). Mr. Owen Nares contributed one of his usual unstable cameos in Act Three.

Miss Minaver will probably write a fine play one day but she must—to quote Sergizot—*"Attends et voir!"*

.

I have often heard Mr. Agate grumbling with utter lack of conviction that "these damned Sunday performances completely ruin his day's golf." This attitude, I am convinced, is a sort of defiant gesture. He doesn't wish us to know that really the Theatre means far more to him than most things and he goes to each play with a heart beating with hope.

On the rare occasions when even some of his yearnings towards the ideal are gratified, then there is no one more generous or enthusiastic . . . To an Author such as myself this is the most necessary thing in the world and I can say with real sincerity that I would rather be blamed by Mr. Agate than praised by most other people.

A couple of years later with *Easy Virtue* there are signs of critical souring setting in . . .

"The higher the brow the narrower the mind. That is if one is a fashionable young playwright familiar with the tawdry round of the Riviera and unable to conceive a world elsewhere . . . Mr. Noel Coward gets

younger with every play, and in *Easy Virtue* has attained to that pure ide-
alism which prompts the schoolboy who has been taken to see *La Dame
Aux Camélias* to believe for the next ten years that a *cocotte* is the noblest
work of man if not of God.

"At first it looked as though he was going to write his best play . . .
Unfortunately, as soon as the play began to move it went to pieces."

Agate was to relent with the 1929 *Bitter Sweet,* which, after many ifs
and buts, he considered "a thundering job."

He went on to say—"Of course, the country may be teeming with people who are capable of doing what Mr. Coward has done. Only nobody
else has done it yet. Nobody else has ever done it, except Wagner."

After that it was a steady downhill ride. Perhaps it was simply a gen-
erational clash of intellects. Agate wanted to feel that he had shaped the
young playwright into the success he became. The young playwright
determined to make it clear that he was his own creation.

There may also be a clue in Agate's quote from *Ego* (4) . . .

"I don't know very much but what I do know I know better than anybody. My mind is not a bed to be made and re-made."

By the early postwar years Agate was less of a factor. When he called
the book of the 1946 *Pacific 1860* "mindless bosh," nobody stirred. In any
case, the show had enough problems of its own.

Noël skewered him in verse . . .

To Mr. James Agate
(to an eminent critic)

Mr. James Agate
Arrived late
As a matter of fact
He missed half the first Act.
Then, in the Circle Bar,
Whence Bacchus beckoned,
He missed most of the Second,
Discussing Milton's blindness,
Thus going too far
From which I reckoned
That he would skip the Third
But I was wrong, far worse occurred,
He fell asleep!

There in his seat on the aisle
He dozed awhile,
Authors may weep
At such unkindness
But other than author's tears;
The ghosts of earlier years,
His own shades, his proprietary ghosts
Whom he reveres;
All those of whom he boasts
Of having seen, remembered; those would cry
More bitterly, more sorrowfully than I.
His Sarah, his Réjane and his Rachel,
(He can't remember her but he can tell
Many an anecdote
About her, and can quote
From *Phèdre*
Alas, he never quotes from *Cavalcedre*!)
How these would sob
To see so "vrai" a critic,
So "blasé" a critic,
So "gonflé" a critic
Let down his job!

Alexander Woollcott (1887–1943)

Then there was Alexander Woollcott, one of New York's leading—in his
view "THE leading"—drama critics of the 1920s and 1930s. Noël met
him on his initial visit to America in 1921 and was embraced as a member
pro tem of the Algonquin Round Table (or the "Vicious Circle," as non-
members dubbed it).

The fact that over the years Noël would write to Woollcott as "Dearest
Acky-wacky-weesa" indicates the fact that a genuine, if theatrical, friendship tended to dominate the strictly professional relationship. Together
they were a verbal double act that could have toured the halls. Woollcott
would sometimes address Noël as "My Blemish."

Noël would level the playing field by recalling that one of Woollcott's critical colleagues had called him "the Seidlitz Powder of Times
Square."

Woollcott, in fact, was also an occasional actor himself and the inspiration for the character of Sheridan Whiteside in the 1939 Kaufman-Hart play, *The Man Who Came to Dinner*. He even got to play himself on occasion.

Noël's acquaintance with the roly-poly Woollcott began in earnest and, fittingly, at a play . . .

"In the interval I contrived, by a casual word, to creep into the heart of Alexander Woollcott. The word was 'vexing.' I said, without any particularly witty intent, that I had found the performance of one of the actors in the play very vexing, whereupon the warm September night was instantly shattered by strange cluckings and gurglings and sharp, shrill wails of pleasure. I was unused to abandoned displays from eminent critics and I regarded this capering figure on the sidewalk with astonishment.

"Later on I became accustomed to such outbursts, finding, to my occasional dismay, that they worked both ways. Alexander Woollcott, in a rage, has all the tenderness and restraint of a newly caged cobra, and when striking, much the same admirable precision. He has written a good deal about me in various newspapers and magazines. He has, in criticism, brought me to the dust and raised me on to high pedestals, usually giving a sly, rococo twist to the pedestals. He has in biographical sketches, sacrificed, without pang of conscience many of my nobler characteristics to pertinent witticisms. He has coaxed, relentlessly, many hundreds of dollars out of me at backgammon and been loudly and urgently clamorous for payment."

In 1928 Noël was playing on Broadway in his own revue, *This Year of Grace!* One of his numbers was "A Room with a View." It was to become one of Noël's classic "hits" but Woollcott took against Noël's rendering of it and found a novel way of expressing his criticism long before he could do so in next day's print . . .

"As a final inducement to me to relinquish it to my understudy, he appeared in a stage box with a party, each member of which buried his or her face in a newspaper the moment I began to sing. All these gestures and many others of like devilishness have, oddly enough, merely served to cement even more strongly my fondness for him, and there he sits, and will probably continue to sit for ever, firmly ensconced in my affections, wearing a dreadful old green dressing-gown, playing to me all the Gilbert and Sullivan records that he knows I hate, and ordering me shrilly from the house whenever I win one point from him at any game of chance."

Woollcott did not, of course, "sit for ever" anywhere—not even at the Round Table. His health was never good since his military service in the First World War. He died during a radio broadcast in 1943.

As an exit he would have given himself a good review.

Later Noël was able to draw a more objective distinction between the character and the critic . . .

"It is wise to listen to other people's opinions but not always wise to be guided by them. Alec adored the witty side of me but distrusted my sentiment. He had a perfect right to say what he thought, but I had no right to allow myself to be so easily swayed by anyone so peculiarly prejudiced as Alec—and a critic into the bargain!"

―――――

Noël was never a fan of American critics . . .

"The New York drama critics Walter Kerr and Brooks Atkinson may best be described as the unhidden persuaders." (The reference would have had relevance at the time, since it referred to Vance Packard's currently successful book on the excesses of advertising: *The Hidden Persuaders*.)

Graham Greene (1904–1991)

And then there was Graham Greene . . .

Noël's relationship with him was problematic—at least in the early years.

Noël found it hard to understand what he was doing to rouse such ire. It seemed to transcend the professional. Greene seemed to find in Noël a repository for everything he personally considered out of date and irrelevant in the theatre and repeatedly said so in print.

Noël was always at a loss to understand what first triggered it—nor did Greene ever explain it in print—but certainly from the early 1940s Greene, at that time a critic for *The Spectator,* was in the habit of dragging him in as a point of reference, often by the most tortuous of means.

Reviewing a 1941 revival of Barrie's *Dear Brutus,* Greene laments the dramatically fallow years since the play's original 1917 production, "disappointing years when no sustained talent more important than Mr. Coward's has appeared in the theatre." Compared to Barrie, Greene believed,

"Mr. Coward's works already bear the lines of time more deeply." Of a costume drama: "This was a period piece in the worst—the Coward—sense." Elsewhere he compared "Coward comedies" to "too expensive cigarette cases." The sniping continued nonstop and finally Noël was moved to retaliate in verse. In June 1941 he sent Greene . . .

The Ballad of Graham Greene

Oh, there's many a heart beats faster, lads
And swords from their sheaths flash keen
When round the embers—the glowing embers
Men crouch at Hallowe'en
And suddenly somebody remembers
The name of Graham Greene.
(A literary disaster, lads
The fall of Graham Greene.)

Oh, there's many a Catholic Priest, my boys
And many a Rural Dean
Who, ages later—long ages later
When all has been, has been.
Will secretly read an old *Spectator*
And pray for Graham Greene.
(Let's hope its sales have decreased, my boys
Because of Graham Greene.)

Oh, one asks oneself and one's God, my lads
Was ever a mind so mean,
That could have vented—so shrilly vented
Such quantities of spleen
Upon a colleague? Unprecedented!
Poor Mr. Graham Greene.
(One's pride forbids one to nod, my lads
To Mr. Graham Greene.)

Oh, there's many a bitter smile, my boys
And many a sneer obscene
When any critic—a first-rate critic,
Becomes a "Might have been"

Through being as harsh and Jesuitic
As Mr. Graham Greene.
(Restrain that cynical smile, my boys,
To jeer is never worthwhile, my boys.
Remember the rising bile, my boys
Of Mr. Graham Greene.)

Was it Greene's bleak Catholicism that frowned on Noël's apparently superficial, overpublicized lifestyle? Hannen Swaffer and other critics had taken that view, confusing the image of the man with his work.

Was Noël's homosexuality an issue?

Greene himself was a highly esteemed novelist by the time in 1941 when he condemned *Blithe Spirit*—one of Noël's most successful plays—as "a weary exhibition of bad taste."

Yes, one might cavil that in wartime a comedy about death and the afterlife was a questionable premise but 1,997 audiences thought otherwise.

Noël eventually decided to retaliate—again in verse . . .

Dear Mr. Graham Greene, I Yearn
Dear Mr. Graham Greene, I yearn
So much to know why you should burn
With such fierce indignation at
This very fact that I exist.
I've been unable to resist
Sitting up later than I need
To read in the *Spectator* what
Appears to be no more, no less
Than shocking manners. I confess
Bewilderment. I've seldom seen
Another brother-writer press
Such disadvantage with such mean
Intent to hurt. You must have been
For years, in secret nourishing
A rich, rip-snorting, flourishing
Black hatred for my very guts!
Surely all these envenomed cuts
At my integrity and taste

Must be a waste of your own time?
What is my crime, beyond success?
(But you have been successful too
It can't be that) I know a few
Politer critics than yourself
Who simply hate my lighter plays
But do they state their sharp dispraise
With such surprising, rising bile?
Oh dear me no, they merely smile.
A patronising smile perhaps
But then these journalistic chaps
Unlike ourselves, dear Mr. Greene,
(Authors I mean) are apt to sneer
At what they fear to be apart
From that which they conceive as art.
You have described (also with keen,
Sadistic joy) my little book
About Australia, one look
At which should prove, all faults aside,
That I had tried, Dear Mr. Greene,
To do a job. You then implied
That I had run away, afraid,
A renegade. I can't surmise
Why you should view your fellow men
With such unfriendly, jaundiced eyes.
But then, we're strangers. I can find
No clue, no key to your dark mind.
I've read your books as they appear
And I've enjoyed them. (Nearly all.)
I've racked my brains in a sincere
But vain endeavour to recall
If, anytime or anywhere,
In Bloomsbury or Belgrave Square,
In Paris or Peking or Bude,
I have, unwittingly, been rude.
Or inadvertently upset you.
(Did I once meet you and forget you?
Have I ever been your debtor?

Did you once write me a letter
That I never got—or what?)
If I knew, I shouldn't worry.
All this anguish, all this flurry,
This humiliating scene
That I'm making, Mr. Greene,
Is a plea for explanation
For a just justification
By what strange Gods you feel yourself empowered
To vent this wild expenditure of spleen
Upon your most sincerely
Noël Coward.

Although they were well aware of each other, they never actually met until 1949, when they were both in middle age. Noël recorded . . .

"Met Graham Greene at long last and belaboured him for being vile about me in the past. Actually he was rather nice."

Four years later he ran into Greene and his then mistress, Catherine Walston, in Jamaica. Further rapprochement.

"He was very agreeable and his beastliness to me in the past I have for-

A Man Planning to Steal a Film.

given but not forgotten. He has a strange, tortured mind but, like most of God's creatures, aches to be loved."

Greene returned to the island the following year with Mrs. Walston and rented Noël's house, Blue Harbour. He spent time talking to Coley—with the obvious intention of having his remarks passed on to Noël. He was clearly in the business of making critical amends.

"We went to *After the Ball* the other night and thoroughly enjoyed it. Personally I like it better than *Bitter Sweet*."

Which makes one query his judgment as a theatre critic . . .

In 1959 Noël was invited to play with Alec Guinness in Carol Reed's film version of Greene's novel *Our Man in Havana*. His part was that of Hawthorne, a not very bright agent of MI5, who decides to recruit Wormold (Guinness) as "our man." Critics were unanimous in praising Noël's performance and one went so far as to say that he had "stolen" the picture from Guinness. Noël was not disposed to argue the point. After all, he said, "it was only petty larceny."

He wrote to Greene . . .

Now that our professional paths have at long last and irrevocably crossed, I feel a tiny celebration is in order. As you know, I have recently finished playing the role of Hawthorne—an experience I must admit I thoroughly enjoyed. Not only was the part beautifully written in your finest Italian hand but it gave me the opportunity to evoke all the hapless, bumbling bureaucrats I stumbled over in the war years. You must have suffered the same fate yourself or even you could not conjure them up from the vasty deep.

I very much fear that we got off to a sticky start all those years ago. You clearly thought that my attitude to life was a little *soufflé-ish* and I must confess I found yours occasionally *al dente*—but enough of this culinary *argot*. (You must forgive me but I have just discovered the joys of cooking—even if my nearest and dearest don't always share my enthusiasm for my own creations!)

Whether one agrees with some of your themes, you are without doubt one of the finest writers in the language we both share. You are also—rather more to my surprise and pleasure—one of the most entertaining companions, as I discovered when you and Catherine visited us in Jamaica . . .

So, my dear Graham, if He should give us a few more years—always supposing there is a He and you would know more about this than I—let us spend them, separately and together, thumbing our respective noses at those who most deserve it.

Yrs. Ever
HAWTHORNE

Kenneth Tynan (1927–1980)

"A good dramatic critic is one who perceives what is happening in the theatre of his time.

"A great dramatic critic also perceives what is *not* happening."

—KENNETH TYNAN

.

"A critic is a man who knows the way but can't drive the car."

.

If anyone was determined to earn the tag "eccentric," it was Kenneth Peacock Tynan. As an undergraduate at Oxford, for instance, he would order a restaurant meal to be served in reverse order, starting with the dessert. Every premise was there to be questioned.

After university he decided he'd like to try his hand as an actor but when he was cast as the First Player in Alec Guinness's disastrous 1951 production of *Hamlet,* he changed his mind. The fact that he suffered from a pronounced stutter, he felt, did not augur well, if he was to challenge the likes of Olivier and Gielgud.

He maintained his emotional connection with the theatre by turning to reviewing. He turned out to be a witty and incisive writer with views that were often at odds with theatrical convention at *The Observer* from 1954—with a period at *The New Yorker* from 1958 to 1960.

Noël received his share of negative comment. Of the 1952 *Quadrille,* starring the Lunts, Tynan felt it suggested "Oscar Wilde rewritten in a rectory garden." Noël, he concluded, "says it all twice over."

At the same time he nurtured a basic admiration which he expressed in a 1953 essay—"A Tribute to Mr. Coward"—that pinned down the essence of Noël's talent better than anyone had to date.

―――

A real point of contention for the two of them was reached at the end of the decade with the rise—accelerated by a hefty supportive push from Tynan in his columns—of the "Angry Young Men" in the British theatre.

Noël had been to see John Osborne's *Look Back in Anger* in 1957. "I expect my bewilderment is because I am very old indeed and cannot understand why the younger generation, instead of knocking at the door, should bash the fuck out of it."

(Ironically, he was echoing what his older generation—in the person of Sir Gerald du Maurier—had said about him at the time of *The Vortex.*)

At this point Noël was still in his own theatrical doldrums, dubbed hopelessly old-fashioned by critics like Tynan. By 1961, when the "Kitchen Sink" school of playwrights, typified by the likes of Osborne, Arnold Wesker, Harold Pinter—with an occasional nudge from Samuel Beckett—was enjoying its continued heyday, Noël had had enough.

By this time he was concentrating most of his theatrical energies on America, so in a sense he was also looking back in anger—at the English stage.

In 1961 he wrote a series of finger-wagging articles for *The Sunday Times* under the umbrella title—"Consider the Public." One was "A Warning to Critics." The reaction was extreme—pro and con. Noël would note—"The Press in London are still squealing like stuck pigs over my articles . . . I really must do some more when I have time."

Kenneth Tynan was equally moved to express his displeasure. "The bridge of a sinking ship, one feels, is scarcely the ideal place . . . to deliver a lecture on the technique of keeping afloat."

In point of fact, Noël was disillusioned about many aspects of postwar Labour Britain.

"I am becoming almighty sick of the Welfare State; sick of general 'commonness,' sick of ugly voices; sick of bad manners and debased values . . . The age of the Common Man has taken over a nation which owes its very existence to uncommon men."

As will happen with fads in anything, the pendulum inevitably swung away from Kitchen Sinks and the debris they contained—and Angry Young Men became Middle-Aged . . . "and that staunch upholder of the revolution, Ken Tynan, has slithered backwards off the barricades and is now enquiring, rather dismally, *where* all the 'destructiveness' is leading us and *what* is to be put in place of what has been destroyed?"

One important thing that was about to be put in place was the long-awaited National Theatre—to be housed temporarily at the Old Vic. It would also turn out to be common ground—at least temporarily—to Noël and Tynan.

They had had a rapprochement a little earlier at the White Elephant club restaurant. Noël reported that Tynan was "amiable. All his views on life and the theatre are diametrically opposed to mine" but there was undoubtedly mutual respect by now.

So much so that it was Tynan who persuaded Laurence Olivier—now ensconced as the first Director of the National—to include in his first season a production of *Hay Fever*.

Noël and Larry had not worked together since *Private Lives* in 1930 and now here they were having the time of their lives, like a couple of overgrown kids. Their mutual exchange of cables were so extravagantly and lovingly worded that Joan Plowright (the new Lady Olivier) warned them both—only half jokingly—that if one of them fell into alien hands, they could both be arrested!

Tynan himself was briefly employed by the National as Artistic Advisor but his choice of plays—Beckett, Brecht, and Rolf Hochhuth—were considered too "radical," as well as too unpopular, and the relationship was terminated.

Tynan never wrote a play—or, at least, a play that was produced—but after his stint at the National, when he had returned to journalism, he did produce a revue called *Oh!, Calcutta!*—a vulgar neo-Gallic pun on the fact that it was played in the nude.

In 1973 the actor Roderick Cook compiled a Coward revue in New York, which he called *Oh Coward!* It was the last show Noël ever saw on his last visit.

In the programme notes for the production Tynan wrote . . .

"Coward took the fat off English comic dialogue; he was the Turkish bath in which it slimmed."

In 1964 Tynan held out the hand of reconciliation when he wrote to Noël . . .

I saw Marlene's [Dietrich] triumphant opening a couple of nights ago and we talked glowingly about you over supper. I then went to bed and had an extraordinary dream in which you confessed to having an affair with Diana Cooper. "She keeps a good pillow," you said reminiscently, "but she's rather lacking in *udge*." At this I nodded sagely, though I hadn't the least idea what "udge" was. Perhaps one day you might care to explain.

Ever yours,
KEN

And so it continued with just the occasional aside . . .

As when Noël wrote to Alfred Lunt in 1967. . .

"I miss you with particular anguish during our Scrabble games. Did you really play against Ken Tynan? Does he *know* any words with as few as seven letters?"

===

Noël's verdict on the subject? Bearing in mind his overriding conviction that few things are serious enough to be taken entirely seriously . . .

"My feelings abut critical attacks have never been very strong because I've been in the theatre too long. Only occasionally could I pick up a hint—but only from a good critic, like Agate. He once or twice said something or other that made me think, but as a general rule, as I only played a three-month season at a time, we were always sold out for the three months before we opened, so it didn't matter what the critics said anyway.

"I'm so terribly, terribly sorry for critics. They have to go to the damned theatre every night, and see all sorts and kinds of nonsense, and I think their senses—if you'll forgive the phrase—get dulled. And I think they suddenly will spring a surprise and you come out with a rave and a long scream. And then very often the play closes. You can't tell."

Although he frequently claimed to "rise above it," the postwar evidence says otherwise.

In 1956 he admitted—"I have been bitterly hurt inside by the English fusillade of critical abuse" and compared it to "the whole-hearted pleased generosity" he received in the U.S. It was that generosity that caused him to turn his attention to American theatre in his later years.

It also caused him to deflect his annoyance with a typical one-liner . . . "Thanks to the vilification poured upon my head . . . I now find myself as big a celebrity as Debbie Reynolds."

===

But perhaps Tynan's most perceptive quote on Noël was . . .

"He was the instant projection of a new kind of human being which had never before existed in print or paint."

Tynan wrote . . .

A TRIBUTE TO MR. COWARD

To be famous young and to make fame last—the secret of combining the two is glandular: it depends on energy. Someone once asked Demosthenes what was the most important quality in an orator. "Action," he said. And the second? "Action." And the third? "Action." So with a talent.

Noël Coward, who was performing in public at ten, has never stopped being in action; at fifty-three he retains all the heady zest of adolescence. Forty years ago he was Slightly in *Peter Pan,* and you might say that he has been wholly in *Peter Pan* ever since. No private considerations have been allowed to deflect the drive of his career; like Gielgud and Rattigan, like the late Ivor Novello, he is a congenital bachelor. He began, like many other satirists (Evelyn Waugh, for instance), by rebelling against conformity, and ended up making his peace with it, even becoming its outspoken advocate.

Any child with a spark of fantasy in its soul is prone to react against the English middle classes, into which Coward was born. The circumstances of his early upbringing, in Teddington, were "liable," he wrote afterwards, "to degenerate into refined gentility unless carefully watched." He promptly reacted against them, and also against his first school-teacher, whom he bit in the arm—"an action which I have never for an instant regretted." From this orgy of rebellion he excepted his mother, a tiny octogenarian who is now comfortably installed in a flat in Eaton Square. With the production of *The Vortex,* in 1924, notoriety hit him. He had already written two other plays and most of a revue, meanwhile announcing that his own wit and Ivor Novello's profile were the first and second wonders of the modern world.

The Vortex, a jeremiad against narcotics with dialogue that sounds today not so much stilted as high-heeled, was described by Beverley Nichols as "immortal." Others, whom it shocked, were encouraged in their heresy by an unfortunate photograph for which Coward posed supine on a knobbly brass bedstead, wearing a dressing-gown and "looking," as he said, "like a heavily-doped Chinese illusionist." From this sprang the myth that he wrote all his plays in an absinthe-drenched coma; in fact, as he has been patiently explaining for nearly thirty years, he drinks little and usually starts punishing his typewriter at seven a.m. His triumph has been to unite two things ever dissociated in the English mind: hard work and wit. Toil is commonly the chum of serious-mindedness; and though, within Coward, a social historian and philosopher are constantly campaigning to be let out, they seldom escape into his work. His wit in print is variable—he has not written a really funny play since *Present Laughter* in 1942—but in private it is unflagging. It took Coward to describe an American adaptation of *The Cherry Orchard,* set in the deep South, as "A Month in the Wrong Country"; and many other theatrical *mots* have been fathered on him. We may never know, for example, whether it was he who, after seeing a certain actress as Queen Victoria, left the theatre murmuring: "I never realized before that Albert married beneath him."

To see him whole, public and private personalities conjoined, you must see him in cabaret. Just before his first season at the Café de Paris, I noticed him watching his predecessor, whose act was not going too well. I asked him how he was enjoying the performances, and, with a stark, stunned, take-it-or-leave-it stare, he hissed: "Sauce! Sheer sauce!" A few weeks later he padded down the celebrated stairs himself, halted before the microphone on black-suede-clad feet, and, upraising both hands in a gesture of benediction, set about demonstrating how these things should be done. Baring his teeth as if unveiling some grotesque monument, and cooing like a baritone dove, he gave us "I'll See You Again" and the other bat's-wing melodies of his youth. Nothing he does on these occasions sounds strained or arid; his tanned, leathery face is still an enthusiast's.

All the time the hands are at their task, affectionately calming your too-kind applause. Amused by his own frolicsomeness, he sways from side to side, waggling a finger if your attention looks like wandering. If it is possible to romp fastidiously, that is what Coward does. He owes little to earlier wits, such as Wilde or Labouchère. Their best things need to be delivered slowly, even lazily. Coward's emerge with the staccato, blind impulsiveness of a machine-gun.

I have heard him accused of having enervated English comedy by making it languid and blasé. The truth, of course, is the opposite: Coward took sophistication out of the refrigerator and set it bubbling on

"I thought somebody like Noël Coward might be able to use it."

"A very Noël Coward sort of person."

the hob. He doses his sentences with pauses, as you dose epileptics with drugs. To be with him for any length of time is exhausting and invigorating in roughly equal proportions. He is perfectly well aware that he possesses "star quality," which is the lodestar of his life. In his case, it might be defined as the ability to project, without effort, the outline of a unique personality, which had never existed before him in print or paint.

Even the youngest of us will know, in fifty years' time, exactly what we mean by "a very Noël Coward sort of person."

(1953)

Noël's avuncular advice to the covey of critics in 1961 . . .

CONSIDER THE PUBLIC
A Warning to Dramatic Critics

In the long history of the arts there have been almost as many harsh things said by artists about critics as there have been by critics about artists. Byron, Pope, Dryden, Coleridge, Hazlitt, to name only a few, have all, in their time, lashed out when driven to exasperation by the carping of those they considered, rightly, to be their inferiors.

Like the cobra and the mongoose, the artist and the critic have always been and will always be Nature's irreconcilables. Occasionally a temporary truce may be established, based insecurely on a sudden burst of enthusiasm from the latter for the work of the former, but these halcyon interludes are seldom of long duration. Sooner or later a dissonant note is sure to be sounded and back we tumble again into the dear old basic status quo.

> *"For never can true reconcilement grow,*
> *When wounds of deadly hate have pierced so deep."*

My personal attitude to the dramatic critics, after fifty years of varying emotions, has finally solidified into an unyielding core of bored resignation. Every now and then the outer edge of this fossilized area in my mind can be twitched into brief sensitivity by an unexpected word of praise or a stab of more than usually vicious abuse, but these occasions are becoming rarer and rarer and the core remains, hardening imperceptibly with the passing of time until, presumably, it will achieve absolute invulnerability.

However, before this state of Nirvana finally sets in, I feel an impulse to rise up, gird my loins and have just one valedictory bash at my natural enemies. Not, I hasten to say, on my own account; I have never been attracted to lost causes—but on behalf of the love of my life which is the theatre.

The Theatre, in all its diverse aspects, fascinates and enchants me today as much as it did when I first became a professional actor at the age of ten. A fine play impeccably acted or a good musical well sung and danced can still send me out into the street in a state of ecstatic euphoria, just as a mediocre play indifferently acted can depress me utterly and rob me, temporarily, of all hope and ambitions.

Naturally, I do not expect dramatic critics to scale such heights of enjoyment or plumb such depths of despair, for in order to do so they would have to know a great deal more than they do about playwriting and acting. And if they did know a great deal more about playwriting and acting, it is highly probable that they would be playwrights or actors themselves and not critics at all, for either of the above occupations are more attractive and financially remunerative, when successful, than journalism.

A dramatic critic is frequently detested, feared, despised, and occasionally tolerated, but he is seldom loved or envied. The awareness of this must, in course of time, lower his morale and corrode his spirit, either consciously or subconsciously.

Unfortunately, I cannot recall any occasion in England when a dramatic critic decided to become an actor, but there is still hope in my heart and my fingers are crossed. Mr. Kenneth Tynan, we know, started as an actor, but was soon forced, by managerial and public apathy, to desist.

In earlier years it was customary for critics, after they had given their opinions of the play and the leading actors, to mention some of the lesser members of the cast. This provided a certain encouragement to supporting players, if only to the extent of bringing their names to the attention of the public and to other managements. That this custom, of late, seems to be gradually dying out is perhaps regrettable, but only up to a point, for the critic is yet to be born who is capable of distinguishing between the actor and the part. A minor actor playing a brief showy role, however ineptly, can always be sure of good notices, whereas a popular favourite, using all the subtle resources of long experience to bring life to a long, unrewarding part, is dismissed with a caution.

Apart from this cruel time limitation, it appears that they are also crushed into a position of cowed subservience by an omniscient being called a Sub-Editor. This Sub-Editor, whose knowledge of the Theatre is probably limited to his local Odeon, holds all these fearsome oracles in deadly thrall. It is he who has the power to slash their columns to pieces and he who is responsible for those sensational headlines which are so often entirely irrelevant to the reviews they preface. Thousands of members of the public I believe seldom read further than these headlines and so when they are confronted by large black-lettered phrases such as "Not This Time, Sir Laurence!" or "Noël Flops Again!" they automatically follow their own instincts and go out to book seats.

In consideration of these circumstances, therefore, it is perhaps unfair to blame critics too much for their lack of selectiveness. They have to sit night after night in different theatres, staring glumly at what is put before them, haunted by the spectre of the Sub-Editor waiting for them, and aware that Time's Wingèd Chariot is goosing them along towards their deadline. All they can do really is to scribble a few hurried notes onto their programmes and run like stags to their desks as the final curtain touches the stage.

For most Theatre people, however, both the Sub-Editor's headline and the criticisms beneath them have an importance far out of proportion to their actual significance. Most playwrights, stars, actors, directors and managers devour avidly every review from *The Times* down to the *Express,* and allow themselves to be either depressed or elated, according to what they read. What few of them seem to realise is that an average member of an average audience seldom takes more than one or, at most, two newspapers, and even then he is more than likely to turn to the latest crime or the sporting page before casting his eye over the theatrical news.

There is no doubt, however, that a unanimously unfavourable press can sometimes do considerable damage to a production, particularly if the play in question happens to have no famous name on the bill, either author or star, to attract the public. Just as a unanimously enthusiastic press can ensure good business for two or three weeks. If the play is good and worthy of the praise it has received, it will run. If not, the public, within a comparatively short space of time will discover that it has been duped and stay away.

It is quite apparent that "The New Movement in the Theatre" with all its potential talent and genuine belief in its own significance, is failing.

For young, aspiring playwrights and actors to be consistently over-praised because what they write and act happens to coincide with the racial, political and social prejudices of a handful of journalists, can only have a disastrous effect on their creative impulse. Very few beginners, however talented, can be expected to survive indiscriminate acclaim without becoming complacent and over-sure of themselves. The wise ones among them will, of course, after a little while, compare their notices with their royalties and decide that they still have a great deal to learn.

To state that the dramatic critics of today are doing a grave disservice to the Theatre and to the public is a sweeping generalization that needs qualifying, although in my, far from humble, opinion it is very largely true. However I will qualify it to the extent of saying that those who write for the more respectable newspapers such as *The Times, The Daily Telegraph, The Sunday Times* and *The Observer,* can at least be relied upon to treat an author or an actor with courtesy.

The critics of the *Daily Mail,* the *Daily Express,* the evening papers and the picture papers, however, have, of late years, flung all thought of courtesy to the winds and devoted themselves, with increasing viru-lence, to witless and indiscriminate abuse. Being myself one of the prin-cipal victims of this vulgarity, I feel perfectly justified in pointing out that they are making cracking idiots of themselves and proving nothing beyond the fact that they are entirely out of touch with the public they are supposed to be writing for.

In conclusion, I would like to suggest that our contemporary crit-ics, if they wish to retain an atom of respect from their readers and the theatrical profession, should rid themselves of their more obvious per-sonal prejudices, endeavour to be more objective and, if possible, more constructive.

In any event they should mind their manners.

——

"It's no use, I must face the fact that I find literary and dramatic criticism tedious and always have. Even Shaw and Max Beerbohm are only, to me, readable in very small doses when they are criticizing their fellow artists. I am unable to work up any real interest in what so-and-so has to say about Shakespeare's object in writing such-and-such. I would rather . . . draw my own conclusions or, better still, draw no conclusions at all; just enjoy it . . . I don't want to peep behind the scenes and scuffle about backstage while the ideas and lyrical phrases are waiting for their entrances. I don't really care if Shakespeare wrote the Sonnets to Willy Herbert or to Mary Fitton. 'Shall I compare thee to a summer's day?' is enough.

"I am not interested in the inevitably prejudiced theories of professional critics. Shaw, with all his brilliance and dynamic talent, was shrill and foolish when he discussed Shakespeare . . . Max Beerbohm, with all his wit and satirical humour, becomes strangely watery when he scratches at the giants. Dear Alec Woollcott's views, when spoken, were amusing and provocative; on paper they are neither, but become rigid and somehow trite.

"Verbal diarrhoea is a major defect . . . [Many writers] have learnt assiduously *too many words* and they wish you to know that they know *far more words* than other people and, what is more, long and complicated words. The crowing becomes quite deafening sometimes and gets between them and what they are trying to say."

—————

The passing years did nothing to change his lack of respect for the breed. Reading a book in 1955 by Walter Kerr of *The New York Times* he could write: "He is an excellent dramatic critic, the best, I think, in America at the moment, but like all critics, poor beasts, he devotes too much time to analyses of motives, largely imagined and, although he begins by being objective, little by little his own ego obtrudes itself and he makes you aware of how much *he* has read and how clever *he* is, none of which is offensive but merely vitiates his arguments."

—————

After *Sail Away* premiered in Chicago he reflected: "The show, considering it was an out-of-town opening, was remarkably slick. But *now* is when I start work. Because what was seen on that stage last night was not a *quarter* of what I'm going to get out of this by the time it gets to New York. And even *then* I'll be in trouble with the critics. I never said I was grateful to the critics in my life—because I'm not. Only occasionally— once or twice—I've had what is called a constructive criticism. Generally they miss the point, poor beasts. They really don't *know* much about it and if they *did* know more about it, they'd be doing it. They're all writing plays like mad and all their plays are failures, so therefore, I know that I know more than they do. But, in fairness to them, they judge what they see and it's up to me to see that they see what I *want* them to see."

9

PRODUCED BY . . .
AND DIRECTED BY . . .

———

Produced by . . . André Charlot · Charles B. Cochran ·
John C. (Jack) Wilson · Hugh (Binkie) Beaumont

Sentimental reasons are not the thing in business, as I have learned to my bitter cost over the years. Cochran, Charlot, John C. Wilson; I have been taken advantage of by all of them and downright cheated by some of them. I am now sixty-one and at last the penny had dropped."

André Charlot (1882–1956)

The first London producer Noël crossed his fledgling sword with was André Charlot.

And for that he had Beatrice Lillie to thank/blame.

"She introduced me to André Charlot. After I had sung several songs with incredible vivacity, Charlot took her aside and said—'Bea, never do that to me again. That boy has no talent whatsoever!' "

It was different after Noël had become friends with Ned Lathom, a stagestruck theatre enthusiast with money he liked to invest. He invited Noël to visit him in Davos, where he was recuperating from a bout of tuberculosis—the first of many.

Knowing Noël's interest in musical theatre matched his own . . .

"He made me play to him all the songs I had written, and when he realized that there were enough comparatively good ones to make up a score, he wired Charlot commanding him to come out immediately."

Since Lathom had funded Charlot's last revue, *A to Z,* he could ensure the producer's serious attention. Noël was understandably nervous after his own earlier encounter but he found Charlot to be "expansive and benign, and a series of cigar-laden conferences ensued, during which *London Calling!* was born."

Noël wrote to his mother, Violet . . .

Darling,

I've just played all the music to Charlot and he's delighted—he sat without a smile and then took me aside and said they were ALL good—so that's that. I now quite definitely enter the ranks of British Composers! . . . it will be very thrilling to hear all my songs done by a good orchestra, won't it? I am very excited as the music IS good.

At the conference it had been agreed that he would share the writing of the book with Ronald Jeans, a writer well established in the field, and the composing of the music with Philip Braham. On reflection Noël came to the conclusion that the arrangement made sense, "as to do a whole show might have proved too heavy a burden on my inexperience."

Casting, though, was a different matter. He knew that the three leads—Gertie Lawrence, Maisie Gay, and Tubby Edlin—were to receive large salaries, whereas his would be a pittance. To resolve this, he argued that to appear in a musical entertainment would undermine his status as a serious actor. He did this, knowing that he had "in my contract as author a clause to the effect that I was to be consulted as to cast. I was able to raise adequate objections to the name of every juvenile suggested, until ultimately, after many weeks' wear and tear, I allowed myself to be persuaded to change my mind."

He also succeeded in persuading Charlot's mind on salary and settled for £40 a week.

London Calling! opened to strong reviews and gave Noël a definite toehold in the world of musical theatre. He was a year or so away from his real breakthrough in *The Vortex.*

Then Charlot created a complication. He decided to take a revue that was to be a compilation of all the best numbers from his earlier revues and stage it on Broadway with Beatrice Lillie, Jack Buchanan, and . . . Gertie Lawrence. Which meant that she would have to leave *London Calling!* . . . and Noël.

André Charlot

He would subsequently leave the show himself and drop in occasionally to see how it was holding up after so many cast changes and different "editions." The view did nothing to encourage him. "The company ambled through the show, the fade-outs and black-outs were untidy, and the smart Molyneux dresses looked as though they had been used to wrap up hot-water-bottles. I talked to Charlot about pepping it up a bit but he wasn't interested, his mind being obviously occupied with more important plans, and so I went down to our cottage in Dockenfield . . . and wrote *Hay Fever.*"

Noël never worked with Charlot again and, in fact, his only subsequent dealings with him involved extricating Gertie from her contract, so that she could appear with him in *Private Lives.*

Charlot was one of the many victims of the Great Depression. He was made bankrupt and later moved to Hollywood, where he became a character actor—often uncredited—in more than fifty films.

J. M. Barrie described him as "the whole British theatrical profession in a nutshell."

Charles B. Cochran (1872–1951)

"Charlot made stars. Cochran turned them into planets."
—DOUGLAS BYNG—REVUE ARTISTE

·

"Cochran was a sentimentalist with taste and a cynic with enthusiasm."
—NOËL

·

Charlot's *bête noire*—and the man soon to elbow him out of the way—was Charles Blake Cochran ("Cockie") . . .

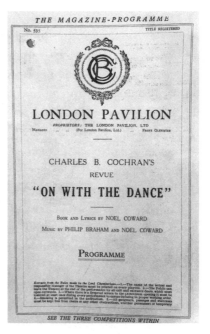

Charles B. Cochran ("C.B."), impresario, by Max Beerbohm at the time of *Bitter Sweet* (1929).

"Oh, Cockie," said Noël, "I've just seen my name in lights."

The producer first crossed Noël's path at the time of *The Young Idea* when he received "a letter of the most generous praise" from him.

"A few days later I had lunch with him . . . flushed with perfectly chosen wine and still more perfectly chosen words of encouragement. I don't remember any premonition sitting behind my chair and nudging me into realisation that this was the first of an endless procession of similar lunches that dotted through future years, that hundreds of restaurant tables, bottles of hock and *entrecôtes minutes* were waiting for us. It only seemed an extremely pleasant hour, significant because I hoped that he might be persuaded to produce a play of mine one day."

That day arrived sooner than he might have suspected. In fact it came right on the heels of his success with *The Vortex.*

Cochran asked him to write another musical revue along the lines of *London Calling!* Noël was now keen to do the whole thing this time but all Cochran wanted from him was the libretto. "He was forced to say that he was very sorry, but he frankly did not consider my music good enough to carry a whole show and that he intended to engage Philip Braham as composer."

But Noël had now developed enough animal cunning to deal with that . . .

"The ideas came swiftly and, oddly enough, nearly every idea carried with it its accompanying song. In my planning of the show almost every scene led up to a number, and so when the revue was complete it was discovered, to the embarrassment of everyone but me that . . . the whole score, book and lyrics were mine."

At the Manchester tryout the show, *On with the Dance,* was billed as—"Charles B. Cochran's Revue." Since this was almost entirely "Noël Coward's Revue," it seemed to him "to be a slight overstatement" and it sent him roaring back to the hotel, where he confronted Cochran in his bathroom. "I'm not at all sure that I didn't deprive him of his towel while I shrieked at him over the noise of the water gurgling down the plug-hole . . . It is odd that in all the years I worked with him that show is the only one over which we ever quarreled. I think the psychological explanation must be that in those early days of our association, we had neither of us estimated accurately enough our respective egos. And a couple of tougher ones it would be difficult to find."

The strength of Noël's would be severely tested by the opening night fiasco of *Sirocco* in 1927. It seemed as though his world—so recently put together—was coming apart but Cochran helped stop that happening. Nobody would care five minutes from now—so would Noël kindly get on with writing his new revue, *This Year of Grace!*? "He was quite sure it would turn out to be a triumphant one in the eye for the lot of them.

"I was grateful to him for this . . . He, more than most people, perceived beneath my business-like nonchalance, a certain vague scurry of apprehension. I was scared inside, scared that perhaps, after all, the Press were right, that I was nothing better than the flash-in-the-pan, the over-bright little star they had so caustically described. . . . I needed outside manifestations of confidence in my ability and Cockie bolstered me generously. No gleam in his eye indicated that he remembered my past shrill quarrel with him, no suggestion of veiled patronage . . . It is, I am sure, through his failures that he has made his friends. No other theatrical manager that I have ever known can rally adherents so swiftly in catastrophe. Temperamental stars demand to be allowed to pawn off their jewellery for him. Chorus girls, stage managers, members of his office staff eagerly offer him their services indefinitely for nothing. Even hard-boiled backers rush through the flames with their cheque-books over their mouths to aid him, regardless of the fact that the flames are probably consuming many of their own investments."

On with the Dance had played for 229 performances. *This Year of Grace!* would play for 316 and go on to a New York production but there was one item neither Noël or Cochran could have anticipated.

The song "A Room with a View" was performed by Sonnie Hale and Jessie Matthews. In her autobiography Matthews records—"At the end of our song Sonnie whispered—'Let's make it come true.' Could we blame Noel Coward for writing this sweet song that we had made our own? For I defy any young couple to sing that song together every night without a strong bond growing between them."

That strong bond caused Hale to divorce his current wife, Evelyn Laye, and marry Matthews. As it happened Laye was top of the list Noël and Cochran had drawn up to play the lead in their forthcoming *Bitter Sweet*. Laye was so upset that she would rather scrub floors than work for either of them again—an opinion she quickly revised when the London production was such a success. She had to beg Noël to let her audition for the subsequent New York production.

There was one further irony. Noël had composed the song while recuperating from a nervous breakdown. He wandered the beach in Hawaii collecting sea shells as the words and music came to him. He intended it to be a satirical pastiche of the love songs of the period but when it turned out to be such a success, he kept that to himself!

═══

Over the next several years Noël and Cockie were often traveling companions. Before the Broadway production of *This Year of Grace!* they made a trip to New York to find new talent for the show. As a business trip it was not an overwhelming success. The highlight of the talent trawl was "one girl who could do the side splits and walk on her hands with a social nonchalance that was exceedingly fetching." As a bonding experience it worked much better.

The two of them turned out to complement one another rather than compete. This became clear on the way home, when they were forced to share a cabin.

"Although we had both viewed this prospect with slight apprehension, it turned out to be extremely cosy. Neither of us snored, apparently, and conversation after lights out was stimulating."

On the voyage Noël wrote the first act of *Bitter Sweet* . . . "and when I read it to Cockie and explained to him the story of the rest of it, he became at once enthusiastic. One of his greatest qualities is his amazing flair for visualizing a play completely from the barest outline, and he decided then and there that he would do it—providing that I could finish it in time—in the spring of the following year, 1929."

═══

In due course rehearsals were under way and finally—the dress rehearsal . . .

"Of all the performances I ever saw of *Bitter Sweet,* that rehearsal was far and away the most exciting . . . At the end Cockie thanked the company in a voice husky with emotion and added that he wouldn't part with his rights in the play for a million pounds."

The show was a palpable hit in both London and New York, despite the fact that it defied so many of the accepted theatrical conventions. The hero killed at the end of Act II!

Cochran's comment on that? "According to the rules it should have failed—but I always contend that there are no rules."

The success of the Coward-Cochran partnership continued with *Private Lives* (1930), *Cavalcade* (1931), another revue, *Words and Music* (1932), and *Conversation Piece* (1934).

Perhaps it was the apparent inevitability of this success that caused Noël to make what turned out in hindsight to be one of his biggest errors of judgment. Perhaps it was the prodding of Jack Wilson, his associate and sometime lover.

Did he need a producing partner at all?

After *Conversation Piece* he wrote to Cochran . . .

My Dear Cocky,

If you were a less understanding or generous person this letter would be very difficult to write; as it is, however, I feel you will appreciate my motives completely and without prejudice.

I have decided after mature consideration to present my own and other people's plays in the future in partnership with Jack. This actually has been brewing in my mind over a period of years, and I am writing to you first in confidence because I want you to understand that there would be no question of forsaking you or breaking our tremendously happy and successful association for any other reason except that I feel this is an inevitable development of my career in the theatre.

Particularly I want you to realise how deeply grateful I am for all the generosity and courage and friendship you have shown me over everything we have done together . . . but above all, dear Cocky, I want to insist upon one important fact which, sentimental as it may seem, is on my part sincere, and that is that without your encouragement and faith in me and my work, it is unlikely that I should ever have reached the position I now hold in the theatre, and that whatever may happen in the future, I feel that there is a personal bond between us which has nothing to do with business or finance or production. Please understand all this and give me the benefit of your invaluable friendship.

Yours affectionately,
NOEL

There followed an ominous silence. Then the eventual reply . . .

My dear Noel,

Many thanks for your letter, which was found this morning under my bed, very much chewed up by my dachshund.

As you say, the development you refer to was inevitable, and I wish you and your associates the best of good fortune.

Meanwhile, believe me,

Yours as ever,

CBC

Noël was not best pleased with the curt tone of Cochran's reply but he should not have expected more. He went on to set up Transatlantic Productions with Jack Wilson, Lynn, and Alfred. In objective retrospect it can be seen that none of Noël's musicals post-Cochran succeeded to the same degree. Nor did their personal relationship. But it had been a remarkable decade for both of them.

In 1951 Cockie made his personal exit in dramatic fashion trapped in a bath of scalding hot water.

John C. (Jack) Wilson (1899–1961)

If there was ever a "horse of another colour," it was Jack Wilson.

He turned up to a performance of *The Vortex* and applauded so loudly that he drew attention to himself . . .

"I remember remarking . . . that he must be an American because he was wearing a turn-down collar with his dinner-jacket. A few days later a mutual friend told me that he knew a young American who was very anxious to meet me, and could he bring him round to my dressing room one night, and the next evening Jack Wilson walked nervously, and with slightly overdone truculence, into my life . . . A few months later he gave up being a stockbroker in order to be my personal manager, in which capacity he has bullied me firmly ever since."

Soon after Jack relocated from New York to London. "We had drawn up an elaborate contract . . . bristling with legal technicalities, options and percentages, so that in the event of sudden unforeseen mutual hatred, we could still continue to work together, however dourly, on a business basis."

Noël wrote this account in the 1937 *Present Indicative*. He would live to qualify that initial assessment.

Or perhaps "bird of prey" might
be a better animal analogy.

Jack became *de facto* a member of the "family" Noël was setting up for himself—secretary Lorn Loraine, designer Gladys Calthrop, later actress Joyce Carey and assistant Cole Lesley.

It was Coley who—years later—summed up the vague disquiet many of the family sensed but hesitated to express—"In addition to his film star looks, Jack had an immense amount of charm, and with his sharp wit he could be so funny that one forgave, or didn't even notice, the mocking irony with which his wit was edged."

Seen objectively, there was a problem from the start but one of Noël's flaws was that, where someone he cared for was concerned, he could only see what he wanted to see—and Jack, as employee-lover, was the prime example.

He was immediately given power of attorney, effectively putting him in charge of Noël's finances, a decision that was to prove costly.

When a few years later Jack had to make a trip back to the U.S., a cable from Noël reached him on the ship. ("Baybay" and "Dab" were the "family" nicknames for him) . . .

> Baybay's gone, the mousies play,
> Fifteen cheques went out today.

Richmond Park is grey with sorrow,
Thirty cheques go out tomorrow.

Darling Baybay, darling Jack,
Just a kleptomaniac
Pinching gifts from Poppa's house
Like a predatory louse.

Taking slyly without stint
Here a photo, there a print.
Still, although you snatch and grab
Poppa loves his darling Dab.

This equivocal undertone was to prevail—until it became an overtone.

Came the war and Jack, as an American citizen, decided he could run Noël's business affairs more conveniently from the safety of New York, which was presumably his excuse for not warning Noël that from its outbreak the British government had passed a law forbidding its citizens from using any financial resources they happened to have in the U.S.

Noël—who had spent a fair amount of time—and his own money—traveling around America in 1940 and 1941 at the behest of the Ministry of Information—found himself in breach of a law he had never heard of. It had been Jack's responsibility, as his financial advisor, to warn him but Jack had more pressing concerns, it appeared.

Noël had to undergo the humiliation of being taken to court and fined. Jack saw no need to apologize.

Back in 1934 he had been the driving force behind the decision to cut ties with Cochran and form Transatlantic Productions. Now back in the U.S. even that seemed merely a stepping-stone.

With Noël otherwise engaged with wartime commitments, Jack directed two of Noël's plays on Broadway—both starring Noël's friend Clifton Webb. *Blithe Spirit* was considered a success with 657 performances—*Present Laughter* (158 performances) less so.

After the war he began to try to produce and direct on Broadway. And then, maybe—Hollywood!

Lorn commemorated his *chutzpah* in verse . . .

Long years ago when first we knew
Our dear John Chapman W,
His latent talents were confined
To efforts of a simple kind.
A homely wit, a merry sense
Of fun at your and my expense . . .
A trifling bagatelle maybe
Of error in accountancy.
Picture and book—a brooch or so,
Those were his limits long ago.

But as the years that speed apace
Have added girth to Baybay's face,
They've stretched the fields of enterprise
On which he casts his penny eyes.
When wicked murmurs once were heard
All Broadway trembles at his word.
The acid jokes that used to be
Reserved for Gladys, you and me
Are now the *bons mots* of the day
In syndicated USA.

It used to be enough for Dab
To pinch, appropriate or grab
Such trifles as he wished to use
From Goldenhurst or Burton Mews.
But as a child outgrows its nurse
So Baybay's pocket and his purse.
Now he finds investors just the thing
To suit light-fingered pilfering
And when he's had his fill from them . . .
OH, DO BE CAREFUL, M-G-M!

To be fair he did make a considerable theatrical success with *Kiss Me,
Kate* and *Gentlemen Prefer Blondes* but his work became increasingly
erratic.

So did his health. Arthritis, Jack claimed. Alcoholism, Noël deduced.

In 1951 Jack also took on the running of the Westport Country Playhouse in Connecticut near to where he lived. Noël heard mixed reviews but set them aside when Jack decided to put on *Island Fling*—the latest version of a play that had been giving Noël trouble—with Claudette Colbert in the lead.

Diary, *July 25, 1951*

"Cable from Jack—my play is apparently a success and Claudette is wonderful in it . . . Have decided to fly to America and see it before it closes. I must know whether it is good or not and what Jack has done with it."

August 26

"Wrote a long letter to Jack accepting his suggestion that we finish our theatrical association. This is a relief as I think very little of him as a theatre man."

Gone were the days when he could write from London—"I would rather you directed than anybody else. I have implicit faith in your taste and discretion."

The personal relationship was a more difficult matter after all these years. He would continue to see Jack and his wife, Natasha, and watch Jack's steady physical deterioration.

Then, in October 1961 . . .

"Natasha found Jack dead on the floor of his bathroom.

"I cannot feel sad that he is dead. He has been less than half alive for the last ten years, a trouble and a bore to himself and to everyone else. Naturally, now that he is dead, my mind is inclined to skip the disintegration and fly back to when he was handsome, witty, charming, good company. What a hideous, foolish waste of life! His character was never good . . . I am almost sure he was aware of inadequacy . . . Of course I am sad. Of course I feel horrid inside. But not nearly as much as I might have. To me he died years ago."

═══

Transatlantic Productions was never a comfortable fit. The Lunts were in a world of their own and Noël never had time to do all he wanted to do. Jack, as we've seen, was distinctly erratic.

Noël was lucky at the end of the 1930s to become involved with—and eventually merge with—the H. M. Tennent agency, headed by the man they called the *éminence grise* of the West End Theatre . . .

Hugh (Binkie) Beaumont (1908–1973)

Their professional paths first crossed in 1937 when Noël was preparing *Operette*.

The show was not one of Noël's successes and it became clear that he was missing the Cochran touch. Binkie seemed like someone who might be able to fill that role, should he be part of a more formal arrangement.

At that time he was with the H. M. Tennent agency. Harry Tennent's name was on the door but it was Binkie who was the driving force.

In 1939 Noël and Binkie entered into a more formal agreement and from then on a genuine friendship evolved—or so Noël thought. His *Diaries* have frequent entries along the lines of . . . "Dinner with Binkie and we had one of our heart-to-heart sessions . . ."

In many ways the two men were very different. Both were their own creations but, whereas Noël had polished his to a fine shine, Binkie still had a number of rough edges. As early as 1942—as they did with Jack Wilson—Noël and Lorn are sending him a teasing verse . . .

Dearest Binkie, dearest Bink,
Lorn and I sincerely think
You have been for long enough
Both illiterate and rough
And in fact for many a year
Very, very common, dear.
So accept from this address
Hints on gentlemanliness.

That which warns of Luftwaffe spleen
Is a SIREN, not SIREEN.
Soldier's furlough, sweet but brief,
We call LEAVE and never LEAF.
Use grammatical restraint
IS NOT is correct . . . not AIN'T.
Words like NOTHING, may we say,
End with "G" and not with "K."
NAPKINS, in the smarter sets,
Are not known as SERVIETTES.
Also, these are not tucked in
Neatly underneath the chin.
May we add that OPPOSITE
Is pronounced to rhyme with "BIT."
Should you belch at lunch or tea,
Never mutter "Pardon me."
Mark these rules and, if you can,
Be a little gentleman.

(With love from Mr. Noël Coward and Mrs. Lorn Loraine)

In the early war years most of Noël's work was presented jointly by Tennent's and Jack Wilson . . . *Present Laughter* . . . *This Happy Breed* . . . *Blithe Spirit* . . .

Then after the war . . . *Sigh No More* . . . *Peace in Our Time* . . .

Binkie writes to Noël that he is not happy with *Peace in Our Time* (1947). The play is Noël's variation on his idol Saki's earlier *When William Came*—a story of how England might have been if the Germans had won the war.

This upset Noël, as he considered this to be the best play he had written so far . . .

"If that play turns out to be a flop, I shall be forced to the reluctant and pompous conclusion that England does not deserve my work. That is a good play written with care and heart and guts and it is beautifully acted and directed . . . I have a sick at heart feeling about England anyhow. We are so idiotic and apathetic and it is nothing to do with 'after the war,' because we were the same at Munich and before that."

The joint production arrangement continued for the next few years . . . *Relative Values* (1951) . . . *Quadrille* (1952) but Binkie was taking over the lead role.

As Coronation Year approached it was Binkie who persuaded Noël that it was time for him to return to the West End as an actor. Why didn't he take a look at Bernard Shaw's *The Apple Cart*? The role of King Magnus would suit him down to the ground.

Noël took up his suggestion and in 1953 had a considerable success in the part. It was a limited run, which pleased him . . .

"I must never play more than three months . . . This loathing of routine is curious but very definite . . . I love acting and I love the theatre but, oh Christ, how people can play heavy parts for long runs I shall never know."

It would be 1956 and *Nude with Violin* before Binkie and H. M. Tennent had Noël all to themselves—and by then he had begun to detect early warning signs . . .

1954

"Dined with Binkie . . . I have a curious feeling of sadness about him. There is no concrete reason for this but an inner instinct tells me that he is due for unhappiness. I may be entirely wrong. I hope I am."

There was to be an unscripted, unproduced solo comedy that relieved the growing tension for a while.

Binkie, his partner John Perry and Terence Rattigan came to stay with Noël in Jamaica in 1957. A fellow guest happened to be Winifred Ashton (the writer-artist known professionally as "Clemence Dane" and a long-time friend of Noël's).

"Winnie" was known as a dropper of verbal bricks—second only to John Gielgud in that regard.

She would emerge for breakfast with an observation such as—"Oh, how wonderful to wake up to see a row of tits on one's windowsill!"

Noël wrote to Joyce Carey to report . . .

"When we were discussing harmlessly at lunch the fact of people having split personalities and secret sides to them, Winifred in her most trilling governess voice said—'Of course, of course, the five John Thomases!' [English slang for 'penis.'] This naturally enough reduced the five John Thomases present to dreadful, ill-concealed hysteria. Binkie choked, great round tears coursed down Coley's face and I talked very very loudly about something quite different."

There wasn't too much to laugh at back in London.

1957

"Binkie is behaving badly and greedily over the American production of *Nude*. He is demanding two per cent of the gross and a share of the subsidiary rights. Both of these demands are unheard of. It is sad that, with all his true capacity for friendship, his over-developed business acumen should let him down. Friendship and business, we know, do not marry comfortably, but I am afraid he has taken a good deal more advantage of me over the years than I realised. This is a discouraging thought but it doesn't really matter. Ethical standards in my mind must be upheld. If they are not, measures must be taken to ensure that they are. In future I fully intend to take them."

1959

"Dined with Binkie and he was at his nicest and we heart-to-hearted until 3 a.m., by which time my friend was pissed as a newt."

═══

The dinners and the heart-to-hearts continued but increasingly there was a third party—alcohol . . .

And perhaps a fourth—Noël's disenchantment . . .

1960

"Production of *The Last Joke* by Enid Bagnold starring Gielgud and Ralph Richardson opens to appalling reviews . . .

"This looks like disaster for Binkie and, as far as I am concerned, serve him bloody well right. He has really behaved badly to me of late . . . In the old days he used to love the theatre and allow himself to be gently advised . . . I am sad about this change in him because I thought he was really a friend. Perhaps he still is deep down, but I'm not very sanguine. Too much power and too much concentration on money grubbing."

In 1960 Noël writes another play he's particularly proud of—and one that expresses the deep emotion he feels for the theatre.

Waiting in the Wings is about a group of elderly actresses living out their remaining years in a "home" appropriately called The Wings. Binkie told Noël he didn't care for it and didn't want to produce it.

It then emerged that not only had he rejected it but that he had actively tried to dissuade senior actresses—many of whom were close to Noël—from taking part . . .

"Gladys Cooper asked me why I had written a play about retired actresses and not offered her a part in it. I explained that I had written it FOR her but that Binkie had told me she had turned it down without comment. This is rather shocking, I'm afraid. I originally planned it with her as Lotta and Sybil [Thorndike] as May. Now Sybil is playing Lotta and Marie Lohr, May. It will probably be as well in the long run because Gladys's trouble with learning lines has certainly not improved, but the point is that Binkie told a black lie. I am making no issue of this, but I am wondering whether or not Edith Evans, whom Binkie told me LOATHED the play, ever had it sent to her? It's not very nice, is it?"

There was to be no "long run." The play was eventually produced by Michael Redgrave's production company and ran for a modest 188 performances.

November 1960

Noël and Binkie have a theatre evening in New York and then return for one of their regular "heart-to-hearts" . . .

"Whatever was possible to put right between us was ignored. He was amiable and gossipy and I didn't really care for him any more. This is sad, but I suddenly saw all the pallid little wheels whizzing round: the fear of me, the lack of moral courage, the preoccupation with money, etc., and there it was, clearly and unmistakably the end of a long friendship. We shall always have an agreeable relationship, I am sure, but no more reality. Perhaps there never was any."

And, indeed, the "agreeable relationship" did continue for another decade. But then, so did another relationship—Binkie's with the bottle.

The last time Noël saw him was at a dinner given at Claridge's in November 1972 to honor Noël. Everyone who was anyone—or wished to be considered so—was there and the evening was emotional in the best sense.

After Noël left, the guests began to disperse but one of them made a somewhat unorthodox exit. Binkie was seen crawling to his car on all fours.

A few weeks later Noël, Graham, and Coley were back in Jamaica when they heard the news that Binkie had died in his sleep.

Noël himself was failing badly but this was something he found hard to take in. Despite their ups and downs, Binkie had been his closest friend and confidant for more than thirty years. Graham and Coley tried their best to distract him—but to no avail.

A few days later Noël made his own exit.

. . . AND DIRECTED BY . . . BASIL DEAN (1888–1978)

BRYAN:

I thought his *Hamlet* was marvelous.

LORRAINE:

All the unbleached linen and kapok.

The Closet scene looked like a tea-tent.

—*STAR QUALITY* (1967)

In March 1913 Noël and his mother, Violet, went to meet "a young man with a rasping voice and dark glasses" who was about to direct a play called *Hannele*—a translation from the German—for the Liverpool Repertory Company.

He would direct five of Noël's plays in the 1920s. His name was Basil Dean.

Noël got the part. "I was engaged at a salary of two pounds a week" and so began a somewhat erratic relationship.

Dean was a martinet-in-the-making and battle lines were soon drawn.

Basil Dean gave Noël his first serious acting role when he directed him in *Hannele* (1913). In the 1920s their professional paths and personal wills would cross several times— with varying results.

Dean said something that displeased Noël and the thirteen-year-old actor told him—"Mr. Dean, if you ever speak to me like that again, I shall go straight home to my mother." Dean never spoke to him like that again, though they were to have many differences of opinion on matters theatrical.

Dean had his own recollection of "a pimply, knobbly-kneed youngster with an assured manner."

By the time of *The Vortex* (1924) they were on a more even professional footing—to the point where Noël entrusted him with the direction of the Broadway production . . . on condition that he keep it close to the original London production, which just happened to have been directed by—N. Coward.

"This really seemed to be the most satisfactory arrangement. I knew Basil well and admired his work, and I didn't want to carry the burden of producing the play myself and acting in it."

It would prove to be a sensible move, for the play turned out to be Noël's triumphant American debut as both playwright and actor. Once again it was a case of Noël asserting himself at the outset.

The play was to be produced by Charles Dillingham and Abe Erlanger in conjunction with Basil Dean but at the first meeting Erlanger explained to Noël that it couldn't be put on until Noël had rewritten the last act.

Noël clearly didn't appreciate that in America mother love was something sacred and any audience would leave the theatre *en masse* at the spectacle of a son abusing the woman who gave him birth. He then reassured Noël that he, Abe Erlanger, would be on hand to tell him what to do.

At which point—to the horror of Dean and Dillingham—Noël told Erlanger what to do and stormed out. The production went on precisely as Noël had written it under the management of Irving Berlin and Sam Harris.

———

1927. Noël and Basil were to work together next on *Easy Virtue*. This was its premiere before taking it to the U.K. The star was Jane Cowl as Larita.

"She and Basil inaccurately measured each other's quality early on and proceeded firmly to misunderstand each other on every possible occasion. The production was tricky, especially the dance scene in the last act which Basil, with his usual passion for detail, polished within an inch of its life."

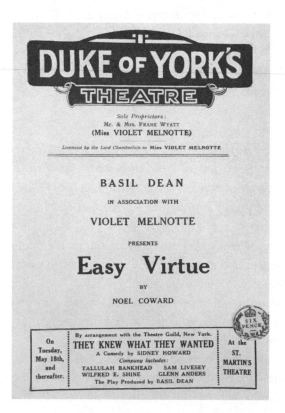

In the event—Noël recorded—it was received with "only moderate acclaim."

Immediately after *Easy Virtue* came *The Queen Was in the Parlour*—Noël's solitary venture into Ruritania.

"By this time I had grown to know him very well, not only as a producer but as a person . . . As a man he was pleasant . . . and in his more relaxed moments exceedingly good company. As a producer he could be and frequently was a fiend . . . A first rate producer should learn early on in his career that most actors wear their intestines on their sleeves."

The Queen ran for 126 performances.

Towards the end of 1926 came a Coward rarity.

This Was a Man was only staged in New York with Basil directing. Noël looked back on it—not with anger but certainly irritation . . .

"The production by Basil Dean was practically stationary. The second act dinner scene made *Parsifal* in its entirety seem like a quick-fire vaudeville sketch."

"A. E. Matthews ambled through *This Was a Man* like a charming retriever who has buried a bone and can't quite remember where."

———

Meanwhile Dean was contemplating *The Constant Nymph*, his adaptation of a popular romantic novel. For the leading role of Lewis Dodd he had John Gielgud in mind and had even offered him the part when Noël—in an effort to help with the publicity—suggested that he should play Dodd for the first month of the run. Dean, realizing the commercial advantage this would involve, agreed—and Gielgud once again found himself playing Noël's understudy.

Noël soon came to regret his own generous offer, though the experience certainly taught him a thing or two . . .

"Basil adamantly refused to allow me to use any of myself in it at all. I wasn't even permitted to smoke cigarettes, but had, with bitter distaste to manoeuvre a pipe."

Even before the month was over he had talked his way out of the part and left it to John Gielgud, who managed the part and the pipe very effectively for a year's run.

But their final collaboration turned out to be as theatrical off-stage as it was on.

Sirocco was one of several plays Noël had written, been unable to place, and then put aside until the success of *The Vortex* had created a sudden demand for other work from this talented new playwright. At that point he should have been a lot more selective in what he took out of that bottom drawer.

The Rat Trap, for instance, written in 1918, lasted for only twelve performances.

Sirocco dated from 1921 and even though Noël did some revisions to it before it was staged in 1927, his theatrically maturer self should have sensed its weaknesses. However, with Ivor Novello as the star and Basil Dean directing, on it went.

To be fair, it probably appeared at the moment when there were the beginnings of an anti-Coward groundswell. There were those who thought that this young man was being praised too much and too indiscriminately and it was time to take him down a peg or two. For many in audience that first night that was the show they'd come to see—not *Sirocco.*

Basil Dean wasn't there to see the fiasco. He made it a habit not to see the first nights of his own productions but to go off and dine quietly. Later he would recall . . .

"Following my usual custom, I returned to the theatre via the stage door towards the end of the last act. As I stood in the wings on one side of the stage I saw Noel standing in the prompt corner opposite, waiting, I presumed, for the customary reception. [In fact, he had come through the pass door to persuade the stage manager NOT to raise the curtain!] Had I been beside Noel, much of what followed might have been avoided. Mistaking the dull roar I heard for applause and cries of 'Author,' I waved to the stage manager to raise the curtain and for Noel to take his call. But the more I waved to him to go on, the more violently he shook his head. I could, of course, hear nothing above the din. Finally, and for quite a different reason from what I supposed, Noel went on to face the music."

Dean would write . . .

"*Sirocco* ended my association with Noel as dramatist. I am sorry that it closed upon such a sour note as far as the public was concerned."

Years later he could even joke about it as a piece of theatrical jargon. "How did the show go?" "Oh, it was a *Sirocco,* old boy!"

But there would be another joke he found less amusing.

During the war he was appointed director of ENSA (Entertainments

National Service Association), an organization briefed to organize entertainments of various kinds—using entertainers of various talents—for the troops in the war zones. So varied and variable were the shows they produced that the organization soon acquired another definition—"Every Night Something Awful."

Noël appeared in numerous entertainments for the armed forces both at home and abroad—but never for ENSA.

("I had no intention of offering my services to ENSA, for I was suspicious of their efficiency.")

On directing Noël the actor . . .

> "Every effect was sharp and clear as a diamond. By way of minor example, he had learned—no one more effectively—how to use the cigarette as an instrument of mood, punctuating witticism with a snap of his lighter, and ill temper with a vicious stabbing-out in a nearby ashtray."
>
> —BASIL DEAN

10

MUSICAL THEATRE, REVUE, AND CABARET

Taking Light Music Seriously

ON TAKING LIGHT MUSIC SERIOUSLY

I was born into a generation that still took light music seriously. The lyrics and melodies of Gilbert and Sullivan were hummed and strummed into my consciousness at an early age. My father sang them, my mother played them, my nurse, Emma, breathed them through her teeth while she was washing me, dressing me and undressing me and putting me to bed. My aunts and uncles, who were legion, sang them singly and in unison at the slightest provocation. By the time I was four years old "Take a Pair of Sparkling Eyes," "Tit Willow," "We're Very Wide Awake, the Moon and I" and "I Have a Song to Sing-O" had been fairly inculcated into my bloodstream.

The whole Edwardian era was saturated with operetta and musical comedy: in addition to popular foreign importations by Franz Lehár, Leo Fall, André Messager, etc., our own native composers were writing musical scores of a quality that has never been equalled in this country since the 1914–18 war. Lionel Monckton, Paul Rubens, Ivan Caryll and Leslie Stuart were flourishing. *The Quaker Girl, Our Miss Gibbs, Miss Hook of Holland, Floradora, The Arcadians* and *The Country Girl,* to name only a few, were all fine musical achievements; and over and above the artists who performed them, the librettists who wrote them and the impresarios who presented them, their music was the basis of

Gladys Calthrop.

their success. Their famous and easily remembered melodies can still be heard on the radio and elsewhere, but it was in the completeness of their scores that their real strength lay: opening choruses, finales, trios, quartettes and concerted numbers, all musicianly, all well balanced and all beautifully constructed.

There was no song-plugging in those days beyond an occasional reprise in the last act; there was no assaulting of the ear by monstrous repetition, no unmannerly nagging. A little while ago I went to an American "musical" in which the hit number was reprised no less than five times during the performance by different members of the cast, as well as being used in the overture, the entr'acte and as a "play-out" while the audience was leaving the theatre. The other numbers in the show, several of which were charming, were left to fend for themselves and only three of them were ever published. In earlier days the complete vocal score of a musical comedy was published as a matter of course, in addition to which a booklet of the lyrics could be bought in the theatre with the programme. These little paper-bound books were well worth the sixpence charged because they helped those with a musical ear to recapture more easily the tunes they wanted to remember and to set them in their minds.

In the years immediately preceding the first world war the American Invasion began innocuously with a few isolated song hits until Irving Berlin established a beach-head with "Alexander's Ragtime Band." English composers, taken by surprise and startled by vital Negro-Jewish rhythms from the New World, fell back in some disorder; conservative musical opinion was shocked and horrified by such alien noises and, instead of saluting the new order and welcoming the new vitality, turned up its patrician nose and retired disgruntled from the arena.

At this moment war began, and there was no longer any time. It is reasonable to suppose that a large number of potential young composers were wiped out in those sad years and that had they not been, the annihilation of English light music would not have been so complete. As it was, when finally the surviving boys came home, it was to an occupied country; the American victory was a *fait accompli.* This obviously was the moment for British talent to rally, to profit by defeat, to absorb and utilize the new, exciting rhythms from over the water and to modify and adapt them to its own service, but apparently this was either beyond our capacity or we were too tired to attempt it. At all events, from the nineteen-twenties until today, there have been few English composers of light music capable of creating an integrated score.

One outstanding exception was the late Ivor Novello. His primary talent throughout his whole life was music, and *Glamorous Night, Arc de Triomphe, The Dancing Years, Perchance to Dream* and *King's Rhapsody* were rich in melody and technically expert. For years he upheld, almost alone, our old traditions of Musical Comedy. His principal tunes were designed, quite deliberately, to catch the ear of the public and, being simple, sentimental, occasionally conventional but always melodic, they invariably achieved their object. The rest of his scores, the openings, finales, choral interludes and incidental themes he wrote to please himself and in these, I believe, lay his true quality; a much finer quality than most people realized. The fact that his music never received the critical acclaim that it deserved was irritating but unimportant. One does not expect present-day dramatic critics to know much about music; as a matter of fact one no longer expects them to know much about drama. Vivian Ellis has also proved over the years that he can handle a complete score with grace and finesse. *Bless the Bride* was much more than a few attractive songs strung together and so from the musical standpoint, was *Tough at the Top*, although the show on the whole was a commercial failure.

Harold Fraser-Simson, who composed *The Maid of the Mountains*, and Frederic Norton, who composed *Chu Chin Chow*, are remembered only for these two outstanding scores. Their other music, later or earlier, is forgotten except by a minority.

Proceeding on the assumption that the reader is interested in the development of my musical talent, I will try to explain, as concisely as I can, how, in this respect, my personal wheels go round. To begin with, I have only had two music lessons in my life. These were the first steps of what was to have been a full course at the Guildhall School of Music, and they faltered and stopped when I was told by my instructor that I could not use consecutive fifths. He went on to explain that a gentleman called Ebenezer Prout had announced many years ago that consecutive fifths were wrong and must in no circumstances be employed. At that time Ebenezer Prout was merely a name to me (as a matter of fact he still is, and a very funny one at that) and I was unimpressed by his Victorian dicta. I argued back that Debussy and Ravel used consecutive fifths like mad. My instructor waved aside this triviality with a pudgy hand, and I left his presence for ever with the parting shot that what was good enough for Debussy and Ravel was good enough for me. This outburst of rugged individualism deprived me of much valuable knowledge, and I have never deeply regretted it for a moment. Had I intended at the outset of my career to devote all my energies to music I would have endured the necessary training cheerfully enough, but in those days I was passionately involved in the theatre; acting and writing and singing and dancing seemed of more value to my immediate progress than counterpoint and harmony. I was willing to allow the musical side of my creative talent to take care of itself. On looking back, I think that on the whole I was right. I have often been irritated in later years by my inability to write music down effectively and by my complete lack of knowledge of orchestration except by ear, but being talented from the very beginning in several different media, I was forced by common sense to make a decision. The decision I made was to try to become a good writer and actor, and to compose tunes and harmonies whenever the urge to do so became too powerful to resist.

I have never been unduly depressed by the fact that all my music has to be dictated. Many famous light composers never put so much as a crotchet on paper. To be born with a natural ear for music is a great and glorious gift. It is no occasion for pride and it has nothing to do with will-power, concentration or industry. It is either there or it isn't. What is so curious is that it cannot, in any circumstances, be wrong where one's own harmonies are concerned. Last year in New York, when I was recording *Conversation Piece* with Lily Pons, I detected a false note in the orchestration. It happened to be in a very fully scored passage and the mistake was consequently difficult to trace. The orchestrator, the conductor and the musical producer insisted that I was wrong; only Lily Pons, who has perfect pitch, backed me up. Finally, after much argument and fiddle-faddle it was discovered that the oboe was playing an A flat instead of an A natural. The greatness and gloriousness of this gift, however, can frequently be offset by excruciating discomfort. On many occasions in my life I have had to sit smiling graciously while some well-meaning but inadequate orchestra obliges with a selection from my works. Cascades of wrong notes lacerate my nerves, a flat wind instrument pierces my ear-drums, and though I continue to smile appreciatively, the smile, after a little while, becomes tortured and looks as if my mouth were filled with lemon juice.

I could not help composing tunes even if I wished to. Ever since I was a little boy they have dropped into my mind unbidden and often in the most unlikely circumstances. The *Bitter Sweet* waltz, "I'll See You Again," came to me whole and complete in a taxi when I was appearing in New York in *This Year of Grace*. I was on my way home to my apartment after a matinée and had planned, as usual, to have an hour's rest and a light dinner before the evening performance. My taxi got stuck in a traffic block on the intersection of Broadway and Seventh Avenue, klaxons were honking, cops were shouting and suddenly in the general din there was the melody, clear and unmistakable. By the time I got home the words of the first phrase had emerged. I played it over and over again on the piano (key of E flat as usual) and tried to rest, but I was too excited to sleep.

There is, to me, strange magic in such occurrences. I am willing and delighted to accept praise for my application, for my self-discipline and for my grim determination to finish a thing once I have started it. My acquired knowledge is praiseworthy, too, for I have worked hard all my life to perfect the material at my disposal. But these qualities, admirable as they undoubtedly are, are merely accessories. The essential talent is what matters and essential talent is unexplainable. My mother and father were both musical in a light, amateur sense, but their gift was in no way remarkable. My father, although he could improvise agreeably at the piano, never composed a set piece of music in his life. I have known many people who were tone-deaf whose parents were far more actively musical than mine. I had no piano lessons when I was a little boy except occasionally from my mother who tried once or twice, with singular lack of success, to teach me my notes. I could, however, from the age of about seven onwards, play any tune I had heard on the piano in the pitch dark. To this day my piano-playing is limited to three keys: E flat, B flat and A flat. The sight of two sharps frightens me to death. When I am in the process of composing anything in the least complicated I can play it in any key on the keyboard, but I can seldom if ever repeat these changes afterwards unless I practise them assiduously every day. In E flat I can give the impression of playing well. A flat and B flat I can get away with, but if I have to play anything for the first time it is always to my beloved E flat that my fingers move automatically. Oddly enough, C major, the key most favoured by the inept, leaves me cold. It is supposed to be easier to play in than any of the others because it has no black notes, but I have always found it dull. Another of my serious piano-playing defects is my left hand. Dear George Gershwin used to moan at me in genuine distress and try to force my fingers on to the right notes. As a matter of fact he showed me a few tricks that I can still do, but they are few and dreadfully far between. I can firmly but not boastfully claim that I am a better pianist than Irving Berlin, but as that superlative genius of light music is well known not to be able to play at all except in C major, I will not press the point. Jerome D. Kern, to my mind one of the most inspired romantic composers of all, played woodenly as a rule and without much mobility. Dick Rodgers plays his own music best when he is accompanying himself or someone else, but he is far from outstanding. Vincent Youmans was a marvellous pianist, almost as brilliant as Gershwin, but these are the only two I can think of who, apart from their creative talent, could really play.

At the very beginning of this introduction I said that I was born into a generation that took light music seriously. It was fortunate for me that I was, because by the time I had emerged from my teens the taste of the era had changed. In my early twenties and thirties it was from America that I gained my greatest impetus. In New York they have always taken light music seriously. There, it is, as it should be, saluted as a specialized form of creative art, and is secure in its own right.

—From the Introduction to *The Noël Coward Song Book* (1953)

MUSIC HALL

When I was a little boy I was lucky enough to be taken to the Theatre quite often. Occasionally the outing would be to a Music Hall instead, and this I loved; there was an excitement about the evening from the noisy, brassy overture onwards. I found it thrilling to watch the numbers of the turns change on the illuminated plaques at both sides of the proscenium, each one filling me with fresh anticipation. Then, at the age of eleven I "went on the Halls" myself in a sketch called "A Little Fowl Play" with Sir Charles Hawtrey, and when I was thirteen in a sketch called "War in the Air." In the latter I played a child with a one-track mind who prayed each night in the prologue, "Please God make me a great big aviator one day." This prayer was answered in a flash, at the beginning of the very next scene to be precise, when I (suddenly grown up and remarkably changed in looks, even to the colour of my eyes) stepped into an aeroplane and whizzed off on a wire round the edge of the Dress Circle, or rather half way round where, on the first night, the whole contraption stuck and the effect was thenceforward abandoned.

With these two sketches I played in most of the London Variety houses, from the Palladium and the Coliseum to the Willesden Hippodrome and the Shoreditch Empire, and I adored every minute. I got to the theatre as early as I possibly could and was usually made up and ready before the overture, so that I could stand at the side and watch the other turns. In this way I saw Nellie Wallace, Maidie Scott, Phil Ray, George Robey, Beattie and Babs, all the great ones in fact, from that special and visually beautiful angle, the wings. I shall never forget them, each turn had for me its special fascination—the performing dogs, the performing seals, the stars who "topped the bill," the snake charmers (I let a whole basket of snakes loose between the matinée and evening performances one wicked day, to the consternation of Madame Alicia Adelaide Needham and her Ladies Choir) and I learnt a great deal.

When I was twenty I went to Paris for the first time, fell in love with it as young people usually do and I have remained in love with it ever since. Mistinguett and Maurice Chevalier were appearing in a revue at the Casino de Paris and of course I went to see them. I hadn't much French but what little I had I was extremely proud of, and that very day I had conducted the purchase of a tie with great fluency and flair. (The friend I was with was deeply impressed; until the end of the transaction that is, when to the saleswoman's final *Bonjour, Monsieur* and to her great surprise and my mortification, I replied before I could stop myself, *Aujourd'hui* with a slight bow from the waist and sickening clarity.)

But my lack of knowledge of *argot* hardly mattered while watching two individual performers as great as Mistinguett and Chevalier. I had by this time seen many of the French stars in London where they had been enjoying a tremendous vogue and much adoration—Gaby Deslys, drenched in pink ostrich feathers, Alice Delysia and Morton at the Ambassadors, Régine Flory at the Palace, Yvonne Arnaud who up till then had been appearing in musical comedies, and Raquel Meller proffering her violets and her vast eyes to the Coliseum audiences.

So I was not altogether unprepared for the shock of seeing the Paris Music Hall for the first time. I already had some idea of the power the French performers injected into their sad love songs, the hilarious low humour into the funny ones, their finesse in the witty ones and above all I had been bowled over by their glamour and the strength of their personalities.

But of all the assaults on the senses made by the Music Hall, the visual impact is for me the most memorable. One after another, quick and fast, the pictures were created; unforgettable, painted on the brain for ever. Most of them sharp, unsubtle, in the primary colours; some of them, in the *café-concerts* and the theatres where smoking was allowed, softened and a little blurred. Through the gauze curtain woven by the smoke from many cigarettes one saw the line of high-kicking girls, glittering in their sequinned *maillots*. Or through the shaft of light thrown on to the touching picture of Mistinguett in her rags, singing "J'en ai marre," the smoke from one cigarette would curl upwards in a spiral; given momentary form, a white solidarity almost, as it hit the spotlight, only to vanish in the darkness above it, or be blown into the auditorium by some resin scented draught from the stage.

Toulouse Lautrec captured all this with paper and chalks, as Sickert captured it for us in England with oils and canvas. In this book it has all been caught by the camera—the singers, the dancers, clowns, acrobats, tight-rope walkers, jugglers, contortionists and trick cyclists; the light, the feathers, *les nus* and the spangles. It seems to me that these photographs give us the pictorial essence of the subjects they set out to portray. For those of us who never saw Damia, for instance, here she is with her chalk-white face and her tight black dress; Dranem, Jenny Golder and Mayol exactly, I am sure, as their public knew and loved them. The ones we shall never see again, Grock, Little Tich, Harry Pilcer and Barbette, are brought back to us vividly as we remember them. And the stars of today, Piaf, Joséphine Baker, Chevalier, Yves Montand, Marlene Dietrich, Charles Trenet, Suzy Solidor, Juliette Gréco, they too are here to remind us of the pleasure they have given us and, more important, the promise of further pleasure to come.

—From the Introduction to *Les Folies du Music-Hall* (1960)

Revue

"A light theatrical entertainment consisting of a series of short (usually satirical) sketches, comic turns, songs, etc."
—*OXFORD ENGLISH DICTIONARY*

.

Before he made a name for himself as a playwright with *The Vortex* in 1924, Noël had already put down a marker in musical theatre.

Admittedly he was only a contributor—albeit a major one—to André Charlot's 1923 revue, *London Calling!* But he managed to capture the reviews.

The Times: "Mr. Noel Coward is the Poo-Bah of the production. He takes a leading part in it, and acts, dances and sings with credit; he helped Mr. Ronald Jeans write the 'book' and also wrote the lyrics and music. To him, therefore, the greatest praise is due, for it was his handiwork that gave the others many of their opportunities of shining."

One of those opportunities was for Gertrude Lawrence to perform "Parisian Pierrot," a song which remains a favorite in the Coward songbook. Cecil Beaton was to call it "the signature tune of the 1920s."

Someone who didn't share *The Times*'s rapture was the young John Gielgud. He was in the habit of writing his own review of a show on his programme and on this occasion . . .

"Very delightfully entertaining. Maisie and Gertrude Lawrence chiefly—Noel Coward is definitely not good, and it is a pity there is no ingenue in the show who can apparently sing in tune."

It was as well Noël didn't see this, as Gielgud would be cast a few months later as his understudy in *The Vortex*!

———

In *The Times* reviewer James Agate wrote . . .

"For years the critics have complained that the people who produce revues persistently ignore the wits whilst paying attention to the wigs, fretting themselves into a fever as to the covering of the actors' heads and indifferent to the clothing to their authors' minds. Latterly, there have been signs of a change, and in his present venture Mr. André Charlot has gone to the length of impressing in the person of Mr. Noel Coward, the youngest, and who shall say that that does not mean the brainiest of our intellectuals. Is dullness the consequence, or is this revue rendered 'screamingly funny'? The answer, I think, is to be found in the serried rows of those grave and reverend signors, the critics, who forsook their glum misanthropy and laughed themselves, so to speak, free of their critical toils.

"There is no reason to despise revue, which springs as much out of the temper of modern minds, as Greek drama from Greek thought, or the morality play from the desire to be preached to. Revue fits the times, and there is no critical sense in being sniffy about this particular form of

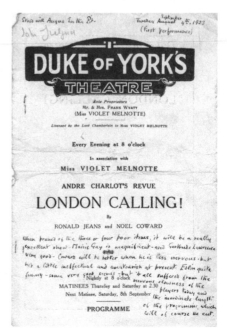

John Gielgud's programme notes.

dramatic art. *London Calling!* is one of the best revues I have ever seen. To begin with it fulfils its function, which is that of slating public vanities and foibles by laughing at them."

Agate went on to praise Gertrude Lawrence . . .

"Miss Lawrence pinks you prettily like an adroit fencer . . . besides being an accomplished actress, she is also a graceful dancer and a charming singer."

Noël fared less well . . .

"Mr. Coward, as actor, is something of a difficulty. He is both self-conscious and self-assertive, and not, I think, a very great success."

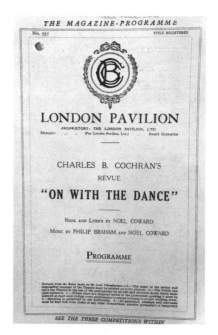

The Times, therefore, spoke with forked tongue. The show was an undoubted success and ran for 316 performances.

With *The Vortex* still running Noël settled into a pattern in which plays and revues alternated. Nineteen twenty-five saw him make the move from Charlot to Cochran with *On with the Dance.* This time, after some heavy bargaining, he was given complete control.

The show ran for 229 performances and added another Coward "classic" with the song "Poor Little Rich Girl."

This Year of Grace! (1928)

This Year of Grace! opened at the London Pavilion in March 1928 and ran for 316 performances.

Cochran wrote to Noël:

> You have given me such brilliant material that the rest was fairly easy, but beyond that, we are all grateful for your help in production. From the moment you read me some of the book and played the tunes, I had no doubt as to the success of the show.
>
> I ask you to promise me one thing, and that is not to undertake a revue or any part of a revue for any other Manager. One revue a year

at the London Pavilion is all you should do; also, let me remind you that you owe me a play with music and a play without music. Don't undertake to write them by Thursday next, but let me have them when the spirit moves you.

Never have I worked with an author with such pleasure as with you on *This Year of Grace!* The same goes for the lyricist and the composer.

Yours as ever,

Charles B. Cochran

When the show was taken to Broadway with a new cast, Noël joined it. His costar was Beatrice Lillie and there were times when "Beattie" could be distinctly problematic . . .

"Before I continue further, I should like to say that she was then, and is now, a much-loved friend. The fact that she was an uppish, temperamental, tiresome, disagreeable, inconsiderate, insufferable friend during that one week of her life in no way sullies my steadfast love for her. It may have temporarily dimmed it to the extent of my wishing ardently to wring her neck . . ."

It introduced some songs that would become Coward standards . . . "A Room with a View" and "Dance, Little Lady"—a further warning to the Poor Little Rich Girl—and "World Weary" on Broadway.

The critical reception was uniformly positive, which was just as well, since after the fiasco of *Sirocco* the previous year, there was ground to be made up. Amid the mutual congratulations there was one small jarring note that was soon set aside.

Cochran—whose experience in this field was far more extensive than Noël's, since he had practically invented the form of the *revue intime*—questioned the validity of the "one man show."

As he wrote in one of his memoirs . . . "I have come to the conclusion that the miscellany which a spectacular revue must be, is best arrived at by employing a multitude of brains and hands to provide the material, with one controlling brain to receive it, edit, arrange, and give it form. It is on this principle that I have worked most successfully."

By *This Year of Grace!* Noël had bargained himself to the position of controlling all the elements—all of which he had created himself! Where was the objectivity?

There would be one more Coward-Cochran revue—the 1932 *Words and Music.*

Again, it added signature Coward songs . . . "Mad Dogs and English-

men" . . . "Mad About the Boy" . . . "Something to Do with Spring" . . .
"The Party's Over Now" . . . but it underperformed *This Year of Grace!*
by running for only 164 performances.

———

Cochran's contention about the nature of revue, continued . . .

"This form of entertainment cannot be entirely a one-man job. Coward had written the whole of the dialogue and most of the music of *This Year of Grace!*, but variety was given to that revue by the introduction of other items, by the employment of several hands on the scene and costume designs, and—I am sure I am right—by the sympathetic collaboration of Coward and myself in every department and at all stages of production.

"In *Words and Music* we had a revue planned, written, composed and directed throughout by one brain . . . If homogeneity was the end aimed at, the end was certainly attained. But in revue homogeneity can lead to monotony . . . Coward's scheme was an interesting experiment, but not sufficiently varied to be popular.

"Some of the satire was bitter rather than stimulatingly acid; some of the items were sad—depressing rather than entertaining."

And then he comes to the crux of the matter . . .

"While *Words and Music* might be a most entertaining Coward revue, it was not a Cochran revue."

MAD DOGS AND ENGLISHMEN

Drawings by Gladys Calthrop.

Gladys Calthrop, a friend from the 1920s
and Noël's designer for many years. Painted
in oils by Sir John Rothenstein.

Set to Music was a Broadway revue based on the 1932 London revue *Words and Music.*

The latter had run for several months "not, as I had hoped, for two years. It was a good revue on the whole and received excellent notices but what it lacked was a big star or, better still, two big stars. The cast included . . . some expert performers but none of them at this time had that indisputable star quality which commands queues at the box office. Later it was produced in New York under the title *Set to Music* with Beatrice Lillie and Richard Haydn. Nobody could question the 'star' status of Beatrice Lillie but even with her name over the marquee the show, after three months capacity business, lingered on for a further month or so and then closed. All of which, I am reluctantly forced to admit, proves that the revue wasn't quite as good as it should have been . . . it didn't hit the jackpot and that was that.

"When I was a very little boy my beloved housemaid-cum-nurse, Emma, used to admonish me by saying—'Don't be too sharp or you'll cut yourself.' This, I think, on looking back, was what was wrong with

Sonnie Hale and Jessie Matthews share "A Room with a View." *This Year in Grace*, London, 1928.

Words and Music. It was too clever by half. It contained too much satire and too little glamour to attract the masses. However, as it didn't exactly flop humiliatingly in either London or New York I can quite happily chalk it up as a near miss and remember it with affection."

Noel Coward Rehearses Beatrice Lillie in *Set to Music*

Applause is heard offstage and Miss Lillie comes on with the line: "Shut it out, Daisy. *Shut—it—out!* I can't bear it!" She puts both hands to her head to drown out the sound. "What's the matter, darling?" one of her

Words and Music by Noël Coward. Adelphi Theatre, 1932. Ivy St. Helier as Lady Mullenty and Gerald Nodin as Sir Ronald Mullenty while Romney Brent as the Reverend Inigo Banks sings "Mad Dogs and Englishmen." First sung by Beatrice Lillie in *The Third Little Show*, 1931. The young man in the white top hat is Graham Payn.

admirers asks. "Nothing," she responds, with tragic mien, and sits down wearily. "Everything." She turns to look at them and slumps back. "Absolutely perfect, Bea-dle-dy," Coward calls out.

He watches them go through it again. This time, as she drops her arm, the fall makes her body jerk in the opposite direction so that she almost slips off the chair. She holds up her hand for the next man to kiss, lets it fall again. "No, that's not good. Let me try it over." Out goes her hand; the man kisses it. This time she leaves her arm suspended for a fraction of a second, then slowly and gracefully lets it float down to the table. This gets an instantaneous laugh from the company and a warm note of approval from Coward. "I'm *afraid* this scene's going to be funny, Bea. . . . *Look,* I've thought of something. When you put out your hand the second time, shift the pearls you're holding, then make a quick grab for them so that he won't get them. You'll vary all these bits, of course, once you get an audience reaction; but let's get as many of them set now as possible. Right!"

When Miss Lillie—alone at last—begins her song: "Weary of It All," Coward dances it out beside her, beating the tempo for the piano player with his hands. She comes to the lines: "Caviar and grouse in an over-heated house" and her whole body seems to crumple with world weariness; then, suddenly, completely unexpectedly, and out of time with the music, she galvanizes herself into a mine of energy and sweeps forward to sing her next lines in a throaty hot-cha voice, her body swaying in swing rhythm. The whole cast, including Coward, break into peals of laughter. Lillie, as swiftly as she has cast it off, replaces the mantle of jaded, sophisticated weariness and walks, with her back to the audience, towards the exit singing: "I'm so weary"—Pause, a droop of her head—"weary"—she picks up her evening cloak in pantomime—"weary"—she is at the door now, she wiggles her hips faintly—"of it"—she starts to go out, then just when you expect the "all" to come out, she suddenly turns so that her profile faces the audience, bursts into harsh, mania-cal laughter and exits. The shock of the laugh—no one has heard it before—renders the cast almost speechless, then the whole company breaks down completely. "That pulled it up, Noel, didn't it?" Lillie says. She cocks one finger in the air, screws her mouth a little, then she, too, starts to laugh.

As you watch Miss Lillie in one incredible absurdity after another, keeping the company convulsed in rehearsals, even when she does the same scene over and over, you begin to realize how much the projection of comedy depends on timing, on the physical line of the body in gesture and movement, and on the sound pattern of a performance. You see, also, how much these elements spring from "the infinite capacity for taking pains," rather than from divine comic inspiration.

"The simple movements on the stage," as Coward explains to an actor in relation to a dance step, "only look spontaneous if they are studied over, and over, and *over*. You must know *exactly* how many steps to take to reach your partner and you must take the same number of steps each time you do it. Otherwise it will look sloppy. Spontaneity on the stage is only possible in movements and nuances which are superimposed *after* you've got a rigid pattern."

To say that Miss Lillie is funny only because she has a superlative comedian's technique is, of course, foolish. The light of real comic genius sparkles from beneath her dark eyelashes, radiates from each of the unexpected angles of her countenance, and illumines every motion and gesture she makes. But she would never be the Mistress of the Absurd if her technique were less sure. Her most inspired moments of spontaneous comic combustion would only pop and fizzle if they were not executed with perfect timing and the use of every trick in the comedian's bag.

Miss Lillie never delivers the comic thrust of a speech without reacting to it by some movement, however imperceptible; she never makes a gesture with her hand which is not reflected in a twist of her torso, a crook of her knee, a tightening, or a loosening, of her muscles. Let her toss her hand absurdly forward and her back will respond (when the laugh has subsided) by a sudden stiffening which throws her posterior into relief, gaining another laugh, which she will top by a slight, but surely a refined, wiggle. The "line" of her performance is always pliable and angular—always, that is, until she wants to get a comic effect by making it motionless and straight. It always has contrast. So it is with the "sound," which is measured to fit and to enrich this "line." It is, with the sound, a question of *crescendo* here and *piano* there; of suddenly beating a slow tempo (or an unresponsive audience) into quivering alertness by an unexpected increase in the volume of tone—one of Miss Lillie's favorite, and most favored, tricks.

There is something else, much harder to put your finger on, which illuminates Miss Lillie's playing—a quality which differentiates the great artist, in any field, from the merely competent one—the power to make some comment of her own on anything she essays. She sings a ditty about a party on the Riviera in which the *dénouement* is, to say the least, unexpected. It always gets a laugh. But the laugh is twice as big when Miss Lillie, either before or after the climax (she varies this at rehearsals), looks at the audience with an expression of horrified amazement or of enraptured understanding, as if to say: "Have you ever *heard* of such a party?" taking them into her confidence. In another scene she stands angrily on stage as the chorus insists on singing "Ah! Ah! Ah!," preventing her from starting in on her next verse, and pushes one foot out in a petulant pose. That is the comic statement; the com-

Noël and cast of *Set to Music* (1939).

ment comes when, a moment later, drawing her shoulders together, she looks down over the peak of her nose and stares at her foot with mock incredulity.

"All right. Let's get on to the next scene," as Coward puts it. "And remember, boys," he is poised on the edge of the runway, "I want sharpness, vitality, brilliance, talent and charm!" He clicks his fingers and hurries into the orchestra. But the next scene has to wait until the evening session because a Mr. Winston, the stage manager announces, is here to measure the men for shirts and to get Mr. Coward's approval of the patterns. And the "fine patrician quartet of us" which sings of England's stately homes goes down to the men's room to be fitted instead of acquainting the company with the fact that:

> *"Our duty to the nation,*
> *It's only fair to state,*
> *Lies not in procreation*
> *But what we procreate.*
> *And so we can cry*
> *With kindling eye,*
> *As to married life we go,*
> What ho! *for the stately homes of England!"*

The curtain fell on *Set to Music* and rose almost immediately on—World War II. Another "war to end all wars."

When it was over Noël decided to give revue one more try. This time in London only.

Sigh No More (1945)

Sigh No More was perhaps not an ideal title, as the production was to give him several. Once again he created most of the material and also directed. Ironically, one of the numbers that survived the show was called "Never Again."

The other was "Matelot," which he wrote specially for Graham Payn. Payn describes how it came to be written by accident . . .

"I was struggling with my solo spot in the second half, a number entitled 'It Couldn't Matter Less.' Frankly, as far as I was concerned, it

couldn't. I told Noel I didn't think the number was good enough. 'Yes, it is,' he snapped, 'it's VERY good!' So I plucked up my courage and challenged him. 'All right, then, let's see YOU do it!' There were indrawn breaths from the others at the rehearsal. Would God, let alone The Master, strike me down?

"Noel gave me a Look, then took up the gauntlet, which, as an actor/director, he was quite capable of doing. After trying the number a couple of times he conceded. 'You're quite right, it isn't strong enough. I'll write you another song.' 'Oh, yes, chum,' I thought. 'I've heard THAT one before.' . . . But a couple of days later he called to say he'd written a new song. 'It's called "Matelot." Come around and I'll play it for you.'

"After hearing the first eight bars I knew we had a hit. Later he would say that it was the one thing about the show he couldn't say goodbye to without a pang."

Sigh No More expired after 213 performances. Noël never attempted the revue medium again in the nearly thirty more years of his life. Charity concerts aplenty but never a revue. Perhaps Cochran's words had been heard after all . . .

"The essence of revue is variety, rapidity, change of mood and contrast of line and colour . . . homogeneity can lead to monotony."

Noël did, however, set down his own evaluation of what was involved in this form that he never quite mastered to his own satisfaction . . .

The art of Revue writing is acknowledged by those unfortunates who have had anything to do with it as being a very tricky and technical business. Everything has to be condensed to appalling brevity. The biggest laugh must be on the last line before the black out. No scene or number should play for more than a few minutes at most, and, above all, the Audience must never be kept waiting. The moment their last splendid laugh at the end of a sketch has subsided into a general chuckle, their attention must immediately be distracted by a line of vivacious chorus girls (preferably with bare legs) or a treble-jointed acrobatic dancer with no bones at all; in fact, anything arrestingly visual that will relax their strained mind and lull them into a gentle apathy, while the next onslaught upon their risibilities is being prepared behind the scenes.

The lessons which have to be learned by aspiring Revue writers are many and bitter. The bitterness really being the eternal bugbear of "Running Order." Running Order is the Sequence in which the various items in the show follow one another, and however carefully the Author may have planned it originally, this sequence is generally completely changed by the time the show reaches dress rehearsal, and frequently drastically after the first night.

For instance, the leading lady upon perceiving that the pretty blonde danseuse will undoubtedly make a tremendous success, resolutely refuses to follow immediately afterwards with her Powder-puff number with the girls, whereupon everything is changed round, and the low-comedy lodging house scene is substituted in place of the Powder-puff number. Then, after a suitable interval, it is discovered that with this rearrangement it is impossible for the chorus to make their change from "The Jungle Scene" to the "Tower of London in 1586" because, according to the original layout, the six-minute lodging house scene came in between, whereas now they only have half a minute's reprise of the Theme song to enable them to get in and out of their wimples. At this point the Author is usually dragged protesting miserably, into a cold office behind the dress circle and commanded to write then and there a brief but incredibly witty interlude to be played in front of black velvet curtains by no more than four minor members of the Cast (the Principals all being occupied with quick changes), without furniture, as there is no time to get it on and off, and finishing with such a gloriously funny climax that the Audience remain gaily hysterical for at least a minute and a half in pitch darkness.

Another problem which the writer has to face is the successful handling of Danger Spots. The principal danger spots in Revue are (1) The opening of the whole show, which must be original and extremely snappy. (2) the sketch immediately following it, which must be so convulsive the Audience are warmed up enough to overlook a few slightly weaker items. (3) The Finale of the first half. This should essentially be the high spot of the evening so that on the first night the bulk of the Audience and the critics can retire to the bars (if not already there) and, glowing with enthusiasm, drink themselves into an alcoholic stupor for the second half. The fourth danger spot is the strong low-comedy scene, which should be placed as near as possible to the second-half finale and should be strong, low, and very comic indeed.

If, upon reading the notices in the newspapers after that first night, it is found that different critics take exception to different scenes, you can safely predict a successful run. If all the critics unanimously take exception to one particular scene, it is advisable to move that scene to a more conspicuous place in the programme. If, on the other hand, no particular critic disliked any particular scene and they all unite in praising the whole production, it either means that you have such a good show that they haven't the face to attack it, or such a bad show that they like it. In either case it will probably be a failure.

Do the grapes taste a little sour?

.

Musical Theatre

"Oscar Hammerstein wrote wisely that the perfect lyric for a musical should be inspired directly by the story and the characters contained in it. In fact, ideally a song in a musical should carry on whenever the dialogue leaves off. Apart from one or two rare exceptions I concur with him entirely . . . Any young potential lyric writer should learn early that if he wishes to write a successful 'book show' he must eschew irrelevance and stick to the script."

On Writing Lyrics

"I can only assume that the compulsion to make rhymes was born in me. There is no time I can remember when I was not fascinated by words 'going together.' Lewis Carroll, Edward Lear, Beatrix Potter, all fed my childish passion, in addition to all the usual nursery rhymes that the flesh is heir to. . . . I can still distinctly recall being exasperated when any of those whimsical effusions were slipshod in rhyming or scansion."

===

"On my fifth birthday my mother injected the 'musical comedy' virus into my bloodstream by taking me to see *The Dairymaids* at the Grand Theatre, Croydon. All I can clearly remember of it is the opening chorus in an elaborate dairy where a number of young ladies were skittishly manipulating butter churns, and the opening chorus of the second act when, confusingly, the same young ladies were vaulting about in a gymnasium in a high school and executing a complicated dance routine with Indian clubs. Delighted but bewildered by all this, I questioned my mother closely, but her explanations were vague and unsatisfying. However, it established in my mind the conviction that 'musical comedy' was gaily irrational to the point of lunacy, a conviction which I have staunchly upheld for over sixty years.

"My mother was what would be described in today's American slang as 'a genuine musical comedy buff.' This is easily accounted for by the fact that, during her early married years, she appeared humbly but repeatedly in the chorus of the Teddington Amateur Dramatic Society's productions of Gilbert and Sullivan. When she took me to the theatre for birthday and other treats it was always to a musical comedy, in fact I never saw a 'straight' play until I was eleven and had already been on the stage professionally for a year. This first 'straight' play I saw was a comedy called *Better Not Enquire,* starring Charles Hawtrey, at the Prince of Wales Theatre. No prescient inner voice whispered to me that within six months I should be appearing at that same theatre with Hawtrey himself, in a play called *The Great Name,* in which I had one line, as a page-boy, in the last act."

===

Noël recalled . . .

"In the days of my youth musical comedy stars were a good deal more

insouciant in regard to their work and their public than they are today. They 'stayed off' on the slightest pretext. I remember waiting for hours in pit and gallery queues to see Lily Elsie in *The Merry Widow, The Dollar Princess* and *The Count of Luxembourg* but I never actually caught up with her until she played *Pamela* at the Palace Theatre during the Great War. She was, of course, enchanting; but I cannot resist sending an affectionate 'Thank you' to Miss Deborah Volar, her understudy, whom I saw so often and knew so much better."

When he was "between jobs"—i.e., unemployed—

I spent a good deal of time, now being an established actor, in writing in to the various theatres for free seats. I had had some professional cards printed with "Master Noel Coward" in the middle, and "Mr. Charles Hawtrey's company, *Where the Rainbow Ends,* Savoy Theatre" in the left-hand corner. These were sent to different managements with a stamped addressed envelope inside and a pompous little note in the third person, usually beginning "Master Noel Coward would be so very much obliged," etc.

Usually they were returned with callous regrets, but every now and then, as though to keep up my spirits, two pink dress circles tickets would arrive with "Complimentary" stamped across them. These were gala days. Mother used to frizz her hair and put on her evening dress. I put on my black suit and Eton collar and off we'd go in the train and bus, always arriving far too early, long before the safety curtain had risen, but content with a box of chocolates and a programme. We used to have supper when we got home and discuss the play over it.

In those early years my favourite musical-comedy actress was Miss Gracie Leigh, who always played second (soubrette) parts. In the window of Keith Prowse I saw a poster advertising *The Quaker Girl* on which she headed the female cast list.

There was another poster overlapping this, and so it was not until Mother and I had forced our way into the front row of the pit and opened our programme that we noticed the four magic words "And Miss Gertie Millar." Presently she made her entrance with all the Quakers, detached herself from them, glided across the stage to Joseph Coyne, who was sitting under a tree, and proceeded to sing and dance their first duet, "When a Good, Good Girl Like Me Meets a Bad, Bad Boy Like You." From that moment onwards I was enslaved.

Miss Gertie Millar.

I was much luckier with my adored Gertie Millar, on one occasion miraculously so. I opened my programme and there was the sinister little slip announcing that "Owing to indisposition, etc., Miss Millar's part would be played by Miss Whoever-it-Was." I groaned with disappointment and contemplated for a moment leaving the theatre, but as I was being taken as a special treat by an old friend who had booked the seats (dress circle, front row) weeks before, I crushed down my gloom and determined to enjoy the show for what it was worth. It was fortunate that I did, because on she came, my beloved star, as magical as ever. Of course the age-old tradition that a star must appear even if he or she is practically dying is an excellent one, although it can be carried too far.

My bedroom was plastered with photographs of Gertie, for ever since the first time I had seen her in *The Quaker Girl*, I had adored her, and in my own memory she is the most graceful and charming artiste I have ever seen. Now that I know her well I can never look at her gay unchanged face without a little stab of the heart, to think that never again will she float down the stage, chuckling lightly and expressing with her hands a joy of living which was her own special charm. I often waited outside the Adelphi stage door for hours to see her come out.

She always smiled at me and said goodnight. Once she gave me a flower from a bouquet she was carrying, which I pressed carefully in a bound volume of CHUMS.

Many years later I went with her to the opening night of a revival of *The Quaker Girl,* which was less than adequately performed and I remember her putting her hand gently on my knee to calm my irritated twitching and quell my muttered imprecations. To me Gertie Millar was and is—now, alas, only in my memory—the epitome of what a musical-comedy star should be, as indeed *The Quaker Girl* was the epitome of what a musical comedy should be. It has a good story, excellent lyrics and, above all, an enchanting score by Lionel Monckton. Embedded in my mind for ever is the vision of Gertie Millar singing "Tony from America" in the moonlit garden of the "Pre-Catalan," moving with such feather-light grace that she seemed to be floating rather than dancing.

A little while ago [in the mid-1930s] a party was given by Gladys and Leslie Henson—a good higgledy-piggeldy theatrical party with a magnificent cast of yesterday and today. Lily Elsie was there and Maurice Chevalier and Violet Loraine and everybody balanced *vol-au-vents* on their knees and drank whatever they wanted and gossiped and sang songs. Gertie Millar (the Countess of Dudley) sat on the stairs in chinchilla, while I was at the piano strumming a few excerpts from bygone musical comedies in which everybody joined.

Suddenly, as I played "Tony from America," the other sounds fell away, and from the semi-gloom of the stairs came "He guessed I was alone, so that's why he came along and found me," in that funny, unvocal little voice, bridging the years and for a strange instant filling our hearts with a pleasurable melancholy. Many of us cried, because it was a most touching moment, and theatrical people are notoriously facile of emotion, frequently victimised by their own foolish sentimentality.

⸻

Diary, April 25, 1952
"Poor Gertie Millar is dead . . . Although she has been so ill for so long, it gave me a horrible pang. She was my childhood's dream girl, after all . . . I can still recall the reed like figure and the tiny, breathless voice, the words half spoken and half sung."

⸻

"In my youth nearly all musical comedies had 'Girl' titles: *The Girl from Kay's, The Girl from Up There, The Girl in the Taxi, The Girl on the Film, The Sunshine Girl, The Girl from Utah, The Girl in the Train,* and so on. Every now and then a 'Maid' or two edged their way on to the posters: *The Spring Maid, My Mimosa Maid, The Maid of the Mountains.* But on the whole the 'Girls' won hands down."

Bitter Sweet (1929)

Noël's first—and many would argue his best—"book" musical was the 1929 *Bitter Sweet.*

"The idea was born in the early summer of 1928. It appeared quite unexpectedly and with no other motivation beyond the fact that I had vaguely discussed with Gladys Calthrop the possibilities of writing a romantic Operette. She and I were staying with her family solicitor in Surrey and an hour or so before we were due to leave, Mr. Peake happened to play to us on the gramophone a new German orchestral record of 'Die Fledermaus.'

"Immediately a confused picture of uniforms, bustles, chandeliers and gas-lit cafés formed in my mind, and later, when we were driving over Wimbledon Common, we drew the car to a standstill by the roadside, and in the shade of a giant horse-chestnut tree mapped out roughly the story of Sari Linden.

"The uniforms, bustles, chandeliers and gas-lit café all fell into place eagerly, as though they had been waiting in the limbo for just this cue to enter."

He sensed that the moment might be right for an entertainment of this kind. The West End theatre was putting on "an endless succession of slick American 'Vo vo deo do' musical farces in which the speed was fast, the action complicated and the sentimental value negligible."

Noël's production partner at the time was C. B. Cochran, who liked the idea, so all that remained to be done—among the many other things that had to be done—was to do it.

———

"During that winter of 1929 I finished *Bitter Sweet* . . . The book had been finished long since, but the score had been causing me trouble . . ."

He was appearing on Broadway in *This Year of Grace!*

And, as usual, trying to balance several things at once . . .

"One day, when I was in a taxi on my way back to the apartment after a matinée, the 'I'll See You Again' waltz dropped into my mind, whole and complete, during a twenty minutes' traffic block. After that everything went smoothly, and I cabled to Cockie in London suggesting that he start making preliminary arrangements regarding theatre, opening date, etc."

His first choice to play Sari was, not surprisingly, Gertrude Lawrence but they both realized that with songs like "I'll See You Again" "her voice, although light and charming, was not strong enough to carry such a heavy singing role.

"In every other way she'll be splendid. It needs a damn good actress, which she is, and someone who can wear clothes and look alluring, which she does, and I do honestly think that if the story is got over properly, half the battle is won."

But G's other contractual commitments ruled it out anyway.

Next choice was Evelyn Laye but here—as we've seen—the London production of *This Year of Grace!* provided the obstacle.

"One afternoon, in the lobby of the Algonquin Hotel, I ran into Peggy Wood. She had just come in from the country and was wearing a rain-

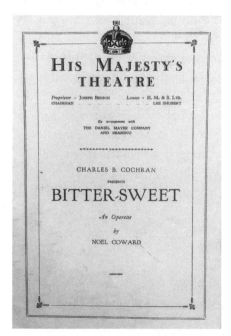

In the early years there seemed to be some doubt whether the show was called *Bitter-Sweet* or *Bitter Sweet*. At Noël's insistence the hyphen was conveniently discarded.

coat, an unbecoming rubbery hat on the back of her head and horn-rimmed glasses, and she looked as far removed from my vision of Sari as Mrs. Wiggs of the Cabbage Patch.

"I had known her on and off for several years, in fact ever since my first visit to New York in 1921, but oddly enough in all that time I had never once seen her on the stage. I had, of course, on all sides enthusiastic accounts of her acting and her looks and the loveliness of her voice, but never having been able to judge for myself, and confronted by that rubber hat, that face devoid of make-up and those horn-rimmed glasses, it was with some trepidation that I hear myself asking her if she would care to come over to London and do an operetta."

Back in his studio in the Hotel des Artistes he hears her sing and "the first few bars she sang assured me that here was the ideal Sari."

And so it proved. Despite the mixed views of the critics who—since *Sirocco* had begun to review the author as much as the work—felt that, having praised *This Year of Grace!*, they must temper their enthusiasm this time. "It would be too bad, after all, if I were encouraged to believe that there was anything remarkable in writing, composing and producing a complete operetta. I might become uppish again and this was an excellent opportunity of putting me gently but firmly in my place."

Bitter Sweet ran for 697 performances . . . and then came the American production . . .

.

> Sentiment is out of fashion. Yet *Bitter Sweet*, which is nothing if not sentimental, has not been a dead failure. Thus we see that things that are out of fashion do not cease to exist. Sentiment goes on; unaffrighted by the roarings of the young lions and lionesses of Bloomsbury. *Bitter Sweet* goes on too; and Mr. Cochran (being a sentimentalist) has wished that this survival should be commemorated by me in some sentimental drawings.
>
> —MAX BEERBOHM

.

(Covering note with his drawings of *Bitter Sweet*)
"On the day of production Florenz Ziegfeld [who was co-producing] asked me to lunch and told me in course of it that, as I had so resolutely refused his offer of a smarter male chorus and twelve ravishing show-girls (an offer, incidentally, which had been made daily since our arrival in America), he was going to refrain from any undue display over the New

The duel scene at Café Schlick. Captain Lutte and Carl Linden.

York first night . . . I received this dispiriting announcement apathetically, being far too exhausted to care whether he gave the seats away with a packet of chewing gum."

Noël never thought the Broadway cast to be the equal of the London one but, nevertheless, the show was a hit . . .

And the hit of the hit was Evelyn Laye—now playing the role she had previously rejected. "It was Evelyn's night from first to last. She played as though she were enchanted."

Noël reported to Violet . . . "I've only got 283 telegrams to answer! Evelyn is weeing down her leg with excitement. She's been such a darling. I'm delighted with her success."

The show ran for 159 performances.

———

Evelyn Laye recalled her nervousness in having to "audition" for Noël for the Broadway part . . .

I tried to sing Noel's lovely melodies in three voices, making it a little breathless and sweet for the young girl, powerful for the woman of forty and deeper and more resonant for the elderly woman.

I went to the theatre on the morning that Noel was going to hear me sing for the first time. Elsie April (Noel's musical amanuensis) was going to play for me. Noel was an isolated figure, sitting in the middle of the empty stalls. I was very nervous. Noel is such an enthusiast, with such a superb flair for knowing what is right that he can be a task master with a whip, or a fiend if things are done badly.

"Well, I'm ready, dear," he said in his clipped, precise voice. "Noel, before I start I want to ask you a favour?" I told him. "Please let me sing the whole score right through, and even if there are passages you don't like, please don't stop me until the end. If you stop me, you won't see what I'm trying to do with it."

"Very well," said the young man who was already dubbed "The Master" by most of the people who worked for him.

I began to sing.

After a while Noel left his seat and started walking up and down the main aisle of the stalls. Elsie nodded at me encouragingly. This was a good sign. He was interested. As I went on his pace increased, till, at the last number, he was marching up and down very quickly, his hands clasped firmly behind his back.

As I finished he wheeled round to come up to the orchestra rail. "Very exciting, very exciting," he said. "That's your personality, your interpretation. It's good, very good. Don't change it. Stay there."

He came round to the stage. "It's good, darling," he repeated. He kissed me and said in a matter-of-fact voice—"Now I'm going to get some lunch"—and vanished.

I looked at Elsie. "There'd have been no lunch for him, or for you, if he hadn't liked it," she observed.

One of the show's biggest fans was Ivor Novello and this seems as good a time as any to fit him into the context of Noël's personal and professional life . . .

Ivor could not have been more generous in his appreciation of this achievement. In a letter he wrote:

I've just come back from seeing *Bitter Sweet* for the second time and I've got to tell you what a *lovely, lovely* thing you have done—it's sheer joy from beginning to end. The music impressed me unbelievably—it's so gay yet full of thought and has the most extraordinary way of reflect-

Drawings by Gladys Calthrop.

Peggy Wood for London, Evelyn Laye for New York, Jane Marnac for Paris: all played Sari (as did Jeanette MacDonald and Anna Neagle on film) in a score that featured "If Love Were All," "I'll See You Again," "Zigeuner," "Ladies of the Town," and "Dear Little Café." In London alone *Bitter Sweet* ran for 697 performances.

The TATLER

Vol. CXVIII. No. 1532. London, November 5, 1930. POSTAGE: Inland 1½d.; Canada and Newfoundland, 1d.; Foreign, 1½d. Price One Shilling

BITTER . . . to lose PEGGY
SWEET . . . to regain EVELYN

Miss Evelyn Laye being greeted on her arrival at Waterloo by Miss Peggy Wood and Mr. C. B. Cochran. The return of Miss Laye from the States to take up the part created by Miss Peggy Wood in Noël Coward's triumphant success has its sad as well as its glad side. While welcoming with rapture the second "Lady Shayne" straight from the plaudits of New York, London will gratefully remember the brilliant rendering of her predecessor, who, after playing this exacting rôle for fifteen months, has been ordered a rest. Au revoir and many, many thanks to Peggy. Pass friend Evelyn: all's well. Another picture of Miss Laye appears on a later page

"The two most beautiful things in the world are Ivor's profile and my mind."

Noël reported to Violet: "Evelyn made the most triumphant success I've ever seen when she made her entrance in the last act in the white dress. They clapped and cheered for two solid minutes. . . . She certainly does knock spots off the wretched Peggy."

ing the story as it goes along. The only disconcerting thing about it is that I cry the moment the first note starts and *cannot* stop—the whole thing is so full of regret—not only for that darling lover who died but for a vanished kindly silly darling age you've re-created. I bless you for it and take off hat, drawers, nay sock suspenders to you for it . . . It's all so clear cut that one remembers the smallest detail. Your own mind is so un-blurred and you've used it like a painter's series of brushes, yet each stroke is so defining.

A few words of context . . .

From the day that Ivor—almost accidentally—wrote *Glamorous Night* (1935), the show that single-handedly revived the fortunes of Drury Lane, he virtually owned the operetta form.

Crest of the Wave (1937), *The Dancing Years* (1939), *Perchance to Dream* (1945), and *King's Rhapsody* (1949) all played to packed houses of middle-class matrons, yearning for romance. Admittedly, Noël had many more different irons in the fire than Ivor by this time but it always irked him that he was never able to repeat the success he had enjoyed with *Bitter Sweet* in this particular *milieu*.

Sandy Wilson probably hit on the reason when he observed that "Noël's wit sprang from his intellect." He had a romantic streak, whereas Ivor was a true *romantic*. In his shows he wore his heart boldly on his sleeve—and his public adored him for it.

In 1951 Noël was asked to write the introduction for a biography of Ivor. He willingly did so but before the book could be published, Ivor, who was appearing in his own *King's Rhapsody,* went home after a performance and died of a heart attack. Ruritania died with him. Noël asked for the preface to be withdrawn . . .

The name Ivor Novello is euphonious; it is pleasant to say, to hear and to see. It is also one of the most famous names in England. Thirty-three years ago in 1917, when my friendship with him just began, it was already famous; already sprinkled with star dust, although at that time he had never set foot upon the professional stage apart from very occasionally, when he would appear at a charity performance looking extremely handsome and a little self-conscious to accompany some piercing soprano in one of her own compositions.

To sustain celebrity value for thirty-three years is a considerable feat. To sustain personal friendships for the same length of time through all the treacherous circumstances of continual success is even more remarkable. The answer, of course, lies in character. Ivor has a strong character; over and above the richness of his talent and the unquestionable force of his personality, he is determined, stubborn and industrious. He is also generous, kind and disarming; beneath several layers of superficial sentimentality, quite ruthless. Added to these paradoxical attributes he possesses what to my mind is the greatest gift of all, an indestructible sense of humour. This, generally directed against himself, is reserved for his personal life and is seldom apparent in public, for curiously enough, in spite of all his successful years, he is shy and self-conscious in front of strangers and, alas, in front of cameras. Apart from a few casual snapshots, I have never seen a photograph of him that gave the slightest indication of what he is really like. Before a camera his face takes on a set look, his eyes become soulful and frequently something quite dreadful happens to his mouth. He dons this lifeless *papier-maché* mask automatically on all public occasions. When perhaps in the cause of a charity he is brought forth or when he is face to face with a member of the Royal Family, his manner becomes strained, and his fluid charm solidifies in an expression of miserable politeness. This startling transformation rarely takes place on the stage, although occasionally I have observed signs of it when for a few moments he has to remain static with nothing to do, I have observed it creeping up on him!

Another strange aspect of his character is his militant anti-snobbism. In his early years, several of his more blue-blooded admirers tore themselves to shreds in an effort to launch him socially. I believe that for a very brief period he partially succumbed and submitted himself to be taken to some of the more *recherché* non-theatrical parties of the period but it didn't last long. He was unimpressed and uncomfortable, the social jargon was alien to his ears and he was bored stiff and aching to get back to the warm, relaxed, theatrical cosiness of his own friends.

This undiminished, passionate love of his "métier" is the most significant key to his character. Theatre, good, bad and indifferent, is the love of his life; to him other human endeavours are mere shadows. Every now and then, spurred on by circumstances or doctor's orders, he journeys to some far off place, never alone, always surrounded by a group of his closest friends. Once there, he settles down to enjoy the climate and bask in the sun, always with the comforting thought at the back of his mind that he will soon be back in his dressing-room. Last year he spent a weekend in my home in Jamaica and we sat on the verandah in the lovely tropical evening light looking out over the mountainous coast, sodden with history and discussing with parochial intensity the return of Lily Elsie to the London stage in the nineteen-twenties.

For many years it has been fairly generally assumed that owing to the fact that both Ivor and I write plays and appear in them, we must inevitably be fierce rivals. Acquaintances who know neither of us well frequently attempt to curry favour by deprecating, usually very clumsily, either me to Ivor or Ivor to me. I warn these well wishers here and now in the coldest of cold print that they are wasting their time. Such a state of affairs never has existed and never will. To begin with, neither of us are temperamentally capable of professional jealousy and we are both far too occupied with doing what we want to do to worry about competition. We are both middle-aged, fortunate, talented and successful. We are both reviled by the Press and respected by the public. Above all, we like each other's company and have been close friends for over a quarter of a century. We have, of course, a lot in common. We were both boy sopranos and we both drink a lot of tea.

All this is a brief preface to the story of Ivor's life. I will add one more comment. The reward of his work lies in the fact that whenever and wherever he appears, the vast majority of the British public flocks to see him. He has provided romance, gaiety, nostalgia and pleasure for many millions of people for many years. He is also, among the few people who really know him, very much loved.

(1950)

Conversation Piece (1934)

Nineteen thirty-three . . . and Noël is traveling back to England . . .

"By the time we had arrived in Plymouth Sound I had completed the libretto of *Conversation Piece*. The idea had come to me when we were two days out of New York and I happened to read a delightful book called *The Regent and His Daughter*."

There was no doubt in his mind who should play the lead—the French star Yvonne Printemps. In the fall of 1933 he began to write the piece—with frequent side trips to Paris to woo the lady into taking the part of Mélanie, the ward of Paul, the Duc de Chaucigny-Varennes, who has brought her to England in the hopes of setting up a good aristocratic marriage for her. The part of Paul would be played by Romney Brent.

The libretto contains an exchange that would prove to be ironic . . .

PAUL: Tell me, do you speak French?
EDWARD: *Oui, un peu.*
PAUL: I never think that's enough, do you?

Mlle Printemps, it emerged, spoke even less English and had to learn the part phonetically.

By the time Cochran produced the show at His Majesty's Theatre in February 1934 Noël had decided to play Paul himself instead of Romney Brent. He wrote to his friend Alexander Woollcott . . .

"I am now giving an exquisite performance as a syphilitic French duke . . . Romney comes occasionally and makes hideous Siamese faces at me from the side of the stage. The play is a great success the music and lyrics are good . . . The play itself, I think, is dull and garbled and I am faintly ashamed of it."

In his introduction to the published version he would write . . .

"There are two startling anachronisms of which, at the time of writing it, I was blissfully unaware. It is never explained, for instance why, in the last scene, Mélanie has completely dismantled a rented house in Brighton, the furniture of which obviously doesn't belong to her! Also, the sentimental emphasis on the gleaming lights of the packet-boat sailing to France is unfortunate, considering that in 1811, the year in which the action of the play passes, England and France were at war!"

Incidentally, by the time the run ended, Mlle Printemps's grasp of English was still tenuous at best but the rest of the company were now speaking excellent French.

Conversation Piece played for 177 performances but has never had a professional revival.

═══

Some years later there was talk of asking her to star in a proposed revival of *Operette*. Although this didn't come to pass, it did cause Noël to reflect on their friendship . . .

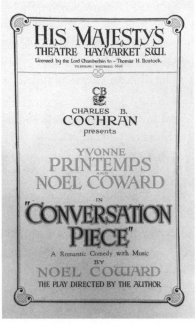

YVONNE PRINTEMPS

According to present day standards of biographical writing, I warn the reader here and now that this essay on Yvonne Printemps will be a disappointment. It should, I know, be witty, analytical and detached; it should, above all, be critical. Praise of her assets should be immediately qualified by sharp emphasis on her defects. It is no longer entertaining to members of the public to read that an artiste sings beautifully unless they are informed in the same paragraph that her diction is faulty and her acting leaves much to be desired; it also delights them to be told that although her phrasing of the aria in act three was quite perfect, she is too old for the part and her legs are too short.

We have in fact nowadays all been hypnotised by the newspapers of the world into believing that "Bad news is Good news and Good news is No news." Personally I do not subscribe to this arbitrary dictum. I am sick to death of bad news. I am weary of hearing artists and works of art belittled by mediocre minds; I prefer abuse to qualified praise and I have long ago given up any hope of finding anything constructive in professional criticism. The opinions of my fellow artists are all that interest me, because experience has taught me that they are the only ones who have enough knowledge of the *métier* to justify them.

Every now and then in our curious world of the theatre a unique star is born. They are rare, these gifted changelings and their uniqueness lies, not necessarily in their talent but in that particular quality they possess which defies comparison with anyone else; and it is of course, this indefinable quality that defeats criticism. Professional critics must have a yardstick with which to measure their values and the yardstick they use with monotonous regularity is comparison. Take this away from them and they are lost, befuddled and liable to make even greater asses of themselves than usual.

It is permissible, obviously, to prefer Eleanora Duse to Sarah Bernhardt, for instance, just as it is permissible to like an oak tree better than an elm tree but it is foolish to say that one is superior to the other. It should, therefore, be possible to discuss an individual artist without dragging in his or her contemporaries or predecessors. I am aware that Kirsten Flagstad sings better than Yvonne Printemps and that Anna Pavlova probably danced better than Tamara Karsivina but I should not care to see Pavlova in *Le Tricorne*, Karsivina in *La Mort du Cygne*, Flagstad in *Les Trois Valses* or Printemps in *The Ring*. In my forty years in the theatre I have known thousands and thousands of fine actors, actresses, singers and dancers but only a few who were great stars. Yvonne Printemps falls into the latter category not because she is in the least like any of them but because she is like none of them. All that she has in common with them is her uniqueness and the fact that her name is part of the structure of her world and the history of her time.

It is for me a difficult task to write a critical analysis of Yvonne Printemps in *Operette* for the simple reason that ever since I first beheld her in the first act of a play sitting up in bed and singing *"J'ai deux amants,"* she has completely disarmed my critical faculties. In the years following I have heard her in *Mozart, Mariette, Les Trois Valses* and my own operette, *Conversation Piece,* which I wrote and composed for her. I have heard her sing when she was so nervous that she could hardly stand. I have heard her sing when she was sad, gay and in every mood in between. But the occasion I will always remember was one occasion when we were lunching at her home. Her husband, Pierre Fresnay was present and the conversation was easy and relaxed. The food was more than perfect and there was a great deal of it. We had exquisite soup, *truite au bleu,* a *tête de veau,* salad and cheese and a chocolate *soufflé.* The sun was rather hot and so we retired indoors for coffee. Suddenly, with her coffee still unfinished, Yvonne, without rising from the sofa, sang the aria from *Madame Butterfly*, unaccompanied and full out. Her voice was pure and effortless and her breathing apparently non-existent. Pierre smiled indulgently and offered me some armagnac but I could neither refuse it nor accept it, because my eyes had filled with tears and I was speechless.

I am grateful to Yvonne Printemps for many such moments. There is something in her voice, not only her singing voice but her speaking voice, that pierces the heart immediately. Only last week when I was in Paris with Vivien Leigh and Laurence Olivier we went to see *Hyménée.* The curtain rose and there was Yvonne, an invalid, seated in a wheel chair. She started to speak, quite ordinarily, quite simply, and the usual magic occurred, clearly and unmistakably. I glanced at Vivien and Larry next to me. Their eyes were shining and Vivien was fumbling silently in her bag for her handkerchief.

By now it must be fairly apparent to the reader that my considered opinion of Yvonne Printemps in *Operette* or out of it is favourable to say the least. But I really cannot allow my personal affection for her to blind me to her faults, one of which is her resolute determination not to sing a note on the stage unless she is forced to. In private life she will sing at the drop of a hat. I have heard her in a restaurant, happy and relaxed, open her mouth and warble like a bird but the thought of singing on the stage sends her into a pathological frenzy. It is a peculiar nervousness I have never encountered before and she is seized with it not only on opening nights, when it would be understandable, but on every other night as well. I have seen her over and over again in *Conversation Piece* waiting in the wings, clasping and unclasping her hands and shaking. There is no apparent reason for this: it is a sort of self-imposed masochism. It isn't that she has ever failed in a singing role; on the contrary, her public love for her to sing, her friends love for her to sing, even the critics love for her to sing. She has never, to my knowledge, had anything but triumphant success as a singer and I am sure that it is only the fact that she is such a fine actress that prevents people from going to the box office and demanding their money back when they have seen her in a straight play in which she doesn't sing one note.

In *Conversation Piece* she had, of course, one supreme reason to be nervous. She was playing and singing a long role in a foreign language. In latter years when I played one of my own plays (*Present Laughter—Joyeux Chagrins*) in Paris in French I understood only too well what she must have suffered. I at least could understand and speak French fairly fluently and still found it a terrible ordeal. She, on the other hand, knew no English at all and, I regret to say, however, that by the end of the run of *Conversation Piece* most of the English company spoke French excellently.

She arrived in London for the first rehearsal word perfect, having been working on the part phonetically for many weeks—but to little avail, as far as their meaning was concerned. I can still see her attacking those inimical English words with tremendous vehemence and then suddenly collapsing in fits of laughter.

The English company adored her from the first day but after two weeks of rehearsal they became a little puzzled by the fact that she never sang. Each day when the time came to do the number Yvonne would stand by the piano mouthing the words to herself but emitting no sound. One evening at the beginning of the third week I was directing the second half ballroom scene from my point of vantage in the front row of the dress circle. The theatre was empty except for a few under-studies sitting in the stalls and my own immediate entourage, consisting of my secretary, Lorn Loraine, John C. Wilson, my manager and G. E. (Gladys) Calthrop, who had designed the production. The ballroom scene was difficult to direct because the whole cast was on the stage at the same time and I was beginning to get rather irritable. The moment came for Yvonne to sing her aria, "Plus de coeur discret" and, as usual, I expected her to stand quite still and mouth it soundlessly. The rehearsal accompanist struck the first introductory chords and suddenly, without warning, she decided to sing. The company who, up to that moment, had never heard her utter a vocal sound, stood transfixed. She sang the whole aria through passionately and divinely and the effect was electrifying. She finished with her arms outstretched and the last lovely B flat echoing though the empty theatre; there was a moment's stunned silence and the whole cast went mad. They shouted and cheered: Yvonne, of course, dissolved into floods of tears immediately. Personally, I was moved beyond words. It was a supreme "theatre" moment for theatre people. No layman living outside the walls of our enchanted citadel could have appreciated the true significance of it.

And in it, curiously enough, lay the essence of Yvonne Printemps. At a command performance she will sing beautifully to the kings and queens of the world. On an opening night she will sing superbly to ill mannered late-comers and cantankerous critics, but to her own people in a half lit, empty theatre she will sing with her whole heart and the heart of Yvonne Printemps is even greater than her talent.

Operette (1938)

In 1937 Noël decided to try his hand at another operetta. *Conversation Piece* had been a vehicle for Yvonne Printemps, so his mind turned to another European *chanteuse* he admired—the Viennese star Fritzi Massary.

He'd met her in Berlin in the early 1920s and they had kept in touch. All he needed now was an idea and one came to him when he went to stay with another old friend, Eleanora von Mendelssohn in her Schloss Kammer-am-Attersee in Austria. Massary was another guest in the house party.

The setting—itself theatrical—inspired him to conceive a storyline there and then for *Operette*, "a play with music." "I am writing Fritzi as herself," he told Eleanora, "giving her three good songs, one in each act . . . It isn't strictly Kammer but a sort of exaggerated theatrical version of it."

From the fragment of it that exists it seems distinctly Chekhovian . . . Noël also allows himself a personal "in-joke."

He is writing this while he and the Lunts are still feeling the bruises from the fiasco of their last joint venture—the 1935 *Point Valaine*.

In this early version, he teases them in the characters of Ruth Vernon and Latymer Chard, a theatrical couple who—like the Lunts—never stop rehearsing . . .

(There is the sound of raised angry voices in the distance and RUTH and LATYMER come on from the direction of the lake)

RUTH: How dare you—how dare you say such cruel things to me!

LATYMER: Because I once loved you and now I hate you—coldly and clearly I *hate* you . . .

RUTH: Go away—go away—

LATYMER: You belong to a race apart from me—it was madness to

Calthrop view of *The Stately Homes of England.*

imagine that we could ever be happy—you breathe different air—you
see different suns, different moons, different stars—you're as alien to
me as the East is alien to the West—you're . . .

RUTH: (*Wildly, crying*) Go away—go away—someone will hear . . .

LATYMER: I would wish the whole world to hear what I have to say
to you—you have no power over me any more, do you understand
that?—I'm free at last—Don't be afraid I shall not remember you—
I shall always remember you, but not as I believed you to be, only as
you are—empty and vain—a courtesan without conviction—a harlot
without warmth!

RUTH: (*Striking him in the face*) You fool!

LATYMER: That wasn't right—do it lower down.

RUTH: Give it to me again.

LATYMER: . . . empty and vain—a courtesan without convictions a harlot
without warmth!

RUTH: (*Striking him again*) You fool!

(*They go into the house*)

———

After writing the first act, Noël put it aside in favor of another treatment
that featured "a play within a play." To costar with Fritzi Massary he

brought back Peggy Wood, his original Sari. Since this was his first musical since the breakup with Cochran, it's quite likely that he was hedging his bets by having two leading ladies instead of one.

Kammer
August 22, 1937

My dear Noël,

Happiness—excitement—gratitude were the feelings released in me when I read your letter. I will sing like mad—learn English till I burst and—as I told you—come when you send for me—so—October in London!

One thing I can promise you—I won't be *kaknaiv* [as naïve as shit]—I won't be *klugscheisserisch* [a smart-ass].

Have a lovely time in America with luck in everything and I hope to meet you in London as charming as only you can be!!! There is one more thing I meant to tell you—I never thought any one would ever be able to stir up so much in me again and if nothing comes of it— I am and always will be your

FRITZI

> *The Stately Homes of England*
> Lord Elderley, Lord Borrowmere,
> Lord Sickert and Lord Camp,
> With every virtue, every grace,
> Ah, what avails the sceptered race.
> Here you see the four of us,
> And there are so many more of us,
> Eldest sons that must succeed . . .

Noël recalled that the song was "what is colloquially known as a 'show stopper' . . . They were all nice looking, their diction was clear and they never went off without resounding applause. Since then I have recorded it and sung it all over the world and it has been popular with everyone with the exception of a Mayoress in New Zealand, who said it let down the British Empire."

In his preface to the published text Noël is refreshingly frank about the outcome . . .

Operette, from my point of view, is the least successful musical play I have ever done. The reason for this is that it is over-written and under-composed. The story of an imaginary "Gaiety Girl" of the early 1900s who achieves overnight stardom and then has to sacrifice her love-life to her career, while not fiercely original, is an agreeable enough background for gay music and lyrics and beguiling period costumes. Unfortunately, however, the plot, which should have been the background, became the foreground, and the music, which should have dominated the action, established the atmosphere, and whirled the play into a lilting success, was meagre and only at moments adequate. The principal waltz song, "Dearest Love" wasn't bad but it wasn't nearly as good as "I'll See You Again" or "I'll Follow My Secret Heart" . . . the only real lyric success of the entertainment was "The Stately Homes of England," which had very little connection with the story.

Another aspect of *Operette* was the triumphant confusion it established in the minds of the audience. This was cunningly achieved by the switching of the action back and forth between the stage play and the real play. I remember peering from my box at the Opera House, Manchester, and watching bewildered playgoers rustling their programmes and furtively striking matches in a frantic effort to discover where they were and what was going on . . .

If the reader is interested in how not to write a musical play, in how to overload a light, insignificant story with long stretches of accurate but uninspired dialogue, and in how to reduce an audience of average intelligence to a state of frustrated confusion, he will probably enjoy it immensely.

Operette ran for 133 performances. What Charles Cochran thought is unrecorded.

Incidentally, the out-of-context "big number" became something of a Coward signature. From "Green Carnation" in *Bitter Sweet,* it would continue through "Three Theatrical Dames" in *Hoi Polloi* . . . "Three Juvenile Delinquents" in *Ace of Clubs* . . . and the Tessie O'Shea "London" sequence in *The Girl Who Came to Supper.*

Pacific 1860 (1946)

By Noël's own reckoning "*Pacific 1860* was a flop. Not, let it be said, a resounding flop, not one of those immediate disasters in which the management is forced to cut its losses and close within a few days or weeks. *Pacific 1860* ran about six months.

"Generally, the play is the basic cause of failure, but in the case of *Pacific 1860* this actually did not apply. The story was light, romantic and without any startling originality but it was pleasant and convincing enough to provide a peg on which to hang the score and the lyrics which, after all, was all that it was intended to be in the first place.

"In Operetta, as in Grand Opera, although to a slightly lesser degree, it is the musical score that counts far and away above everything else. The fabulous success of the Gilbert and Sullivan operas would hardly have been achieved on the strength of their plots, construction and dialogue; it was the continued genius of the lyrics and music that spread them so triumphantly across the civilized world. That is a fact that our present day critics, among so many other things, overlook. I am convinced

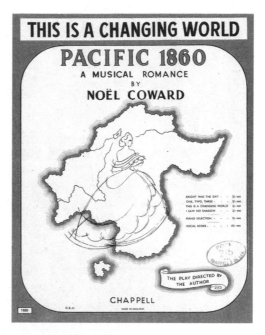

Pacific 1860 (1946). Noël and designer Gladys Calthrop look at Mary Martin in one of the period dresses Gladys has created for the show.

Mary didn't like her wardrobe. She wanted to use her regular *couturier*, Mainbocher. She refused to wear a hat—until Noël pointed out that in that period the only woman who didn't wear a hat would be a lady of ill repute.

Mary wore the hat.

Gladys Calthrop and Noël study the costumes Gladys has designed for *Pacific 1860*.

that the slow decay of English musical comedy is largely attributable to this complete ignorance of light music. Why should an ambitious young composer spend months conceiving and evolving a full musical score when he knows at the outset that the highest praise he can hope to get for it will be the adjectives 'Tuneful' or 'Pleasantly reminiscent.'

"In America, on the other hand, when a new musical is produced out of town for its try-out, the first question put to those who have attended the opening is invariably 'How was the score?' Light music is important in America, is treated with proper respect and criticized accordingly. Here it is treated with no respect and criticized, if at all, with contemptuous ignorance."

In retrospect it's obvious that the odds were stacked against *Pacific 1860* from the outset.

Noël was anxious to make a major mark. He would reopen the Theatre Royal Drury Lane, the scene of one of his greatest triumphs—*Cavalcade*. It would be a musical and it would star Irene Dunne. The lady was not available? Well, then—Yvonne Printemps. But then he remembered the trouble she had with her English. Well—Mary Martin. He wrote to her immediately and signed her for the part of the diva—Elena, Madame Salvador.

There was the problem of Drury Lane itself.

Badly bomb-damaged and with a chill winter wind blowing through the cracks and no heating, it was in no fit state to put on a major show. The cast in their flimsy tropical costumes were literally turning blue.

But the real problem was the show itself. Noël lost his objectivity somewhere along the creative way. What he turned up with was a typical prewar operetta set in his mythical South Sea island, Samolo.

He invented it for one of the short plays in the *Tonight at 8:30* sequence and became besotted by his own creation. He labored over its "history" and even invented its language. If in *Conversation Piece* he'd overindulged his French, he went even further with his Samolan and it unbalanced the piece.

===

Later, when the text came to be published, he tried to rationalize what went wrong . . .

Pacific 1860 ran about six months, although the last three of these were less of a run than a convulsive stagger. It is one of the few failures of my career for which a number of genuine alibis can be offered.

Any theatrical production that fails automatically produces a crop of alibis—it is in the wrong theatre, there is not enough advertising, there is a general slump, the International Situation is cloudier than usual, the weather is too wet or too hot or too cold, or else, according to the Calendar, Ascot, Goodwood, the Boat Race, Lent or the usual doldrums immediately preceding Christmas can be blamed. All of these excuses are trotted out regularly by loyal members of the Company and the loyal members of the Company's loyal relations and friends. The fact that the existing smash hits of the town are continuing to play to capacity at every performance, regardless of sporting events, political unrest, climate, hell or highwater is ignored, but long afterwards, when the ill-fated entertainment has closed and been consigned to oblivion, even the most vociferous defenders may look back and admit that it wasn't really very good and deserved its sad destiny.

This, I am sure, is why our once glorious heritage has run dry and why, with a very few rare exceptions, we are producing nothing indigenous, nothing that does not slavishly attempt to imitate American rhythms and Negro-Jewish harmonies, so vital and exciting in themselves and so pallid and lifeless in carbon copy.

Where, oh where in our musically satellite welfare state are the famous English light waltzes that everyone was humming when we were young? Where are our melodic, nostalgic English ballads that charmed so many gentle drawing-rooms? . . .

Where, above all, are those rollicking, bawdy music-hall tunes in six-eight time which were once so deeply engrained in our British tradition? A rhetorical question indeed with a sad, monosyllabic answer. "Dead."

In the score of *Pacific 1860* I tried, and at times succeeded, in recapturing a little of the earlier charm. Musically it is one of the best things I have ever done. The trio in Act Two "This Is a Night For Lovers," "This Is A Changing World," "My Horse Has Cast a Shoe" and several of the concerted numbers are not, in my considered opinion, entirely unworthy of the traditions of English light music. The score was brilliantly orchestrated, played by a large and expert orchestra conducted by Mantovani and totally ignored in all the criticisms excepting one which said that the music was sugary and Ivor Novello-ish. That, on the whole, was the nicest printed compliment I received on the entire production.

Then there was Mary Martin . . .

Mary was actually miscast, although I am convinced that, as things were, the play wouldn't have lasted three weeks without her. "Elena Salvador," a famous nineteenth century Prima Donna, should have been played by an actress much older and more genuinely sophisticated than Mary was or ever could be. When, a few years later, she returned to Drury Lane as "Nellie Forbush" in *South Pacific* the English public was able to see for the first time the warm, lovable toughness which is her essential quality as an artist and which my intricate Victorian furbelows had laced in, restricted and obscured.

Mary Martin's artistry, which I place second to none within its own scope, has a direct personal appeal to an audience and this appeal is the very reverse of so-called "sophistication." Wise and witty and experienced Women of the World are not her dish at all; her own inner truth repudiates artificial social graces. She is fundamentally "innocent" and will remain so until the end of her days.

This, it should be noted, is Recollection in the Relative Tranquillity of 1958. In the heat of 1946 Noël's reaction to his star was rather different.

He and his leading lady bickered endlessly and ended up barely speaking. He expressed his frustration in a verse . . .

I Resent Your Attitude to Mary

I resent your attitude to Mary.
It betrays a very ugly sort of mind.
She is innocent and pure
And her husband, I am sure,
Would consider your behaviour rather crude and most unkind

He resents and I resent
And all the passers-by resent
Your hideous attitude to Mary.

I resent your attitude to Mary
You only send her flowers once a day
Tho' her voice is apt to jar,
She's a very famous star
And she's only taking ten per cent for acting in your play.
Tho' her husband's heel is rather hairy,
He does very nicely on her pay.
He resents and she resents . . .
Your beastly attitude to Mary.

There was to be a rapprochement a few years later and they would star together in the 1955 live TV special *Together with Music*.

January 29, 1946

"Came to the sad conclusion that the fundamental trouble with the show is that Mary, charming and sweet as she is, knows nothing about Elena, never has and never will, and that although she has a delicious personality, she cannot sing. She is crammed with talent but she is still too 'little' to play sophisticated parts.

"She is a good trooper and works hard but has no conception of Elena's character and no technical experience as an actress. Her charm and personality are not enough to put her over in a big theatre in a period part. She should be crooning through a microphone."

Pacific 1860 finally opened on December 19, to tepid reviews all round.

The consensus was that the postwar West End didn't need prewar Coward. It limped along for 129 performances and by the time it closed Noël declared that he was "sick to death of *Pacific 1860* and everything to do with it."

Ironically, the show that took over Drury Lane next was *Oklahoma!* That—although it was an import—caught the upbeat postwar mood precisely, as Noël himself recognized. He went to see it several times and, looking round at the beautifully restored theatre couldn't help but feel a little pang for "poor old *Pacific 1860.*"

———

After *Pacific 1860* Noël was to leave the musical theatre behind him for a while. Then 1949 found him writing *Hoi Polloi:* A Love Song to London—variously called *Over the Garden Wall* and *Come Out to Play.*

It was to be a sort of sequel to the 1939 *This Happy Breed,* which had followed the fortunes of a typical London lower-middle-class family until the outbreak of war. *Hoi Polloi* would show Londoners picking up the bomb-damaged pieces of their lives and putting them back together. It was terrain he knew well and cared about.

It would tell the story of a sailor (Harry Hornby) in London on a twenty-four-hour leave, who meets a girl (Pinkie Macklin), the daughter of a greengrocer. They spend the day together, meet a variety of other Londoners and, predictably, fall in love.

By this time the critics had decided they had fallen out of love with Noël and—though he would never admit it—they had shaken his self-confidence. He put *Hoi Polloi* aside and decided to write something more "contemporary."

That "something" was *Ace of Clubs.*

Ace of Clubs (1950)

"I have just finished writing an entirely new book for the Musical and it really is jolly good and quite different from anything I have done before . . . It was very complicated and difficult to construct but the actual writing of it was fairly painless and I managed to do the whole thing in a week! . . . It is robust, 'tough' and not a bit bittersweet but I think it is pretty exciting . . . the plot is intricate and rather complicated."

He took the basic storyline of *Hoi Polloi*—the sailor and his one-day leave—but this time the setting is a seedy nightclub run by gangsters and Pinkie is a slightly used chanteuse in the club. Many of the songs from *Hoi Polloi* find their way into the score as "numbers" in the club's floor show.

It was a milieu Noël didn't really understand and for which he had little sympathy. (It would take *Guys and Dolls* to show him how the underworld could be used sympathetically.) His "lovable little Cockney sparrows" were notable for their absence.

Noël's own recollection in relative tranquillity . . .

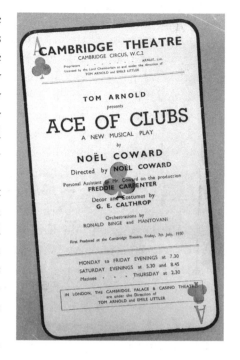

CAMBRIDGE THEATRE
CAMBRIDGE CIRCUS, W.C.2

Proprietors .... ARNLIT, Ltd.
Licensed by the Lord Chamberlain to and under the direction of
TOM ARNOLD and EMILE LITTLER

TOM ARNOLD
presents

ACE OF CLUBS
A NEW MUSICAL PLAY

by

NOËL COWARD

Directed by NOËL COWARD

Personal Assistant to Mr. Coward on the production
FREDDIE CARPENTER

Decor and Costumes by
G. E. CALTHROP

Orchestrations by
RONALD BINGE and MANTOVANI

First Produced at the Cambridge Theatre, Friday, 7th July, 1950

MONDAY to FRIDAY EVENINGS at 7.30
SATURDAY EVENINGS at 5.30 and 8.45
Matinee - - - THURSDAY at 2.30

IN LONDON, THE CAMBRIDGE, PALACE & CASINO THEATRES
are under the Direction of
TOM ARNOLD and EMILE LITTLER

"My only musicals to date had been in period—Victoria, Regency, Edwardian, Victorian Colonial—I considered the time had come to write a musical play in a modern setting with contemporary songs. Most of the contemporary songs were good but the book was uninspired . . . The situation is not entirely without merit and the whole show had a certain breeziness, but something went wrong somewhere along the line and the finished product fell far short of what I hoped it would be . . . I can always comfort myself with the reflection that it was 'Before Its Time.'"

But its 211 performances were cold comfort.

After the Ball (1954)

July 1953. "I have decided to turn *Lady Windermere's Fan* into a musical . . . Binkie is delighted with the idea and so am I, because it really is up my musical alley."

Later he records that "I have cut out the more glaringly melodramatic of Oscar Wilde's lines and divided the remainder into sections ending with a suitable 'cue for a song.'" He was enjoying the experience and even surprising himself—"I can scarcely go to the piano without a melody seeping from my fingers, usually in keys that I am not used to and can't play in; it is most extraordinary and never ceases to surprise me."

In January—"Now all is done and the relief is immense, particularly as I know that it is very good indeed. I have been very much *en veine* and have turned out some of the best lyrics I have ever written."

Sadly disillusion set in when it was discovered that Mary Ellis— whom he had known for years as the glittering star of *Rose Marie* and many other operettas—no longer had the voice to sing the material he had written for her. One by one her numbers had to be cut. "Seven minutes of my best music and most charming lyrics sacrificed . . ." Then, when he saw an actual performance of the revised show—"Mary Ellis acted well but sang so badly that I could hardly bear it."

In a letter to his old friends the Lunts he felt he could express his true feelings and disappointment . . .

"I have been having a terrible time with *After the Ball*, mainly on account of Mary Ellis's singing voice which, to coin a phrase, sounds like someone fucking the cat. I know that your sense of the urbane, sophisticated Coward wit will appreciate this simile."

To compensate he tried to inject more comedy into Ellis's performance but even that didn't work. "She couldn't get a laugh if she were to pull a kipper from her twat."

There is no evidence that Miss Ellis attempted this particular feat.

The show lasted 188 performances. It was to be the last Coward musical to have its premiere in London. Broadway would become his new musical home.

———

In early 1956 sitting in his beloved Jamaica . . .

"I have decided to use my peaceful mornings by writing a film script . . . a brittle, stylized, sophisticated, insignificant comedy-with-music. It will be called *Later than Spring* . . . from the suspense point of view it will be as unexpected as *Cosi Fan Tutte*. It will be of Mozartian subtlety and a splendid vehicle for Marlene [Dietrich]—and, of course, myself."

Two years later the film is forgotten . . . also Mozart . . . even Marlene. Now it will be a stage musical. In the new show the heroine would be Mrs. Wentworth-Brewster (from his song "A Bar on the Piccola Marina"). We would follow her exploits now that she has discovered that "life was for living."

Naturally, there would be a few changes. She would lose a few pounds and a few years. Oh, and she'd be Americanized. And she'd be played by Ethel Merman. No? Well then, Rosalind Russell.

While he was waiting for Miss Russell to make up her mind, he wrote . . .

"The book is causing me trouble . . . books for musicals invariably cause trouble . . . In a straight play you have time to develop your characters and lead up to and away from moments of crisis. In a musical you hardly have any time at all. The music and lyrics, on which the show really depends, interrupt all flow and sequence . . . I have no worries about the score or lyrics . . . and ideas for numbers come thick and fast.

"The dialogue scenes already written are quite good, as I can't help writing good dialogue, but whether they are leading anywhere is my principal worry. I am sure the only thing to do is to finish the whole thing roughly and then go back and see what has to be pointed up, filled out, cut or redone."

In the event he found there were too many troubles. Rosalind Russell said no . . . he toyed with the idea of Judy Holliday or Irene Dunne (again), then decided on Kay Thompson . . .

"I have decided to change the title from *Later than Spring* to *Sail Away,* which is a gayer title and more appropriate. I wrote yesterday a wonderful opening number for Kay Thompson . . ."

But neither title persuaded Miss Thompson to come aboard.

It's surprising that Noël failed to see that mature leading ladies don't see themselves playing the ugly duckling—even though the swan is waiting in the wings.

In retrospect it becomes obvious that most of Noël's successful shows emerged fully formed. Some may have enjoyed a significant gestation period but the process of setting them down on paper was mercifully short and painless. *Hay Fever, Private Lives,* and *Blithe Spirit* took only a few days—but *Later than Spring* occupied him for the better part of two years before he set it aside and turned to *Sail Away.*

Sail Away (1961)

"It is always a mistake to try to rehash yesterday's cold mutton," Noël wrote. "Polly (Wentworth-Brewster) and Max are now, happily, dead as Dodos."

But they were not to be the only ones who would suffer from *mal de mer.*

The two leading characters in *Sail Away* were Verity Craig, an attractive but unhappily married woman, who is traveling alone. She meets a younger man, Johnny van Mier on the cruise ship and they have a brief affair before she decides to return to her husband.

The Boston audience warmed to the show as a whole but found the leading couple's story depressing. "They sang beautifully but were far from convincing as actors. Also the love story is not right and I have been busy revising and reconstructing it. They were, after all, engaged for their voices and I fear I have asked too much of them. It is madness to ask two singers to play subtle 'Noel Coward' love scenes with the right values and sing at the same time. However, all this will be worked on."

When Philadelphia returned the same verdict—even to the reworked version—it became clear that tinkering was not enough. Major surgery was needed.

By the time the SS *Coronia* docked at the Broadhurst Theatre in New York in October 1961 it was time for Verity to disembark. Noël had taken the secondary character of Mimi Paragon, the cruise social director, who would provide most of the comedy, and turned her into the romantic as well as the comedy lead. She would now be Johnny's love interest.

Her performance as Mimi made a star out of Elaine Stritch overnight.

The show itself was not the monster hit Noël had hoped for to "finance his old age." He tried to analyze what had gone wrong . . .

"I know, with my deepest instinct, that there is something about *Sail Away* that doesn't satisfy me. I am proud of the music and the lyrics, I am not especially proud of the 'book,' but it is adroitly constructed, does not drag and fulfills its purpose, which is to carry the show through to its conclusion. The 'books' of musicals, with one or two notable exceptions, are always unsatisfactory. There is never enough time to develop characters, and the music and the dancing, which is after all what the public come for, take up the major portion of the time allotted. In this instance I have deliberately kept the 'book' down to the minimum, in the belief that the public would be relieved not to have to sit through acres of dialogue between numbers. In fact I have used a revue formula with a mere thread of story running through it. Presumably I was wrong. Most of the critics seemed to mourn the lack of 'strong' story without realizing that a 'strong' story was never intended in the first place. I planned a light musical entertainment with neither undertones or overtones of solemnity, and this, so help me, is exactly what I have achieved. It will have to succeed or fail on its own merits, there is nothing more to be done with it. It is, of course, disappointing that it didn't get raves and become an

immediate smash, but I have had disappointments before and a great deal worse than this."

Sail Away ran for 167 performances on Broadway and was followed by a London production.

⸻

It would be the last pure "Coward" musical. He would be deeply involved in two more Broadway shows but not as the only creator.

⸻

"Herman Levin [successful producer of *My Fair Lady*] has called me up from New York and asked me to do the score and lyrics for *The Sleeping Prince*, which is being turned into a musical by Harry Kurnitz [a Hollywood screenwriter]."

The original play by Terence Rattigan had received tepid notices at best. Surprisingly, Olivier decided to play the role of the Regent in a film version, *The Prince and the Showgirl*, opposite Marilyn Monroe.

"I feel rather torn about this. At the moment I naturally feel that I

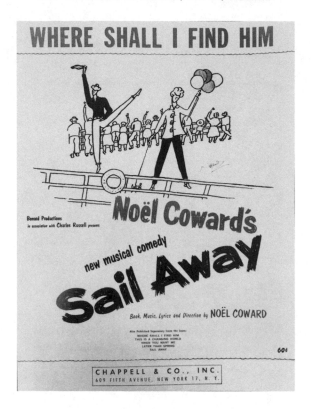

don't want to have anything to do with an American musical ever in my life again but this, of course, will pass and I have always loved *The Sleeping Prince . . .*"

That also would pass . . .

"Also it is period and a perfect period, what's more, for my music and lyrics. I have given an evasive answer." Shortly after, however, he agreed to meet with Levin and Kurnitz, who persuaded him to agree to write the score.

The Girl Who Came to Supper (1963)

The first run-through he considered "disastrous. Vastly over-directed. Too much movement, too many props and everybody overacting like mad and trying to be funny. So much of it is brilliant and the brilliance was obscured by Joe [Layton]'s choreographic passion for incorrect movement."

His admiration for Layton's abilities had suffered a sea change through the experience on *Sail Away.*

Rehearsing *The Girl Who Came to Supper* with José Ferrer and
Florence Henderson (1963).

"Why do choreographers have no respect for words or lyrics? Anyway,
I let fly, lost my temper and flounced off and the next day refused to go
near the theatre."

His personal theatrical "performance" seemed to have the desired
effect, because he found the Boston opening "quite palpably a smash
hit . . . The whole show is now much better.

"Tessie O'Shea stopped the show cold . . . Florence Henderson is
miraculous and I love her every minute. José Ferrer a bit inaudible and
an ugly voice and appearance, but great charm, a fine comedian."

The New York critics were generally positive about the show and, for
once, kind to Noël personally. "None of them has really been very good
for the book. Poor Harry. He is such a dear, but he is a writer of lines and
jokes, rather than a writer of plays."

"It has all been rather a grueling and frustrating experience for me and
I shall never again put myself into such a tricky position."

The notices were put up in March 1964 . . .

"Three factors have contributed to this disaster. José Ferrer, the book
and the Broadway Theatre; all three of which I have shrieked about from

the beginning. Florence didn't really come off either. I think, however, she would have had a better chance with a physically attractive leading man. I tried to wishful think myself into believing that José would be good, but I knew in my heart from the very beginning that he was miscast. Another factor—which I hate to have to admit—is that dear Joe Layton really directed it wrong from the very first. He staged it brilliantly but the actual direction was common and farcical, whereas it should have been witty and romantic. However, that is that and it's definitely spilt milk department."

What Noël did not choose to see was the show's unfortunate resemblance to Levin's only major previous success—*My Fair Lady*. The story of an older, cynical man redeemed by a simple girl reminded audiences of Higgins and Eliza, with the nonsinging Ferrer standing in for the nonsinging but more charming Rex Harrison and with Florence Henderson as a less interesting Julie Andrews.

Unfortunately comparisons didn't stop there.

O'Shea and her Cockney numbers were reminiscent of Stanley Holloway's Alfred Doolittle, while Roderick Cook and Irene Browne replicated the characters played by Robert Coote and Cathleen Nesbitt in the original. There was even a second half set piece in the Coronation scene

Tessie O'Shea as the quintessential Cockney, the larger-than-life Ada Cockle, introduces "London" (1963).

to replace *My Fair Lady*'s Ascot. A sense of *déjà vu* loomed over the whole enterprise and when it had to compete with new arrivals like *Hello, Dolly!* and *Funny Girl*, it came up short.

The Girl ran for 112 performances.

High Spirits (1964)

In early 1963 Noël received a visit in New York from composer Hugh Martin and lyricist Timothy Gray. They proposed to turn *Blithe Spirit* into a musical called *Faster Than Sound*. Desultory conversations on the subject had been going on for some time and by now it was very near the back of Noël's mind . . .

"I was all set to turn it down, because it really has been going on far too long and I was sick of all the frigging about."

To his amazement Martin and Gray weren't there to simply talk. They had the whole score, which they proceeded to play for him.

"Coley and I sat with our mouth open. It is quite brilliant. The music is melodic and delightful, the lyrics really witty, and they have done a complete book outline keeping to my original play and yet making it effective as a musical. I am not only relieved but delighted."

He agreed to direct it and as work began—"I intend to keep a firm eye on it from the word go." The title of the show was now *High Spirits*.

And there turned out to be plenty to occupy his eye . . . and ear. Above all there was his leading lady, his old friend Beatrice Lillie. He finally went on record with his frustrations . . .

"I am patient, kind, forebearing, sensible and decisive. If I were not all these things, I should now be nestling cosily in a straight-jacket in a Loony Bin. Day after day I have sat quietly with my nails dug into the palms of my hands while Miss Lillie stumbles, flounders, forgets, remembers, drives the company mad and is as much like Madame Arcati as I am like Queen Victoria."

He was not to know that the lady was in the early stages of dementia. Even so she was receiving rave reviews on the out-of-town performances. "The news from the *High Spirits* front is curious. Tammy [Grimes, the show's Elvira] spent the last Philadelphia week in hospital suffering from self-induced hysteria and Beattie's notices."

At this point Noël's own health was giving him problems and he

Tammy Grimes (Elvira), Beatrice Lillie (Madame Arcati), and Edward Woodward (Charles Condomine) bring new spirit to *Blithe Spirit*.

had developed an ulcer. It came as a timely relief when the producers approached him "and asked if I minded them calling in Gower Champion to pull the show together. I said I would be only too delighted. In due course he arrived and, at the first conference, listed everything that I have been saying for eight weeks.

"After plodding through two musicals I am really very tired indeed. I took on far too much. I am sick to death of *High Spirits* and everyone connected with it. I think, galvanized by Gower, it may be a success. At any rate I have done all I can do."

High Spirits did turn out to be a success, running for 375 performances. It was to be Noël's final contribution to musical theatre.

By the time the show had made its successful Broadway opening—and was on the way to making a great deal of money—he could be more objective.

His irritation with Bea Lillie faded and he could reflect that she was "unquestionably a great star and has that indestructible capacity for making audiences love her . . . so far as the public is concerned, it doesn't matter how many lines she forgets and how many mistakes she makes. She is adored."

With Bea Lillie rehearsing *High Spirits,* at the Alvin Theatre, New York, April 1964.

BEATRICE LILLIE—AN APPRECIATION

The explanation of the word "unique" in *Chamber's Twentieth Century Dictionary* is as follows—"Single or alone in any quality; without a like or equal." This word, in my opinion, applies to Beatrice Lillie more than to any other star in the world, with the possible exception of Charlie Chaplin. She is supremely single and alone and most certainly without a like or equal.

When she first comes onto the stage she imposes herself immediately and effortlessly on the audience. Her manner is a mixture of assurance and humility; she smiles not tentatively but hopefully, and suddenly, in a split second, she is *loved,* not merely laughed at or respected or admired, but *loved.* From that moment on whatever disasters, embarrassments, grotesqueries may bedevil her in the course of the performance, the sympathy and affection of the public is firmly ranged on her side. She may stray widely from the written script; she may interpolate on the spur of the moment words and phrases of her own which are far removed from the author's original intention and, as often as not, entirely irrelevant but the instinctive accuracy of her touch and her impeccable taste sweeps the by now hysterical audience into transports of laughter.

For an author, if he is wise, and not too obsessed with the sanctity of his own words, will stay resigned in his seat and laugh. If not he will fly out into the lobby and beat his head against the wall. In my own case, when faced with the erratic fantasies of Beatrice Lillie, I have found the former less agitating and the more sensible.

For an author or director to attempt to pin Beatrice down to a meticulous delineation of character is a direct invitation to nervous collapse. It isn't that she is unwilling or too sure of herself to take the trouble to learn "written" lines accurately. On the contrary, she tries with every fibre of her being to memorise every word. For the last many months and all through the rehearsal and try-out period for *High Spirits* she could be observed on the side of the stage or in her dressing room with her spectacles on her nose and her eyes glued to the script. Indeed, I am convinced that, even as I write these words, she is struggling away somewhere or other.

Deep down in her subconscious there is and always has been a sort of mental block about memorising lines accurately. As far back as 1928, when we were appearing together in *This Year of Grace!*, I remember having a blazing row with her because she was singing my lyrics the wrong way round. In the forty-seven years that I have known her we have had three or four violent quarrels, none of which endured for more than twelve hours. During this recent production of *High Spirits* we have had none at all, with the exception of one black moment in New Haven, when she was under the impression that I had cut a scene which I hadn't cut and flew at me in no uncertain terms. Within an hour, however, she telephoned me at the hotel, admitted that she had completely misunderstood the situation and apologised with loving grace.

I have never encountered a star yet, including myself, who could not be a fiend when nervous and overwrought with pre-opening night tensions but I have known very few who were capable in so short a time of admitting they were wrong with such beguiling sincerity.

Beatrice Lillie has frequently been described by enthusiastic critics as "the funniest woman in the world." We have, of course, no absolute proof that that statement is correct. There may be, for all we and the critics know, Dyak matrons in the forests of Borneo, hilarious female pygmies lurking in the jungles of the Amazon or jolly veiled priestesses in some far flung spots to challenge the verdict that she is, in fact, the funniest woman of our time and our civilisation.

When I first met her in the latter part of World War I, she was not, on the stage, funny at all. She was appearing in a revue at the Alhambra

Theatre in London as a male impersonator. She was young, slim and as shiningly groomed as she is today. Her silk hat, white tie and tails were impeccable and she sang, irrelevant even at that early age, "I Want to Go Back to Michigan." The picture of that elegantly attired dandy yearning to return to a middle Western farm struck me, young as I was, as fairly incongruous.

Later, in the summer of 1917 when I, a reluctant recruit to the Armed Forces, was incarcerated in the First London General Military Hospital, I remember climbing over a gap in the wall one morning, rushing home and changing from my hospital "blues" to a civilian suit and going to an opening matinée performance of an André Charlot revue called *Cheep!* at the Vaudeville Theatre. That performance turned out to be, in the light of later events, an historic occasion because it was the first time the sleek and urbane Beatrice Lillie appeared in her true colours as a comic genius of the first order.

In the first part of the revue she appeared as usual in her immaculate tails and sang, if I remember rightly, a song written specially for her by her sister Muriel, called "Take Me Back to the Land of Promise." The lyric, inspired by Muriel's obviously deep-seated fascination, dealt nostalgically with the blessings of being born a Canadian. The refrain ran as follows:

> *Oh, take me back to the la-and of Promise,*
> *Back to the land of the ice and the snows,*
> *There you and I together will wander*
> *Down lover's lane where the maple leaf grows.*
> *Skating—baseball and canoeing,*
> *That's the place to do your billing and cooing,*
> *Oh, take me back to the land I love be-est,*
> *Back to my little grey home in the west.*

When I explain that Beattie sang this with charm and sincerity and without the slightest humorous implication, the startling metamorphosis she achieved in the second act will be clearly understood. This metamorphosis occurred in a burlesque musical act called "The Dedleighdul Quartette." I forget the names of the other three performers but Miss Lillie, with high piled auburn hair, and a green satin evening gown from the bosom of which protruded a long stemmed chrysanthemum, will stay in my memory for ever. She sang, in a piercing soprano, a straight popular ballad called "Bird of Love Divine." She sang this also with apparently the utmost sincerity, but it did just occur to her during the second verse to prop her music up against the chrysanthemum. I believe I was still laughing when, a couple of hours later, I clambered back over the hospital wall in order to be discovered demurely in bed for evening roll call.

In the fairly long interim between 1918 and 1964 Beattie has sung many of my songs and played many of my sketches. I have appeared frequently with her not only on the professional stage in *This Year of Grace!*, but at countless charity performances and troop entertainments during World War II. On one occasion many years ago I actually joined her, at her own request, on her opening night in cabaret at the Rainbow Room, where we proceeded to sing, unrehearsed, with almost total inaccuracy, two duets which we had performed in the past.

I have directed her on three different occasions. *This Year of Grace!* 1928, *Set to Music* 1938 and now *High Spirits* in 1964. I have known her gay and sad, bad tempered, good tempered, sober as a judge and high as a kite, but I have never known her do anything consciously vulgar or deliberately unkind.

And what, in this particular analysis, is perhaps most important of all, I have very very seldom known her fail to conquer and hold the public. Perhaps only two or three times I have seen an audience die on her. The reason for this being because she either stayed on too long or was insecure in her material. But those occasions have been very very rare.

I stated blithely a paragraph or two back that I directed her in three shows. This actually is a mis-statement. I have never really directed Beatrice Lillie any more than anyone else has. I have guided her, argued with her and, on occasion, squabbled with her but direction *qua* direction in her case is an academic term. She is not in the least non-cooperative. She listens attentively when told when to move and where to move and how to end a certain line and tries willingly and earnestly to comply, but the results are short-lived. Her instincts and her talent take command and her instinctive obedience to them is absolute. Her timing, contrary to what many critics have affirmed, is by no means always faultless. She is frequently guilty of ruining a comedy line by imposing on it a visually comic gesture. This is largely because her inventiveness is always moving ahead of what she is actually doing or saying.

She has little or no knowledge of "acting" in the technical sense. Her experience in "legitimate" comedy is naturally limited because she has only appeared in straight plays three or four times in her life. The trained give and take of a number of experienced actors playing a concerted scene is foreign to her. She establishes little or no contact with her fellow players on the stage, not from any delusions of superiority or conceit, but because it seldom occurs to her to look at them. She is the product of a different and, in many ways, a much harder school. Her own personal genius and experience have trained her to establish immediate contact with the audience. This, obviously enough, can be achieved much more easily when she is alone on the stage and has nobody else near her to deflect her primary and instinctive intention.

With one other person only she has no problems, providing always that she likes and respects that one other person enough to relax. On the various occasions I have appeared with her, I have found her completely unselfish and great fun to work with. But with more than one other person and with perhaps a complicated scene to play, she is subconsciously ill at ease.

However, the sum total of all this meticulous analysis becomes automatically null and void when she can still, after a long and triumphant career, walk on to a stage and completely subjugate hundreds of people eight times a week. Star quality is and always has been indefinable. In Beattie's case it is authentic and valid and allied to a disciplined professionalism which is wholly admirable and completely reliable. I have never known her be late for a rehearsal. I have never actually known her to miss a performance and I can only say that, if she ever has, it must have been for a very good reason. She belongs to a great and rare theatrical vintage which is fast running out. Nor for her the easy and prevalent self-indulgences of hypochondria. Not for her the sudden onslaught of nervous exhaustion brought on by bad temper and being spoilt and too newly successful. When you read the name "Beatrice Lillie" over a theatre marquee, you can be fairly certain, even if you have had to book your seat months ahead, that she will be there. And she will make her first entrance (unbeknownst to you, nervous as a kitten) and you will be aware, either consciously or unconsciously, that you are in the presence of a gallant, shining and indestructible star.

(1964)

Cabaret

"I can't sing but I know how to, which is quite different."
—*THE OBSERVER* (1969)

.

"It is a composer's voice. It has a considerable range but no tone, little
music but lots of meaning."

.

WHERE ARE THE SONGS WE SUNG?
Where are the songs we sung
When Love in our hearts was young?
Where, in the limbo of the swiftly passing years,
Lie all our hopes and dreams and fears?
Where have they gone—words that rang so true
When Love in our hearts was new?
Where in the shadows that we have to pass among
Lie those songs that once we sung?
—*OPERETTE*

.

Although he only made his formal cabaret debut in 1951, Noël had been
auditioning for it for years. The war had taken him to all the war zones
to entertain the troops . . . ("I occasionally hurtle up to the front and
sing firmly to the troops who are so sunk in mud that they can't escape.")
It also created the need for him to compose a number of new songs to
complement his familiar material. So when he was booked to appear in
London's Café de Paris in October 1951, he was ready.

In a sense he had already opened "out of town." As part of his duties
as president of the annual Theatrical Garden Party he had taken to giving half hour concerts in a tent with a placard that read—*Noël Coward at
Home.* He was joined by Norman Hackforth, his wartime accompanist,
and the reunion was something that pleased them both. ("My shows
were happily triumphant and all of them rapturously received.") It was
the war without the audio distraction of enemy gunfire.

The Café de Paris had its memories for Noël. As a teenage performer
thirty-five years earlier he had appeared, partnered by an equally *ingénue*
young lady called Eileen Dennis, dancing and singing through dinner
and supper at what was then called the Elysée Restaurant. Their reception was at best mixed, so Noël felt he had something to prove second
time round!

Things didn't look promising to begin with . . .

"In the afternoon rehearsed at the Café de Paris—everything perfect except my voice, which is failing fast. Came straight home feeling dreadfully worried. This is the cruelest luck. I feel fine, the microphone is perfect, all London is fighting to get in and see me—and now this happens. I am heartbroken."

His throat specialist came round to give him emergency treatment. "He pulled out my vocal chords and twiddled about with them." He also forbade Noël to say a single word until he was standing on the stage at the stroke of midnight.

"He padded down the celebrated stairs of the Café de Paris, halted before the microphone on black-suede-clad feet, and, upraising both hands in a gesture of benediction, set about demonstrating how these things should be done."—Kenneth Tynan

"Went to the Café feeling slightly tremulous. Really triumphant success—tore the place up. Glittering audience headed by Princess Margaret and the Duchess of Kent. All very glamorous . . . all very enjoyable."

Whatever the surgeon had done did the trick. He was in fine voice. Kenneth Tynan described him as "cooing like a baritone turtle dove." One of the very few negative reviews he received accused him of "massacring his own material." To which Noël replied—by way of his *Diary*— "If so, it was the most profitable massacre since the St. Valentine's Day massacre."

His season ran for twenty-four performances and he was to repeat it for the next three years. It was cabaret that restored Noël to the eminence he had worked so hard to achieve in the first place. While he might have been written off, he had never written himself off. Instead he had done what he always promised he would—"pop up through another hole in the ground."

═══

In 1954 Marlene Dietrich followed Noël's example and made her own cabaret debut at the Café de Paris.

She was introduced by . . . Noël Coward . . .

Ladies and Gentlemen. Thank you so much. I am so very happy to be home again and particularly happy to have got back in time for this special occasion, because I have got myself into an absurd habit which, try as I may, I cannot break, the habit of introducing Marlene. Glamour is an overworked word. Like so many other evocative and charming words, it has been insulted and debased by enthusiastic journalists until to-day it is used, monotonously and inaccurately to describe every protuberant starlet who leers at us from the pages of a movie magazine. Nevertheless, authentic glamour is still rare and exciting. It is an abstract quality, evanescent and indefinable and Marlene possesses more of it than anyone else I know. It endows the brilliance of her technical performance and everything she does with an extra magic.

In all the many years I have belonged to the Theatre I have seen many great stars give many great performances. It is not their performances that I remember in detail but certain, detached, glamorous moments that they emblazoned on my memory for ever and a day. I can remember when I was very young seeing Gertie Millar flitting across a moonlit stage singing "Tony from America," Lily Elsie dancing, with ineffable grace, the staircase waltz in *The Count of Luxembourg,* Anna Pavlova flying onto the stage like a living flame in "The Bacchanal" and, in later years, my beloved Gertrude Lawrence, sun-tanned and radiant in a white Molyneux dress, moving towards me across the stage of the Phoenix Theatre. These, and many other moments, I shall always treasure and I like to think that to-day, in London, there are young people, and middle-aged ones too, for that matter, who, many years hence, will suddenly say, with a note of fond nostalgia "Ah, yes—but *I* remember seeing Marlene Dietrich walk down the stairs of the Café de Paris."

In cabaret at the Café de Paris.

Tribute to Marlene Dietrich

We know God made trees
And the birds and the bees
And the seas for the fishes to swim in
We are also aware
That he has quite a flair
For creating exceptional women.
When Eve said to Adam
"Start calling me Madam"
The world become far more exciting
Which turns to confusion
The modern delusion
That sex is a question of lighting
For female allure
Whether pure or impure
Has seldom reported a failure

As I know and you know
From Venus and Juno
Right down to La Dame aux Camélias.
This glamour, it seems,
Is the substance of dreams
To the most imperceptive perceiver
The Serpent of Nile
Could achieve with a smile
Far quicker results than Geneva.
Though we all might enjoy
Seeing Helen of Troy
As a gay, cabaret entertainer
I doubt that she could
Be one quarter as good
As our legendary, lovely Marlene.

November 1954

===

"A character called Joe Glaser flew in from New York to sign me up for Las Vegas. A typical shrewd, decent, sharp agent type."

What Noël didn't know at the time was that Glaser was a man with a problem. He was on a retainer from the Desert Inn and had failed to deliver his candidate of choice, Liberace. He'd heard of Noël's success and thought this Brit might fill the bill. When he came backstage to meet Noël, it was obvious that he couldn't see what all the fuss was about, but he was running out of options.

"The discussion was satisfactory financially, everything being contingent on whether or not I like Las Vegas, so he is escorting me there for a couple of days, so that I can case the joint . . . If I can salt away £20,000 free of tax by appearing there for three weeks in the spring, I have a strong feeling that I should do it, whether I like it or not . . . we are getting together in New York."

Obviously he did do it—and described his impressions of this mad Alice in Wonderland world . . .

"This is a fabulous madhouse. All around is desert sand with pink and purple mountains on the horizon. All the big hotels are *luxe* to the last degree. There are myriads of people tearing away at the fruit machines and gambling gambling gambling for twenty-four hours a day . . . In the classier casinos, beams of light shine down from baroque ceilings on the masses of earnest morons flinging their money down the drain . . . Every instinct and desire is concentrated on money. I expected that this would exasperate me but oddly enough it didn't. The whole fantasia is on such a colossal scale that it is almost stimulating. I went from hotel to hotel and looked at the supper rooms. They are all much of a muchness: expert lighting and sound and cheerful appreciative audiences.

"Joe Glaser, whom I have taken a great shine to, never drinks, never smokes and adores his mother. My heart and reason go out to him, because he at least took the trouble to fly over to London and see me at the Café and give me a concrete offer. If it all ends in smoke, I don't think it will be his fault. I believe him to be honest according to his neon lights."

Having accepted the engagement—for $40,000 a week—Noël was told that he could not get an American work permit for his longtime accompanist, Norman Hackforth.

Marlene Dietrich promptly recommended her own cabaret accompanist—Peter Matz. Noël took to him from the beginning but was somewhat taken aback at their first meeting. Looking at the music arrangements Noël had brought over, Matz remarked—"You're not going to use these, are you?" Noël thought fast enough to say airily—"No, no, I'd like you to redo them all."

Matz duly did, pitched them appropriately for the mature Coward voice and almost certainly extended his cabaret and recording "shelf life."

"Pete Matz, at the age of twenty-six, knows more about the range of various instruments and the potentialities of different combinations than anyone of any age I have *ever* met in England. I suppose music is in the air more here and the mixture of Jewish and Negro rhythms has become part of the national consciousness because it is a goulash of all races. Very exciting and stimulating."

"Well, it is all over bar the shouting, which is still going on. I have made one of the most sensational successes of my career and to pretend that I am not absolutely delighted would be idiotic. I have had screaming rave notices and the news has flashed round the world. I am told continually, verbally and in print, that I am the greatest performer in the world, etc., etc. It is all very, very exciting and generous, and when I look back at the grudging dreariness of the English newspaper gentlemen announcing, when I first opened at the Café de Paris, that I massacred my own songs, I really feel that I don't want to appear at home much more.

"Here, a rave notice is not considered bad news as it is at home. Here also there is a genuine respect for, and understanding of, light music. I am not gibed at for not being a 'Singer,' because they recognise immediately here that not being a 'singer' is one of my greatest assets. They know I know how to sing, and they are used to, and largely prefer, performers who perform songs rather than 'sing' them. Light music has been despised and rejected in England for years . . . Here light music has its own genuine values, which are recognized not only by the public but by the Press.

"On Friday I was driven out into the Nevada desert, where I was photographed for *Life* magazine in my dinner jacket sipping a cup of tea. The temperature was 118 degrees."

But perhaps the review that touched him most of all was when Frank Sinatra suggested publicly that anyone who wanted to hear how a song should be sung should "get the hell over to the Desert Inn."

Las Vegas was a significant turning point in Noël's career. In the following year he would leave England and become a tax exile. His professional focus would increasingly become America.

"Smile! You never know who's looking!" Noël and Jane Powell pose by the pool at the Desert Inn, Las Vegas. (The 1955 swimsuit fashion had still to discover the itsy-bitsy bikini.)

"The first night, from the social-theatrical point of view, was fairly sensational. Frank Sinatra chartered a special plane and brought Judy Garland, the Bogarts, the Nivens, etc.; then there were Joan Fontaine, Zsa Zsa Gabor, the Joe Cottens, Peter Glenville, Larry Harvey, etc. The noise was terrific. The next day there was a quarter of an hour's radio talk devoted to me in course of which they all lavished paeans of praise on me with the most uninhibited and heart-warming generosity. The Press have been courteous and the photographers insistent but considerate."

Television

Las Vegas turned out to be only the beginning of Noël's winning streak. Television offers came pouring in from General Motors . . . Chrysler ($600,000) . . . and CBS ($450,000 for three live TV broadcasts of his own choosing). He decided to go with CBS.

Up to this point he had been wary of TV as a medium. In his *Diary* that same year . . .

"What I have learned so far is that, apart from a few special personalities and talents, the standard of entertainment is poor, the lighting unpredictable, and the commercial emphasis very overstressed. I have seen to date very few evidences of imagination in production and no sense of experimentation."

His reservations about the medium echoed his previous concerns about film as a medium—concerns that had been set aside with the experience of *In Which We Serve.*

But *television?*

What would that do for his plays? In later years he would conclude . . .

"The cutting of my plays down for television is certainly a salutary experience, and I believe that the next time I embark on a full-length play for the theatre, I shall find that I have profited by it.

"I shall have learned, for instance, to dispense with amusing irrelevancies that have no direct bearing on the story and to get back to my original method of saying what I have to say in as few lines as possible with a minimum of atmospheric padding and linguistic flourishes."

But that insight would come later. Right now the learning process was about to begin . . .

He decided he would start off by taking the approach of transferring what he knew worked in terms of cabaret to television. The time slots he had signed up for—ninety minutes including commercials—were clearly too long for a solo performance. But perhaps a show for two people . . . ?

"*Together with Music,* the TV spectacular I am going to do with Mary Martin will be completely spontaneous. The kind of spontaneity I like best—the kind that comes after five weeks' rehearsal."

He decided to approach Mary Martin to costar with him. Their

"The Chairman of the Board" and "The Master"—Las Vegas (1955). "Judy Garland . . . told me she and Frank Sinatra decided that I was better than anyone they had ever seen and could give them lessons, which couldn't have been more comforting or more sweet."

Together with Music (1955)

feud after *Pacific 1860* was long
since over and their mutual
admiration—both personal and
professional—had been reestab-
lished. Mary was happy to accept.

Although their opening
number—"Ninety Minutes Is a
Long, Long Time"—might seem
to be pushing their luck, since
the ninety minutes would be live,
with no opportunity for retakes,
the time seemed to fly by.

Luckily they were able to film
a rehearsal on kinescope, which
gave Noël the chance to make
some firm suggestions for improvement . . .

"A great many of the camera shots were muddled and diffuse and
taken from too far off, and the sound balance was appalling. I therefore
spent the rest of the day re-rehearsing the whole show and insisting that
practically all of it should be done in close-ups. It is no use me trying to
sing witty lyrics if you can't see my eyes."

When it came to the live performance . . .

"The atmosphere was sizzling . . . When the moment came to start I noticed that Mary was quivering, so I gave her a sharp, loving lecture and on we went. I discovered to my relief that whatever nerves I had had were stilled and that I was in complete control and determined to enjoy myself. I remembered my kinescope lesson and sang everything slap into the cameras. I knew from the outset that I was giving a good performance, and thank God, I kept it up.

"At the end of the performance chaos set in . . . I have never had such varied praise in my life. . . . I was terribly touched by the messages from strangers all over the continent. What an extraordinary medium. It is hard to imagine all those millions and millions of people all looking at me at the same moment. Then the reviews came out . . . When I think of the grudging patronage of the English Press compared with this whole-hearted PLEASED generosity, my heart does sink a little."

But not for very long. As he once said—"I can take any amount of criticism—as long as it is unqualified praise."

There was money in the bank and two more shows to go.

Noël and Mary Martin—
Together with Music—
CBS TV (October 1955).

Some years earlier he had written a song called "I Like America." Now he liked it even more . . .

.

HOW I WRITE MY SONGS

Musical inspiration is a peculiar sort of thing. It just comes. One cannot sit down and think and think until melodies come to the mind. I am much too busy for that, and, besides, that method would never bring success—at least, not in my case.

I just go on with the business of living, like other people do, until something occurs to me. It may be while I am at dinner, or on a 'bus, or even while I am having a bath. If I am anywhere near a piano I fly to it and play the tune with one hand. That "fixes" it, as a photographer would say, and I can proceed with the rest in a more leisurely way.

The next step is to get the harmony exactly as I want it, playing it over and over again if necessary. After that my task is practically ended. I play it to a trained musician, who writes the notes down and then repeats the piece to me so that I can make quite sure that he has reproduced it correctly.

I may be asked why I do not do this theoretical work myself. How boring! Besides, I happen to know practically nothing about such matters. I have never had a lesson in pianoforte playing in my life. I once went to the Guildhall School of Music for a few lessons in harmony and composition, but found them so dull and tiresome that I gave them up.

One does not need a deep knowledge of the mysteries of theory and musical form in order to compose light songs of the revue and musical comedy type. What *is* necessary is a perfect ear for pleasant sounds. When I think of what seems to me to be a good tune, the most suitable harmony suggests itself at the same time—in a rough form, at any rate. I don't know whether I am breaking conventional rules of theory, and care less. The sound's the thing.

Nearly all my life I have been able to pick tunes up readily after hearing them at a music-hall or theatre, and to play them on the piano. Lots of people can do that to a certain extent, though the difficulty in most cases is to reproduce the harmony correctly, for every popular success has some little peculiarity in that respect that may cause trouble. But the right gift, an absolutely correct musical ear, solves the problem in a moment.

I do not know when I began to compose, but I must have been

How I Write My Songs

By
NOEL COWARD

MUSICAL inspiration is a peculiar sort of thing. It just comes. One cannot sit down and think and think until melodies come to the mind. I am much too busy for that, and, besides, that method would never bring success—at least, not in my case.

I just go on with the business of living, like other people do, until something occurs to me. It may be while I am at dinner, or on a 'bus, or even while I am having a bath. If I am anywhere near a piano I fly to it and play the tune with one hand. That "fixes" it, as a photographer would say, and I can proceed with the rest in a more leisurely way.

The next step is to get the harmony exactly as I want it, playing it over and over again if necessary. After that my task is practically ended. I play it to a trained musician, who writes the notes down and then repeats the piece to me so that I can make quite sure that he has reproduced it correctly.

I may be asked why I do not do this theoretical work myself. How boring! Besides, I happen to know practically nothing about such matters. I have never had a lesson in pianoforte playing in my life. I once went to the Guildhall School of Music for a few lessons in harmony and composition, but found them so dull and tiresome that I gave them up.

One does not need a deep knowledge of the mysteries of theory and musical form in order to compose light songs of the revue and musical comedy type. What *is* necessary is a perfect ear for pleasant sounds. When I think of what seems to me to be a good tune, the most suitable harmony suggests itself at the same time—in a rough form, at any rate. I don't know whether I am breaking conventional rules of theory, and care less. The sound's the thing.

Nearly all my life I have been able to pick tunes up readily after hearing them at a music-hall or theatre, and to play them on the piano. Lots of people can do that to a certain extent, though the difficulty in most cases is to reproduce the harmony correctly, for every popular success has some little peculiarity in that respect that may cause trouble. But the right gift, an absolutely correct musical ear, solves the problem in a moment.

I do not know when I began to compose, but I must have been very young. I used to write songs in collaboration with Miss Esme Wynne, who has been my friend since my nursery days. She wrote lyrics, and I tried to set them to music. I remember she wrote one which ran:

Our little love is dying,
On his head bloom lately crimson roses faded quite.

I knew nothing about rhythm in those far-off days; the tune seemed to me the only thing that mattered. The music I composed caused the words to read like this:

Our little love is dying on his head.
Lately crimson roses faded quite.

Perhaps I was in a hurry. Unfortunately, I have always been pressed for time, and I usually work at a rapid rate. I wrote the whole of " On With the Dance " (now being presented at the London Pavilion)—music, lyrics and book—in a month. My play, " I'll Leave it to You," was written in a few weeks.

It was really through hurry that a certain unfortunate incident happened on the river some time ago. Miss Betty Chester and I were engaged to appear in " The Knight of the Burning Pestle," and as the time for preparation was so short we decided to go to Oxford, where we could study our parts without interruption.

We were in a canoe one day, studying for all we were worth, when the craft upset, and our manuscripts got so wet that they were useless. Result, several days' delay until we obtained new copies.

But I was talking about musical inspiration. One of my greatest successes was " Parisienne Pierrot," sung in " London Calling." The idea of that came to me during a visit to a cabaret in Berlin. I noticed a doll hanging on a curtain, and it seemed to impress itself on my mind. Soon afterwards, a melody which appeared to associate itself with the doll incident occurred to me, and—well, I just played it.

I thought of the tune of my latest success, " Poor Little Rich Girl," while I was having tea. The usual dash for the piano, and the thing was done. But for some reason I wrote this song in four flats, whereas I had always kept to three flats previously.

There is no scientific explanation of it at all. Some of us have these strange peculiarities, and some have not. I don't even know how I got my musical talent, unless it has been handed down from a grandfather who was organist for many years at the Crystal Palace.

But I wonder if it is fair to his memory to say so ?

[Maurice Beck and Helen Macgregor
NOEL COWARD
Photo]

"Popular tunes probe the memory more swiftly than anything else."

very young. I used to write songs in collaboration with Miss Esmé Wynne, who has been my friend since my nursery days. She wrote lyrics, and I tried to set them to music. I remember she wrote one which ran:

Our little love is dying.
On his head bloom lately crimson roses faded quite.

I knew nothing about rhythm in those far-off days; the tune seemed to me the only thing that mattered. The music I composed caused the words to read like this:

Our little love is dying on his head.
Lately crimson roses faded quite.

Perhaps I was in a hurry. Unfortunately, I have always been pressed for time, and I usually work at a rapid rate. I wrote the whole of "On with the Dance" (now being presented at the London Pavilion)—music, lyrics and book—in a month. My play, *I'll Leave It to You,* was written in a few weeks.

It was really through hurry that a certain unfortunate incident happened on the river some time ago. Miss Betty Chester and I were engaged to appear in *The Knight of the Burning Pestle,* and as the time for preparation was so short we decided to go to Oxford, where we could study our parts without interruption.

We were in a canoe one day, studying for all we were worth, when the craft upset, and our manuscripts got so wet that they were useless. Result, several days' delay until we obtained new copies.

But I was talking about musical inspiration. One of my greatest successes was "Parisian Pierrot," sung in *London Calling!* The idea of that came to me during a visit to a cabaret in Berlin. I noticed a doll hanging on a curtain, and it seemed to impress itself on my mind. Soon afterwards, a melody which appeared to associate itself with the doll incident occurred to me, and—well, I just played it.

I thought of the tune of my latest success, "Poor Little Rich Girl," while I was having tea. The usual dash for the piano, and the thing was done. But for some reason I wrote this song in four flats, whereas I had always kept to three flats previously.

There is no scientific explanation of it at all. Some of us have these strange peculiarities, and some have not. I don't even know how I got my musical talent, unless it has been handed down from a grandfather who was organist for many years at the Crystal Palace.

But I wonder if it is fair to his memory to say so?

(1925)

LONDON MORNING
A Ballet
Story and Music by Noël Coward

When I was first invited by Anton Dolin and Julian Braunsweg to write a Ballet for London's Festival Ballet Company they suggested, reasonably and politely, that although any idea I might conceive could be acceptable, they would prefer something typical of England in general and of London in particular.

Being a Londoner this naturally appealed to me immediately and I began trying to think of some special aspect of our proud city that would lend itself most easily to light music and dancing. There are indeed many such aspects: From the friendly cockney pub life of the East End, the sedate nanny and perambulator charm of Kensington Gardens, to the jocular noisy gaiety of Hampstead Heath on a Bank Holiday.

Then suddenly a nursery jingle obligingly dropped into my mind "Pussy cat, pussy cat, where have you been?" "I've been to London to see the Queen," and I realised that really the most appropriate place to set a London ballet would be outside the gates of Buckingham Palace, for here, every morning of every day of the year, not only Londoners themselves but visitors of all nations and creeds and colours from all over the world, gather to watch the Changing of the Guard, and catch, if possible, a glimpse of our Royal Family.

Personally, as an incurably middle-class Englishman, I always experience a thrill of pride in this traditional daily performance of our London pageantry. To me, a London where I could no longer see a cavalcade of Horse Guards clattering along the Mall, or suddenly turn the corner of a quiet square and see a Royal limousine drive by with the wave of a white gloved hand at the window, would be a duller and sadder place. I am perfectly aware that to many this attitude of mine must appear reactionary, unrealistic and sentimental, but I have lived by now for many years, and I have as much right to state my sentimental pride as others have to state their shrill contempt.

This really is all there is to say about *London Morning*. There is little story in it. A variety of characters pass and re-pass: a suburban family out for the day, some school girls, an invalid in a wheel chair, a trio of ladies of the town and some business men with brief-cases and bowler hats: a young American girl teases a sentry, a policeman remonstrates with her, an English sailor on leave falls in love with her. Some rain falls because in London some rain always falls, some bells chime because in London some bells always chime and the Palace guard is changed, because in London the Palace guard is always changed, at precisely the same time on every morning of every day of every year.

That is all really, merely an attempt to set to music and dancing half an hour of an average London morning in spring outside the gates of Buckingham Palace, with as a basic theme, the idea that, to many people even in these difficult turbulent years, it is still exciting to go to London to see the Queen.

(1958)

11

ON WRITING A PLAY (4)
(1960–1970)

"Dad's Renaissance"

———

Volcano (1957) · *Suite in Three Keys* (1966)

"I am now more of a perfectionist than I used to be; I take pride in being a professional. I don't write plays with the idea of giving some great thought to the world and that isn't just coy modesty. As one gets older one doesn't feel quite so strongly any more, one discovers that everything is always going to be exactly the same with different hats on.

"When the public is no longer interested in what I have to write, then it will be brought home to me that I am out of touch; not before."

·

"Who would have thought the landmarks of the Sixties would include the emergence of Noël Coward as grand old man of British drama? There he was one morning flipping verbal tiddlywinks with reporters about 'Dad's Renaissance' . . . the next, he was there again . . . slightly older than the century in which he sits, his eyelids wearier than ever, hanging beside Forster, Eliot and the O.M.s, demonstrably the great-est living English playwright."

—RONALD BRYDEN (NEW STATESMAN)

·

"Whenever I reflect with what alarming rapidity I am trundling toward old age and the dusty grave, I find it comforting to count my blessings. And although the future, like the late Mrs. Fiske, is heavily veiled, my blessings, up to date, have been considerable."

(1965)

Although it was written in 1957, *Volcano* was not produced until 2012, thus it should be considered as a late play . . .

"I am halfway, or nearly halfway through a new play. The idea came to me quite suddenly . . . in about twenty minutes the whole story had set itself into three acts and six scenes without any conscious effort from me. And then the title obligingly dropped into my mind, *Volcano,* and I started right away and wrote the first scene. It is a serious play, so far I think, very well written . . . The story is concerned with the emo-tional problems of six people, notably four of them, and is played against the background of a minor volcanic eruption.

"The second act takes place in a guest house on the volcano itself, good old Fumfumbolo. I know that my psychology is sound and, for the first time in a long while, I am conscious of the magic of my gift. It always surprises me each time it happens and I shall never cease to marvel at it. Why suddenly, after months of barrenness, should the right words flow out of me with so little effort beyond concentration. I am sure, by the way this is absorbing my mind, and by the pleasure that it is giving me to write it, that it is intrinsically right. All of which, not unnaturally, makes me very happy."

———

The reason why it came so easily should have been apparent. Many of the elements in the play were from Noël's own life.

The heroine, Adela Shelley, an attractive widow, runs the guesthouse on Noël's fantasy island, Samolo—a thinly disguised Jamaica. The character was based on Blanche Blackwell, the native white Jamaican who was a close friend and neighbor to Noël and sold him the land on which he built his house Firefly.

A year or so before the play begins Adela had foolishly indulged in a casual affair with Guy Littleton, the island's would-be Lothario. Now Guy's wife, Melissa, has made the trip from London to assess what is going on.

These two characters are clearly based on Noël's friend Ian Fleming, author of the James Bond novels, and his wife, Ann. In real life Ann was Ann Rothermere, wife of the press baron, Lord Rothermere. She and Ian had conducted what they considered to be a discreet cross-continent affair for some time to the interest and amusement of the locals.

Noël was to revisit the subject in more detail—and with rather more humor—when he wrote his only published novel, *Pomp and Circumstance,* in 1960.

In the play the guests survive the volcano but the experience causes them all to rethink aspects of their present lives. Catharsis, in a word, for all but one of them. Melissa leaves, having decided to divorce Guy, Guy tries to reinstate his relationship with Adela, only to have her reject him out of hand.

In the event Noël wrote two versions of *Volcano.* On reflection he decided that Adela did not have an affair with Guy prior to the opening of the story, as she had in Version 1. And in that version Melissa leaves, undecided about divorcing Guy.

———

In Noël's mind the play was a natural to be produced by his friend Binkie Beaumont, who had steered so much of his work to the West End. Binkie, however, didn't share his enthusiasm. He had little sympathy for the characters and felt Noël should have made it a comedy. This was not what theatregoers wanted. (John Osborne's *Look Back in Anger* was the current theatrical touchstone.)

His reaction obviously disappointed Noël. "There are still many million middle-aged, middle-class English people who would, I think, appreciate the values of *Volcano*. However, perhaps I am more old-fashioned than I realise."

The play was eventually given a single rehearsed reading on June 29, 1989, with Judi Dench as Adela, her husband, Michael Williams, as Guy.

In May 2012 Bill Kenright and Thelma Holt produced a national tour of eight cities culminating in a short run at the Vaudeville Theatre, London. The production starred Jenny Seagrove and (fittingly) Judi Dench's daughter, Finty Williams, played a supporting role.

He was determined to play one last time in London "where I first started more than fifty years ago, to sort of round off the dinner . . . I would like to act once more before I fold my bedraggled wings."

1962

"I really must get back to my pens and paper and typewriter. I have an idea of doing a series of short plays, two a night, under the collective title of *Neutral Territory,* each play, separate in itself, will take place in a hotel suite in Switzerland. I intend to write them for myself as a sort of acting orgy swan-song. It is a fascinating project if I can get enough variety into it . . ."

Then silence until three years later . . .

"I have written the first act of a play called *A Song at Twilight.* So far it is good, I know, and I've got the fireworks to come in the last act. The original idea has been in my mind for some time. It was suggested by a scene in David Cecil's biography of Max Beerbohm when Constance Collier, after years of non-contact, suddenly descends on him when he is an old man and flattens him with her vitality. My play is more sinister, and there is Maugham in it as well as Max.

"All this is very exciting, but what is most exciting of all is my extraordinary facility for writing dialogue. Too great a facility, really. I have to force myself to go slowly. And oh, how much easier it is to write than prose. Anyhow, at the moment I'm functioning happily."

March 28

"I am wagging my tail hard. Yesterday I finished the play and I really think it's a rouser. Of course, it may turn out not to be and everyone will hate it, but I doubt this. In the first place I intend to play it myself with, if possible, Maggie Leighton and Irene Worth.

"I am now preparing two long one-acters to play as contrast in the same set. One, *Concert Pitch,* about a great conductor, and the other, *Shadows of the Evening,* about a north-country business tycoon. We shall see."

Concert Pitch was replaced by the broadly comic *Come into the Garden, Maud.*

"I have this morning finished *Shadows of the Evening* and I think it is one of the best plays I have ever written. I may have to eat these words later and consider myself a proper Charlie for having written them but this is how I feel at the immediate moment. It is a sad theme but not entirely a sad play. It also has wonderful parts for all three of us, particularly me. I really do think that to have written one full-length and two one-act plays in the same set with three characters and a waiter is a remarkable theatrical feat and I am mighty proud of myself."

In the end he found it impossible to pin down the increasingly scatty Margaret Leighton. Currently married to Michael Wilding, she could only come to London if she could bring him—at the company's expense. The company—Noël and producer Binkie Beaumont—declined the offer and settled on Lilli Palmer. Irene Worth was already confirmed.

("Oh dear, what a silly, silly girl is Miss Margaret Leighton. Actually I am very relieved. Lilli is very intelligent, untiresome and a bloody good actress, whereas poor Maggie has, I fear, already become tainted by those awful Hollywood values . . .")

Then the real problems began. In October 1965 Noël took time off for a vacation—solo for once. In the Seychelles he contracted amoebic dysentery and was extremely ill. When he was able to travel Coley met an emaciated Noël at Geneva airport. For several weeks he was confined to a hospital in Lausanne. The intended opening in January 1966 had to be put back to April and even that would be touch-and-go.

The setup was now fixed. Under the overall heading of Noël Coward's *Suite in Three Keys* would be the full-length *A Song at Twilight* and the two shorter plays—*Shadows of the Evening* and *Come into the Garden, Maud.*

Then a rehearsal pattern that was beginning to be repetitive . . .

Lilli hadn't acted onstage for more than ten years and had trouble converting film technique to stage. Noël remarked that she was acting like something out of the German silent cinema . . . "She has a gesture for every word."

And while he had thwarted Michael Wilding's involvement, he was to suffer the Spouse Syndrome anyway when Carlos Thompson—Lilli's current husband—suggested that Noël fire the director, since he (Carlos) could bring "music" to the play, if he were to direct it. Noël's reply was commendably succinct. "It's not a musical. So shut up!"

There was one lighter note. Casting the role of the hotel waiter, Felix, in *A Song at Twilight* they found a well-qualified Italian actor. Unfortunately, his grasp of certain English pronunciation was not always the surest. He insisted on referring to Sir Hugo's "tastes" as Sir Hugo's "tes-

tes." Noël quipped—"I know the play is about homosexuality but that is going too far! Also it gives away the plot far too soon."

A Song at Twilight opened on April 14.

"Well, the most incredible thing has happened. Not only has *A Song at Twilight* opened triumphantly but the Press notices have on the whole been extremely good. Most particularly the *Express* and the *Evening Standard*! Fortunately the *Sun* struck a sour note and said 'Coward's Return Very Tedious,' which convinced me that I hadn't entirely slipped . . . The play is such a sell-out smash that we have had to engage extra people to cope with the ticket demand. On the opening night I gave an excellent, unnervous, controlled performance, thank God. I am back again, like Dolly, where I belong and have always belonged.

"My letters of praise have been fabulous. Irene was brilliant, Lilli still shrill and insecure but much better. Her notices were tepid. London really feels as though it were *en fête,* with my success, and it is a warming and lovely feeling. . . . I haven't experienced anything like it for many a long day and it made everything worthwhile. People came pouring onto the stage afterwards and it was altogether a heart-warming triumph."

What failed to warm his heart was playing opposite Lilli Palmer. Their relationship deteriorated steadily until he vented in his *Diary*—"I have made a truce . . . because I have to play with her. But I have never—with

Irene Worth, Noël, and Lilli Palmer in *Come into the Garden, Maud,* a play in the sequence *Suite in Three Keys* (1966). It would be Noël's last appearance on any stage.

the possible exception of Claudette Colbert [in the American TV production of *Blithe Spirit*]—worked with such a stupid bitch."

It was a fitting finale but it was most definitely a finale. Noël's health would continue to plague him in the years that remained and the embarrassing experience he had had remembering his own lines was not lost on him.

The plays were meant to transfer to Broadway the following season but that was now too much for him. *Song* and *Maud* finally appeared there as *Noël Coward in Two Keys* in 1974—a year after his death.

The vainglorious leading lady was something of a thread in Noël's professional life.

At one point he even wrote a short sketch about the lady . . .

A VIVID STUDY OF THEATRICAL LIFE

Mademoiselle Lola, the Tragedy Queen, sat in her rose-tinted dressing room, her richly bejeweled hand lying carelessly across a diamond-studded makeup box and her daintily-shod foot tapping the floor impatiently. She was smoking one of her favorite Russians and blowing the scented smoke in clouds about her.

Suddenly a loud knock came at the door.

"Entrez," she murmured in the soft cooing voice for which she was famed!

The call boy in pale blue uniform with gold buttons respectfully crossed the threshold. "Madame," he said, "the Great British Public are clamoring for you!" With that he withdrew. "Oh, la la la la," cried she. "How too droll!" And picking up a sapphire-studded fan, she swept from the room.

On her way down the long passage a sound of sobbing arrested her. It seemed to come from a door on the right. She opened it and beheld a poor painted chorus girl crying bitterly. Heavens, what a scene of squalor and filth! Lola's heart was touched to compassion.

"What ails thee, child?" she asked. The poor girl looked up through tear-dimmed eyes at the beautiful vision before her. "The Manager has bid me go," she sobbed. "But how too cruel," cried Lola, enraged. "Here, child, take heart. I will see to it that you are re-engaged as my fifth understudy!" The girl, with a hoarse cry of thanks, fell on her knees and kissed the hem of her Benefactress's sequined robe.

"God bless you," she murmured brokenly. "God bless you!"

"La la, child," laughed Lola gaily. "It is naught!" And with that she was gone.

Such is an episode in the career of one of our most famous actresses.

12

CURTAIN CALLS

T here would be no more performances . . . simply some valedictory appearances . . .

On the evening of his birthday—December 16, 1969—there was a gala midnight matinee to honor not merely his seventieth birthday but a life in the theatre.

Fittingly it took place on the stage of the Phoenix Theatre, which had opened in 1930 with his *Private Lives* . . .

In his words of thanks . . .

"Very many years ago, when I first went on the stage, I was told by my master, the late Sir Charles Hawtrey . . . He said—'When you are faced

"You'll have to call me SIR Noely now!"
In the 1970 Honours List came the
long-delayed knighthood.

Noël and Dick Cavett.

with an emotional scene, keep it down,' and he added—'In fact, lose yourself, lose your audience.'

"And I would rather not run the risk of losing this audience—and certainly not this time.

"Thank you all so very, very much for making this, quite obviously, the most moving theatrical moment of my life."

The award was presented by his old friend Cary Grant—his wartime "control" when they were both spies and two of "Little Bill" Stephenson's "boys."

(But that's a whole other story . . .)

In his acceptance speech Noël teased his audience . . .

"This is my first award—so please be kind."

Then there was his guest appearance on *The Dick Cavett Show*—in which he was joined by the Lunts . . . almost fifty years after their first meeting.

CAVETT: You're—you—what is the word when one has such terrific, prolific qualities?

NOËL: *Talent.*

CAVETT: It's these big words that trip me up!

—*The Dick Cavett Show,* ABC-TV, February 10, 1970

Noël with the Lunts at dinner after the Tony Awards (1970).

With Marlene at *Oh Coward!,* the last show he saw (1973).

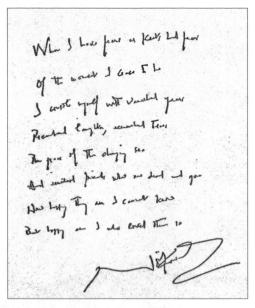

NOËL'S LAST VERSE.
When I have fears, as Keats had fears,
Of the moment I cease to be,
I console myself with vanished years,
Remembered laughter, remembered tears,
The peace of the changing sea
And remembered friends who are dead and gone.
How happy they are I cannot know
But happy am I who loved them so.

On his last night in New York he attended a performance of *Oh Coward!,* a revue based on his own material. On his arm was Marlene Dietrich; surrounding him the palace guard of his "family"—Graham Payn, Cole Lesley, and the rest.

As they left the theatre a fan asked Noël if he had enjoyed the show.

"One does not laugh at one's own jokes," Noël replied with mock seriousness. Then added, smiling—"But I did come out humming the tunes."

Chalet Coward 1973

In his last TV interview Noël was asked to sum his life up in one word. He paused uncharacteristically, then said—

"Now comes the terrible decision as to whether to be corny or not.

"There *is* one word. LOVE.

"To know that you are among people you love and who love you.

"That has made all the successes wonderful—much more wonderful than they'd have been anyway.

"And that's it, really. That's it.

"To love and be loved is the most important thing in the world but it is often painful."

Noël always said that he didn't mind where it all ended—"just that I would prefer Fate to allow me to go to sleep when it's my proper bedtime. I never have been one for staying up too late."

In the early morning of March 26, 1973, at his home, Firefly, in his beloved Jamaica he slipped away from the century he had done so much to define.

It had been a marvelous party . . .

When Graham Payn thanked the Queen Mother for attending the memorial service for Noël in Westminster Abbey, she replied: "I came because he was my friend." March 28, 1984.

ENVOI

During his 1954 run in cabaret at London's Café de Paris Noël introduced a song that posed the question no one in the theatre should
ever ask . . .

Why Must the Show Go On?
The world for some years
Has been sodden with tears
On behalf of the Acting profession,
Each star playing a part
Seems to expect the "Purple Heart,"
It's unorthodox
To be born in a box
But it needn't become an obsession,
Let's hope we have no worse to plague us
Than two shows a night at Las Vegas.
When I think of physicians
And mathematicians
Who don't earn a quarter the dough,
When I look at the faces
Of people in Macy's
There's one thing I'm burning to know:

Why must the show go on?
It can't be all that indispensable,

To me it really isn't sensible
On the whole
To play a leading role
While fighting those tears you can't control,
Why kick up your legs
When draining the dregs
Of sorrow's bitter cup?
Because you have read
Some idiot has said,
"The Curtain must go up!"
I'd like to know why a star takes bows
Having just returned from burying her spouse.
Brave boop-a-doopers,
Go home and dry your tears,
Gallant old troupers,
You've bored us all for years
And when you're so blue,
Wet through
And thoroughly woe-begone,
Why must the show go on?
Oh Mammy!
Why must the show go on?

We're asked to condole
With each tremulous soul
Who steps out to be loudly applauded,
Stars on opening nights
Sob when they see their names in lights,
Though people who act
As a matter of fact
Are financially amply rewarded,
It seems, while pursuing their calling,
Their suffering's simply appalling!
But butchers and bakers
And candlestick makers
Get little applause for their pains
And when I think of miners
And waiters in "Diners"
One query for ever remains:

Why must the show go on?
The rule is surely not immutable,
It might be wiser and more suitable
Just to close
If you are in the throes
Of personal grief and private woes.
Why stifle a sob
While doing your job
When, if you use your head,
You'd go out and grab
A comfortable cab
And go right home to bed?
Because you're not giving us much fun,
This "Laugh Clown Laugh" routine's been overdone,
Hats off to Show Folks
For smiling when they're blue
But more *comme-il-faut* folks
Are sick of smiling through,
And if you're out cold,
Too old
And most of your teeth have gone,
Why must the show go on?
I sometimes wonder
Why must the show go on?

Why must the show go on?
Why not announce the closing night of it?
The public seem to hate the sight of it,
Dear, and so
Why you should undergo
This terrible strain we'll never know.
We know that you're sad,
We know that you've had
A lot of storm and strife
But is it quite fair
To ask us to share
Your dreary private life?
We know you're trapped in a gilded cage

But for Heaven's sake relax and be your age,
Stop being gallant
And don't be such a bore,
Pack up your talent,
There's always plenty more
And if you lose hope,
Take dope
And lock yourself in the John,
Why must the show go on?
I'm merely asking
Why must the show go on?

The question—needless to say—was strictly rhetorical . . .

The New Theatre (1903–1972) begat the Albery
(1973), which finally begat the Noel Coward
Theatre in June 2006. Coward's first West End
play, *I'll Leave It to You,* was produced there in
July 1920 and ran for thirty-seven performances.

Appendix

The Decline of the West End

In these stirring days of astronautical adventure, nuclear fission, social equality, sexual abandon, the Common Market, the very Common Man, Apartheid, Centre 42, the Beatles and the Royal Court Theatre; when the winds of change are whistling through the thinning hair of our elder actors and tangling intolerably the very long hair of our younger ones, I feel that the moment has come for someone to step forward authoritatively and say a few kindly words in defence of what is now contemptuously described as "The Commercial Theatre."

Today the "Commercial Theatre" has become, in the eyes of everyone but the public, a shameful and sordid business. From the viewpoint of our modern theatrical intellectuals, Shaftesbury Avenue, Charing Cross Road, St. Martin's Lane and the Strand have become almost unmentionable areas. No Victorian missionary could have regarded the red light district of an alien city with more lofty disdain. The playgoers in search of cultural refreshment may travel East and South, possibly North, but never never West. He may bumble along in a tube or a taxi to Stratford Atte Bowe, he may be jerked through the English countryside in a dusty nationalised British railway carriage to sit in draughty converted aeroplane hangars or inadequately transformed country chapels for his entertainment and pleasure, but for him to book two stalls at Keith Prowse and proceed in a comfortable manner to the Globe Theatre, Wyndham's Theatre or the Savoy Theatre stamps him ineradicably as a reactionary clot. He may even find, as the merry years go marching on, that Sloane Square is a tiny bit too near.

I am perfectly prepared to admit that the West End of London has of late acquired a certain shoddy, red-light-district atmosphere compared with its glamour of earlier days, but in those squalid thoroughfares it is still possible to find pleasantly upholstered theatres in which a playgoer can sit at ease and enjoy the age-old pleasure of seeing the lights go down and an actual curtain go up. He may even, when it has gone up, have quite a good time. At least, if he doesn't have a good time, he can go out and return home without beating his way through muddy fields.

There has been a lot of talk during the past few years about "The Theatre of Ideas" as opposed to the "Theatre of Entertainment." And a lot of very silly talk at that. In the first place it is arbitrary to assume that the "Theatre of Ideas" must necessarily be opposed to the "Theatre of Entertainment." A play of "Ideas" can be just as entertaining as a play of "Pure Entertainment" can be boring. Everything depends, as always, on how it is written, directed and acted. But the basic error in all the argument is the assumption that a commercial enterprise is a bad thing and a non-commercial enterprise, a good thing. In the old days, when the critics were happily presumed to be Philistines, the theatrical skies were clearer.

Now, when the critics have become pseudo-intellectuals and range themselves firmly on the side of the experimenters to the virtual exclusion of every other form of production, the values have become badly muddled. In any case, while we're on the subject, what exactly *is* a play of ideas? I have read and seen a number of the *avant-garde* plays of the last few years, some of which interested me and some of which did not. *Look Back in Anger,* for instance, which rightly caused a tremendous sensation, cannot be described as a play of ideas. It is a brilliant essay in invective and psychology and provides a super-star part for an intelligent actor. Is *The Caretaker* a play of ideas? If so, where and what are they? To me it was a theatrical *tour de force* of intricate interplay of character upon character and a fascinating experiment in photostatic dialogue impeccably acted and directed. Mr. Pinter's idea in writing it was certainly excellent but so, in a slightly different way, was Baroness Orczy's idea of writing *The Scarlet Pimpernel.*

However much the "Theatre of Ideas" may be considered to be opposed to the "Theatre of Entertainment," I am personally very vigorously opposed to the assumption, prevalent among some of our *avant-garde* pioneers, that what the large public enjoys must inevitably be bad and what the critics enjoy must be good. This is a perilous point of view for those who wish their talents to be generally recognized, and I have yet to meet an actor, writer or director who, in the depths of his base and secret heart, would not prefer success to failure.

I am perfectly aware, of course, that there are varying degrees of success just as there are varying degrees of failure. A highly intelligent serious play at the Royal Court Theatre cannot expect to achieve so long a run as a popular West End farce or musical but if it is good enough it will attract a large enough public to pay its production and probably make a little profit. If it is not good enough, it won't. If it is so boring, abstruse, esoteric and pretentious that it fails to satisfy even the conditioned public who are accustomed to enjoying the theatre the hard way, it will close because nobody will go, and a play to which nobody will go, however worthy, idealistic, experimental and intellectual the motives that inspired it, is a flop. No paeans of articulate praise will revive its failing pulse, no indignant letters to *The Times* or impassioned pleas on the radio will save it. It's a goner, and, without the slightest apology for my flippancy, I say serve it bloody well right.

There have been far too many plays of this calibre presented to us during the last few years, several of which I have been trapped into seeing, either by my own curiosity or by the misguided advice of other people. I have invariably left the quarter-full theatre irritated and depressed and sadly bewildered by the conceit and silliness of some of my hitherto respected colleagues. Naturally, I have often been equally disillusioned by productions in the commercial theatre but in those cases the irritation and boredom were less painful, principally, I suspect, because the productions, however badly written and acted, were at least untainted by false reverence.

I do not wish to give the impression that I am unsympathetic to those who are trying to inject fresh blood and new techniques into the Theatre and I am the first to acknowledge it when they produce something of genuine value, but I must admit I become a little fractious when I hear it suggested that certain of our experimental drama groups should be subsidised by a government department such as the Arts Council, which in effect means that they would be subsidised by the British tax payer.

Playwriting, directing and acting are surely professional jobs and should be recognised as such. In England, as in many continental countries, a National Theatre and an Opera house are subsidised, to my mind, very sensibly, because they both present in the best manner possible classics that are too well known to attract the public for a straight run. Occasionally these establishments allow themselves a little experimental flutter or two, but their main *raison d'être* is the keeping alive of tried and true masterpieces. If Government subsidies were to be granted to every producing company that asked for them, the Theatre would inevitably cease to be a profession at all. Nobody up to date has suggested seriously that the Government subsidise fishmongers, grocers, stock-brokers or truck drivers during the early years of their apprenticeship and I see no reason why any theatrical groups, however high-minded and well intentioned, should be given public funds to fiddle about with when they should, in fact, be earning their living in a profession which after all they themselves have chosen. If a certain Management of a certain Theatre voluntarily decides to present a series of different plays to the public, all good luck to them, but it must be remembered that nobody asked them to.

As far as I can recall no subsidies were granted to Sir Henry Irving, Sir Herbert Tree, Sir Charles Cochran, Vedrenne and Eadie, Granville-Barker, Jack Hylton or Emile Littler. I cannot believe that at any moment of their careers Shaw, Maugham, Barrie, Ibsen, Pinero or Galsworthy sat back comfortably in their stalls during rehearsals reflecting that, whatever might happen to their plays, the financial side of the business was generously taken care of. And I am quite quite sure that I have never found myself in such a cosy situation.

If a commercial manager produces a play that fails to attract the public, he closes it and endeavours to recoup his losses by producing something else. Whatever wailing and gnashing of teeth this entails is generally confined to the cast and the backers and others immediately concerned. There are never protests in the public Press by critics or anyone else. But it seems that the commercial theatre nowadays is deserving of neither pity nor praise. Whatever good it may inadvertently do for the reputation of the British drama by presenting a play with taste and elegance, this good is automatically negated by the fact that it happens to be a financial success. The basic truth that the theatre is and should be a money-making business is no longer regarded as valid. This new snobbism that has grown lately about the theatre only being good when it is *not* a money-making business is both pretentious and unrealistic.

Success in the theatre, as in every other trade, is an essential goal to strive for. "To fail gloriously" is a vapid, defensive cliché. There is little glory in failure. "To succeed triumphantly" has a happier ring to it and it is much rarer and more difficult to achieve. Speaking for myself I have never had a "glorious" failure in my life. I've just had failures, and the inescapable reason for these failures was that the plays in question were just not quite good enough. Whenever a "flop" occurs in the theatre there is always a number of the faithful, a group of fervent loyalists to affirm that the play is far and away the best thing one has ever done, that the theatre was too big or too small, that the leading lady was miscast and that the critics are pigs. These facile alibis must be dismissed and the injured author must waste no time in wound-licking but sit down and write something else as soon as possible.

I am prepared cheerfully to admit that I have never once achieved an intellectual success, or an intellectual failure for that matter, which is not surprising because I am not, never have been and never could be described as an Intellectual. I am, however, talented, observant, technically proficient, emotional, intelligent and industrious, and the sensible application of these qualities has brought me many comforting rewards. Not the least of these is the knowledge and experience I have gained in a profession that I have loved and respected for fifty-five years. It is because of this knowledge and experience that I felt myself entitled to express my profound gratitude to The Commercial Theatre and to the cheerful, entertainment-loving public who so stubbornly supports it.

I've been to a marvelous party . . . I couldn't have liked it more.

Acknowledgments

This book would not have been possible without the help of my friend and agent—in that order—Alan Brodie. His wry Scots charm makes the path passable. I would also like to thank Robert Hazle and the entire team at ABR for their support and patience. I'm indebted to too many members of the ever-growing Coward "family" to mention by name, but they know who they are and what they contributed. I hope I've done you justice.

Once again, I'd like to thank the editorial team at Knopf—in particular Marc Jaffee and Kathy Zuckerman, publicist and perceptive reader of minds. And—prima inter pares—my friend and editor (in that order), Victoria Wilson—a lady who manages to nudge you into expressing that little bit more than you thought you knew!

And always, my wife, Lynne, my sine qua non . . .

Sources and Permissions

Extracts and quotations are taken from the following sources, courtesy of Methuen Drama:

The Noël Coward Autobiography

The Lyrics of Noël Coward

Noël Coward in His Own Words, edited by Barry Day

The Letters of Noël Coward, edited by Barry Day

Collected Plays, volumes 1–9

Theatrical Companion to Coward: A Pictorial Record of the Theatrical Works of Noël Coward, 2nd edition, updated by Barry Day and Sheridan Morley

Extracts from *The Noël Coward Diaries*, edited by Graham Payn and Sheridan Morley, are courtesy of Weidenfeld & Nicolson.

The author gratefully acknowledges permission to quote from these titles.

All sheet music covers are reproduced by kind permission of Faber Music Limited.

Other text references and images not specifically acknowledged herein are courtesy of the Noël Coward Archive Trust (www.noelcoward.com/archive-trust).

Index

(Page references in *italics* refer to illustrations.)

Ace of Clubs (Coward), *349*, *372*, 378–9, *379*
acting, Noël on, 135–68, 193–201
  advice to actors, 229–30
  American vs. English comedy style, 45
  appearance of spontaneity in, 342
  the art of acting, 136–40
  auditions, 140–2, 162–3
  being booed off the stage, 164–5
  busy-ness on the stage, 230
  casting period's disappointments, 185–6
  clarity of delivery, 154, 189
  control, 157–61
  "corpsing," 157–8, 205–6
  dealing with disappointments, 230
  emotional acting vs. comedy, 51
  first-night nerves, 163–4
  giggling onstage, 157–8
  hamming, 172
  instinct, 229
  intellectual or psychological approaches,
    188–9
  learning the lines, 150–4, 165–8, 203
  mannerisms, xvi, 48, 159
  Method and, 195–7, 198, 200–1
  other actors playing parts created by
    Noël, 178–9
  performances differing from playwright's
    intentions, 184–5
  playing Americans, 230
  playing and singing in a foreign
    language, 367
  range, 161–2
  repertory approach, 139
  sense of style, 177–8
  stage fright, 162–8
  star quality, 231–8
  stars "staying off" on the slightest
    pretext, 350
  talent (or the lack of it), 143–6, 162–3,
    229
  thinking of many things simultaneously,
    230
  timing, 45, 154–6
  "Touring Days" song, 26–7
  upstaging, 155
  varying the performance, 155–6
  verses:
    "The Boy Actor," 6–7
    "The Child Prodigy," 17
  "A Warning to Actors" ("Consider the
    Public" essay originally published
    in *The Sunday Times* under the
    title "The Scratch-and-Mumble
    School"), 194–200
  see also leading ladies
Actor Prepares, An (Stanislavski), 196
Actors' Orphanage, 265
Actors Studio, 225
Adelphi Theatre, London, *340*, 351
advertising:
  Noël's Rheingold ad, *262*
  Packard's *Hidden Persuaders* on, 281
After the Ball (Coward), 38, 61, 286,
  379–80
After the Fall (Miller), 75–6
Agate, James, 274–9, 290
  London Calling! reviewed by, 333–5
  "To Mr. James Agate (to an eminent
    critic)," 278–9
  The Vortex reviewed by, 50–1, 275

Albee, Edward, 73–4, *74*
Albert, Prince, 292
Aldrich, Richard, 210, 253
Alexander, Sir George, 177
"Alexander's Ragtime Band" (Berlin), 326
Algonquin Round Table, 44, 279, 354
Allen, Adrianne, *109*, 110, 155, 205
Alvin Theatre, New York, *389*
Amherst, Jeffery, 103–4
Andrews, Bobbie, *211*
Andrews, Julie, 386
Angry Young Men, 68–72, 78, 288
    see also Osborne, John; Wesker, Arnold
Apple Cart, The (Shaw), 58–60, *59*, 138–9,
    315
April, Elsie, 357
Arcadians, The, 324
Arcati, Madame (character), Noël's acting
    ambitions and, 56, 244
Arliss, George, 58
Arnaud, Yvonne, 331
Around the World in 80 Days (film), 204
Ashton, Winifred ("Winnie," known
    professionally as "Clemence
    Dane"), 315–16
Ashwell, Lena, Players, 205–6
Astaire, Fred and Adele, 44
Astley-Cooper, Mrs., 34–5, *35*, 36
"Astonished Heart, The" (Coward), 129
As You Like It (Shakespeare), 193
Atkinson, Brooks, 262, 264, 281
A to Z (Charlot revue), 301
audiences, Noël on, 168
    in America vs. England, 262–3
    being booed off the stage by, 164–5
    charity "theatre parties" and, 263
    drawn to star quality, 233
    listening to reactions of, 173–4
auditions:
    of Laye for *Bitter Sweet*, 305, 356–7
    Noël on, 140–2
    Noël's own approach to, 25, 28, 142
    stage fright and, 162–3
Autumn Idyll, An, 17–18, *18*

Bacall, Lauren, *243*
Badel, Alan, 252
Bagnold, Enid, 317
Balcon, Michael, 50
Bankhead, Tallulah, 92, *93*, 172
Barefoot in the Park (Simon), 76
Barnard, Ivor, *50*
"Bar on the Piccola Marina, A" (Coward),
    380

Barrie, J. M., 62–3, 224, 275, 281–2, 302,
    432
    Peter Pan, 15, 291
        Noël playing Slightly in, *5*, 22–3, *24*,
        62, 63, 291
Barrymore, John, 179
Baum, Vicky, 97
Beaton, Cecil, 220, 332
Beaumont, Hugh (Binkie), 153, 244–5, 253,
    254, *313*, 313–18, 379, 413, 415
    Nude with Violin and, 315, 316
    Peace in Our Time and, 315
    teasing verse for, 314
    Waiting in the Wings and, 317
Beckett, Samuel, 73, 74–5, 79, 288, 289
Beerbohm, Max, 66, 297, 298, *303*, 355, 414
Benchley, Robert, 179
Berlin, Irving, 326, 329
Bernhardt, Sarah, 365
Best, Edna, 92, *93*, 159, *161*, 171, 172
Better Not Enquire ("straight" play), 348
Birmingham Rep, 41
Bitter Sweet (Coward), 103, 191, 214, 286,
    306, 328, *349*, 353–60, *354*, 356, *358*,
    359, 372
    Agate's review of, 278
    casting of Sari, 354–5, 358
    dress rehearsal for, 306
    idea for, 353
    "I'll See You Again" in, 214–15, 292, 328,
        354, 358, 371
    Laye's audition for, 305, 356–7
    New York production of, 305, 355–7
    Novello's praise for, 357–60
Blackwell, Blanche, *221*, 412
Blithe Spirit (Coward), 239, *241*, 241–5,
    242, 283, 310, 314
    literary quotations and, 42, 56
    Madame Arcati character in, 56, 153,
        242, 244–5, 387
    musical version of, *see High Spirits*
    TV version of, 152, *243*, 244, 247, 417
    writing of, 33, 241–3, 252, 381
Blue Harbour, Jamaica, 286
Boer War, 114
Bolt, Robert, 71, 79
"Bon Voyage" (Coward), 47
Boom (film), 77
Braham, Philip, 301, 304
Braithwaite, Lilian, 50, *50*, 51, 160–1, 171,
    201
Braunsweg, Julian, 407–8
Brecht, Bertolt, 289
Brent, Romney, *340*, 363

Brief Encounter (film), 95, 133, 249
Brown, Ivor, 56, 122–3
Browne, Graham, *89*
Browne, Irene, 386
Browning Version, The (Rattigan), 78
Brunel, Adrian, 50
Bryan, Dora, 252
Bryden, Ronald, 411
Brynner, Yul, 212
Buchanan, Jack, 208
Bunny Lake Is Missing (film), 158–9, 207
Burton, Richard, 77
Byron, George Gordon, Lord, 56

cabaret, 163, 212, 264, 292, 394–404
    at Desert Inn, Las Vegas, 398–401, *400,*
        401, 402
    Noël's accompanists for, 394, 399
    reviews of Noël's performances, 399–400
    television performances, 401–4, *403, 404*
    see also Café de Paris, London
Café de Paris, London, 31, 292, 394–8, *395,*
        397, 399, 424
    Dietrich's cabaret debut at, 396–8
    Noël as teenage performer at, during
        its days as Elysée Restaurant, 30–1,
        31, 394
    "Why Must the Show Go On?"
        introduced at, 424–7
Cakes and Ale (Maugham), 65
Calthrop, G. E. (Gladys), 35, 116, 120, 309,
        325, 338, 339, 353, 367, *373, 374*
    drawings by, *337, 339, 358, 359, 369*
Campbell, Judy, 152, *246*
Cape Playhouse, Dennis, Mass., 210
Caretaker, The (Pinter), 79, 83–4, 430
Carey, Joyce, 240, 241, 316
Carroll, Joan, 18, *18*
Carroll, Lewis, 348
cartoons, *293*
Caryll, Ivan, 324
casting period, Noël on disappointments
        of, 185–6
Castlerosse, Lord and Lady, 106
Cat on a Hot Tin Roof (Williams), 76
Cavalcade (Coward), 77–8, 79, 113, *113,*
        114–18, *115,* 179, 210, 308, 374
Cavett, Dick, 420, *420*
CBS-TV:
    Blithe Spirit broadcast by, *243,* 244, 247
    Noël's performances on, 401–4, *404*
    Present Laughter rejected by, 245–7
Cecil, David, 66, 414
celebrity, Noël on his experience of, 51–3

censorship, 49–50, 97
Centre 42 venture, 70, 71
Chalet Coward, 214
Chamberlain, Neville, 134, 247, 249
Champion, Gower, 388
Channing, Carol, 264
Chapel Royal choir, 8–9
Chaplin, Charlie, 389
charity "theatre parties," Noël on, 263
Charley's Aunt (Thomas), 25–6, 41, 161
Charlot, André, 208, 300–2, *302,* 335, 391
    London Calling! and, 301–2, 332, 333
Chase, Pauline, 26
Chekhov, Anton, 61–2, 224, 368
Cherry Orchard, The (Chekhov), 62, 292
Cherry Pan (Coward), 23–5
Cherwell, 78
Chester, Betty, *31, 42,* 407
Chevalier, Maurice, 330–1, *332,* 352
child actors:
    Noël as, 8–32, 208, 291, 318, 330
        breakthrough from amateur to
            professional, 10
        first public appearance, 8
        in Griffith's film *Hearts of the World,*
            29–30, *30*
        in Hawtrey's company, 14–15, *16,*
            18–19, 330
        in Miss Lila Field's Company, 10–14
        as mushroom in *An Autumn Idyll,*
            17–18, *18*
        playing Slightly in *Peter Pan,* 5, 22–3,
            24, 62, *63,* 291
        "Touring Days" verse about, 26–7
    Noël's verses on:
        "The Boy Actor," 6–7
        "The Child Prodigy," 17
    stage fright not experienced by, 162, 164
"Childe Harold's Pilgrimage" (Byron), 56
Christie, Agatha, 243
Chrysler, 401
Churchill, Winston, 249
cinema, Noël on theatre vs., 191
Citizens Theatre, Glasgow, 98
Claridge's, London, 207
clarity of delivery, Noël on, 154, 189
classical music, Noël's early suspicion of,
        39–40
Clements, John, 253
Cochran, Charles B. ("Cockie"), 108, 148,
        274, 300, 302–8, *303,* 372, 432
    Bitter Sweet and, 305, 306, 353, 355
    Cavalcade and, 114, *115,* 307
    Conversation Piece and, 307, 363

Cochran, Charles B. ("Cockie")
    (continued)
  on nature of revue, 336, 337, 345
  Noël's cutting of ties with, 307–8, 310,
    313, 370
  On with the Dance and, 304, 335
  Private Lives and, 108, 307
  This Year of Grace! and, 305, 306, 335–6,
    337
  Words and Music and, 148, 307, 336–7
Cocktail Party, The (Eliot), 67
Colbert, Claudette, 96, 152, 243, 254, 254,
    255, 256, 312, 417
Coley, see Lesley, Cole
Coliseum, London, 18–19, 115, 330, 331
Collection, The (Pinter), 80
Collier, Constance, 66, 171, 414
Collier, Patience, 229
comedic acting vs. emotional acting, Noël
    on, 51
comedy, Noël on, 172–4
Come into the Garden, Maud (Coward),
    414, 415, 416, 417
"Commercial Theatre," Noël on, 429
Compton, Frank, 219
Compton Burnett, Ivy, 80
Concerto (Coward), 191
Concert Pitch (Coward), 414
confidence in your writing, 179–80
Confidential Clerk, The (Eliot), 67
Congreve, William, 61
consecutive fifths, 327
"Consider the Public" (Noël's essays for
    The Sunday Times), 69, 267, 288
  "A Warning to Actors" (originally
    published under the title "The
    Scratch-and-Mumble School"),
    194–200
  "A Warning to Dramatic Critics," 288,
    294–7
  "A Warning to Pioneers," 82–6
Constant Nymph, The (Kennedy and
    Dean), 151, 159, 160, 161, 203, 321
constructing a play:
  Miller's lessons on, 41, 43
  Noël on, 182
Contemporary Theatre, 1924, 275
Conti, Italia, 16–17, 21–2
  Noël's ode to, 16–17
control in acting, Noël on, 157–61
Conversation Piece (Coward), 307, 328,
    362–3, 364, 365, 366–8, 375
Cook, Roderick, 289, 386
Cooper, Diana, 289–90

Cooper, Gladys, 92, 152, 172, 257, 258, 317
Coote, Robert, 386
Corbett, Leonora, 179
Coronation Year, 58, 213, 315
Coronet Theatre, New York, 259
"corpsing," 157–8
  of Olivier, 205–6
Count of Luxembourg, The (Lehár), 350,
    397
Country Girl, The, 8, 324
Courtneidge, Cicely, 27
Courtneidge, Robert, 27–8
Coward, Noël:
  as actor, 301, 315, 321
    Agate's reviews of, 50–1, 274, 335
    allowing understudy to play for him,
      159, 201
    approach to auditions, 25, 28, 142
    averse to long runs that limited his
      creative versatility, 97
    awkward fit with The Constant
      Nymph, 159–61
    being and not being Noël Coward
      and, 178–9
    in childhood, 8–32, 208, 291, 318, 330;
      see also child actors
    Dean on directing Noël, 323
    in films, 29–30, 30, 77, 204, 207, 285,
      286
    first engagements as adult, 41,
      42–3, 48
    forgetting words he had written
      himself, 154
    Gielgud's assessments of, 201–3, 332–3
    impromptu performance of leading
      role in Sherriff's Journey's End,
      111–12
    last appearance on stage, 414, 416,
      416
    Madame Arcati role and, 56, 244
    mannerisms of, xvi, 48, 159, 203
    Shakespearean roles and, 42, 56
    in Shaw's The Apple Cart, 58–60, 59,
      138–9, 315
    writing more important to Noël
      than, 47
    see also acting, Noël on
  ballet written by (London Morning), 349,
    407–9
  cabaret, 163, 212, 264, 292, 394–404
    accompanists for, 394, 399
    at Desert Inn, Las Vegas, 398–401,
      400, 401, 402
    reviews of, 399–400

television performances, 401–4, *403*, *404*
  see also Café de Paris, London
class boundaries and background of, 34–5
as dancer, 30–1, *31*, 394
death of, 423, *423*
essays and articles:
  on Beatrice Lillie, 389–93
  "How I Wonder What You Are," 232–8
  "How I Write My Songs," 405–7, *406*
  introduction for biography of Novello, 360–2
  introduction to *Contemporary Theatre, 1924*, 275
  "Music Hall," 330–2
  "On Taking Light Music Seriously," 324–30
  "The Decline of the West End," 429–33
  on Yvonne Printemps, 364–8
  see also "Consider the Public"
filmmaking and, 380–1
  Brief Encounter, 95, 133, 249
  In Which We Serve, 191, 402
  lack of interest in, 191
  Later than Spring, 380–1
financial affairs of, 57–8, 309–10
fortieth birthday of, 191–2
knighthood for, 79, 221, 249, 419
literary quotations used by, 55–6
musical theatre:
  Ace of Clubs, 349, 372, 378–9, *379*
  After the Ball, 38, 61, 286, 379–80
  Conversation Piece, 307, 328, 362–3, *364*, 365, 366, 367, 368, 375
  High Spirits, 153–4, 387–90, *389*, 392
  Operette, 133, 313, 363, 365, 366, 368–72, 394
  Pacific 1860, 278, 349, 372–8, *373*, *374*, 403
  see also *Bitter Sweet*; musical theatre—Noël on
New York first visited by, 44–6
novels:
  Cherry Pan (juvenilia), 23–5
  Pomp and Circumstance, 256, 412, *413*
Paris first visited by, 330–2
plays:
  Cavalcade, 77–8, 79, 113, *113*, 114–18, *115*, 179, 210, 308, 374
  Come into the Garden, Maud, 414, 415, *416*, 417

Design for Living, 113, 118–23, *120*, *121*, *123*, *151*, 155–6, *156*, 218, 252
The Dope Cure, 39, 40, 41
Easy Virtue, 49, 88, 90, 94–5, 277–8, 320, 320–1
Fallen Angels, 49, 92–4, *93*
Home Chat, 99
Humoresque, 39–40, 41
I'll Leave It to You, 32, *32*, 34, 43–4, 48, 274, 407, 427
The Impossible Wife, 34
The Last Trick, 33–4
Look After Lulu!, 264–5
The Marquise, 100–1
Nude with Violin, 204, 260–4, 315, 316
Peace in Our Time, 249–52, *251*, 315
Point Valaine, 123–4, *125*, 220, 368
Post-Mortem, 113, 179, 249
Quadrille, 220, 258–60, *259*, 287, 315
The Queen Was in the Parlour, 49, 96, 321
The Rat Trap, 34, 88, 322
Relative Values, 152, 173, 256–7, 315
Salute to the Brave, 240
Semi-Monde, 97–9, 176
Shadows of the Evening, 414–15
Sirocco, 63, 101–3, 180, 305, 321–2, 336, 355
A Song at Twilight, 66, 414, 415–16, 417
Suite in Three Keys, 69, 154, 415–17, *416*
This Happy Breed, 42, 55, 134, 162, 195, 239, 244, 247–9, *248*, 314, 378
This Was a Man, 40, 55, 96–7, 272, 321
The Unattainable, 36–8, 41
Volcano, 411–13
Waiting in the Wings, 62, 265–7, *266*, 268, 317
The Young Idea, 47–8, *48*, 57, 274, 304
see also *Blithe Spirit*; *Hay Fever*; *Present Laughter*; *Private Lives*; *South Sea Bubble*; *Tonight at 8:30*; *Vortex, The*
as playwright:
  celebrity early in Noël's career and, 51–3
  construction problems in Noël's early works, 41
  indications of Noël's stamping grounds marked out in his early works, 39–41
  Miller's lessons and, 41, 43, 46
  more important to Noël than acting, 47

Coward, Noël:
  as playwright (continued):
    perspective on, gained during Noël's
      first American trip, 46–7
    quick writing and, 33, 46, 56, 252–3,
      381
    stylistic excesses in Noël's early work,
      35–9, 60
    see also writing, Noël on
  political views of, 85, 288
  as producer, 149–50
  revues:
    London Calling!, 208, 301–2, 304,
      332–5, 333, 334, 407
    Noël on art of, 346–7
    On with the Dance, 56, 303, 304, 305,
      334, 335, 335, 407
    Set to Music, 133, 334, 338–44, 340,
      343, 392
    Sigh No More, 315, 334, 344–5
    Words and Music, 147, 307, 336–9,
      340
    see also This Year of Grace!
  seventieth birthday of, 207, 419–20
  short stories:
    "Aunt Tittie," 64
    "Bon Voyage," 47
    "What Mad Pursuit?," 273
  sixties entered by—his own and the
    century's, 268–70
  songs:
    "A Bar on the Piccola Marina," 380
    "Dance, Little Lady," 336
    "Dearest Love," 371
    "Forbidden Fruit," 28–9, 36
    "Green Carnation," 372
    "I Like America," 405
    "I'll Follow My Secret Heart," 371
    "I'll Remember Her," 215–16
    "I'll See You Again," 214–15, 292, 328,
      354, 358, 371
    "It Couldn't Matter Less," 344–5
    "Later than Spring," 268–70
    "London" sequence, 372, 386
    "Mad About the Boy," 147, 337, 337
    "Mad Dogs and Englishmen," 336–7,
      338, 340
    "Matelot," 334, 344–5
    "Men About Town," 132
    "Mrs. Worthington," 143–6, 144
    "My Horse Has Cast a Shoe," 376
    "Ninety Minutes Is a Long, Long
      Time," 403
    Noël on how he writes, 405–7, 406

  "Parisian Pierrot," 332, 407
  "Poor Little Rich Girl," 335, 336, 407
  "A Room with a View," 280, 305–6,
    336, 339
  "Something to Do with Spring," 337
  "Stately Homes of England," 344, 369,
    370, 371
  "The Party's Over Now," 337
  "This Is a Changing World," 376
  "This Is a Night for Lovers," 376
  "Three Juvenile Delinquents," 372
  "Three Theatrical Dames," 226–9,
    372
  "Touring Days," 26–7
  "Weary of It All," 341
  "Why Must the Show Go On?,"
    424–7
  "World Weary," 336
  as songwriter:
    "How I Write My Songs," 405–7, 406
    Noël's first complete song
      ("Forbidden Fruit"), 28–9, 36
    on writing lyrics for musical theatre,
      347–8
  as tax exile, 206, 256, 261, 265, 400
  television, 401–4
    Blithe Spirit broadcast by CBS, 243,
      244, 247
    The Dick Cavett Show, 420, 420
    Present Laughter rejected by CBS,
      245–7
    Together with Music, 377, 402–4, 403,
      404
  Tony award for "lifetime achievement,"
    221, 264, 421
  verses:
    "The Boy Actor," 6–7, 140
    "The Child Prodigy," 17
    "Epitaph for an Elderly Actress,"
      225–6
    "I Resent Your Attitude to Mary," 377
    last written, 422, 422
    "Ode to Italia Conti," 16–17
    "Routine for a Critic (Dirge)," 272–3
    "Social Grace," 169–70
    "Three Theatrical Dames," 226–9
    "To Mr. James Agate (to an eminent
      critic)," 278–9
    "Touring Days," 26–7
    "Tribute to Marlene Dietrich," 397–8
  vocal chord problem of, 395
  wartime missions, 57–8, 239–40, 310,
    322–3, 394
  wit of, 60, 61, 292, 360

Coward, Violet (mother), 8, 9, 10, 14, 25–6, 34, 216–17, 291, 301, 318, 319, 329, 348, 350, 356, 359
Cowl, Jane, 320
Coyne, Joseph, 350
Crawford, J. R., 25
creativity after forty, Noël on, 191–2
Crest of the Wave (Novello), 360
Criterion Theatre, London, 100
Critic, The (Sheridan), 137
critics:
    confusing Noël the man with his work, 273, 283, 355
    Noël on, 271–99
        in America vs. England, 290, 404
        constructive criticism from, 298–9
        feelings about critical attacks of, 290
        good reviews from, as fortification, 273
        "Routine for a Critic (Dirge)," 272–3
        "A Warning to Dramatic Critics" ("Consider the Public" essay for The Sunday Times), 288, 294–7
    see also specific critics
Cutler, Kate, 48

Daily Express, 93, 297
Daily Express, The, 93
Daily Mail, 42, 297
Daily Mirror, 10
Dairymaids, The, 348
Damita, Lili, 96
"Dance, Little Lady" (Coward), 336
Dancing Years, The (Novello), 360
Davenport, Bromley, 50
Dean, Basil, 22, 99, 102, 103, 159, 203, 318–23, 319, 322, 323
    The Constant Nymph and, 159, 321
    on directing Noël the actor, 323
    Easy Virtue and, 320–1
    The Queen Was in the Parlour and, 321
    Sirocco and, 321–2
    This Was a Man and, 321
    The Vortex and, 319–20
    wartime entertainments directed by, 322–3
Dear Brutus (Barrie), 63, 281
"Dearest Love" (Coward), 371
Death of a Salesman (Miller), 75
Debussy, Claude, 327
"Decline of the West End, The" (Coward), 429–33
Deep Blue Sea, The (Rattigan), 78
Delysia, Alice, 331

Dench, Dame Judi, 413
Dennis, Eileen, 30, 394
De Profundis (Wilde), 60
Desert Inn, Las Vegas, 398–401, 400, 401, 402
Design for Living (Coward), 113, 118–23, 120, 121, 123, 151, 155–6, 156, 218, 252
Deslys, Gaby, 331
Devine, George, 72
dialogue, Noël on:
    overlapping lines, 174–6
    writing, 182, 191
Dick Cavett Show, The, 420, 420
Dietrich, Marlene, 289, 332, 380, 399, 421, 422
    cabaret debut of, at Café de Paris, 396–8
    Noël's "Tribute to Marlene Dietrich," 397–8
Dillingham, Charles, 319–20
directing:
    Noël on, 140, 183, 185
    see also specific directors
Doble, Frances "Bunny," 102–3
Dolin, Anton, 407–8
Dope Cure, The (Coward), 39, 40, 41
Douglas, Lord Alfred, 60
Downton Abbey, 118
Draper, Ruth, 230
"Drawing-room Dramas," 94
"Drop in for Drinks" (Coward), 175–6
drug taking, censorship of The Vortex and, 49–50, 97
Drury Lane Theatre, London, 115, 116, 360
Duke of York's Theatre, London, 266
Dulcy (Kaufman), 216
du Maurier, Daphne, 214
du Maurier, Sir Gerald, 128, 171–2, 177, 258, 265, 277, 288
Dumb Waiter, The (Pinter), 79
Dunne, Irene, 374, 381
Duse, Eleanora, 365

Eadie, Dennis, 258
Easy Virtue (Coward), 49, 88, 90, 94–5, 320, 320–1
    Agate's review of, 277–8
Edlin, Tubby, 301
Ego (Agate), 274, 278
Eliot, T. S., 67–8
Elizabeth, the Queen Mother, 221, 221, 222, 222, 423
Ellis, Mary, 380

Ellis, Vivian, 326
Elsie, Lily, 9, 350, *351*, 352, 362, 397
Elysée Restaurant (now Café de Paris), London, 30–1, *31*
ENSA (Entertainment National Service Association), 322–3
Entertainer, The (Osborne), 68
epigrams, 38, 60–1, 173
Erlanger, Abe, 319–20
Ethel Barrymore Theatre, New York, *120*, *121*, 122
Evans, Edith, *92*, 137, 152–3, 171, 226, 317
Everyman Theatre, Hampstead, 50, *50*, 88
explicit language, Noël on, 172

failure in the theatre, Noël on, 182–90
    being booed off the stage, 164–5
Fall, Leo, 324
Fallen Angels (Coward), 49, 92–4, *93*
"Family Album" (Coward), 133
fans, Noël on, 169–70
Faster Than Sound, 387
Ferber, Edna, 44, 62
Ferrer, José, *385*, 385–6
Festival Ballet Company, 407–9
Feydeau, Georges, 264
fiction writing, Noël on, 180
Field, Lila, 10–14, *11*
first-night nerves, Noël on, 163–4
Flagstad, Kirsten, 365
Flames of Passion, 95
Fleming, Ian, 412
Floradora, 324
Folies du Music-Hall, Les (Damase), Noël's Introduction to, 330–2
Fontanne, Lynn, 44, 45, 127, 216–24, *217*, *221*, 308, 312, *421*
    Design for Living and, 118–20, *121*, *123*, *151*, 155–6, 218, 220
    Noël on acting with, 155, 219–20
    Operette and, 368–9
    plays modified by, 258–9
    Point Valaine and, 123–4, *125*, 220, 368
    Quadrille and, 220, 258–60, *259*, 287
    varying the performance, 155
    Zolotow's *Stagestruck* and, 223–4
"Forbidden Fruit" (Coward), 28–9, 36
forty, Noël on creativity after, 191–2
Fraser-Simson, Harold, 327
Fresnay, Pierre, 365–6
Fry, Christopher, 233
"Fumed Oak" (Coward), 131, *131*, 178
Funny Girl (Styne and Merrill), 387
Future Indefinite (Coward), xvi, 182

Gaiety Theatre, Manchester, 43
Galsworthy, John, 21, 275, 432
Garland, Judy, 401, 402
Gay, Maisie, 301, 332
General Motors, 401
Gentlemen Prefer Blondes, 311
George, King, 249
Gershwin, George, 329
Gershwin, Ira, 210
Gielgud, Sir John, xiii, 159, 193, 201–4, *202*, *204*, 262, 272, 287, 291, 316, 317, 321
    The Constant Nymph and, 159, 203, 321
    as dropper of verbal bricks ("Gielgoodies"), 203–4, 316
    London Calling! reviewed by, 332–3, *333*
    on Noël's acting, 201–3, 334–5
    as Noël's understudy, 159, 261, 321, 333
    Nude with Violin and, 261–2
    "Terry voice" ascribed to, 203, 261
    Vortex and, 333
giggling onstage, Noël on, 157–8
Gilbert and Sullivan, 280, 324, 348, 372
Ginner, Ruby, 17
"Girl" titles, musical comedies with, 353
Girl Who Came to Supper, The, 215–16, 372, 384–7, *385*, *386*
    "I'll Remember Her" in, 215–16
Gish, Lillian, 29, 30
Glamorous Night (Novello), 326, 360
Glaser, Joe, 398, 399
Globe Theatre, London, 262, 429
Goldenhurst (Noël's country house), xv, 134, *211*, 213
Goldfish, The (Field), 10–14, *11*
Goossens, Eugene, 159
government subsidies, 432
Grand Hotel (Baum), 97
Grand Theatre, Croydon, 348
Grant, Cary, 420
Gray, Timothy, 387
Great Name, The (Hawtrey), 14, 348
"Green Carnation" (Coward), 372
Greene, Graham, 244, 281–7
    film version of *Our Man in Havana*, *285*, 286
    Noël's acquaintance with, in Jamaica, 285–6
    Noël's retaliatory verses:
        "The Ballad of Graham Greene," 282–3
        "Dear Mr. Graham Greene, I Yearn," 283–5
    sniping at Noël, 281–2, 283

Gregg, Everley, *133*
Griffith, D. W., *Hearts of the World* and, 29–30, *30*
Grimes, Tammy, 264, 387
Guildhall School of Music, 327, 405
Guinness, Alec, 286, 287
Guys and Dolls (Loesser), 379

Hackforth, Norman, 394, 399
Hale, Sonnie, 305, *339*
Hambleton Hall, *35*
Hamlet (Shakespeare), 42, 49, 135, 154, 193, 194, 287
Hammerstein, Oscar, 212, 347
hamming, Noël on, 172
Hammond, Kay, 253
Hampden, Burford, 13
"Hands Across the Sea" (Coward), 130–1, 133, 211
handwriting, Noël on, 181
Hannele (Hauptmann), 21–2, 318–19
Harrison, Rex, 137, 386
Hawtrey, Sir Charles, *16*, 154, 177, 258, 348, 350
    I'll Leave It to You and, 43
    Noël as child actor performing in company run by, 14–15, *16*, 18–19, 330
    Noël on what he learned from, 15, 137, 157, 419–20
Haydn, Richard, 338
Hay Fever (Coward), 49, 56, 60, 62, 88–92, *89, 91, 92,* 94, 100, 173, 252, 302, 381
    National Theatre's 1964 revival of, 78, *90, 92,* 150, 153, 179, 206–7
    Noël's visits with Hartley Manners and, 44–5
Hearts of the World (film), 29–30, *30*
Hello, Dolly! (Herman), 387, 416
Helpmann, Robert, 61, 262
Henderson, Florence, 385, *385,* 386
Henson, Gladys and Leslie, 352
"Hernia Whittlebot," *55*
Hicks, Seymour, 258
Hidden Persuaders (Packard), 281
High Spirits (Coward), 153–4, 387–90, *389,* 392
    Lillie's difficulty with learning the lines for, 153–4, 387, 388, 389–90
Hochhuth, Rolf, 289
Hoi Polloi (Coward), 372, 378, 379
    "Three Theatrical Dames" in, 226–9, 372
Holliday, Judy, 381
Hollis, Alan, *50*

Holloway, Stanley, 386
Holt, Thelma, 413
Home and Colonial (Coward), 253–4, 255
    See also *South Sea Bubble*
Home Chat (Coward), 99
Homecoming, The (Pinter), 80
Hope, Anthony, 96
Horne, David, 261
Howard, Trevor, 95
Humoresque (Coward), 39–40, 41
Hunter, Ian, *256*
Hyménée (Bourdet), 366

Iago (character), Noël's acting ambitions and, 56
Iceman Cometh, The (O'Neill), 77
Ida Collaborates (Coward and Wynne), 29
"I Like America" (Coward), 405
"I'll Follow My Secret Heart" (Coward), 371
I'll Leave It to You (Coward), 32, *32,* 34, 43–4, 48, 274, 407, 427
"I'll Remember Her" (Coward), 215–16
"I'll See You Again" (Coward), 214–15, 292, 328, 354, 358, 371
Illustrated London News, 114, 118
Importance of Being Earnest, The (Wilde), 38, 61
Impossible Wife, The (Coward), 34
In Which We Serve, 191, 402
Ionescu, Eugène, 72
Isis, The, 78
Island Fling (Coward), 213, *254,* 254–5, 312
    See also *South Sea Bubble*
"It Couldn't Matter Less" (Coward), 344–5

Jamaica, 315–16, 318, 380, 412
    Greene's acquaintance with Noël in, 285–6
    Noël's Blue Harbour home in, 286
    Noël's Firefly home in, 412
        Noël's death at, 423
        Queen Mother's visit to, 221, *221,* 222
James, Henry, 190, 224
Jeans, Ronald, 301, 332
Johnson, Celia, 95
Journey's End (Sherriff), 111–12, 113
Joyeux Chagrins (Roussin), 247, 367
Julius Caesar (Shakespeare), 55, 205–6

Karsivina, Tamara, 365
Kaufman, George S., 44
Kazan, Elia, 76
Kenright, Bill, 413

Kern, Jerome D., 329
Kerr, Molly, *50*
Kerr, Walter, 262, 264, 281, 298
King and I, The (Rodgers and
    Hammerstein), 181, 212–13
King's Rhapsody (Novello), 360
Kiss Me Kate (Porter), 311
Kitchen (Wesker), 72
Kitchen Sink school of playwrights, 70,
    154, 162, 195, 288
Knight of the Burning Pestle, The
    (Beaumont), 41, 42, 42–3, 407
Knoblock, Edward, 204
Kommer, Rudolph, 97
Kurnitz, Harry, 383, 384

Labouchère, Henry, 292
Lady in the Dark (Weill and Gershwin),
    210
Lady Windermere's Fan (Wilde), 60–1
    Noël's musical based on (*After the Ball*),
        38, 60–1, 286, 379–80
Last Joke, The (Bagnold), 317
Last Trick, The (Coward), 33–4
Las Vegas:
    Noël's first impressions of, 398–9
    Noël's performances at Desert Inn in,
        398–401, *400, 401, 402*
Later than Spring (Coward), 380–1
"Later than Spring" (Coward), 268–70
Lathom, Ned, 300–1
Lawrence, Gertrude (Gertie), 155, 157, 205,
    207–16, *208, 211, 212, 214,* 253, 256,
    354, 397
    biographical film on life of (*Star!*), 36
    Home and Colonial, later *South Sea
        Bubble,* and, 253, 256
    illness and death of, 213–15
    "I'll Remember Her" and, 215–16
    The King and I and, 181, 212–13
    London Calling! and, 301, 302, 332, 335
    marriage of, 210
    Noël's assessment of, 209–10
    Noël's first meeting with, 22
    Noël's first professional collaborations
        with, 208
    Noël's obituary for, 207, 213
    Noël's theatrical partnership with, 208
    Private Lives and, *104,* 104–6, *105,* 107,
        109, 111, 125–7, 208, 212, 302
    Tonight at 8:30 and, 125–7, *126,* 128, *129,
        130,* 130–1, *131, 132, 133,* 209, 211
Lawrence of Arabia, 78
Laye, Evelyn, 305, 354, 356–7, *358, 359*

Layton, Joe, 384, 386
leading ladies:
    Noël on, 225–9
        "A Vivid Study of Theatrical Life," 418
        difficult dealings with, 184, 185–8,
            416–18
        "Epitaph for an Elderly Actress,"
            225–6
        musical comedy stars, 348–52
        Running Order in revues and, 346–7
        star quality of, 231–8
        "Three Theatrical Dames," 226–9
    see also specific actresses
Lear, Edward, 348
learning the lines, 150–4
    first-night nerves mitigated by, 165–8
    Gielgud's questioning of Noël's
        emphasis on, 203
    Lillie's difficulty with, 153–4, 387, 388,
        389–90
    Noël's difficulty with, in his farewell
        roles, 154
    Noël's insistence on, 150–4
Lee, Bernard, 252
Lehár, Franz, 324
Leigh, Gracie, 350
Leigh, Vivien, 206, 253, 255, 256, *256,* 264,
    366
Leighton, Margaret, 58, 414, 415
Lesley, Cole (Coley), 213, 286, 309, 316,
    318, 387, 415, 422
Levin, Herman, 383, 384, 386
Liberace, 398
Life magazine, 400
Light Blues, The (Courtneidge), 27–8
light music, 324–407
    Noël on:
        in America vs. England, 326, 374,
            399–400
        "How I Write My Songs," 405–7, *406*
        memories of Music Hall (from his
            Introduction to *Les Folies du
            Music-Hall*), 330–2
        taking light music seriously (from his
            Introduction to *The Noël Coward
            Song Book*), 324–30
    see also cabaret; musical theatre; revues
Lillie, Beatrice ("Beattie"), 208, *211,* 300,
    302, 330, 340, *389*
    Noël's 1964 "Appreciation" for, 389–93
    Set to Music and, 338, 339–44
    This Year of Grace! and, 103, 336
    unable to learn her lines for *High Spirits,*
        153–4, 387, 388, 389–90

literary quotations, 55–6
Little Fowl Play, A, 18, 330
Little Theatre, London, 10–11
Liverpool Repertory Company, 21–2, 318
Lives of the Impressionists (Wilenski), 260
Lohr, Marie, 267, 317
London Calling! (Charlot revue), 208,
    301–2, 304, 332–5, *333, 334*, 407
London Morning (Coward), *349*, 407–9
London Pavilion, 335, 336, 407
Long Day's Journey Into Night (O'Neill), 77
Lonsdale, Frederick, 77, 182
Look After Lulu (Coward), 264–5
Look Back in Anger (Osborne), 64, 68, 288,
    413, 430
Loraine, Lorn, *55*, 181, 309, 310–11, 314, 367
Loraine, Violet, 352
Lord Chamberlain's Office, 49
Losey, Joseph, 77
Lunt, Alfred, 44, 45, 127, *156*, 216–24, *217*,
    221, 289, 308, 312, *421*
    Design for Living and, 118–20, *121, 123*,
        151, 155–6, 218, 220
    Noël on acting with, 155, 219–20
    Operette and, 368–9
    plays modified by, 258–9
    Point Valaine and, 123–4, *125*, 220, 368
    Quadrille and, 220, 258–60, *259*, 287
    varying the performance, 155
    Zolotow's *Stagestruck* and, 223–4
Lyons, Leonard, *67*

Macbeth (Shakespeare), 55, 56
MacDonald, Jeanette, 358
MacLaine, Shirley, 264
MacLiammóir, Micheál, 10–11
MacOwan, Michael, 59, 138–9
"Mad About the Boy" (Coward), 147, 337,
    337
"Mad Dogs and Englishmen" (Coward),
    336–7, *338*, 340
Mainbocher, 373
Malvolio (character), Noël's acting
    ambitions and, 56
Manchester Watch Committee, 95
Mander, Raymond, 78
Manners, Hartley, 44–5
Mantovani, 376
Man Who Came to Dinner, The (Kaufman
    and Hart), 280
March, Elspeth, 252
March, Fredric, 96
Margaret, Princess, 396
Marnac, Jane, 358

Marquise, The (Coward), 100–1
Marshall, Herbert, *48*, 172
Marshall, Norman, 149–50
Martin, Hugh, 387
Martin, Mary, 224
    Noël's television spectacular with
        (*Together with Music*), 377, 402–4,
        403, 404
    Noël's verse "I Resent Your Attitude to
        Mary," 377
    Pacific 1860 and, *373*, 374, 376–7, 403
Massary, Fritzi, 368, 369, 370
"Matelot" (Coward), *334*, 344–5
Matthews, A. E., 321
Matthews, Jessie, 305
Matz, Peter, 399
Maugham, Liza, 66
Maugham, Somerset, 64–7, *67*, 77, 95, 123,
    182, 272, 275, 414
Maugham, Syrie, 66
Meiser, Edith, *254*
Meller, Raquel, 331
"Men About Town" (Coward), *132*
Mendelssohn, Eleanora von, 368
Merman, Ethel, 381
Merry Widow, The (Lehár), 9, 350, *351*
Messager, André, 324
"messages," Noël on plays with, 179
Method acting, Noël on, 195–7, 198, 200–1
Metropolitan magazine, 34
Michael, Ralph, 252
Milk Train Doesn't Stop Here Anymore, The
    (Williams), 77
Millar, Gertie, 9, 350–2, 396–7
Miller, Arthur, 75–6
Miller, Gilbert, 32, 34, 41, 43, 46
Miller, Henry, 41
Mills, John, 112
Miss Hook of Holland, 324
"Mrs. Worthington" (Coward), 143–6, *144*
Mistinguett (Jeanne Florentine Bourgeois),
    330–1
Mitchenson, Joe, 78
Molyneux, Edward, 104, 106
Monckton, Lionel, 324, 352
Monroe, Marilyn, 75, 76, 383
More, Kenneth, 252
Morosco Theatre, New York, *242*
Mousetrap, The (Christie), 243
Moxie, see Relative Values
Mozart, Wolfgang Amadeus, 380
musical theatre, 347–93
    Ace of Clubs, *349*, 372, 378–9, *379*
    After the Ball, 38, 61, 286, 379–80

musical theatre *(continued)*
   Conversation Piece, 307, 328, 362–3, *364*,
      365, 366–8, 375
   High Spirits, 153–4, 387–90, *389*, 392
   Noël on, 347–53
      book for operetta is traditionally a
         soufflé, 60–1
      his childhood introduction to musical
         comedy, 348
      musical comedies with "Girl" titles,
         353
      musical comedy stars, 348–52
      primacy of musical score in, 372–4
      writing lyrics for, 347–8
   Noël's ploy for getting free seats to, 350
   Operette, 133, 313, 363, 365, 366, 368–72,
      394
   out-of-context "big number" in, as
      Coward signature, 372
   Pacific 1860, 278, *349*, 372–8, *373*, *374*,
      403
   see also Bitter Sweet
Music Hall, Noël's memories of (from
   his Introduction to *Les Folies du
   Music-Hall*), 330–2
My Fair Lady (Lerner and Loewe), 383,
   386–7
"My Horse Has Cast a Shoe" (Coward),
   376
My Life in Art (Stanislavski), 196

National Theatre, London, 78, 92, 241
   Hay Fever revival at (1964), 78, *90*, 92,
      150, 153, 179, 206–7, 289
Natwick, Mildred, *243*
Neagle, Anna, 358
Needham, Alicie Adelaide, 330
Nesbitt, Cathleen, 386
"New Movement in the Theatre," 194,
   267, 297
   Noël's essays on, *see* "Consider the
      Public"
New Theatre, London, 44, *161*, *427*
New Year's Honours List, 221, 419
New York:
   Noël's East River apartment in, *252*
   Noël's first trip to, 44–6, 49
   speed and tempo of comedy in, 174
   theater audiences in London vs., 168
   see also specific theatres and productions
New Yorker, The, 287
Nichols, Beverley, 291
Nichols, Dandy, 252
"Ninety Minutes Is a Long, Long Time"
   (Coward), 403

Nodin, Gerald, *340*
Noël Coward in Two Keys, 417
Noël Coward Song Book, 145, 324–30
Noel Coward Theatre, London, 44, *427*
Normandie, SS, *205*
Novello, Ivor, 101–3, 277, 291, 305, 322,
   326, 357–62, *359*, 362, 376
   Bitter Sweet praised by, 357–60
   death of, 360
   Noël's introduction for biography of,
      360–2
novels:
   Cherry Pan (juvenilia), 23–5
   Noël on writing plays vs., 190–1
   Pomp and Circumstance, 256, 412, *413*
Nude with Violin (Coward), 204, 260–4,
   315, 316

Observer, The, 22, 287, 394
Occupe-toi d'Amélie (Feydeau), 264
Oh!, Calcutta!, 289
Oh Coward! (Cook), 289, *421*, 422
Oklahoma! (Rodgers and Hammerstein),
   378
Old Vic, London, 72, 84, 92, 206, 289
Olivier, Laurence, xiii, 56, 92, *109*, 110, 137,
   157–8, *158*, 163, 193, 201, 204, *205*,
   205–7, 253, 272, 287, 289, 366, 383
   "corpsing" of, 205–6
   Home and Colonial and, 253
   obsessed with changing his physical
      appearance onstage, 206
   The Prince and the Showgirl and, 383
O'Neill, Eugene, 77
On with the Dance (Cochran revue), 56,
   303, 304, 305, *334*, 335, *335*, 407
Operette (Coward), 133, 313, 363, 365, 366,
   368–72, 394
   "Stately Homes of England" in, 344,
      369, 370, 371
Osborne, John, 64, 68–70, 79, 81, 178, 265,
   288, 413
O'Shea, Tessie, 372, 385, 386, *386*
Othello (Shakespeare), 56
Our Man in Havana (film), *285*, 286
Our Miss Gibbs, 324
overlapping dialogue, Noël on, 174–6

Pacific 1860 (Coward), 278, *349*, 372–8, *373*,
   374, 403
   Noël's examination of failures in, 375–6,
      377
   Noël's reaction to Martin in, 376–7
Packard, Vance, 281
Paley, Bill, 245–7

Palmer, Lilli, 415, *416*, 416–17
Pamela (musical comedy), 350
Paramount, 96
Paris:
  Noël in, shortly after Liberation, 250
  Noël's first visit to, 330–2
"Parisian Pierrot" (Coward), 332, 407
Parker, Dorothy, 44
Patrick, Nigel, 178
Pavlova, Anna, 365, 397
Payn, Graham, 211, *340*, 344–5, 422, 423
Peace in Our Time (Coward), 249–52, *251*, 315
Peile, Kinsey, *50*
Perchance to Dream (Novello), 360
Period of Adjustment (Williams), 77
Perry, John, 315
Peter Pan (Barrie), 15, 291
  Noël as Slightly in, *5*, 22–3, *24*, 62, 63, 291
Pharall, Aishie, 41
Phoenix Theatre, London, 110, 126, *126*, 208, 233, 259, *259*, 397, 419–20
Pinero, Arthur, 77, 95, 122, 228, 432
Pinter, Harold, 79–81, 83–4, 241, 288, 430
place-names, Noël's fascination with sound of, 40
Playfair, Nigel, 41
Play Parade (Coward), 190, 244, 272
Plowright, Joan, 289
Point Valaine (Coward), 123–4, *125*, 220, 368
politics:
  postwar, Noël's disillusionment with, 288
  theatre's role in relation to, 3, 71, 82, 85–6, 140, 194–5, 199–200
Pomp and Circumstance (Coward), 256, 412, *413*
Pons, Lily, 328
"Poor Little Rich Girl" (Coward), 335, 336, 407
Post-Mortem (Coward), 113, 179, 249
Potter, Beatrix, 348
Powell, Jane, *400*
Preminger, Otto, 158, 207
Present Indicative (Coward), 135, 217–18, 308
Present Laughter (Coward), 12, 61, 87, 90, 134, 162, 179, 182, 193, 195, 229–30, 239, *245*, 245–7, *246*, 264, 292, 314
  Broadway revival of (1982), 178–9
  CBS's refusal to broadcast, 245–7
  London revival of (1947), *245*, *246*
  New York production of, 310

title of, 42, 55
translated into French (Roussin's *Joyeux Chagrins*), 247, 367
Prince and the Showgirl, The (film), 383–4
Prince of Wales Theatre, London, 14, 348
Printemps, Yvonne, 362–8, *364*, 374
Private Lives (Coward), 90, 103–11, *105*, *108*, *109*, *111*, 114, 116, 127, 155, 157–8, *158*, 182, 205, 208, *212*, 252, 289, 308, 381
  balcony scene as revelation to Pinter, 80–1
  Noël's assessment of, 110–11
  revival at Hampstead Theatre (1963), 268
  writing of, 33, 56, 104, 107
Producer and the Play, The (Marshall), 149–50
Prout, Ebenezer, 327

Quadrille (Coward), 220, 258–60, *259*, 287, 315
Quaints, The, 111
Quaker Girl, The (musical comedy), 9, 324, 350, 351, 352
Queen Mother, 221, *221*, 222, *222*, 423
Queen Was in the Parlour, The (Coward), 49, 96, 321

range, Noël on, 161–2
Rattigan, Terence, 77–9, 82–3, 291, 315, 383
Rat Trap, The (Coward), 34, 88, 322
Ravel, Maurice, 327
Ray, Phil, 330
Reader, Raph, 127
Redgrave, Michael, 317
"Red Peppers, The" (Coward), 129–30, *132*
Reed, Carol, 286
Regent and His Daughter, The (Creston), 362
rehearsals, 146–50
  accounts of Noël's working methods in, 147–50
  arguments about how play should be played in, 188
  dress, 148–9, 183–4
  learning the lines before, 150–4, 165–8, 203
  loss of confidence during, 179–80
  Noël on rehearsing Lillie in *Set to Music*, 339–44
  playwright's troubles during, 183–5
Reinhardt, Max, 97, 98
Relative Values, previously titled *Moxie* (Coward), 152, 173, 256–7, 315
Restoration Playwrights, 275, 276

revivals, Noël on, 179
revues, 332–47
  Cochran on nature of, 336, 337, 345
  On with the Dance (Cochran), 56, *303*,
    304, 305, *334, 335, 335*, 407
  Danger Spots in, 347
  London Calling! (Charlot), 208, 301–2,
    304, 332–5, *333, 334*, 407
  Noël on art of, 346–7
  Noël's pattern of alternating plays and,
    335
  Oh Coward! (Cook), 289, *421, 422*
  Running Order in, 346–7
  Set to Music (Coward), 133, *334*, 338–44,
    340, 343, 392
  Sigh No More (Coward), 315, *334*, 344–5
  Words and Music (Cochran), 147, *307*,
    336–9, *340*
  see also This Year of Grace!
Rheingold advertisement, *262*
Rhinoceros (Ionescu), 72
rhymes, Noël on compulsion to make, 348
Richard II (Shakespeare), 55
Richardson, Ralph, xiii, 193, 201, 317
Ritchard, Cyril, 264
Robey, George, 330
Robson, Mary, *50*
Rodgers, Richard, 212, 329
Romeo and Juliet (Shakespeare), 56
Room, The (Pinter), 79
"Room with a View, A" (Coward), 280,
  305–6, 336, *339*
Ross (Rattigan), 78, 84
Rothenstein, Sir John, *338*
Rothermere, Ann, 412
Roussin, André, 247
Royal Court Theatre, London, 72, 79, 85,
  265, 429, 431
Royal Hunt of the Sun, The (Shaffer), 81
Rubens, Paul, 324
Russell, Rosalind, 381
Rutherford, Margaret, *242*, 244–5

Sail Away (Coward), 162, 221, 298, 381–3,
  383, 384, 384
  Later Than Spring screenplay as
    precursor to, 380–1
St. Helier, Ivy, *340*
Saki (Hector Hugh Munro), 250, 315
Salute to the Brave (Coward), 240
Sandringham, Queen Mother's invitation
  to, 222, *222*
Savoy Theatre, London, 15, *18*, 48, 258,
  350, 429

Scott, George C., 178–9
Scott, Maidie, 330
Seagrove, Jenny, 413
Seagull, The (Chekhov), 62
Searle, Alan, 66
Second Mrs. Tanqueray, The (Pinero), 95
Selwyn Theatre, New York, *108*
Semi-Monde (Coward), 97–9, 176
  Preface to, 98–9
Set to Music (Coward), 133, *334*, 338–44,
  340, 343, 392
  Noël on rehearsing Lillie in, 339–44
"Shadow Play" (Coward), 80, 131, *131*, 211
Shadows of the Evening (Coward), 414–15
Shaffer, Peter, 81–2
Shakespeare, William, xiii, 4, 49, 56, 71, 84,
  172, 229, 244, 298
  Hamlet, 42, 49, 135, 154, 193, 194, 287
  Noël's acting ambitions and, 42, 56
  titles of Noël's plays taken from, 42, 55
Shaw, George Bernard, 57, 57–60, 77,
  138–9, 182, 191, 273, 275, 315
  as critic, Noël on, 297, 298
  Noël's evolution as playwright and,
    47, 49
Shelley, Percy Bysshe, 56
Sheppey (Maugham), 64–5
Sherriff, R. C., 111
Sickert, Walter, 331
Siddons, Sarah, 196
Sigh No More (Coward), 315, *334*, 344–5
Sim, Millie, *50*
Simon, Neil, 76
Sinatra, Frank, 400, 401, *402*
Sinclair, Hugh, 178
Sinden, Donald, 178
Sirocco (Coward), 63, 101–3, 180, 305,
  321–2, 336, 355
Sitwell, Edith, *55*
Sleeping Prince, The (Rattigan), 79, 383
  film version of *(The Prince and the
    Showgirl)*, 383–4
Smith, Maggie, *92*
"Something to Do with Spring" (Coward),
  337
Song at Twilight, A (Coward), 66, 414,
  415–16, 417
songwriting, Noël on:
  "How I Write My Songs," 405–7, *406*
  writing lyrics for musical theatre, 347–8
Sound of Music (Rodgers and
  Hammerstein), 224
South Pacific (Rodgers and Hammerstein),
  376

South Sea Bubble, previously titled *Home and Colonial* and *Island Fling* (Coward), 253–6, *256*, 261–2, 264
  Home and Colonial version of, 253–4, 255
  Westport Country Playhouse production of (as *Island Fling*), 213, *254*, 254–5, 312
Spectator, The, 281
spontaneity on stage, Noël on, 342
stage fright, Noël on, 162–8
  being booed off the stage as cure, 164–5
  child actors and, 162, 164
  first night nerves, 163–4
  mitigated by learning the lines, 165–8
Stagestruck (Zolotow), 223–4
Stanislavski, Constantine, 4, 196, 198
Star! (film), 36
"Star Chamber" (Coward), 128
star quality:
  ascribed to Noël by Tynan, 294
  Noël on, 231–8
  "How I Wonder What You Are," 232–8
Star Quality (Coward), 135, 190, *232*, 318
"Stately Homes of England" (Coward), 344, *369*, 370, 371
Stephenson, William, 420
"Still Life" (Coward), 133, *133*
Strange Interlude (O'Neill), 77
Strasberg, Lee, 4, 225
Stratford, 56, 84, 137, 185, 414
Stratton, Chester, *254*
Stritch, Elaine, 382, *383*
Stuart, Leslie, 324
style, Noël on actors' sense of, 177–8
Suddenly Last Summer (Williams), 77
Suite in Three Keys (Coward), 69, 154, 415–17, *416*
Summer's Cloud, A (Coward), 55
Sunday Times, The, 69, 70, 93
  see also "Consider the Public"
Swaffer, Hannen, 283
Sweet Bird of Youth (Williams), 76
Swinburne, Algernon Charles, 56

talent (or the lack of it), Noël on, 143–6, 162–3
  star quality and, 231–8
taste, Noël on, 181
Tatler, The, *358*
Taylor, Elizabeth, 77
Taylor, Laurette, 44–5, 216, *218*
Teddington, Noël's early upbringing in, 9–10, 247, 291

Teddington Amateur Dramatic Society, 348
television, 401–4
  Blithe Spirit broadcast by CBS, *243*, 244, 247
  The Dick Cavett Show, 420, *420*
  Present Laughter rejected by CBS, 245–7
  Together with Music, 377, 402–4, *403*, *404*
Tempest, Dame Marie, xvi, 88–90, *89*, 100–1, 135
Tempest, The (Shakespeare), xiii
Tennent, H. M., 150, 312, 313, 314, 315
Theatre Arts Monthly, 122–3
Theatre Guild, 118
"Theatre of Ideas" vs. "Theatre of Entertainment," 430
"theatre parties," Noël on, 263
Theatre Royal, Aldershot, 29
Theatre Royal Drury Lane, London, 210, 374–5, 378
Theatre World, *251*
Theatrical Companion to Coward (Mander and Mitchenson), 78
Theatrical Garden Party, 394
"The Party's Over Now" (Coward), 337
Third Little Show, The (Coward), 340
This Happy Breed (Coward), 22, 55, 134, 162, 195, 239, 244, 247–9, *248*, 314, 378
"This Is a Changing World" (Coward), 376
"This Is a Night for Lovers" (Coward), 376
This Was a Man (Coward), 40, 55, 96–7, 272, 321
This Year of Grace! (Cochran revue), 103, 305–6, 335–6, 337, 354, 355
  New York production of, 103, 280, 305, 306, 328, 336, 353–4, 390, 392
  "A Room with a View" in, 280, 305–6, 336, *339*
Thompson, Carlos, 415
Thompson, Kay, 381
Thorndike, Sybil, 171, 226, 267, 317
"Three Juvenile Delinquents" (Coward), 372
"Three Theatrical Dames" (Coward), 226–9, 372
Time Remembered (Coward), 56, 240
Times (London), 18, 207, 213, 332–5
timing, Noël on, 45, 154–6
Tiny Alice (Albee), 73
Titheradge, Madge, 22–3, 92, 99, 171
"To a Skylark" (Shelley), 56
Todd, Mike, 204

Together with Music (CBS TV), 377,
    402–4, *403, 404*
Tonight at 8:30 (Coward), 80, 125–33, *126,
    127, 130,* 375
    one-act plays in:
        "The Astonished Heart," 129
        "Family Album," 133
        "Fumed Oak," 131, *131,* 178
        "Hands Across the Sea," 130–1, 133,
            211
        "The Red Peppers," 129–30, *132*
        "Shadow Play," 80, 131, *131,* 211
        "Star Chamber," 128
        "Still Life," 133, *133*
        "Ways and Means," *129,* 133
        "We Were Dancing," 129, *349*
    revival of (1947), 211
Tonight Is Ours, 96
Tony award "for lifetime achievement,"
    221, 264, *421*
"Tony from America" (song), 352, 397
Toulouse-Lautrec, Henri de, 331
"Touring Days" (Coward), 26–7
Transatlantic Productions, 308, 310, 312
Travers, Ben, 67
Tree, Sir Herbert, 177
Tree, Viola, 172
Trevor, Ann, *48*
"Tribute to Mr. Coward, A" (Tynan), 287,
    291–4
"triple bill" formula, 126
    See also Tonight at 8:30; plays
Twelfth Night (Shakespeare), 55, 56
Tynan, Kenneth, 22, 84, 287–94, 295, 395,
    396
    National Theatre and, 289
    Noël's points of contention with,
        287–8
    Noël's reconciliation with, 289–90
    "A Tribute to Mr. Coward" by, 287,
        291–4

Unattainable, The (Coward), 36–8, 41
Unions and Equity impact on American
    theatre, Noël on, 267–8
upstaging, Noël on, 155
Upstairs, Downstairs (television), 118

Vaudeville Theatre, London, 391, 413
"verbal bricks," 203–4, 316
verse writing, Noël on, 180–1
vice and squalor in the theatre, Noël on,
    170–2
Victoria, Queen, 292

Vidal, Gore, 76
Volar, Deborah, 350
Volcano (Coward), 411–13
Vortex, The (Coward), xiii, 12, *49,* 49–53,
    50, 52, 62, 63, 88, 90, 96, 101, 164,
    171, 201–3, 248, 288, 291–2, 301,
    304, 308, 322
    Agate's review of, 50–1, 275
    censorship and, 49–50, 97
    film version of, 49–50, 103
    Gielgud as Noël's understudy in, 333
    New York production of, 319–20
    reception in Chicago, 160–1

Waiting for Godot (Beckett), 74
Waiting in the Wings (Coward), 62, 265–7,
    266, 268, 317
Wallace, Nellie, 330
Walston, Catherine, 285, 286
"War in the Air" (sketch), 330
"Warning to Actors, A" ("Consider the
    Public" essay originally published
    in *The Sunday Times* under the
    title "The Scratch-and-Mumble
    School"), 194–200
Waugh, Evelyn, 291
Way of the World, The (Congreve), 91,
    275
"Ways and Means" (Coward), *129,* 133
"Weary of It All" (Coward), 341
Webb, Clifton, 161, 310
Weill, Kurt, 210
Welfare State, 85, 288
Welles, Orson, 72
"well-made" play, 77, 182
Wesker, Arnold, 70–2, 79, 81
West End of London, Noël on decline of,
    429–33
Westport Country Playhouse,
    Connecticut, *254,* 254–5, 310–11
"We Were Dancing" (Coward), 129, *349*
"What Mad Pursuit?" (Coward), 273
When William Came (Saki), 250, 315
Where the Rainbow Ends (Mills and
    Ramsay), 15–16, 19, *20, 21,* 350
"Why Must the Show Go On?" (Coward),
    424–7
Wilde, Oscar, 60–1, 82, 95, 287
    Noël's ambivalence toward, 38, 60–1
    Noël's musical based on *Lady
        Windermere's Fan* (*After the Ball*),
        38, 60–1, 286, 379–80
    stylistic excesses of Noël's early plays
        and, 36–8, 60

Wilding, Michael, 262, 415
Williams, Flinty, 413
Williams, Michael, 413
Williams, Tennessee, 76–7, 123
Willmore, Alfred, 13
Wilson, John C. (Jack), 127–8, 254–5, 300, 307, 308–12, *309*, 314, 367
  health problems and death of, 311, 312
  Loraine's verse on *chutzpa* on, 310–11
  Noël's finances and, 309–10
Wilson, Natasha, 312
Wilson, Sandy, 360
Winslow Boy, The (Rattigan), 78
Woman and Whiskey (Coward and Wynne), 29
Wood, Peggy, 354–5, *358*, 370
Woods, Al, 54
Woollcott, Alexander, 44, 223, 252, 279–81, 298, 363
wordplay, in Noël's early plays, 38–9, 60, 173
Words and Music (Cochran revue), 147, 307, 336–9, *340*
  Broadway revue based on (*Set to Music*), 133, *334*, 338–44, *340*, *343*, 392
World of Paul Slickey, The (Osborne), 68
World War I, 98, 99, 249
  Saki's *When William Came* and, 250, 315
World War II, 134, 210, 218–19, 249, 344, 378, 392, 394
  Dean's ENSA shows in, 322–3

Noël's missions during, 57–8, 239–40, 310, 322–3, 394
  Peace in Our Time and, 249–52
"World Weary" (Coward), 336
Worth, Irene, 414, 415, *416*
Writer's Notebook (Maugham), 65
writing, Noël on, 179–92
  for ballet, 407–9
  confidence and, 179–80
  constructing a play, 41, 43, 182
  dialogue, 182, 191
  explicit language and, 172
  failure in the theatre, 182–90
  fiction, 180
  handwriting, 181
  lyrics for musical theatre, 347–8
  overlapping dialogue, 174–6
  plays modified by actors to suit themselves, 258–9
  plays vs. novels, 190–1
  songs, 405–7
  theatre vs. cinema, 191
  verse, 180–1
Wynne, Esmé, 16, 19–21, 22, 41, 43, 406

Youmans, Vincent, 329
You Never Can Tell (Shaw), 47
Young Idea, The (Coward), 47–8, *48*, 57, 274, 304

Ziegfeld, Florenz, 355–6
Zolotow, Maurice, 223–4

'I'll see you again' Duet

Refrain

I'll see you again.
whenever Spring breaks through again
Time may lie heavy between
But what has been
Is past forgetting.
This sweet memory
Across the years will come to me
'Though the world may pass us by
In our hearts will ever lie
Just the echo of a sigh
Good-bye

Bitter Sweet (1929).

A NOTE ON THE TYPE

This book was set in Adobe Garamond. Designed for the Adobe Corporation by Robert Slimbach, the fonts are based on types first cut by Claude Garamond (ca. 1480–1561). Garamond was a pupil of Geoffroy Tory and is believed to have followed the Venetian models, although he introduced a number of important differences, and it is to him that we owe the letter we now know as "old style." He gave to his letters a certain elegance and feeling of movement that won their creator an immediate reputation and the patronage of Francis I of France.

Composed by North Market Street Graphics,
Lancaster, Pennsylvania

Printed and bound by Berryville Graphics,
Berryville, Virginia

Designed by Cassandra J. Pappas